52 Weeks of Chunky Knits

52 Weeks of Chunky Knits

Hardie Grant
BOOKS

Contents

To Our Readers

It is time to get super cosy as we dive into the world of chunky knitwear! *52 Weeks of Chunky Knits* is the latest addition to Laine Publishing's popular *52 Weeks* book series. It presents 52 patterns for chunky knits (including one crochet piece as well) that are fun and quick to make. The book includes 25 patterns for sweaters, cardigans, slipovers and vests, as well as accessories and a few home decor items.

The designs are contemporary, stylish and relaxed, using a variety of techniques and constructions. Bold cables, beautiful colourwork, fascinating textures, generous proportions – and more! The patterns are written by 46 talented designers from all over the world.

But what do we actually mean by 'chunky'? In this collection, the patterns typically have a gauge of 12–14 stitches, or fewer, to 4" / 10 cm. Most of the designs are worked in worsted-weight, chunky or super-chunky yarns or by holding multiple strands of thinner yarns together. This gives you that lusciously plump feel when holding them in your hands!

As meditative as the process of knitting is, the moment of finishing your project is equally rewarding. Chunky knits are perfect for those not patient enough to make a whole sweater in fingering-weight yarn. (Or maybe looking for an idea for a Christmas gift that would be ready in, say, two nights ... ?)

Chunky knitwear has been a huge trend in recent years, introducing many young and fashionable makers to the craft. But even though chunky knits are often seen as easy or simple, this book proves that they are not just for beginners or knitters looking for an effortless project. The patterns' skill level ranges from easy to intermediate and more advanced, featuring many elaborate details and interesting techniques that will challenge and captivate all knitters.

In Finnish, we have the word 'vilukissa', which translates roughly to a 'chilly cat' – referring to a person who easily feels cold. This book is dedicated to all you 'chilly cats' out there, looking for something extra warm and thick to wrap yourselves in.

Let's keep the cold at bay and have some fun!

Laine Team

Abbreviations & Notes

approx.
Approximately

bef
Before

beg
Begin(ning)

BN
Bottom needle

BO
Bind off

BOR
Beginning of the round

C1, C2, etc.
Colour 1, colour 2, etc.

CC
Contrast(ing) colour

CDD
Central double decrease: Slip 2 stitches together as if to knit to your right-hand needle. Knit the next stitch. Pass the slipped stitches over the knitted stitch. (2 stitches decreased)

CN
Cable needle

CO
Cast on

cont
Continue(s)/continuing

dec('d)
Decrease(d)/decreasing

DPN(S)
Double-pointed needle(s)

DS
Double stitch

est
Establish(ed)

foll
Follows / following

inc('d)
Increase(d) / increasing

k
Knit

k2tog
Knit 2 stitches together (1 stitch decreased)

k3tog
Knit 3 stitches together (2 stitches decreased)

kDS
Knit double stitch: Knit both legs together

kfb
Knit into front of the stitch without dropping it from the needle, then knit into back of the same stitch, then drop it from the needle (1 stitch increased)

kfbf
Knit into the front of the stitch without dropping it from the needle, then knit into the back of the same stitch, then knit into the front of the same stitch again, then drop it from the needle (2 stitches increased)

ktbl / k1tbl
Knit through back loop of the stitch (twisted stitch)

kwise
Knitwise

LH
Left hand

LHN
Left-hand needle

m
Marker

m1l(p)
Make 1 left: With your left-hand needle pick up the bar between the last stitch you knitted (purled) and the next stitch on the left-hand needle, bringing the needle from the front to the back, knit (purl) into the back of the stitch you just picked up (1 stitch increased)

m1r(p)
Make 1 right: With your left-hand needle pick up the bar between the last stitch you knitted (purled) and the next stitch on the left-hand needle, bringing the needle from the back to the front, knit (purl) into the front of the stitch you just picked up (1 stitch increased)

MC
Main colour

mDS
Make double stitch: Slip the next stitch with yarn in front. Bring the yarn over the right needle to the back and pull on the slipped stitch until it looks like a double stitch (two legs)

N / N1 / N2, etc.
Needle / needle 1 / needle 2, etc.

p
Purl

p2sso
Pass 2 slipped stitches over (2 stitches decreased)

p2tog
Purl 2 stitches together (1 stitch decreased)

p3tog
Purl 3 stitches together (2 stitches decreased)

patt
Pattern

pDS
Purl double stitch: Purl both legs together

pfb
Purl into the front and back of the same stitch (1 stitch increased)

pl
Place

PM
Place marker

prev
Previous

psso
Pass slipped stitch over (1 stitch decreased)

ptbl / p1tbl
Purl through back loop (twisted stitch)

PUW
Pick up wrap: Insert right-hand needle upwards through the wrap around the bottom of the next stitch and the front leg of the next stitch. On a purl row, insert right-hand needle from the back of your work through the wrap around the bottom of the next stitch and the front leg of the next stitch. Purl the two loops as if they were one stitch. On a knit row, insert needle from the front of your work. Knit the two loops as if they were one stitch.

pwise
Purlwise

rem
Remain(ing)

rep
Repeat

RH
Right hand

RHN
Right-hand needle

rib
Ribbing

RM
Remove marker

rnd(s)
Round(s)

RS
Right side of fabric

sk2po
Slip 1 stitch, knit 2 stitches together, pass the slipped stitch over (2 stitches decreased)

skpo
Slip 1 stitch, knit the next stitch, pass the slipped stitch over (1 stitch decreased)

sl
Slip (purlwise with yarn in back on RS and yarn in front on WS, unless otherwise stated)

SM
Slip marker

ssk
Slip, slip, knit: Slip 2 stitches one at a time as if to knit, knit them together through back loops (1 stitch decreased)

ssp
Slip, slip, purl: Slip 2 stitches one at a time as if to knit, purl them together through back loops (1 stitch decreased)

sssk
Slip, slip, slip, knit: Slip 2 stitches one at a time as if to knit, knit them together through back loops (2 stitches decreased)

st(s)
Stitch(es)

St St
Stockinette Stitch

tbl
Through the back loop

TN
Top needle

tog
Together

tw
Turn work

WS
Wrong side of fabric

wyib
With yarn in back

wyif
With yarn in front

w&t
Wrap & turn: Slip the next stitch on your left-hand needle to the right-hand needle. If you are on a knit row, bring the yarn from back to front; if you are on a purl row, bring the yarn from front to back. Slip the stitch back to your left-hand needle so that the yarn 'wraps' that stitch, then turn your work so the other side is facing you.

yds
Yards

yo
Yarn over: Bring yarn between needles to the front, then over right-hand needle ready to knit the next stitch (1 stitch increased)

[ ] / ( )
Repeat instructions in brackets stated number of times

_
Repeat from * to *

GENERAL INFORMATION

Charts are read from bottom to top and from right to left, unless otherwise stated. When knitting flat, they are read from right to left on RS rows and from left to right on WS rows.

If you cannot find the yarn(s) as used in the pattern, or want to use something else, you can substitute with similar yarn(s) of your choosing. Yardage information and recommended yarn substitutes are given in all patterns. Note, however, that yardages are always estimates, especially if using another yarn than used for the sample.

If the pattern states a specific cast-on or bind-off method, you can substitute it with your preferred technique unless otherwise noted.

Most accessory patterns are written for either DPNs or the Magic Loop method. However, you can use your preferred needles and method of knitting. Note that if you use a technique other than the one the pattern is written for, you may need to make adjustments when following the pattern.

The pattern instructions list any special notions you will need. You will also need a tapestry needle to weave in all the ends, a pair of scissors for cutting the yarn and a measuring tape to check the gauge and dimensions.

It is recommended to block your finished item. Soak the knit in lukewarm water for about 20 minutes. Gently squeeze the excess water out and place your knit on a towel. Roll up the towel to press more water out. Be careful not to stretch or twist your knit. Lay out to dry to the required measurements. Alternatively, you can steam block your knit. You can also use mitten blockers, blocking wires and pins to block the finished piece.

You can find more pictures of the patterns featured in this book at lainepublishing.com.

1

Sweaters

Vicky M — Pauliina Leisti — Veera Välimäki

Klara Nilsson — Sara Markkula — Orlane Sucche — Jaime Dorfman — Marie Régnier

Brenda Lam — Esti Juango — Bernice Lim — Arianna Frasca

Vicky M

01 Erika

This oversized, beginner-friendly sweater has a repeated stripe sequence, making it a relaxing knit. It was designed by Vicky M, also known as Vicky Knits.

SIZES

1 (2, 3, 4, 5) (6, 7, 8)

Recommended ease: 14" / 35 cm of positive ease.

FINISHED MEASUREMENTS

Chest Circumference: 45.5 (50, 54.75, 58.25, 63) (66.75, 70.5, 75)" / 115.5 (127, 139, 148, 160) (169.5, 179, 190.5) cm.
Length (Back Neck to Hem, not incl. Collar): 22 (23, 23.5, 24.5, 25) (26, 27, 27.5)" / 56 (58, 60, 62, 64) (66, 68, 70) cm.
Sleeve Length: 17.25 (16.5, 16.25, 15.75) (15, 14.5, 13.75, 13.5)" / 44 (42, 41, 40, 38) (37, 35, 34) cm.
Upper Arm Circumference: 15.25 (15.75, 16.25, 16.75, 17.25) (17.75, 18, 18.5)" / 39 (40, 41, 42.5, 43.5) (45, 46, 47) cm.
Length from Underarm to Hem: 13 (13.75, 14.25, 14.5, 15.25) (15.75, 16.25, 16.5)" / 33 (35, 36, 37, 39) (40, 41, 42) cm.

MATERIALS

Yarn: Air by Drops Design (65% alpaca, 28% polyamide, 7% wool, 164 yds / 150 m – 50 g).
C1: 2 (2, 2, 2, 3) (3, 3, 3) balls of colourway 13 Orange.
C2: 2 (2, 2, 2, 3) (3, 3, 3) balls of colourway 51 Desert Rose.
C3: 2 (2, 2, 2, 3) (3, 3, 3) balls of colourway 46 Dark Olive.
C4: 2 (2, 2, 2, 3) (3, 3, 3) balls of colourway 42 Pistachio Ice Cream.
C5: 2 (2, 2, 2, 3) (3, 3, 3) balls of colourway 35 Clay.

Or approx. 245 (270, 285, 305, 335) (360, 390, 420) yds / 225 (245, 260, 280, 305) (330, 355, 385) m each in five different colours of fluffy aran-weight yarn. Alternative yarn suggestions are for example Ice Yarns Baby Alpaca Air, Sandnes Garn Kos and Wool and the Gang Feeling Good Yarn.

Needles: US 8 / 5 mm and US 6 / 4 mm 32–40" / 80–100 cm circular needles.

Notions: Locking stitch markers, stitch holders or waste yarn. Crochet hook or tapestry needle for seaming.

GAUGE

17 sts x 30 rows to 4" / 10 cm on US 8 / 5 mm needles in Garter St, after blocking.

STRIPE PATTERN

C1 (Orange): 2 rows.
C2 (Desert Rose): 2 rows.
C3 (Dark Olive): 2 rows.
C4 (Pistachio Ice Cream): 2 rows.
C5 (Clay): 2 rows.
Rep throughout unless indicated otherwise.

NOTES

To avoid cutting the yarn between each colour, bring the threads along as you are knitting, staying aware of the tension.

The placement of stitch markers is to guide the knitter without having to count stitches or rows.

It is very important to match row gauge in order to have a matching bind-off edge at the neck and cuffs.

CONSTRUCTION

This sweater is first knitted up in two panels: a front and a back panel. The shoulder seams are seamed together and the sleeves are completed by picking up stitches along the front and back panels. The neckline is knitted along the edge of the collar and the sides are seamed together to finish.

DIRECTIONS

BACK

Note! Leave a very long tail for seaming the sides later.
With C1, and US 6 / 4 mm needles, CO 100 (110, 120, 128, 138) (146, 154, 164) sts using the Long-Tail CO method.

Rib

Row 1 (WS): *K1, p1* to end.
Row 2 (RS): *K1, p1* to end.
Work in est 1 x 1 rib until it measures 5" / 13 cm ending after a WS row.
Note! Remember to switch yarn colours throughout.

BODY

Switch to US 8 / 5 mm needles. Remember to maintain the stripe sequence as you work.

Work in Garter St until the back measures 13 (13.75, 14.25, 14.5, 15.25) (15.75, 16.25, 16.5)" / 33 (35, 36, 37, 39) (40, 41, 42) cm from CO edge, ending after a WS row. Last row worked should be in C5 (2, 4, 1, 3) (5, 2, 4).
PM on the first and last st of the row: this is where the CO will start for the sleeves.

Cont in Garter St until the piece measures 22 (22.75, 23.5, 24.25, 25) (26, 26.75, 27.5)" / 56 (58, 60, 62, 64) (66, 68, 70) cm.

BO all sts.

FRONT

Follow the instructions exactly as for the back until the front measures 19 (19.75, 20.5, 21.25, 22) (23, 23.75, 24.5)" / 48 (50, 52, 54, 56) (58, 60, 62) cm, ending after a RS row. Make sure to place the sleeve m's on exactly the same colour stripe. Last row worked on front bef neckline shaping should be in C2 (5, 3, 1, 4) (2, 5, 3).

NECKLINE SHAPING

Next Row (WS): K60 (65, 70, 76, 81) (85, 90, 95) then sl last 20 (20, 20, 24, 24) (24, 26, 26) sts worked to a st holder or spare needle. This will be the base of the neckline. K to end of row. [40 (45, 50, 52, 57) (61, 64, 69) sts for each front]

Left Front Neck Shaping

Next Row (RS, Dec): K to last 4 sts, k2tog, k2. (1 st dec'd)
Next Row (WS): K to end.
Rep last 2 rows another 5 times. (5 sts

dec'd) [34 (39, 44, 46, 51) (55, 58, 63) sts]
Cont without shaping for another 10 rows. BO all sts.

Right Front Neck Shaping
Next Row (RS): K2, ssk, k to end. (1 st dec'd)
Next Row (WS): K to end.
Rep last 2 rows another 5 times. (5 sts dec'd) [34 (39, 44, 46, 51) (55, 58, 63) sts]

Cont without shaping for another 10 rows. BO all sts.

SEAMING (SHOULDERS)

Note! If preferred, use safety pins at both ends to hold the panels together during seaming.

Using the crochet hook or tapestry needle, join the two sets of shoulders using the Horizontal Invisible Seam. [32 (32, 32, 36, 36) (36, 38, 38) sts rem at back neck]

SLEEVES

With C1 and US 8 / 5 mm circular needles, start at the back m, and pick up, without knitting, 68 (72, 72, 76, 76) (80, 80, 84) sts as foll: 1 st for every colour block, working around to front m. If you have altered the armhole depth, make sure to pick up a multiple of 4 sts. Do not join: the sleeves are worked flat.

Remembering to switch yarns for the stripe patt, work in Garter St until the sleeve measures 12.5 (11.75, 11.5, 11, 10.25) (9.75, 9, 8.75)" / 32 (30, 29, 28, 26) (25, 23, 22) cm, or desired length, ending after an RS row. The cuff will add 4.75" / 12 cm. Last row worked should be C3 (1, 4, 2, 5) (3, 1, 4).

Cuff
Switch to US 6 / 4 mm needles.

Sizes 1, 3, 5 and 7 only
Dec Row (WS): *K2tog, p2tog* to end. [34 (–, 36, –, 38) (–, 40, –) sts]

Sizes 2, 4, 6, and 8 only
Dec Row (WS): K3tog, *p2tog, k2tog* to last 3 sts, p3tog. [– (36, –, 38, –) (40, –, 42) sts]

[34 (36, 36, 38, 38) (40, 40, 42) sts]

Rib Row (RS): *K1, p1* to end.
Work in est 1 x 1 rib for another 33 rows, or until cuff measures 4.75" / 12 cm. Last row worked should be in C1 (4, 2, 5, 3) (1, 4, 2).

Loosely BO all sts in the same colour as last row worked.

Work second sleeve alike, starting at the front m and working around the armhole to the back m. Make sure to match the stripe colour at the end of the main sleeve and cuff.

NECKLINE

With US 6 / 4 mm needles and the yarn colour that comes after the last row at the centre front neck, starting on the left shoulder seam and pick up and k sts as foll:
1 st for every colour block down the left neck edge (11 sts);
20 (20, 20, 24, 24) (24, 26, 26) sts along the held sts on the front panel;
1 st for every colour block up the right neck edge (11 sts);
33 sts along the back panel. [74 (74, 74, 82, 82) (82, 86, 86) sts]
PM for BOR and join for working in the rnd.

Rib Rnd: *K1, p1* to end.
Cont in est 1 x 1 rib for another 14 rnds.
Last rnd worked should be in C1 (4, 2, 5, 4) (1, 4, 2).

Loosely BO all sts in the same colour as last rnd worked.

SEAMING

Seam the sides. First, pin the underarm points tog.

Working with the long tail from the CO, seam from the bottom of the body edge up to the underarm point and then along the sleeve edge as foll: Start from the bottom of the body rib with the Half Stitch Weave (aka Half Mattress Stitch) and then seam the rest using Mattress St or a Vertical Invisible Seam, finishing off with Half Stitch Weave on the cuffs.

FINISHING

Weave in ends. Block to measurements.

Pauliina Leisti

02 Bluma

Bluma is a generously sized sweater with an all-over lace pattern. The yarn is chunky yet light, keeping the pullover from becoming too heavy.

SIZES

1 (2, 3, 4, 5) (6, 7, 8, 9)

Recommended ease: 10" / 25 cm of positive ease.

FINISHED MEASUREMENTS

Bust Circumference: 40.5 (43.5, 47.5, 51.5, 56) (60.75, 64.5, 67.75, 72.5)" / 101.5 (109, 118.5, 129, 140) (152, 161.5, 169.5, 181.5) cm.
Yoke Depth: 9.25 (9.5, 10.5, 11.25, 12.25) (13.25, 13.5, 14.5, 15.25)" / 23 (24, 26.5, 28, 30.5) (33, 34, 36.5, 38) cm.
Length from Underarm to Hem: 14.5 (14.5, 13.75, 13.75, 13.5) (12.5, 12.5, 11.75, 11.75)" / 36.5 (36.5, 34.5, 34.5, 33.5) (31.5, 31.5, 29.5, 29.5) cm.
Total Length (High Neck to Hem): 23.75 (24.25, 24.5, 25, 25.5) (25.75, 26.25, 26.5, 27)" / 59.5 (60.5, 61, 62.5, 64) (64.5, 65.5, 66, 67.5) cm.
Upper Arm Circumference: 14.75 (15.5, 16.5, 17.25, 18.25) (19.5, 21, 21.75, 22.75)" / 37 (39, 41, 43, 45.5) (49, 52.5, 54.5, 57) cm.
Sleeve Length (from Underarm): 16.5 (16.5, 16.5, 16.5, 16.5) (17, 17, 17, 17)" / 41.5 (41.5, 41.5, 41.5, 41.5) (43, 43, 43, 43) cm.

MATERIALS

Yarn: 5 (6, 6, 7, 7) (8, 8, 9, 9) skeins of Unelma by Vuonue (100% Finnish lambswool, 131 yds / 120 m – 100 g), colourway Hiekka.

Or approx. 620 (675, 730, 800, 875) (950, 1030, 1090, 1180) yds / 565 (615, 665, 730, 800) (870, 940, 995, 1080) m of bulky-weight, soft unspun/light wool yarn. Alternative yarn suggestions are for example Ístex Plötulopi held double, Patons Classic Wool Roving held single and CaMaRose Snefnug held double.

Needles: US 10 / 6 mm 32–40" / 80–100 cm circular needles (for body) 16" / 40 cm circular needles (for sleeves and neckband) and DPNs (for sleeves in smallest sizes), US 9 / 5.5 mm 32–40" / 80–100 cm circular needles (for body trim) 16" / 40 cm circular needles (for neckband trim as well as cuffs in larger sizes) and DPNs (for cuffs in smallest sizes), US 8 / 5 mm needles (for BO).

Notions: Removable stitch markers, waste yarn or stitch holders.

GAUGE

13 sts x 16 rows to 4" / 10 cm on US 10 / 6 mm needles in Lace St Patt, after wet blocking. *Note!* Stretch the fabric gently to open the lace patt when blocking.

Knit a swatch using the red-outlined box of Chart D with approx. 25 sts and calculate the gauge measuring the whole swatch, as it is difficult to count sts from the lace patt. Make sure to have a balanced number of increases and decreases. Count rows from the straight stitch columns.

SPECIAL ABBREVIATIONS

skpo: Sl 1 st kwise, k1, psso. (1 st dec'd)

sk2po: Sl 1 st kwise, k2tog, psso. (2 sts dec'd)

SPECIAL TECHNIQUES

Icelandic Bind-Off
K 1 st and pl it back on LHN. *Insert the tip of the RHN pwise into the front loop of the first st on LHN and then kwise into the front loop of the second st. K the second st. Sl both sts off LHN. Pl the new st back on LHN.* Rep *–* until all sts have been BO. Cut yarn and pull yarn tail through the last st.

NOTES

Charts show only the odd-numbered rows/rounds. The even-numbered rows/rounds are purled on the WS and knitted on the RS, unless otherwise stated.

Occasionally, several charts will be worked on the same row. A removable marker can be used on the knitting to mark where charts change. The marker should not be put on the needle, as decreases and yarn overs move markers. It may be helpful to make copies of the charts to be able to place them in the correct order, so reading them is easier in each section.

Be careful to work charts as instructed. In some charts, the whole row is worked repeating the outlined pattern repeat for a requested number of times. In some charts, only the stitches inside the outlined box are repeated, not the whole row. If working from a chart with an outlined box and the box is not mentioned in the written instructions, work the whole row from the chart without repeating the outlined box again.

When picking up stitches for the shoulders and neckband, be careful to pick up from the centre of a knit column with an upside-down 'V'. This way there won't be any large gaps near the yarn over eyelets.

If between sizes, it is recommended to size up.

The lace pattern is simple to work and remember once getting through the first increases.

CONSTRUCTION

This lace sweater is knitted seamlessly from the top down. First, the back neck is knitted increasing to the full width of the back. The front stitches are picked up from the shoulder lines, and after shaping the neckline, the fronts are joined and worked flat to the underarms. The front and back are joined at the underarm and worked in the round. The sleeve and neckband stitches are picked up from the body and worked in the round. The hem, sleeves and neck opening have a minimal simple trim with an Icelandic BO.

DIRECTIONS

BACK

With US 10 / 6 mm 32–40" / 80–100 cm circular needles, CO 22 sts using the Long-Tail CO method. Pl a removable m in the first and last st.
Note! Work edge sts loosely on each row to avoid the shoulder line becoming too tight.

Set-Up Row (WS): P to end.
Row 1 (RS, Inc): K2, work row 1 of Chart A to 2 sts bef end, k2. (2 sts inc'd)
Row 2 (WS, Inc) and all WS Rows: P2, m1r(p), p to 2 sts bef end, m1l(p), p2. (2 sts inc'd)
Work as est until row 19 of Chart A has been worked. Work 1 more WS row as est. (40 sts inc'd in total since CO) (62 sts)

Sizes 2–9 only
Cont with the Lace patt according to Chart D in the middle and start working according to Charts B and C on each side as foll, until row – (1, 5, 9, 11) (17, 17, 19, 23) from Charts B, D and C has been worked, ending after an RS row:

Row 1 (RS, Inc): K2, work row 1 of Chart B, work row 1 of Chart D working the blue-outlined patt rep 2 times, work row 1 of Chart C, k2. (2 sts inc'd)
Row 2 (WS, Inc) and all WS Rows: P2, m1r(p), p to 2 sts bef end, m1l(p), p2. (2 sts inc'd)

After working to specified row of charts, – (2, 10, 18, 22) (34, 34, 38, 46) sts have been inc'd in total.

Sizes 2, 3, 5, 7 and 8 only
Work 1 more WS row as est. (2 sts inc'd)

All sizes
[62 (66, 74, 80, 86) (96, 98, 102, 108) sts] Back inc's are finished. Pl a removable m on the first and last st.

Sizes 4, 6 and 9 only
Next Row (WS): P to end.

Sizes 1, 2 and 9 only
Next Row (RS): K3 (5, –, –, –) (–, –, –, 4), skpo, work row 1 (3, –, –, –) (–, –, –, 1) of Chart D working the blue-outlined patt rep 2 (2, –, –, –) (–, –, –, 4) times, skpo, k3 (5, –, –, –) (–, –, –, 4).
Next Row (WS) and all WS Rows: P to end.
Next Row: K3 (5, –, –, –) (–, –, –, 4), skpo, work next row of Chart D working the blue-outlined patt rep 2 (2, –, –, –) (–, –, –, 4) times, skpo, k3 (5, –, –, –) (–, –, –, 4).
Cont as est until 14 (14, –, –, –) (–, –, –, 15) rows in total have been worked after the end of back increases.

Sizes 3, 4, 6, 7 and 8 only
Next Row (RS): K– (–, 2, 5, –) (2, 3, 5, –), work row – (–, 1, 5, –) (1, 1, 3, –) of Chart – (–, E, E, –) (M, M, M, –), work row – (–, 7, 11, –) (19, 19, 21, –) of Chart D working the blue-outlined patt rep 2 times, work row – (–, 1, 5, –) (1, 1, 3, –) of Chart – (–, F, F, –) (N, N, N, –), k– (–, 2, 5, –) (2, 3, 5, –).
Next Row (WS) and all WS Rows: P to end.
Next Row: K– (–, 2, 5, –) (2, 3, 5, –), work next row of Chart – (–, E, E, –) (M, M, M, –), work next row of Chart D working the blue-outlined patt rep 2 times, work next row of Chart – (–, F, F, –) (N, N, N, –), k– (–, 2, 5, –) (2, 3, 5, –).

Cont as est until – (–, 14, 13, –) (13, 14, 16, –) rows have been worked in total after the end of back inc's.

Size 5 only
Next Row (RS): Work row 1 of Chart G, work row 13 of Chart D working the blue-outlined patt rep 2 times, work row 1 of Chart H.
Next Row (WS) and all WS Rows: P to end.
Next Row: Work next row of Chart G, work next row of Chart D working the blue-outlined patt rep 2 times, work next row of Chart H.
Cont as est until 14 rows in total have been worked after the end of back increases.

All sizes
Last worked row is a WS row, row 14 (16, 20, 22, 2) (6, 8, 12, 14) of Chart D. The back measures approx. 8.75 (9.25, 10.25, 10.75, 11.75) (12.75, 13.25, 14.25, 14.75)" / 22 (23, 25.5, 27, 29.5) (32, 33, 35.5, 37) cm from the neck edge CO m. Make a note of the last row worked on Chart D. Break yarn and leave sts on a st holder or waste yarn.

LEFT FRONT SHOULDER

With the RS of back facing, US 10 / 6 mm needles and starting at the neck edge of the shoulder slope from the st marked with a m after CO, pick up and k 22 (24, 28, 31, 34) (39, 40, 42, 45) sts along the left shoulder line until the removable m at the end of incs. Pick up 1 st per row.

Set-Up Row (WS): P to end.

Sizes 1 and 2 only
Row 1 (RS): Work row 1 of Chart I, skpo, k3 (5, –, –, –) (–, –, –, –).
Row 2 and all WS Rows: P to end.
Row 3: Work next row of Chart I, skpo, k3 (5, –, –, –) (–, –, –, –).
Cont as est until row 15 of Chart I has been worked (to red line on chart). Work 1 more WS row. (3 sts inc'd overall)

Sizes 3 and 4 only
Row 1 (RS): Work row 1 of Chart I, work row 7 of Chart F, k– (–, 2, 5, –) (–, –, –, –).
Row 2 (WS) and all WS Rows: P to end.
Row 3: Work next row of Chart I, work next row of Chart F, k– (–, 2, 5, –) (–, –, –, –).
Cont as est until row 15 of Chart I has been worked (to red line on chart). Work 1 more WS row. (3 sts inc'd overall)

Sizes 5–8 only
Row 1 (RS): Work row 1 of Chart K, work row – (–, –, –, 1) (7, 7, 7, –) of Chart – (–, –, –, H) (N, N, N, –), k – (–, –, –, 0) (2, 3, 5, –).
Row 2 (WS) and all WS Rows: P to end.
Row 3 (RS): Work next row of Chart K, work next row of Chart – (–, –, –, H) (N, N, N, –), k – (–, –, –, 0) (2, 3, 5, –).
Cont as est until row 19 of Chart K has been worked (to red line on chart). Work 1 more WS row. (3 sts inc'd overall)

Size 9 only
Row 1 (RS): Work row 1 of Chart K, sk2po, work the first row of the purple-outlined box of Chart A, skpo, k4.
Row 2 and all WS Rows: P to end.
Row 3 (RS): Work next row of Chart K, sk2po, work next row of the purple-outlined box of Chart A, skpo, k4.
Cont as est until row 19 of Chart K has been worked (to red line on chart). Work 1 more WS row. (3 sts inc'd overall)

All sizes
[25 (27, 31, 34, 37) (42, 43, 45, 48) sts]
Cut yarn and leave sts on a st holder or waste yarn. *Note!* Row 17 (17, 17, 17, 21) (21, 21, 21, 21) of charts (marked by the red line) is worked later.

RIGHT FRONT SHOULDER

With the RS of back facing, US 10 / 6 mm needles and starting at the st at the right end of back inc's marked by a removable m, pick up and k 22 (24, 28, 31, 34) (39, 40, 42, 45) sts along the right shoulder line, until the m at the CO neck edge. Pick up 1 st per row.

Set-Up Row (WS): P to end.

Sizes 1 and 2 only
Row 1 (RS): K3 (5, –, –, –) (–, –, –, –), skpo, work row 1 of Chart J.
Row 2 (WS) and all WS Rows: P to end.
Row 3: K3 (5, –, –, –) (–, –, –, –), skpo, work next row of Chart J.
Cont as est until row 15 of Chart J has been worked. Work 1 more WS row. (3 sts inc'd overall)

Joining Row (RS): K3 (5, –, –, –) (–, –, –, –), skpo, work row 17 of Chart J, CO 12 sts using the Backwards Loop CO method, then across left front sts, work row 17 of Chart I, skpo, k3 (5, –, –, –) (–, –, –, –).

Sizes 3 and 4 only
Row 1 (RS): K– (–, 2, 5, –) (–, –, –, –), work row 7 of Chart E, work row 1 of Chart J.
Row 2 (WS) and all WS Rows: P to end.
Row 3: K– (–, 2, 5, –) (–, –, –, –), work next row of Chart E, work next row of Chart J.
Cont as est until row 15 of Chart J has been worked. Work 1 more WS row. (3 sts inc'd overall)

Joining Row (RS): K– (–, 2, 5, –) (–, –, –, –), work next row of Chart E, work row 17 of Chart J, CO 12 sts using the Backwards Loop CO method, then across left front sts, work row 17 of Chart I, work next row of Chart F, k– (–, 2, 5, –) (–, –, –, –).

Size 5–8 only
Row 1 (RS): K– (–, –, –, 0) (2, 3, 5, –), work row – (–, –, –, 1) (7, 7, 7, –) of Chart – (–, –, –, G) (M, M, M, –), work row 1 of Chart L.
Row 2 (WS) and all WS Rows: P to end.
Row 3: K– (–, –, –, 0) (2, 3, 5, –), work next row of Chart – (–, –, –, G) (M, M, M, –), work next row of Chart L.
Cont as est until row 19 of Chart L has been worked. Work 1 more WS row. (3 sts inc'd overall)

Joining Row (RS): K– (–, –, –, 0) (2, 3, 5, –), work next row of Chart – (–, –, –, G) (M, M, M, –), work row 21 of Chart L, CO 12 sts using the Backwards Loop CO method, then across left front sts, work row 21 of Chart K, work next row of Chart – (–, –, –, H) (N, N, N, –), k – (–, –, –, 0) (2, 3, 5, –).

Size 9 only
Row 1 (RS): K4, skpo, work row 1 of blue-outlined box in Chart D, work row 1 of Chart L.
Row 2 (WS) and all WS rows: P to end.
Row 3: K4, skpo, work next row of the blue-outlined box in Chart D, work next row of Chart L.
Cont as est until row 19 of Chart L has been worked. Work 1 more WS row. (3 sts inc'd overall)

Joining Row (RS): K4, skpo, work next row of blue-outlined box in Chart D, work row 21 of Chart L, CO 12 sts using the Backwards Loop CO method, then across left front sts, work row 21 of Chart K, sk2po, work next row of the purple-outlined box in Chart A, skpo, k4.

All sizes
[62 (66, 74, 80, 86) (96, 98, 102, 108) sts for the front]

From now on, work only according to rows 11–22 of Chart D (red-outlined box) every time working Chart D. (Row 22 is the last WS row of the patt rep, not shown on the chart). Rep these rows according to the instructions for chosen size.

Next Row (WS): P to end.

Sizes 1, 2 and 9 only
Next Row (RS): K3 (5, –, –, –) (–, –, –, 4), skpo, work row 19 (19, –, –, –) (–, –, –, 11) of Chart D working the red-outlined patt rep 2 (2, –, –, –) (–, –, –, 4) times, skpo, k3 (5, –, –, –) (–, –, –, 4).
Next Row (WS) and all WS Rows: P to end.
Next Row: K3 (5, –, –, –) (–, –, –, 4), skpo, work next row of Chart D working the red-outlined patt rep 2 (2, –, –, –) (–, –, –, 4) times, skpo, k3 (5, –, –, –) (–, –, –, 4).

Sizes 3, 4, 6, 7 and 8 only
Next Row (RS): K– (–, 2, 5, –) (2, 3, 5, –), work row – (–, 1, 1, –) (5, 5, 5, –) of Chart – (–, E, E, –) (M, M, M, –), work row – (–, 19, 19, –) (11, 11, 11, –) of Chart D working the red-outlined patt rep 2 times, work row – (–, 1, 1, –) (5, 5, 5, –) of Chart – (–, F, F, –) (N, N, N, –), k– (–, 2, 5, –) (2, 3, 5, –).
Next Row (WS) and all WS Rows: P to end.
Next Row: K– (–, 2, 5, –) (2, 3, 5, –), work next row of Chart – (–, E, E, –) (M, M, M, –), work next row of Chart D working the red-outlined patt rep 2 times, work next row of Chart – (–, F, F, –) (N, N, N, –), k– (–, 2, 5, –) (2, 3, 5, –).

Size 5 only
Row 1 (RS): Work row 11 of Chart G, work row 11 of Chart D working the red-outlined patt rep 2 times, work row 11 of Chart H.
Row 2 (WS) and all WS Rows: P to end.
Row 3: Work next row of Chart G, work next row of Chart D working the red-outlined patt rep 2 times, work next row of Chart H.

All sizes
Cont working as est until the front measures approx. 9.75 (10.25, 11.25, 11.75, 12.75) (13.75, 14.25, 15.25, 15.75)" / 24.5 (25.5, 28, 29.5, 32) (34.5, 35.5, 38, 39.5) cm from the shoulder pick-up line (front is 1" / 2.5 cm longer than the back), ending after a WS row. Last lace patt row worked should be the same as the last lace patt row worked for the back.

JOINING FRONT AND BACK

Sizes 1, 2 and 9 only

Next Row (RS): *K3 (5, –, –, –) (–, –, –, 4), skpo, work next row of Chart D working the red-outlined patt rep 2 (2, –, –, –) (–, –, –, 4) times, skpo, k3 (5, –, –, –) (–, –, –, 4)*, CO 4 (5, –, –, –) (–, –, –, 10) sts for left underarm using the Backwards Loop CO method, put the sts held for the back to needles, rep *–* on the back sts, CO 4 (5, –, –, –) (–, –, –, 10) sts for right underarm using the Backwards Loop CO method, PM for BOR.

Sizes 3 and 4 only

Next Row (RS): *K– (–, 2, 5, –) (–, –, –, –), work next row of Chart E, work next row of Chart D working the red-outlined patt rep 2 times, work next row of Chart F, k– (–, 2, 5, –) (–, –, –, –)*, CO – (–, 3, 4, –) (–, –, –, –) sts for left underarm using the Backwards Loop CO method, put the sts held for the back to needles, rep *–* on the back sts, CO – (–, 2, 4, –) (–, –, –, –) sts for right underarm using the Backwards Loop CO method, PM for BOR, CO – (–, 1, 0, –) (–, –, –, –) st(s).

Size 5 only

Next Row (RS): *Work next row of Chart G, work next row of Chart D working the red-outlined patt rep 2 times, work next row of Chart H*, CO 5 sts for left underarm using the Backwards Loop CO method, put the sts held for the back to needles, rep *–* on the back sts, CO 5 sts for right underarm using the Backwards Loop CO method, PM.

Sizes 6–8 only

Next Row (RS): *K– (–, –, –, –) (2, 3, 5, –) work next row of Chart M, sk2po, work next row of Chart D working the red-outlined patt rep 2 times, work the next row of Chart N, k– (–, –, –, –) (2, 3, 5, –)*, CO – (–, –, –, –) (3, 7, 8, –) sts for left underarm using the Backwards Loop CO method, put the sts held for the back to needles, rep *–* on the back sts, CO – (–, –, –, –) (2, 7, 8, –) sts for right underarm using the Backwards Loop CO method, PM, CO – (–, –, –, –) (1, 0, 0, –) st(s).

All sizes

[132 (142, 154, 168, 182) (198, 210, 220, 236) sts for the body]

From now on, work in the rnd, working Chart D in the middle of the front and back sts and with side sts according to chosen size.

Make sure to beg working from the side st patt row that corresponds to the patt on the next Chart D row – be aware that the row numbers might be different.

When working rows from the green-/orange-/brown-outlined boxes, work only the sts inside the outlined box.

Use a removable m for the BOR m, as for some sizes it will move regularly.

Sizes 1 and 2 only

Next Rnd: K to BOR m.

Partial Set-Up Rnd: K3 (5, –, –, –) (–, –, –, –), *skpo, work next row of Chart D working the red-outlined patt rep 2 times, skpo*, k10 (15, –, –, –) (–, –, –, –), k1, rep *–* once, PM (new BOR m), remove the earlier m.

Next Rnd: K to BOR m, RM, sl1, PM (new BOR m).

Next Rnd: *K0 (3, –, –, –) (–, –, –, –), work the row from the brown-outlined box on Chart H that corresponds with the row that will be worked next on Chart D, ko (2, –, –, –) (–, –, –, –), sk2po, work next row of Chart D working the red-outlined patt rep 2 times, sk2po*, k1, rep *–* once.

Next Rnd: K to BOR m, RM, sl1, PM (new BOR m).

Next Rnd: *Ko (3, –, –, –) (–, –, –, –), work the next row from the brown-outlined box on Chart H, ko (2, –, –, –) (–, –, –, –), sk2po, work next row of Chart D working the red-outlined patt rep 2 times, sk2po*, k1, rep *–* once.

Size 3 only

Next Rnd: K to BOR m, RM, sl1, PM (new BOR m).

Next Rnd: *Work the row from the brown-outlined box on Chart H that corresponds with the row that will worked next on Chart D, sk2po, work next row of Chart D working the red-outlined patt rep 2 times, sk2po, work the same row from the green-outlined box on Chart G that will be worked at the beg of rnd from Chart H, sk2po*, k1, rep *–* once.

Next Rnd: K to BOR m, RM, sl1, PM (new BOR m).

Next Rnd: *Work the next row from the brown-outlined box on Chart H, sk2po, work next row of Chart D working the red-outlined patt rep 2 times, sk2po, work the next row from the green-outlined box on Chart G, sk2po*, k1, rep *–* once.

Size 4 only

Partial Set-Up Rnd: K to 2 sts bef M, pl a new BOR m. (Remove earlier m.)

Next Rnd: *K3, skpo, work the row from the green-outlined box on Chart G that corresponds with the row that will worked next on Chart D, sk2po, work next row of Chart D working the red-outlined patt rep 2 times, sk2po, work the same row from the green-outlined box on Chart G worked at the beg of rnd, skpo, k3*, rep *–* once.

Next Rnd: K to BOR m.

Next Rnd: *K3, skpo, work the next row from the green-outlined box on Chart G, sk2po, work next row of Chart D working the red-outlined patt rep 2 times, sk2po, work the next row from the green-outlined box on Chart G, skpo, k3*, rep *–* once.

Size 5 only

Next Rnd: K to BOR m.

Partial Set-Up Rnd: *Work next row of Chart G, work next row of Chart D working the red-outlined patt rep 2 times*, work next row of Chart H, k5, rep *–* once, work the first 12 sts from next row of Chart H, PM (new BOR m), remove the earlier m.

Next Rnd: K to BOR m, RM, sl1, PM (new BOR m).

Next Rnd: *K1, work the row from the orange-outlined box on Chart L that corresponds with the row that will be worked next on Chart D, k1, sk2po, work the row from the green-outlined box on Chart G that corresponds with the row that will be worked next on Chart D, sk2po, work next row of Chart D working the red-outlined patt rep 2 times, sk2po, work the same row from the green-outlined box on Chart G that will be worked at the beg of rnd, sk2po*, k1, rep *–* once.

Next Rnd: K to BOR m, RM, sl1, PM (new BOR m).

Next Rnd: *K1, work the next row from the orange-outlined box on Chart L, k1, sk2po, work the next row from the green-outlined box on Chart G, sk2po, work next row of Chart D working the red-outlined patt rep 2 times, sk2po, work the next row from the green-outlined box on Chart G, sk2po*, k1, rep *–* once.

Sizes 6 and 7 only

Next Rnd: K to BOR m.

Next Rnd: *Work next row of Chart D working the red-outlined patt rep 4 times, k- (–, –, –, –) (0, 3, –, –), sk2po, k - (–, –, –, –) (0, 3, –, –)*, rep *–* once. [*Size 6 only:* Bef making the last sk2po, move the m 1 st to left. M is now just after the last sk2po.] [*Size 7 only:* RM, move it 2 sts to the right, to the left side of the last worked sk2po.]

Next Rnd: K to BOR m.

Next Rnd: K - (–, –, –, –) (0, 3, –, –), *work next row of Chart D working the red-outlined patt rep 4 times, k - (–, –, –, –) (0, 3, –, –), sk2po*, k - (–, –, –, –) (0, 3, –, –), rep *–* once. Bef making the last sk2po, move the m 1 st to left. M is now just after the last sk2po.

Size 8 only

Next Rnd: K to BOR m, RM, k2, PM (new BOR m).

Next Rnd: Work next row from the red-outlined box of Chart D working the red-outlined patt rep 10 times. *Note!* Only work the sts inside the red box. Bef making the last sk2po, move the m 1 st to left. M is now just after the last sk2po.

Next Rnd: K to BOR m.

Size 9 only

Next Rnd: K to BOR m.

Partial Set-Up Rnd: K4, *skpo, work next row of Chart D working the red-outlined patt rep 4 times, skpo*, k18, rep *–* once, PM (new BOR m), remove the earlier m.

Next Rnd: K to BOR m, RM, sl1, PM (new BOR m).

Next Rnd: *K3, work the row from the green-outlined box on Chart G that corresponds with the row that will be worked next on Chart D, k4, sk2po, work next row of Chart D working the red-outlined patt rep 4 times, sk2po*, k1, rep *–* once.

Next Rnd: K to BORM, RM, sl1, PM (new BOR m).

Next Rnd: *K3, work the next row from the green-outlined box on Chart G, k4, sk2po, work next row of Chart D working the red-outlined patt rep 4 times, sk2po*, k1, rep *–* once.

All sizes

Rep the last 2 rnds for chosen size until the body measures approx. 14 (14, 13.25,

13.25, 12.75) (12, 12, 11.25, 11.25)" / 35 (35, 33, 33, 32) (30, 30, 28, 28) cm from the underarm or 0.5" / 1.5 cm less than desired length slightly stretched, ending after a lace patt rnd.

Hem

Change to US 9 / 5.5 mm needles and k 3 rnds.

Next Rnd: *With RHN, pick up the WS purl bump 1 row below the next st and pl it on the LHN. K2tog*, rep *–* to BOR.

With US 8 / 5 mm needles, BO all sts using the Icelandic BO method.

NECKBAND

With the back of the work facing, beg from the right shoulder seam and with US 9 / 5.5 mm 16" / 40 cm circular needles, pick up and k 64 (64, 64, 64, 70) (70, 70, 70, 70) sts along the neck edge as foll:
Pick up approx. 4 sts for every 5 rows along vertical edges, 1 st for each st on CO edge and along the shaped edges, pick up 1 st per each row but skip the bigger holes to avoid holes in the picked-up edge. *Note!* Pick up sts from the centre of a knit column with an upside down 'V'. The exact number of picked up sts isn't crucial.

Next Rnd: PM, k to BOR. If the picked-up sts feel too loose, work sts from the back loop on the first rnd.

K 2 rnds.

Next Rnd: *With RHN pick up the WS purl bump 1 row below the next st on the LHN and pl it on the LHN. K2tog*, rep *–* to BOR.

With US 8 / 5 mm needles, BO sts using the Icelandic BO method.

SLEEVES

With US 10 / 6 mm 16" / 40 cm circular needles or DPNs, beg at the right edge of the underarm and pick up and k 1 st just bef the CO sts, 4 (5, 3, 4, 5) (3, 7, 8, 10) sts from the CO sts, and 1 st just after them. Then cont to pick up and k 42 (44, 48, 50, 52) (55, 57, 61, 62) sts around the armhole (approx. 4 sts per 5 rows). [48 (51, 53, 56, 59) (60, 66, 71, 74) sts]

On the next rnd, work the sts tbl if the picked-up sts feel loose. If there is a hole at the shoulder seam on the back, pick up an extra st and work it tog with the next st.

Set-Up Rnd: K3 (4, 3, 3, 4) (5, 6, 5, 6), PM for BOR, k to BOR.

Beg working in the lace patt, with St St at the underarm, while AT THE SAME TIME working the Sleeve Shaping. Read through the whole section bef starting.

Sizes 1–5 only
Next Rnd: K7 (8, 9, 11, 12) (–, –, –, –), skpo, PM, work the first row (row 5) of the pink-outlined box from Chart D once, skpo, k to BOR.
Next Rnd: K to m, RM, k1, PM, k to BOR.
Next Rnd: K to 2 sts bef m, skpo, SM, work next row of the pink-outlined box from Chart D once, skpo, k to BOR.

Rep rows 5–16 from Chart D for the lace patt.

Sizes 6–9 only
Next Rnd: K– (–, –, –, –) (4, 6, 7, 9), skpo, PM, work row 11 of Chart D working the red-outlined patt rep 2 times, skpo, k to BOR.
Next Rnd: K to m, RM, k1, PM, k to BOR.
Next Rnd: K to 2 sts bef m, skpo, sm, work next row of Chart D working the red-outlined patt rep 2 times, skpo, k to BOR.

Rep rows 11–22 from Chart D for the lace patt.

Sleeve Shaping

Work in lace patt and St St as set for 7 (7, 7, 7, 7) (4, 4, 4, 4) rnds.

Dec Rnd: K1 (0, 0, 1, 0) (1, 1, 0, 1), k2tog, work as est to 3 sts bef BOR, ssk, k1. (2 sts dec'd)
Rep the dec rnd, every 13 (11, 11, 9, 9) (7, 6, 5, 5)th rnd, 3 (4, 4, 5, 5) (7, 9, 10, 11) times. Change to DPNs if needed. [6 (8, 8, 10, 10) (14, 18, 20 22) sts dec'd] [40 (41, 43, 44, 47) (48, 48, 49, 50) sts after final dec]

Rep last 2 rnds for chosen size, working the lace patt and decs as instructed until the sleeve measures approx. 16 (16, 16, 16, 16) (16.5, 16.5, 16.5, 16.5)" / 40 (40, 40, 40, 40) (41.5, 41.5, 41.5, 41.5) cm from the underarm or 0.5" / 1.5 cm less than desired length when slightly stretched, ending after a lace patt rnd.

Cuff

Change to US 9 / 5.5 mm needles or DPNs and k 3 rnds.

Next Rnd: *With RHN pick up the WS purl bump 1 row below the next st and pl it on the LHN. K2tog*, rep *–* to BOR.

With US 8 / 5 mm needles, BO sts using the Icelandic BO method.

Work second sleeve alike.

FINISHING

Weave in ends. Wet block to measurements opening the lace patt by stretching the fabric gently.

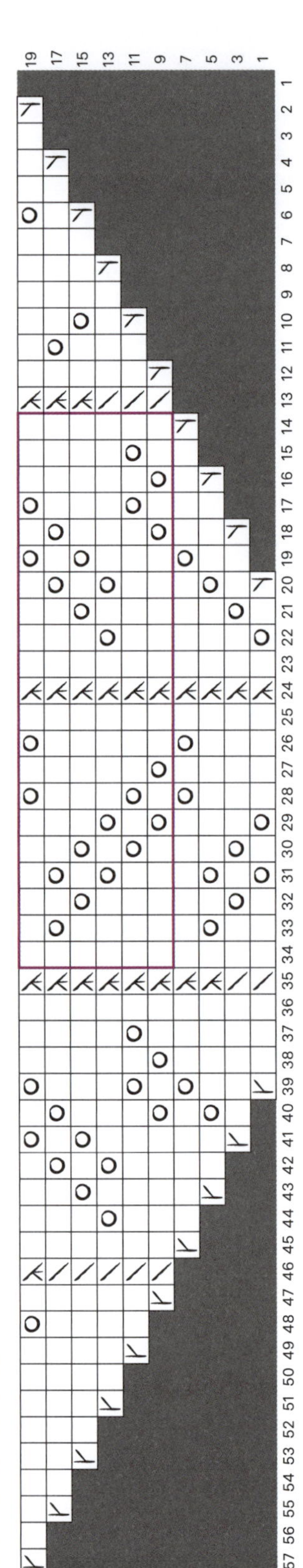

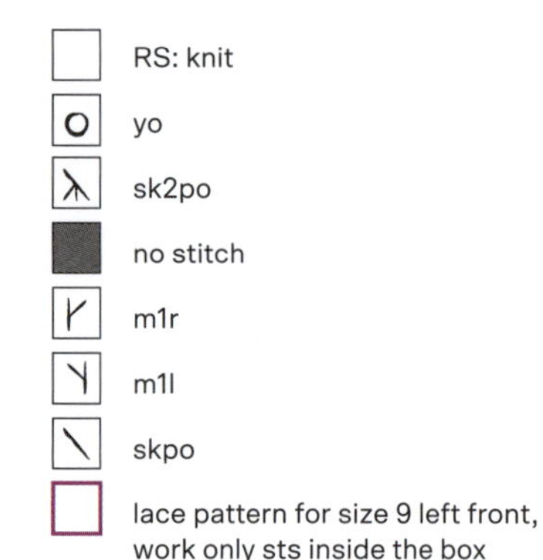

CHART E - LEFT BACK AND RIGHT FRONT SIDE (SIZES 3-4)

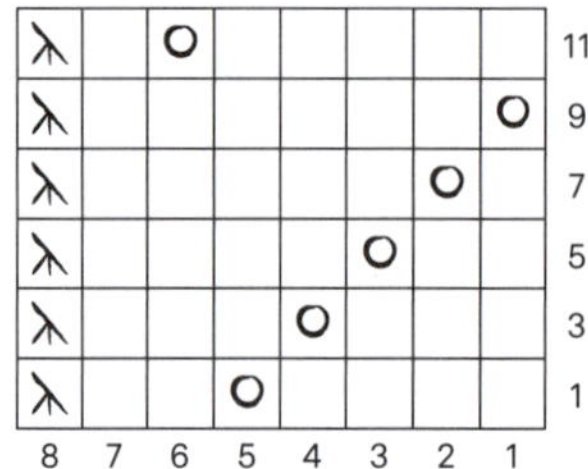

CHART F - RIGHT BACK AND LEFT FRONT SIDE (SIZES 3-4)

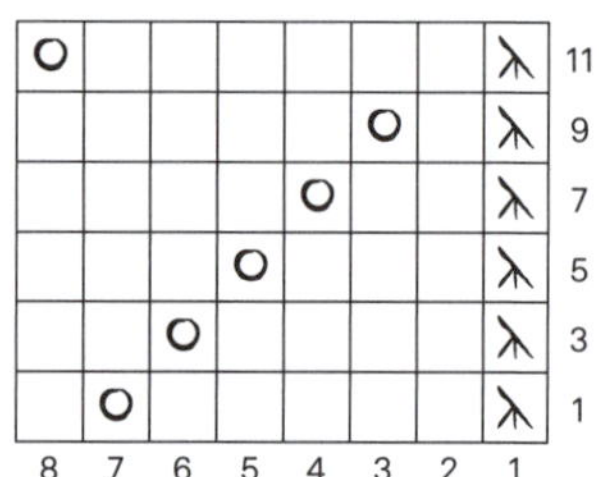

CHART G - SIDE CHART

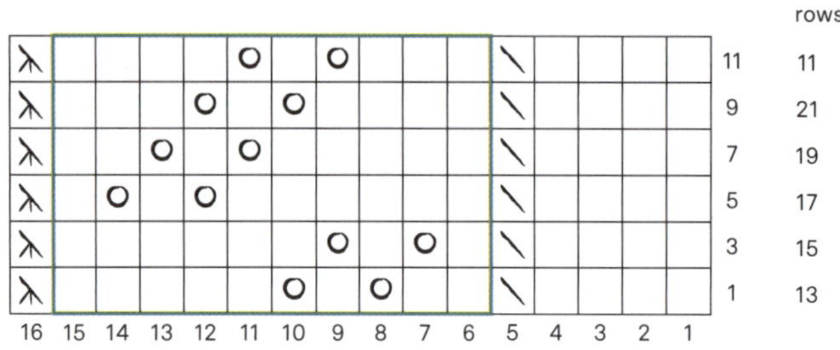

lace pattern for side sts, work only sts inside the box

lace pattern for sleeves (sizes 1-5)

pattern repeat

pattern repeat

CHART B - LEFT BACK INCREASE

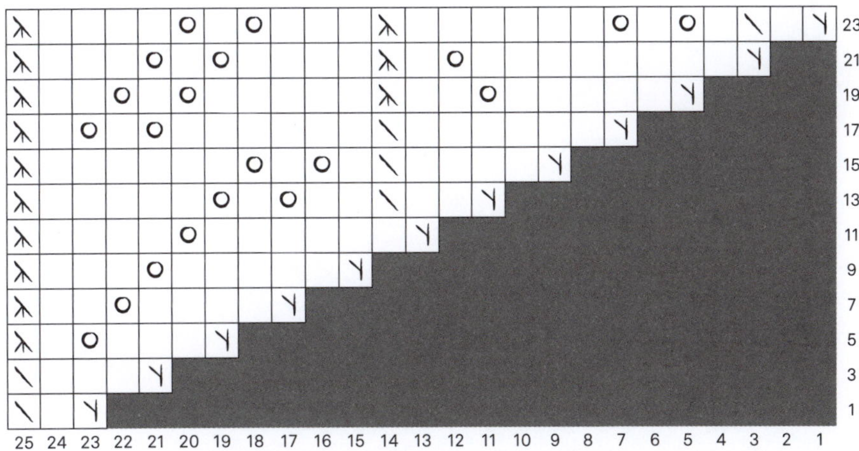

CHART C - RIGHT BACK INCREASE

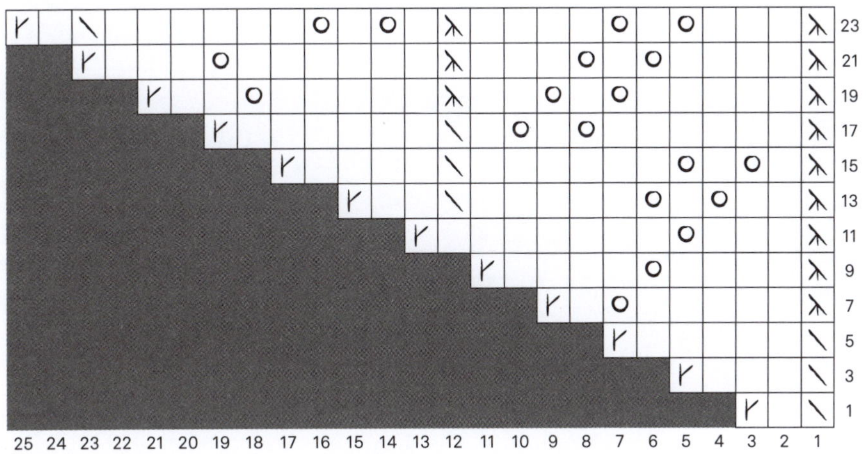

CHART D - MAIN CHART

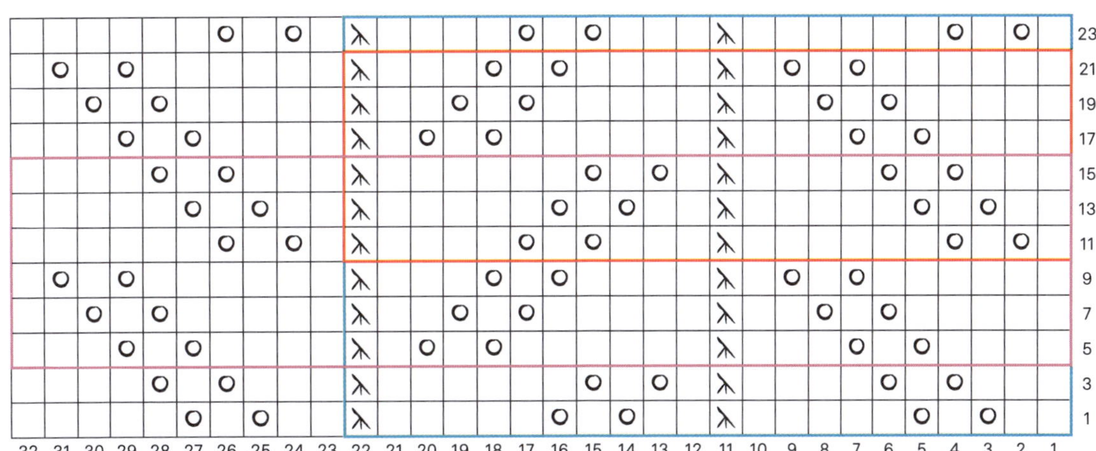

CHART H - SIDE CHART

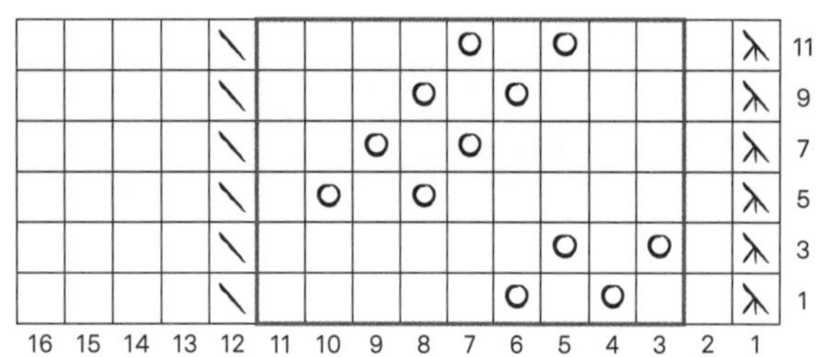

Corresponding rows for Chart D

11
21
19
17
15
13

☐ lace pattern for side sts, work only sts inside the box

CHART I - LEFT FRONT CHART (SIZES 1-4)

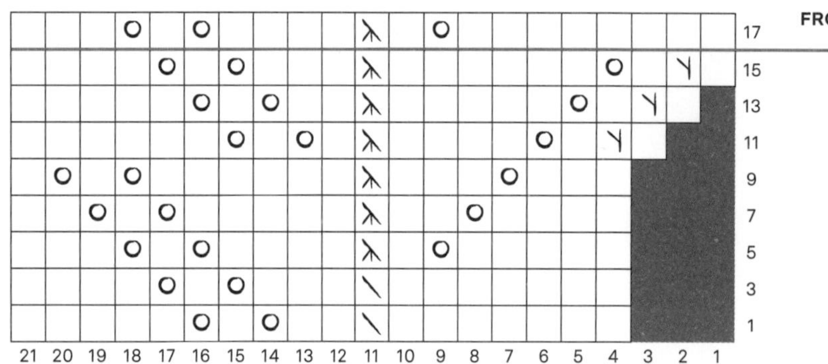

FRONT

CHART J - RIGHT FRONT CHART (SIZES 1-4)

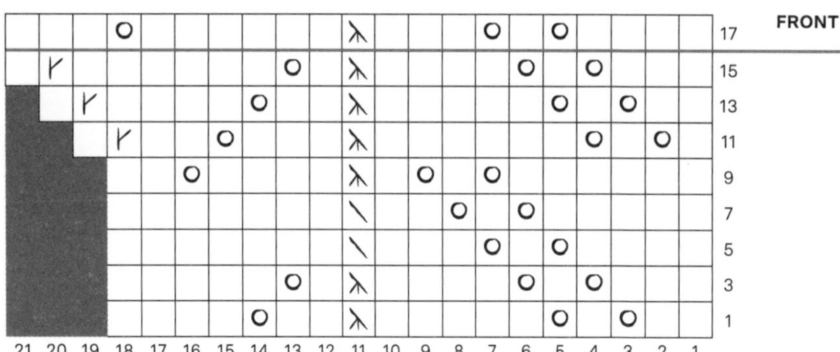

FRONT

CHART M - LEFT BACK SIDE CHART (SIZES 6-8)

19	18	17	16	15	14	13	12	11	10	9	8	7	6	5	4	3	2	1	
⋋		O		O							⋋				O				11
⋋							O		O		⋋					O			9
⋋						O		O			⋋						O		7
⋋					O		O				⋋							O	5
⋋				O		O					⋋		O						3
⋋			O		O						⋋			O					1

CHART K - LEFT FRONT CHART (SIZES 5-9)

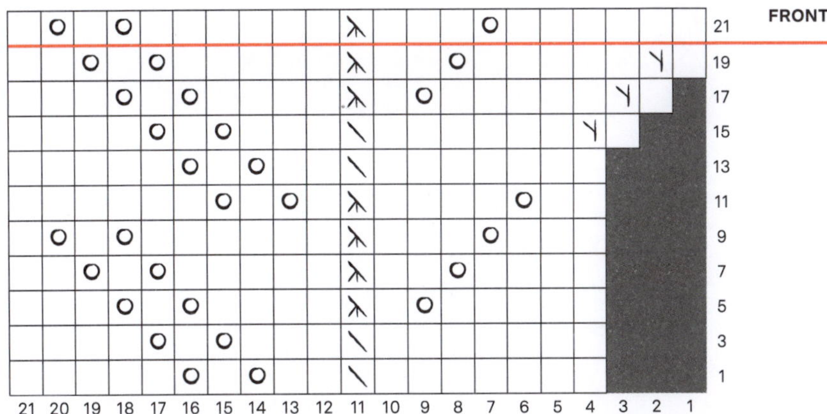

CHART L - RIGHT FRONT CHART (SIZES 5-9)

Row	21	20	19	18	17	16	15	14	13	12	11	10	9	8	7	6	5	4	3	2	1
21						O					⋏		O		O						
19		Y			O						⋏			O		O					
17	■		Y								⋏				O		O				
15	■	■		Y					O		⋏					O		O			
13	■	■	■					O			⋏						O		O		
11	■	■	■				O				⋏							O		O	
9	■	■	■			O					⋏		O		O						
7	■	■	■								\			O		O					
5	■	■	■								\				O		O				
3	■	■	■						O		⋏					O		O			
1	■	■	■					O			⋏						O		O		

FRONT

Corresponding rows for Chart D

21
19
17
15
13
11

□ lace pattern for side sts, work only sts inside the box

CHART N - RIGHT BACK SIDE CHART (SIZES 6-8)

Row	19	18	17	16	15	14	13	12	11	10	9	8	7	6	5	4	3	2	1
11			O					⋏		O		O							⋏
9				O				⋏							O		O		⋏
7					O			⋏						O		O			⋏
5						O		⋏					O		O				⋏
3	O							⋏				O		O					⋏
1		O						⋏			O		O						⋏

Veera Välimäki

03 Limelight

Easy, boxy and with two versions to choose from – that is what the Limelight sweater is all about! You can make it with any chunky yarn, with or without intarsia add-ons.

SIZES

1 (2, 3, 4, 5) (6, 7, 8, 9, 10)

Recommended ease: 8–10" / 20.5–25.5 cm of positive ease.

FINISHED MEASUREMENTS

Chest Circumference: 36 (40, 44, 48, 52) (56, 60, 64, 68, 72)" / 90 (100, 110, 120, 130) (140, 150, 160, 170, 180) cm.
Yoke Depth: 7.75 (9, 9.5, 10, 10.75) (11.5, 12, 12.75, 13.5, 14)" / 19.5 (23, 24.5, 26, 27.5) (29.5, 30.5, 32.5, 34, 36) cm.
Upper Arm Circumference: 12 (13.25, 14.25, 14.75, 16) (17.25, 18.25, 18.75, 20, 20.5)" / 30 (33, 35.5, 37, 40) (43, 45.5, 47, 50, 51.5) cm.
Back of the Neck Width: 5.75 (5.75, 5.75, 6.25, 6.25) (6.75, 6.75, 7.5, 7.5, 7.5)" / 14.5 (14.5, 14.5, 15.5, 15.5) (17, 17, 18.5, 18.5, 18.5) cm.
Body Length from Underarm to Hem: 16" / 40.5 cm.

MATERIALS

Yarn: 4 (4, 4, 5, 5) (5, 6, 6, 6, 7) skeins of Big Kid Mohair by Walk Collection (78% mohair, 13% wool, 9% nylon, 219 yds / 200 m – 100 g), colourway Secret.

Or approx. 700 (770, 850, 920, 1000) (1080, 1150, 1230, 1310, 1390) yds / 640 (705, 775, 840, 915) (990, 1050, 1125, 1200, 1270) m of bulky-weight yarn.

Intarsia version
Big Kid Mohair by Walk Collection (78% mohair, 13% wool, 9% nylon, 219 yds / 200 m – 100 g).

3 (3, 4, 4, 4) (4, 5, 5, 5, 6) skeins colourway Grace (MC) and 1 (1, 1, 1, 1) (1, 2, 2, 2, 2) skein(s) of colourway Lime Soda (CC).

Or approx. 530 (630, 700, 750, 810) (870, 920, 980, 1040, 1100) yds / 485 (575, 640, 685, 740) (795, 840, 895, 950, 1005) m (in MC) and 130 (140, 150, 170, 190) (210, 230, 250, 270, 290) yds / 120 (130, 135, 155, 175) (190, 210, 230, 245, 265) m (in CC) of bulky-weight yarn.

Alternative yarn suggestions are for example Kokon Chunky Mohair and Wool and the Gang Take Care Mohair.

Needles: US 7 / 4.5 mm and US 10 / 6 mm 32" / 80 cm or longer circular needles. DPNs in each size if not using the Magic Loop method for small circumference knitting.

Notions: Stitch markers (2 locking stitch markers, 2 regular), stitch holders or waste yarn, blocking aids.

GAUGE

14 sts and 24 rows to 4" / 10 cm on US 10 / 6 mm needles in St St, after blocking.

SPECIAL TECHNIQUES

Tubular BO for 2 x 2 Rib

Work set-up rnds first.

Note! After Set-Up Rnd 1, sts are aligned for 1 x 1 rib.

Set-Up Rnd 1 (Re-Arrange Sts, RS): *K1, insert the RHN into the second st on LHN from back and slip the 2 sts off RHN holding onto the first st (a k st), catch the dropped k st to LHN and k it, sl1 wyif*, rep *–* to end.

Set-Up Rnds 2 and 4 (RS): *Sl1 wyib, p1* to end.

Set-Up Rnd 3 (RS): *K1, sl1 wyif* to end.

Measure and cut a tail of the working yarn approx. 3 times the length of BO and work Tubular BO.

NOTES

Modifications for Intarsia version

Below are instructions for sections worked in CC. All other parts are worked in MC.

Front Left Shoulder

Work the left front shoulder in CC. When joining the fronts (on WS), work the left front shoulder stitches in CC, CO the front neck stitches in CC and then work the remaining front stitches in MC. Continue working intarsia as established changing colour at the point where you casted on the front neck stitches until you reach the point of 1" / 2.5 cm before joining for lower body. Continue in MC only and place a marker to the point where the colour change was.

Lower Body

Work in MC only until the body measures 1" / 2.5 cm. Then split the body at right underarm as follows. Turn work at BOR to WS.

Next Row (WS): CO 1 extra st to the BOR using MC, p to front m with MC, RM, p3 with MC, PM and attach CC, p to BOR with CC and CO 1 extra st to the end.

Next Row (RS): K to front m in CC, change to MC twisting the yarns at change, and k to end of row in MC.

Continue as established changing colour at the front marker, until the change to smaller needles. With the smaller needle, join in the round again, place the BOR marker and decrease the extra stitches at each end on the joining round. Continue as for the single-colour version.

Right Sleeve

Work the right sleeve flat. Pick up 2 extra stitches at each end of the pick-up (each at underarm), starting with MC but working the last 14 (14, 16, 16, 18) (20, 22, 24, 26, 28) stitches in CC. Continue working as established, back and forth in MC and CC keeping the colour change at the same spot. With the decreases each colour section will decrease at same rate. Continue as established until changing to smaller needles. With the smaller needles, join in the round again, place the BOR marker and decrease the extra stitches at each end on the joining round. Continue as for the single-colour version.

CONSTRUCTION

This sweater with a high 2 x 2 rib neck is worked from the top down, mostly in the round. First, the upper back is worked back and forth without any shaping. Then the stitches for shoulders are picked up along the top of the upper back. Short rows are worked for the shoulders for a better fit. Choose between two versions: a simpler plain knit in one colour and another with intarsia.

DIRECTIONS

BACK

With US 10 / 6 mm needles and MC, CO 62 (70, 76, 84, 90) (98, 104, 112, 118, 126) sts using the Long-Tail CO method. Do not join. Work back and forth in St St.

When knitting the first RS row, pl a locking st m for the end of the left shoulder (LSM) after 21 (25, 28, 31, 34) (37, 40, 43, 46, 50) sts and another locking st m for the beg of the right shoulder (RSM) after 41 (45, 48, 53, 56) (61, 64, 69, 72, 76) sts. [20 (20, 20, 22, 22) (24, 24, 26, 26, 26) sts between m's]

Work in St St until the piece measures 6 (7, 7.5, 8, 8.5) (9, 9.5, 10, 10.5, 11)" / 15 (18, 19, 20.5, 21.5) (23, 24, 25.5, 26.5, 28) cm ending with a WS row. Cut working yarn and place sts on holder.

RIGHT SHOULDER

With US 10 / 6 mm needles and the RS of the back facing, pick up and k 21 (25, 28, 31, 34) (37, 40, 43, 46, 50) sts from the right shoulder, starting from the end of the CO edge of the back and ending at the first st m (RSM). Remove RSM.

Beg working German Short Rows to shape the shoulder.

Set-Up Short Row (WS): P 6 (8, 10, 12, 14) (14, 16, 18, 18, 20) sts, tw.

Short Row 1 (RS): MDS, k to end.

Short Row 2: P to prev DS, p the DS as a single st, p2, tw.

Rep short rows 1–2, 6 (7, 7, 8, 8) (10, 10, 11, 12, 13) times more. Work row 1 once more.

Next Row (WS): P to end working the last DS as a single st.

Cont in St St until the piece measures 6 (6, 6.5, 6.5, 7) (7, 7.5, 7.5, 8, 8)" / 15 (15, 16.5, 16.5, 18) (18, 19, 19, 20.5, 20.5) cm measured from the longer edge (the neck edge).

Inc for the neck.
Inc Row (RS): K to 4 sts bef end, m1r, k to end. (1 st inc'd)
Rep the inc row on every RS row 3 more times. [25 (29, 32, 35, 38) (41, 44, 47, 50, 54) sts]

Work two more rows in St St, ending with a RS row. Cut yarn and pl right front sts on holder.

LEFT SHOULDER

With US 10 / 6 mm needles and RS of the back facing, pick up and k 21 (25, 28, 31, 34) (37, 40, 43, 46, 50) sts from the left shoulder, starting from the second st m (LSM) to the end of the CO edge of the back. Remove LSM.

P to end of next row (WS). Beg short rows to shape the shoulder.
Set-Up Short Row 1 (RS): K 6 (8, 10, 12, 14) (14, 16, 18, 18, 20) sts, tw.
Set-Up Short Row 2 (WS): MDS, p to end.
Short Row 1: K to prev DS, k the DS as a single st, k2, tw.
Short Row 2: MDS, p to end.
Rep short rows 1–2, 6 (7, 7, 8, 8) (10, 10, 11, 12, 13) times more.

Next Row (RS): K to prev DS, k the DS as a single st, k to end.

Cont in St St until the piece measures 6 (6, 6.5, 6.5, 7) (7, 7.5, 7.5, 8, 8)" / 15 (15, 16.5, 16.5, 18) (18, 19, 19, 20.5, 20.5) cm measured from the longer edge (the neck edge).

Inc for the neck.
Inc Row (RS): K4, m1l, k to end. (1 st inc'd)
Rep inc row on every RS row 3 more times. [25 (29, 32, 35, 38) (41, 44, 47, 50, 54) sts]

Work two more rows in St St, ending with a RS row. Keep yarn attached.

JOIN FRONTS

With US 10 / 6 mm needles, join the fronts as foll (WS): P the left front sts, CO 12 (12, 12, 14, 14) (16, 16, 18, 18, 18) sts using the Backwards Loop CO method, p the right front sts.

[62 (70, 76, 84, 90) (98, 104, 112, 118, 126) sts for the front]

Work even in St St until the front measures 6 (7, 7.5, 8, 8.5) (9, 9.5, 10, 10.5, 11)" / 15 (18, 19, 20.5, 21.5) (23, 24, 25.5, 26.5, 28) cm, measured from the sleeve ends of the piece (the short ends). End with a WS row. Keep yarn attached.

LOWER BODY

Join the pieces for lower body (RS): K the front sts, CO 1 (0, 1, 0, 1) (0, 1, 0, 1, 0) st(s) using the Backwards Loop CO method, PM, k the back sts, CO 1 (0, 1, 0, 1) (0, 1, 0, 1, 0) st(s) using the Backwards Loop CO method, PM for BOR. [126 (140, 154, 168, 182) (196, 210, 224, 238, 252) sts]

Cont in St St in the rnd until the body measures 14" / 35.5 cm from underarm, or 2" / 5 cm less than desired length of the sweater.

Sizes 1, 3, 5, 7 and 9 only
Dec on Last Rnd: K2tog, k to m, SM, k2tog, k to end. (2 sts dec'd)

All sizes
Change to US 7 / 4.5 mm needles and k 1 more rnd.

Rib Rnd: *K2, p2* to end.
Cont to work 2" / 5 cm in est 2 x 2 rib.

BO body sts using the Tubular BO method.
Note! Make sure to rearrange the sts for the BO. See Special Techniques for further instructions.

SLEEVES

With US 10 / 6 mm needles and MC, pick up sts for the sleeve starting from the centre of the underarm (RS): Pick up and k 21 (23, 25, 26, 28) (30, 32, 33, 35, 36) sts from underarm to top of shoulder, pick up and k 21 (23, 25, 26, 28) (30, 32, 33, 35, 36) sts down to the centre of the underarm. PM for BOR and join to work in the rnd. [42 (46, 50, 52, 56) (60, 64, 66, 70, 72) sts]

Work 1" / 2.5 cm in St St, then beg working sleeve dec's:
Dec Rnd: K1, ssk, k to 3 sts bef end, k2tog, k1. (2 sts dec'd)
Rep the dec rnd 4 (6, 6, 7, 7) (7, 9, 10, 10, 11) more times on every 10th (8th, 8th, 6th, 6th) (6th, 4th, 4th, 4th, 4th) rnd. [32 (32, 36, 36, 40) (44, 44, 44, 48, 48) sts]

Cont in St St in the rnd until the sleeve measures 14 (14, 14, 14, 14) (14, 14, 15, 15, 15)" / 35.5 (35.5, 35.5, 35.5, 35.5) (35.5, 35.5, 38, 38, 38) cm from underarm, or 3" / 7.5 cm less than the desired length of the sleeve.

Change to US 7 / 4.5 mm needles and k 1 rnd.

Rib Rnd: *K2, p2* to end.
Cont to work 3" / 7.5 cm in est 2 x 2 rib.

BO sleeve sts on next rnd using the Tubular BO method.

COLLAR

With US 7 / 4.5 mm needles and MC, RS of the sweater facing and starting at the back of the neck edge, pick up and k 20 (20, 20, 22, 22) (24, 24, 26, 26, 26) sts from the back neck, pick up and k 18 (18, 20, 20, 22) (22, 24, 24, 26, 26) sts down to front of the neck edge, pick up and k 12 (12, 12, 14, 14) (16, 16, 18, 18, 18) sts from the front neck edge, and pick up and k 18 (18, 20, 20, 22) (22, 24, 24, 26, 26) sts up to the back of the neck. PM for BOR and join to work in the rnd. [68 (68, 72, 76, 80) (84, 88, 92, 96, 96) sts]

Rib Rnd: *K2, p2* to end.
Cont to work in est 2 x 2 rib until the collar measures 2" / 5 cm.

BO collar sts using the Tubular BO method.

FINISHING

Intarsia version only
Seam the side seam on right side of the body and on the right sleeve.

Both versions
Weave in ends. Wet block to measurements.

Klara Nilsson

04 Net

This playful, oversized sweater was designed by Klara Nilsson, better known as Klarybarry. The fluffy cabled net pattern is worked using intarsia.

SIZES

1 (2, 3, 4, 5) (6, 7, 8, 9)

Recommended ease: 4–8" / 10–20 cm of positive ease.

FINISHED MEASUREMENTS

Bust Circumference: 33.5 (38.5, 43, 47.75, 52.75) (57.5, 62.5, 67.25, 71.75)" / 85 (97.5, 109.5, 121.5, 134) (146, 158.5, 170.5, 182.5) cm.
Armhole Depth: 7.25 (7.25, 7.25, 7.25, 9.75) (9.75, 9.75, 12, 12)" / 18.5 (18.5, 18.5, 18.5, 24.5) (24.5, 24.5, 30.5, 30.5) cm.
Length from Underarm to Hem: 9.75 (10, 10.25, 10.5, 8.5) (8.75, 8.75, 7, 7)" / 24.5 (25.5, 26, 27, 21.5) (22, 22, 17.5, 17.5) cm.
Sleeve Length: 17 (16.25, 16.25, 16.25, 15.25) (15.25, 14.25, 14, 12.75)" / 43 (41.5, 41.5, 41.5, 38.5) (38.5, 36.5, 35.5, 32.5) cm.
Upper Arm Circumference: 14.25 (14.25, 14.25, 14.25, 19) (19, 19, 24, 24)" / 36.5 (36.5, 36.5, 36.5, 48.5) (48.5, 48.5, 61, 61) cm.

MATERIALS

Yarn: Puno by Gepard Garn (68% baby alpaca, 10% fine merino wool, 22% polyamide, 120 yds / 110 m – 50 g).
Colour A: 8 (9, 9, 10, 12) (12, 13, 15, 15) balls of colourway 845 Light Aqua.

Or approx. 935 (1000, 1040, 1165, 1350) (1445, 1480, 1690, 1725) yds / 855 (915, 950, 1065, 1235) (1320, 1355, 1545, 1570) m of similar bulky-weight yarn.

Teddy Dear by Gepard (50% merino wool, 40% superfine alpaca, 10% polyamide, 82 yds / 75 m – 50 g).
Colour B: 3 (4, 4, 4, 5) (5, 5, 6, 6) balls of colourway 214 Orange.
Colour C: 3 (4, 4, 4, 5) (5, 5, 6, 6) balls of colourway 420 Bubblegum.

Or approx. 240 (265, 280, 305, 350) (370, 390, 440, 450) yds / 220 (240, 255, 280, 320) (340, 355, 400, 410) m in each colour of similar bulky-weight yarn.

Each yarn is held double throughout the pattern.

Alternative yarn suggestions are for example Knit Picks Y2K (held double) or Illimani Yarn Amelie (held double) for Colour A and Knit Collage Serenity Boucle Yarn (held double) or Urth Yarns Lanalpaca (held single) for Colours B and C.

Needles: US 13 / 9 mm (for rib) and US 15 / 10 mm (for body) 32" / 80 cm and 16" / 40 cm circular needles.

Notions: Cable needle, stitch holders or waste yarn.

GAUGE

9.5 sts x 14 rows to 4" / 10 cm on US 15 / 10 mm needles in St St, after blocking.

12 sts x 18 rows to 4" / 10 cm on US 15 / 10 mm needles in cable patt, after blocking.

SPECIAL ABBREVIATIONS

2/1 RC: Sl 1 st to CN and hold behind, k2, k1 from CN.
2/1 LC: Sl 2 sts to CN and hold in front, k1, k2 from CN.

2/2 LC: Sl 2 sts to CN and hold in front, k2, k2 from CN.

NOTES

Chart

Work the red-boxed repeat (stitches outside this repeat are for visual reference only).

On row 25 of the chart, stop 2 stitches before the end of row. This will be the start and end of the row during rows 26–28.

When working flat, make sure to work even-numbered (cable) rows on RS rows and odd-numbered rows on WS rows.

Other

Make sure to hold each colour double throughout.

Colour A is used throughout and is knitted as stranded colourwork, meaning the yarn creates a float behind the work when not in use.

Each section of Colours B and C will need its own ball.
For the body, prepare 7 (8, 9, 10, 11) (12, 13, 14, 15) balls each for Colour B and Colour C (each ball weighs approx. 10 g in sample yarn). Either hold 2 strands of the yarn together as you wind, or prepare the ball so there is a strand coming from the inside and another from the outside.
For the sleeves, prepare 3 (3, 3, 3, 4) (4, 4, 5, 5) balls each of Colour B and Colour C (again, each approx. 10 g).

When working in intarsia, make sure to twist yarns when changing colour to avoid holes.

The cables move over 1 stitch at a time until they cross with a 2 x 2 cable (see chart).

CONSTRUCTION

This sweater features an all-over cabled net pattern. The cables have different colours to the background and are worked in intarsia. The knit is worked from the bottom up, in the round until armholes. Then, the piece is divided into front and back and knitted back and forth separately, continuing the cable pattern. The sweater has a cropped boxy look with almost no shaping, to really let the pattern shine. The only shaping is worked at the neckline. After the back and front are completed, the shoulders are sewn together and the neckline is knitted in 1 x 1 ribbing. The sleeves are knitted from bottom up in the round without any shaping and are then sewn into the armholes.

DIRECTIONS

HEM

Using US 13 / 9 mm circular needles and Colour A held double, CO 98 (112, 126, 140, 154) (168, 182, 196, 210) sts. Join to work in the rnd, being careful not to twist sts. PM for BOR.

Rib Rnd: *K1, p1* to end.
Work in 1 x 1 rib as est for 3 rnds in total.

BODY

Change to US 15 / 10 mm circular needles.

Start working from chart as foll:
Row 1: *K2 in Colour B, k10 in Colour A, k2 in Colour C*, rep *–* to end.
Cont to work from chart until the body measures 9.75 (10, 10.25, 10.5, 8.5) (8.75, 8.75, 7, 7)" / 24.5 (25.5, 26, 27, 21.5) (22, 22, 17.5, 17.5) cm from CO edge. Make sure to end after an odd-numbered chart row, not a cable row.

Divide for Front and Back

Sizes 1, 3, 5, 7 and 9 only
Work 3 sts in patt, work 50 (–, 64, –, 78) (–, 92, –, 106) sts in patt. Pl next 48 (–, 62, –, 76) (–, 90, –, 104) sts, including the first 3 sts worked, on a st holder or waste yarn. Tw.

Sizes 2, 4, 6 and 8 only
Work – (56, –, 70, –) (84, –, 98, –) sts in patt. Pl rem – (56, –, 70, –) (84, –, 98, –) sts on a st holder or waste yarn. Tw.

[48 (56, 62, 70, 76) (84, 90, 98, 104) sts on hold for the front and 50 (56, 64, 70, 78) (84, 92, 98, 106) sts ready to work for the back]

BACK

Keep working back and forth in patt, working cable rows on the RS and purling across in patt on the WS rows.

Note! Gauge might change when working flat compared to in the rnd. Change to different needles, if needed.

Keep working back and forth in patt until piece measures 16.5 (17, 17, 17.25, 17) (17.25, 17.25, 17.75, 17.75)" / 42 (43, 43, 44, 43) (44, 44, 45, 45) cm from CO, ending after a WS row.

Note! Sizes 1, 3, 5, 7 and 9 don't have whole repeats on front and back. Work as chart: if one of the cables goes 'outside' of the piece, end it and introduce it again when it 're-enters' in the piece further up.

Neck Shaping

Cont working chart during the next section.

Note! If the turn for the shaping is in the middle of a cable: Pl sts onto CN as though to work the cable, k the sts you have left bef the turn as chart, sl the rem cable sts back onto LHN (these will not be knitted), tw.

Right Back Neck

Row 1 (RS): Work 18 (20, 24, 27, 34) (37, 41, 44, 48) sts, tw, leaving rem 32 (36, 40, 43, 44) (47, 51, 54, 58) sts on needle.
Row 2 (WS): Sl1, p to end.

Sizes 1–4 only
BO all sts.

Sizes 5–9 only
Row 3 (RS): Work – (–, –, –, 30) (33, 36, 39, 43) sts, tw.
Row 4 (WS): Sl1, p to end.
BO all sts.

All sizes
Pl the next 14 (16, 16, 16) (10, 10, 10, 10) sts on a st holder for back neck.

Left Back Neck

Row 1 (RS): With RS facing, rejoin yarn and work across rem 18 (20, 24, 27, 34) (37, 41, 44, 48) sts.

Sizes 1–4 only
Row 2 (WS): P to end.
BO all sts.

Sizes 5–9 only
Row 2 (WS): P– (–, –, –, 29) (32, 35, 38, 42) sts, tw.
Row 3 (RS): Sl1, work to end.
Row 4: P to end.
BO all sts.

FRONT

Pl the 48 (56, 62, 70, 76) (84, 90, 98, 104) sts from hold back onto needles. Rejoin yarn ready to work an RS row.

Work back and forth from chart as bef until the front measures 15.25 (15.75, 15.5, 16, 15.5) (15.75, 15.25, 15.75, 15.25)" / 39 (40, 39.5, 40.5, 39.5) (40, 38.5, 40, 39) cm from CO, ending after a WS row.

Neck Shaping

Cont to work chart during the next section.

Note! If the turn for the shaping is in the middle of a cable: pl sts onto CN as if knitting the cable, k the sts you have left bef the turn as chart, sl the rem cable sts back onto LHN (these will not be knitted), tw.

Left Front Neck

Row 1 (RS): Work 21 (25, 28, 32, 35) (39, 41, 45, 48) sts, tw, leaving rem 27 (31, 34, 38, 41) (45, 49, 53, 56) sts on the needle.
Row 2 (WS): Sl1, p to end.
Row 3: Work 19 (22, 25, 29, 32) (36, 39, 43, 46) sts, tw.
Row 4: Sl1, p to end.
Row 5: Work 17 (20, 23, 27, 30) (34, 37, 41, 44) sts, tw.
Row 6: Sl1, p to end.

Sizes 1 and 2 only
BO.

Sizes 3–9 only
Row 7 (RS): Work - (–, 23, 27, 29) (33, 36, 40, 43) sts, tw.
Row 8 (WS): Sl1, p to end.

Sizes 3 and 4 only
BO.

Sizes 5–9 only
Row 9 (RS): Work - (–, –, –, 29) (33, 35, 39, 42) sts, tw.
Row 10 (WS): Sl1, p to end.

Sizes 5 and 6 only
BO.

Sizes 7–9 only
Row 11 (RS): Work - (–, –, –, –) (–, 35, 39, 42) sts, tw.
Row 12 (WS): Sl1, p to end.
BO.

All sizes
Pl next 6 (6, 6, 6) (6, 8, 8, 8) sts on a st holder for front neck.

Right Front Neck

Row 1 (RS): With RS facing, rejoin yarn and work across rem 21 (25, 28, 32, 35) (39, 41, 45, 48) sts.
Row 2 (WS): P19 (22, 25, 29, 32) (36, 39, 43, 46), tw.
Row 3: Sl1, work to end.
Row 4: P17 (20, 23, 27, 30) (34, 37, 41, 44), tw.
Row 5: Sl1, work to end.

Sizes 1 and 2 only
Row 6 (WS): P to end.
BO.

Sizes 3–9 only
Row 6 (WS): P17 (20, 23, 27, 29) (33, 36, 40, 43), tw.
Row 7 (RS): Sl1, work to end.

Sizes 3 and 4 only
Row 8 (WS): P to end.
BO.

Sizes 5–9 only
Row 8 (WS): P- (–, 23, 27, 29) (33, 35, 39, 42), tw.
Row 9 (RS): Sl1, work to end.

Sizes 5 and 6 only
Row 10 (WS): P to end.
BO.

Sizes 7–9 only
Row 10 (WS): P- (–, –, –, 29) (33, 35, 39, 42), tw.
Row 11 (RS): Sl1, work to end.
Row 11: P to end.
BO.

All sizes
Sew shoulders together using Mattress St.

COLLAR

Using Colour A held double and US 13 / 9 mm needles, start at the left shoulder seam and pick up, without knitting, 32 (36, 38, 38, 44) (44, 50, 50, 50) sts around the neckline, including the sts on hold.

Rib Rnd: *K1, p1* to end.
Work in 1 x 1 rib until it measures approx. 3.25" / 8 cm.

BO using the Italian Tubular BO method.

SLEEVES

Using Colour A held double and US 13 / 9 mm needles, CO 42 (42, 42, 42, 56) (56, 56, 70, 70) sts. Join to work in the rnd being careful not to twist sts. PM for BOR.

Rib Rnd: *K1, p1* to end.
Work in 1 x 1 rib for 3 rnds in total.

Change to US 15 / 10 mm needles and start working from chart.

Work from chart in the rnd until the sleeve measures 17 (16.25, 16.25, 16.25, 15.25) (15.25, 14.25, 14, 12.75)" / 43 (41.5, 41.5, 41.5, 38.5) (38.5, 36.5, 35.5, 32.5) cm from CO.

BO.

Attach sleeve using Mattress St.

Work second sleeve in the same way.

FINISHING

Weave in ends. Steam block to measurements.

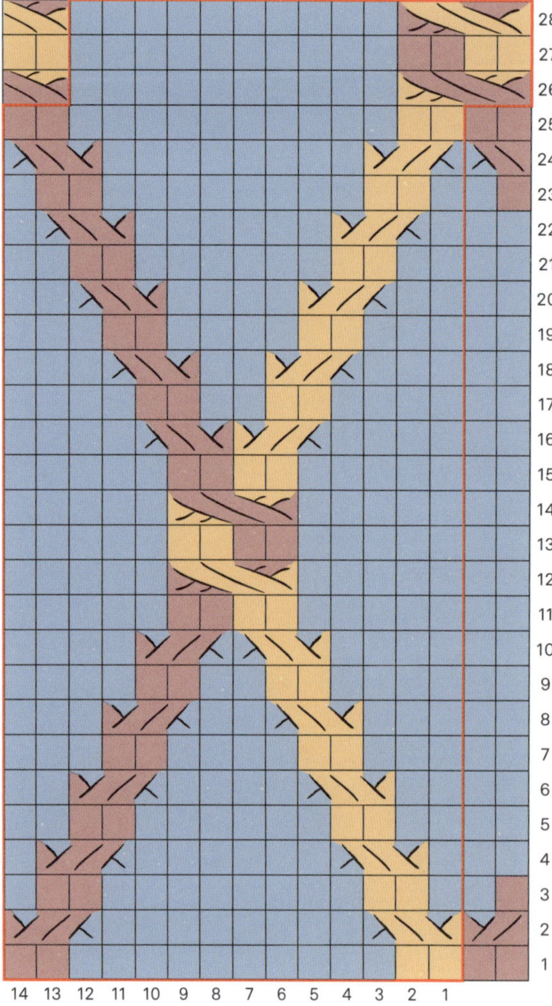

Note!
Row 25: Stop 2 sts bef end of row.
Rows 26–28: Starts and ends 2 sts bef end of row.

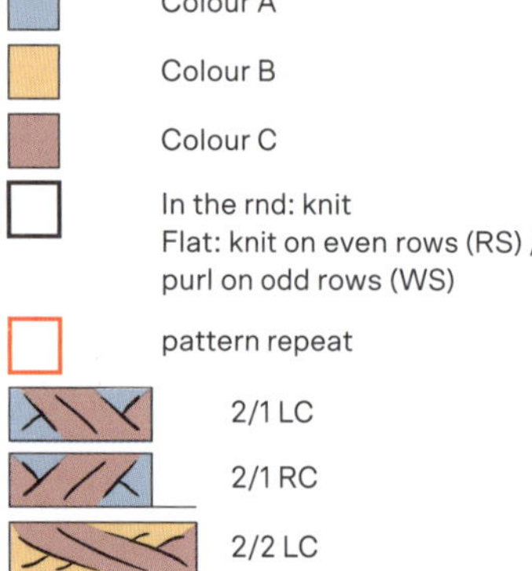

Sara Markkula

05 Erin

Erin is like a warm hug on a winter day. This chunky yet light pullover has generous ease and oversized sleeves. A striking cable panel runs along the front.

SIZES

1 (2, 3, 4, 5) (6, 7, 8, 9)

Recommended ease: 9.75–13.75" / 25–35 cm of positive ease.

FINISHED MEASUREMENTS

Bust Circumference: 43 (47, 51.25, 55, 59) (63, 67.25, 71, 75)" / 109.5 (119.5, 130, 140, 150) (160, 70.5, 180.5, 190.5) cm.
Yoke Depth: 8.25 (8.75, 9.75, 10, 10) (11, 11.5, 11.75, 11.75)" / 21 (22, 24.5, 25.5, 25.5) (28, 29, 30, 30) cm.
Length from Underarm to Hem: 13.5 (13.5, 13.5, 13, 12.5) (12.5, 12.5, 12.5, 12.5)" / 34 (34, 34, 33, 32) (32, 32, 32, 32) cm.
Upper Arm Circumference: 14.75 (15.25, 16.75, 18, 18.75) (20.75, 22, 22.75, 23.25)" / 37.5 (39, 42.5, 46, 47.5) (52.5, 56, 57.5, 59) cm.
Sleeve Length: 16.5 (17, 17, 17.5) (18, 18.25, 18.25, 19, 19)" / 42 (43, 43, 44.5, 45.5) (46.5, 46.5, 48, 48) cm.

MATERIALS

Yarn: 5 (5, 6, 6, 7) (7, 8, 8, 9) rolls of Plötulopi by Ístex (100% wool, 328 yds / 300 m - 100 g), colourway 1026.

The yarn is held double throughout the pattern.

Or approx. 720 (790, 865, 930, 995) (1085, 1170, 1260, 1335) yds / 660 (720, 790, 850, 910) (990, 1070, 1150, 1220) m of chunky-weight yarn (held single). Alternative yarn suggestions are for example Sandnes Garn Poppy and Wool and the Gang Feeling Good Yarn.

Needles: US 11 / 8 mm (for body and sleeves) and US 10 / 6 mm (for rib) 32–40" / 80–100 cm circular needles.

Notions: Cable needle, stitch markers, stitch holders or waste yarn.

GAUGE

12 sts x 18 rnds to 4" / 10 cm with US 11 / 8 mm needles in St St, after blocking.

20 sts x 18 rnds to 4" / 10 cm with US 11 / 8 mm needles in Cable patt, after blocking.

SPECIAL ABBREVIATIONS

4/4 LC: Left cross. Sl 4 sts to CN and hold in front, k4, k4 from CN.
4/4 RC: Right cross. Sl 4 sts to CN and hold in back, k4, k4 from CN.

CONSTRUCTION

This sweater is knitted from top down with two strands of unspun yarn held together. A cable panel runs from neckline to hem on the front. After a few rounds of working the neck opening, the back neck is shaped with a few short rows. The upper body is then shaped with raglan increases. After separating the body and sleeves, the body is knitted straight to the ribbed hem. Sleeves are then worked and shaped with decreases towards the ribbed cuffs. The sweater is finished with an i-cord edging at the neck.

DIRECTIONS

NECK

With 2 strands of yarn held tog and US 11 / 8 mm needles, CO 70 (74, 82, 82, 82) (86, 94, 98, 98) sts using the Long-Tail CO method or preferred method. Join to work in the rnd and PM for BOR. BOR m is at right back shoulder. Don't be afraid if the neck circumference appears large – the cables on the front will reduce it.

Set-Up Rnd: K5 (for right sleeve), PM, p1 (for raglan st), PM (for beg of front panel), p1 (2, 1, 1, 1) (2, 1, 2, 2), k32 (32, 40, 40, 40) (40, 48, 48, 48), p1 (2, 1, 1, 1) (2, 1, 2, 2), PM (for end of front panel), p1 (for raglan st), PM, k5 (for left sleeve), PM, p1 (for raglan st), PM, k22 (24, 26, 26, 26) (28, 30, 32, 32) (for back), PM, p1 (for raglan st).

[70 (74, 82, 82, 82) (86, 94, 98, 98) sts: 34 (36, 42, 42, 42) (44, 50, 52, 52) sts for front, 5 sts for each sleeve, 22 (24, 26, 26, 26) (28, 30, 32, 32) sts for back and 4 raglan sts]

Now work the short turtleneck, foll the Cable Chart for knitted size between m's on front. Work all other sts as est.
Rnd 1: K to m, SM, p1, SM, p1 (2, 1, 1, 1) (2, 1, 2, 2), work Cable Chart, p1 (2, 1, 1, 1) (2, 1, 2, 2), SM, p1, SM, k to m, SM, p1, SM, k to m, SM, p1.
Rnd 2: Work as est to end.
Rep rnds 1–2, 4 more times.

German Short Rows

Work German Short Rows to shape the back neck as foll:
Row 1 (RS): K2, tw.
Row 2 (WS): MDS, p1, SM, work as est to left sleeve m, SM, p2, tw.
Row 3: MDS, work as est to DS, kDS, k3, tw.
Row 4: MDS, work as est to DS, pDS, p3, tw.
Row 5: MDS, work as est to BOR.

YOKE

Now the body and sleeves will be shaped by inc on every 2nd rnd at raglan seams. At the same time, cont to work the Cable Chart on the front.

On the first rnd, resolve the DSs as you come to them. 2 final markers will be added at the inc's on the front.
Rnd 1: M1l, k to m, m1r, SM, p1, PM, m1l, SM, p1 (2, 1, 1, 1) (2, 1, 2, 2), work Cable Chart, p1 (2, 1, 1, 1) (2, 1, 2, 2), SM, m1r, PM, p1, SM, m1l, k to m, m1r, SM, p1, SM, m1l, k to m, m1r, SM, p1. (8 sts inc'd)
Rnd 2: Work as est to end.
Rnd 3: M1l, k to m, m1r, SM, p1, SM, m1l, k to m, SM, p1 (2, 1, 1, 1) (2, 1, 2, 2), work Cable Chart, p1 (2, 1, 1, 1) (2, 1, 2, 2), SM, k to m, m1r, SM, p1, SM, m1l, k to m, m1r, SM, p1, SM, m1l, k to m, m1r, SM, p1. (8 sts inc'd)
Rnd 4: Work as est to end.
Rep rnds 3–4, 16 (16, 18, 18, 16) (19, 20, 20, 18) more times.

[214 (218, 242, 242, 226) (254, 270, 274, 258) sts: 70 (72, 82, 82, 78) (86, 94, 96, 92) sts for front, 41 (41, 45, 45, 41) (47, 49, 49, 45) sts for each sleeve, 58 (60, 66, 66, 62) (70, 74, 76, 72) sts for back and 4 raglan sts]

Now, inc on every rnd on the body and every 2nd rnd on the sleeves as foll:
Rnd 1: M1l, k to m, m1r, SM, p1, SM, m1l, k to m, SM, p1 (2, 1, 1, 1) (2, 1, 2, 2), work Cable Chart, p1 (2, 1, 1, 1) (2, 1, 2, 2), SM, k to m, m1r, SM, p1, SM, m1l, k to m, m1r, SM, p1, SM, m1l, k to m, m1r, SM, p1. (8 sts inc'd)
Rnd 2: K to m, SM, p1, SM, m1l, k to m, SM, p1 (2, 1, 1, 1) (2, 1, 2, 2), work chart, p1 (2, 1, 1, 1) (2, 1, 2, 2), SM, k to m, m1r, SM, p1, SM, k to m, SM, p1, SM, m1l, k to m, m1r, SM, p1. (4 sts inc'd)
Rep rnds 1–2, 0 (1, 1, 2, 4) (3, 3, 4, 6) more time(s).

[226 (242, 266, 278, 286) (302, 318, 334, 342) sts: 74 (80, 90, 94, 98) (102, 110, 116, 120) sts for front, 43 (45, 49, 51, 51) (55, 57, 59, 59) sts for each sleeve, 62 (68, 74, 78, 82) (86, 90, 96, 100) sts for back and 4 raglan sts]

SEPARATING BODY AND SLEEVES

Next, pl sleeve sts on hold, CO sts at underarm and remove all raglan markers.
Next Rnd: RM (BOR m), pl 43 (45, 49, 51, 51) (55, 57, 59, 59) sleeve sts on st holder or scrap yarn, RM, using the Backwards Loop CO method, CO 1 (1, 1, 2, 3) (4, 5, 5, 6) st(s) for underarm, PM for BOR, CO another 1 (1, 1, 2, 3) (4, 5, 5, 6) st(s), k1 (raglan st), RM, k to m, SM, p1 (2, 1, 1, 1) (2, 1, 2, 2), work Cable Chart, p1 (2, 1, 1, 1) (2, 1, 2, 2), SM, k to m, RM, k1 (raglan st) RM, pl 43 (45, 49, 51, 51) (55, 57, 59, 59) sleeve sts on st holder or scrap yarn, RM, using the Backwards Loop CO method, CO 2 (2, 2, 4, 6) (8, 10, 10, 12) sts for underarm, k1 (raglan st), RM, k to m, RM, k1, k to new BOR m.

[144 (156, 172, 184, 196) (208, 224, 236, 248) sts]

BODY

Cont working the body straight as est, with Cable Chart on front, until the body measures 11 (11, 11, 10.75, 10.25) (10.25, 10.25, 10.25, 10.25)" / 28 (28, 28, 27, 26) (26, 26, 26, 26) cm from underarm, or desired length. The hem will add 2.25" / 6 cm.

Change to US 10 / 6 mm needles.

Next Rnd: K to m, RM, p1 (2, 1, 1, 1) (2, 1, 2, 2), ko (0, 2, 2, 2) (2, 0, 0, 0), *k1, k2tog*, rep *–* 9 (9, 11, 11, 11) (11, 15, 15, 15) more times, k2 (2, 2, 2, 2) (2, 0, 0, 0), p1 (2, 1, 1, 1) (2, 1, 2, 2), RM, k to end. [10 (10, 12, 12, 12) (12, 16, 16, 16) sts dec'd] [134 (146, 160, 172, 184) (196, 208, 220, 232) sts]

Hem Rib

Rib Rnd: *K1, p1* to end.
Work in est 1 x 1 rib until hem measures 2.25" / 6 cm.

BO using a stretchy BO method of choice.

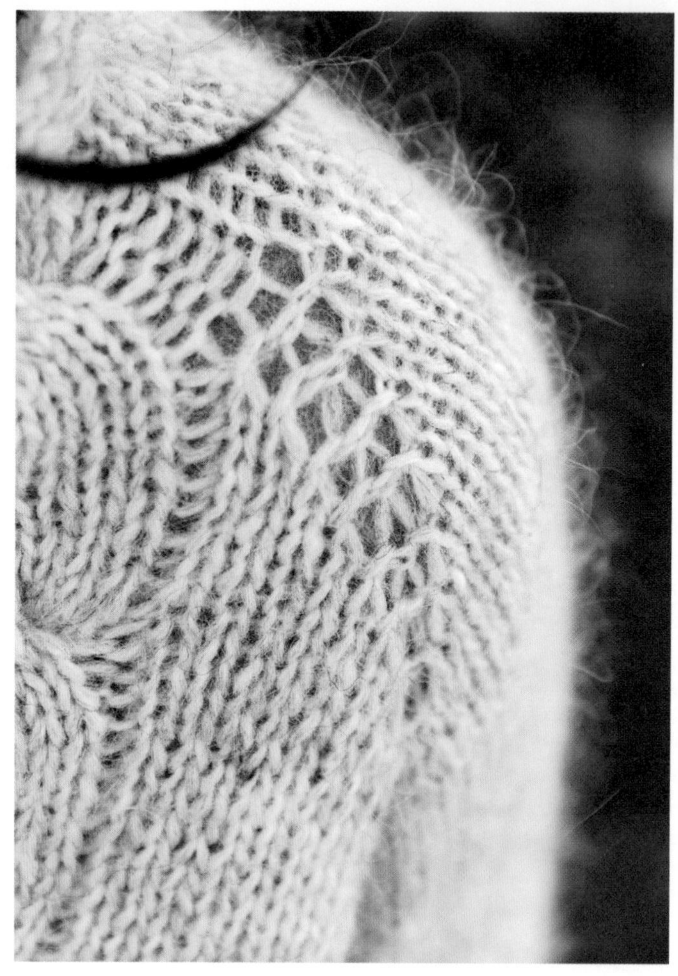

SLEEVES

Note! The sleeves are quite oversized. If shorter or more fitted sleeves are preferred, work dec's more frequently to reach desired length and circumference.

Put the 43 (45, 49, 51, 51) (55, 57, 59, 59) sleeve sts on the US 11 / 8 mm needles.

Set-Up Rnd: Starting at beg of CO sts at underarm, join yarn (2 strands held tog) and pick up and k 1 (1, 1, 2, 3) (4, 5, 5, 6) st(s) from CO sts, PM for BOR, pick up and k 1 (1, 1, 2, 3) (4, 5, 5, 6) st(s) from rem CO sts, k across sleeve sts to end. [45 (47, 51, 55, 57) (63, 67, 69, 71) sts]

Work 3 rnds in St St. Then beg to dec as foll:
Dec Rnd: K1, ssk, k to 3 sts bef m, k2tog, k1. (2 sts dec'd)
Work in St St for 25 (17, 13, 10, 9) (6, 5, 5, 4) rnds.

Rep last 26 (18, 14, 11, 10) (7, 6, 6, 5) rnds another 1 (2, 3, 1, 5) (3, 9, 5, 3) time(s). [41 (41, 43, 51, 45) (55, 47, 57, 63) sts]

Sizes 4, 6, 8 and 9 only
Work a Dec Rnd (2 sts dec'd), then work – (–, –, 11, –) (7, –, 6, 5) rnds in St St.
Rep last – (–, –, 12, –) (8, –, 7, 6) rnds another – (–, –, 2, –) (3, –, 3, 6) times. [– (–, –, 45, –) (47, –, 49, 49) sts]

All sizes
[41 (41, 43, 45, 45) (47, 47, 49, 49) sts]

Work in St St until the sleeve measures 14.25 (14.5, 14.5, 15.25, 15.5) (16, 16, 16.5, 16.5)" / 36 (37, 37, 38.5, 39.5) (40.5, 40.5, 42, 42) cm from underarm, or desired length. The cuff will add 2.25" / 6 cm.

Cuff

Change to US 10 / 6 mm needles.

Rnd 1: K to end.
Rnd 2: K2tog, p1, *k1, p1* to end. (1 st dec)
Rnd 3: *K1, p1* to end.
Work in est 1 x 1 rib until cuff measures 2.25" / 6 cm.

BO using a stretchy BO method of choice.

Work second sleeve alike.

NECKLINE

Using US 11 / 8 mm needles and

SIZES 1 AND 2

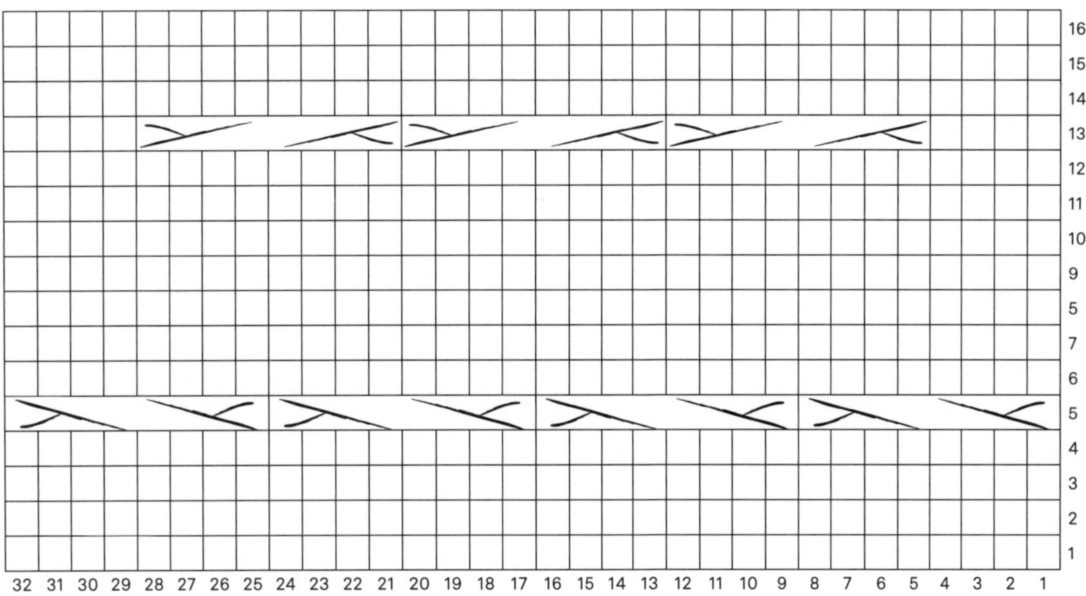

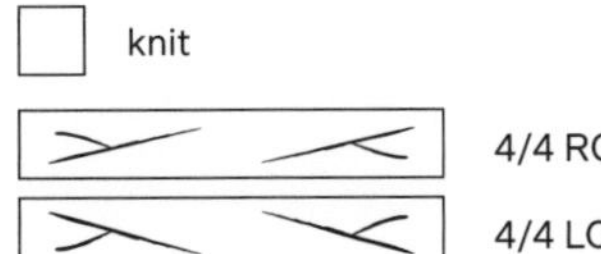

2 strands of yarn held tog, beg at raglan st (p st) on right back shoulder with RS facing and pick up and k 1 st from every st all the way round the back to cable panel on front. Pick up and k 24 (24, 30, 30, 30) (30, 36, 36, 36) sts from the cable panel section (approx. 3 sts for every 4 sts). Then cont to pick up and k 1 st from every st to end. [62 (66, 72, 72, 72) (76, 82, 86, 86) sts]

Next, work the i-cord edge as foll:
K1, sl st back to LHN, rep *–* once more.
K2, k2tog tbl, sl 3 sts back to LHN, rep *–* to end. 3 sts rem on the needles. BO joining i-cord edges into a rnd.

FINISHING

Weave in ends. Wet block to measurements.

SIZES 3–6

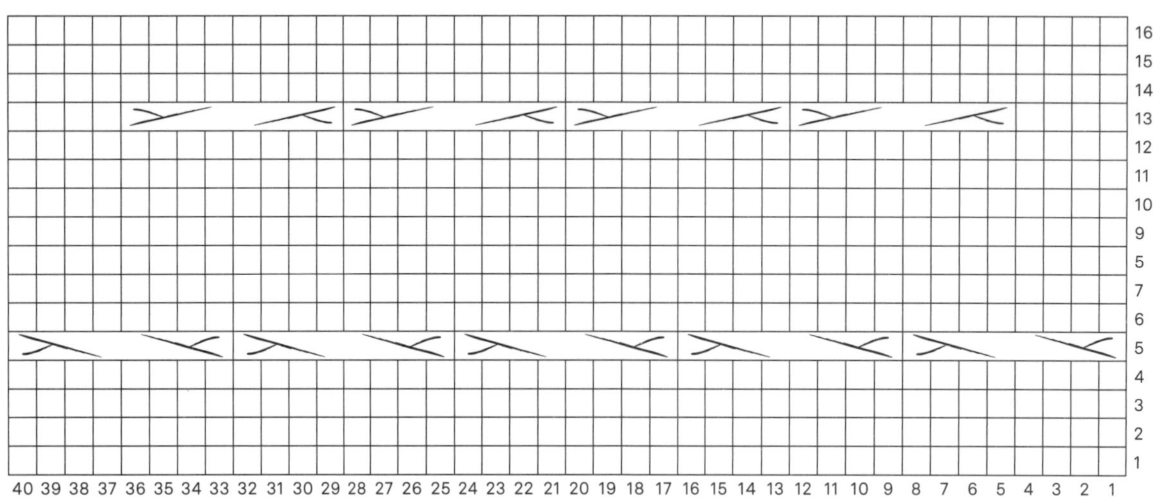

SIZES 7–9

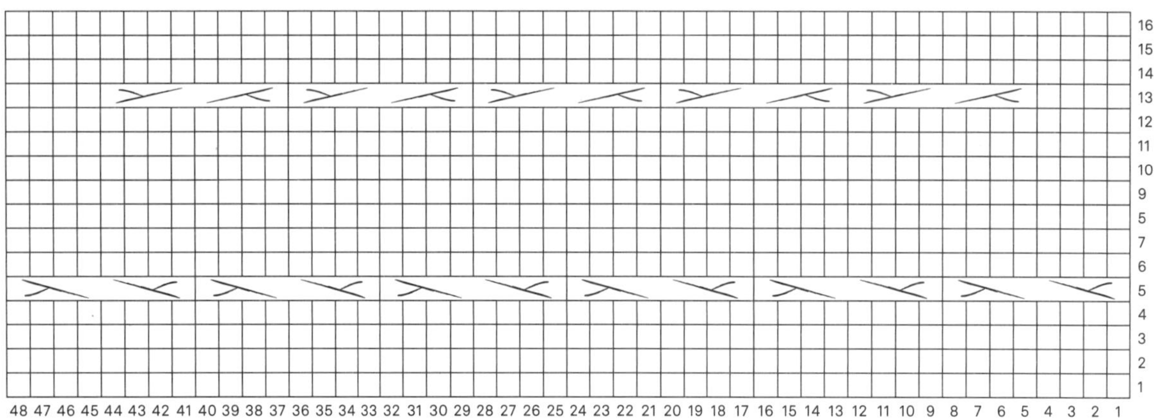

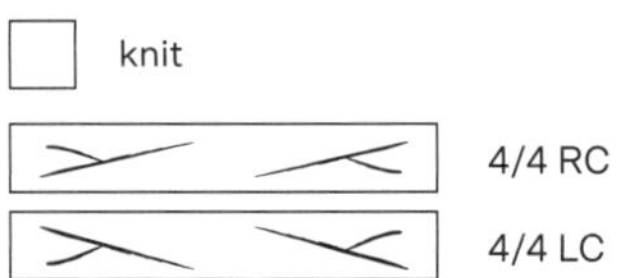

Orlane Sucche

06 Nubo

With its boxy shape and straightforward construction, Nubo is a great sweater for beginners. However, the technical cuff detail makes it interesting for any knitter!

SIZES

1 (2, 3, 4, 5) (6, 7, 8, 9, 10)

Recommended ease: 8–14" / 20–35 cm of positive ease.

FINISHED MEASUREMENTS

Bust Circumference: 45.25 (49.25, 52, 54.75, 57.25) (61.25, 65.25, 69.25, 73.25, 77.25)" / 113.5 (123.5, 130, 136.5, 143.5) (153.5, 163.5, 173.5, 183.5, 193.5) cm.
Yoke Depth: 13 (13.5, 13.5, 14, 14) (14.5, 15, 15.5, 16, 16.5)" / 32.5 (33.5, 33.5, 35, 35) (36, 37.5, 38.5, 40, 41) cm.
Upper Arm Circumference: 17.25 (18.75, 19.25, 20.75, 21.25) (22.75, 23.25, 24.75, 26, 26.75)" / 43.5 (46.5, 48.5, 51.5, 53.5) (56.5, 58.5, 61.5, 65, 66.5) cm.
Length from Underarm to Hem: 9.5" / 24 cm (adjustable).
Sleeve Length: 15" / 38 cm.
Cuff Circumference: 7.5 (8, 8, 8.5, 8.5) (9.25, 9.25, 10, 10, 10.5)" / 18.5 (20, 20, 21.5, 21.5) (23.5, 23.5, 25, 25, 26.5) cm.

MATERIALS

Yarn: 3 (3, 3, 3, 4) (4, 4, 4, 4, 5) skeins of Domitilla by Colori Naturali (90% baby suri alpaca, 10% silk, 243 yds / 225 m – 100 g), colourway Caffelatte.

Or approx. 600 (650, 680, 725, 745) (795, 840, 895, 945, 995) yds / 550 (595, 620, 665, 680) (725, 765, 815, 860, 910) m of very fluffy DK-weight yarn (see Notes). Suggested alternatives are for example Drops Melody and Sandnes Garn Børstet Alpakka.

Needles: US 10.5 / 7 mm (for main fabric) and US 9 / 5.5 mm 32" / 80 cm circular needles (for rib). US 8 / 5 mm DPNs (for cuff BO). Additionally, shorter cable needles and DPNs, if preferred for smaller circumference knitting.

Notions: Stitch markers, cable needle, stitch holders or waste yarn.

GAUGE

12 sts x 16 rows to 4" / 10 cm on US 10.5 / 7 mm needles in St St, after blocking.

24 sts x 24 rnds to 4" / 10 cm on US 9 / 5.5 mm needles in Basketweave patt, after blocking.

SPECIAL ABBREVIATIONS

2/2 RC: 4-st right-crossed cable. Sl 2 sts onto CN and keep in back of the work, k2, k2 from CN.

2/2 LC: 4-st left-crossed cable. Sl 2 sts onto CN and keep in front of the work, k2, k2 from CN.

NOTES

The Domitilla yarn is labelled as a DK-weight but knits up as chunky-weight as the brushed alpaca is so fluffy. If using an alternative yarn, make sure it has the same qualities to match the style of this sweater.

CONSTRUCTION

This sweater is worked seamlessly from the top down. The neckline is shaped with German Short Rows. The pullover is worked in Stockinette Stitch with a raglan construction with deep armholes. The sleeves are put on hold and the short body ends with ribbing. A Basketweave pattern is featured on the sleeve cuffs.

DIRECTIONS

COLLAR

With US 9 / 5.5 mm needles, loosely CO 66 (68, 70, 70, 72) (72, 74, 74, 76, 78) sts with the Long-Tail CO method. Join to work in rnd and PM for BOR. The BOR is at the centre back.

K 2 rnds.

Rib Rnd: *K1tbl, p1* to end.
Rep twisted 1 x 1 rib rnd 7 times more.

YOKE

Neckline Shaping

Change to US 10.5 / 7 mm needles. In the foll instructions, use m's that are distinct from the BOR m.

Work German Short Rows to shape the neckline as foll:
Set-Up Rnd: K11 (11, 11, 11, 11) (11, 12, 12, 12, 12), PM, k10, PM, k24 (26, 28, 28, 30) (30, 30, 30, 32, 34), PM, k10, PM, k11 (11, 11, 11, 11) (11, 12, 12, 12, 12).
Short Row 1 (RS, Inc): *K2, m1l*, rep *–* 0 (1, 2, 2, 3) (3, 2, 2, 3, 4) more time(s), k to m, m1r, SM, k to m, SM, m1l, k3, tw. [3 (4, 5, 5, 6) (6, 5, 5, 6, 7) sts inc'd]
Short Row 2 (WS, Inc): MDS, p to BOR m, SM, *p2, m1l(p)*, rep *–* 0 (1, 2, 2, 3) (3, 2, 2, 3, 4) more time(s), p to m, m1l(p), SM, p to m, SM, m1r(p), p3, tw. [3 (4, 5, 5, 6) (6, 5, 5, 6, 7) sts inc'd]
Short Row 3 (Inc): MDS, k to BOR m, SM, k to m, m1r, SM, k to m, SM, m1l, k to DS, kDS, k3, tw. (2 sts inc'd)
Short Row 4 (Inc): MDS, p to BOR m, SM, p to m, m1l(p), SM, p to m, SM, m1r(p), p to DS, pDS, p3, tw. (2 sts inc'd)
Short Rows 5 and 6 (inc): Rep rows 3 and 4. (4 sts inc'd)
Short Row 7: MDS, k to BOR m.
Short rows are now completed. [80 (84, 88, 88, 92) (92, 92, 92, 96, 100) sts: 30 (32, 34, 34, 36) (36, 36, 36, 38, 40) sts each for front and back and 10 sts for each sleeve]

Cont working in the rnd.

Raglan Shaping

Note! During the first rnd, kDS when encountered.
Rnd 1: *K to last st bef m, kfb, SM, kfb*, rep *–* 3 more times, k to end. (8 sts inc'd)
Rnd 2: K to end.
Rep rnds 1–2, 11 (12, 14, 17, 17) (17, 20, 22, 23, 23) more times. [176 (188, 208, 232, 236) (236, 260, 276, 288, 292) sts: 54 (58, 64, 70, 72) (72, 78, 82, 86, 88) sts each for front and back and 34 (36, 40, 46, 46) (46, 52, 56, 58, 58) sts for each sleeve]

Sizes 1–7 only
Rnd 1: *K to last st bef m, kfb, SM, kfb*, rep *–* 3 more times, k to end. (8 sts inc'd)
Rnds 2–4: K to end.
Rep rnds 1–4, 4 (4, 3, 2, 2) (2, 0, –, –, –) more times. [216 (228, 240, 256, 260) (260, 268, –, –, –) sts: 64 (68, 72, 76, 78) (78, 80, –, –, –) sts each for front and back and 44 (46, 48, 52, 52) (52, 54, –, –, –) sts for each sleeve]

Sizes 6–10 only
Rnd 1: *K to last st bef m, kfb, SM, k to m, SM, kfb*, rep *–* once, k to end. (4 sts inc'd)
Rnd 2: K to end.
Rep rnds 1–2, – (–, –, –, –) (0, 2, 3, 3, 4) more times. [– (–, –, –, –) (264, 280, 292, 304, 312) sts: – (–, –, –, –) (80, 86, 90, 94, 98) sts each for front and back and – (–, –, –, –) (52, 54, 56, 58, 58) sts for each sleeve]

[216 (228, 240, 256, 260) (264, 280, 292, 304, 312) sts: 64 (68, 72, 76, 78) (80, 86, 90, 94, 98) sts each for front and back and 44 (46, 48, 52, 52) (52, 54, 56, 58, 58) sts for each sleeve]

SEPARATING BODY AND SLEEVES

Remove BOR m, k to m, RM, pl the 44 (46, 48, 52, 52) (52, 54, 56, 58, 58) right sleeve sts on hold, CO 2 (3, 3, 3, 4) (6, 6, 7, 8, 9) sts using the Backwards Loop CO method, PM for new BOR, CO 2 (3, 3, 3, 4) (6, 6, 7, 8, 9) sts, RM, k across front sts to next m, RM, pl the 44 (46, 48, 52, 52) (52, 54, 56, 58, 58) left sleeve sts on hold, CO 4 (6, 6, 6, 8) (12, 12, 14, 16, 18) sts, RM, k across back sts to new BOR m. [136 (148, 156, 164, 172) (184, 196, 208, 220, 232) sts]

BODY

Work in St St until the body measures 7.5" / 19 cm, or 2" / 5 cm less than desired length from underarm.

Change to US 9 / 5.5 mm needles.

Hem

Rib Rnd: *K1tbl, p1* to end.
Rep rib rnd 7 times more.

K 2 rnds, then BO all sts.

SLEEVES

Pl the 44 (46, 48, 52, 52) (52, 54, 56, 58, 58) held sleeve sts onto US 10.5 / 7 mm needles. Beg at centre of underarm with RS facing, pick up and k 2 (3, 3, 3, 4) (6, 6, 7, 8, 9) sts from underarm CO, then 2 extra sts from body, work across held sleeve sts, pick up and k 2 extra sts from body, then 2 (3, 3, 3, 4) (6, 6, 7, 8, 9) sts from underarm CO, PM to indicate BOR. [52 (56, 58, 62, 64) (68, 70, 74, 78, 80) sts]

Next Rnd: K2 (3, 3, 3, 4) (6, 6, 7, 8, 9), k2tog, k to last 4 (5, 5, 5, 6) (8, 8, 9, 10, 11) sts bef m, ssk, k to m. (2 sts dec'd) [50 (54, 56, 60, 62) (66, 68, 72, 76, 78) sts]

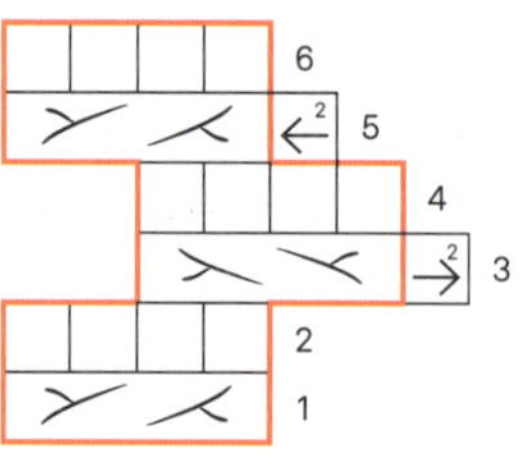

knit

2/2 RC

2/2 LC

move marker 2 sts to the right

move marker 2 sts to the left

pattern repeat: work rows 3–6 a total of 3 times

Work 4 rnds in St St.

Work sleeve dec's as foll:

Dec Rnd: K1, k2tog, k to last 3 sts, ssk, k1. (2 sts dec'd)

Now cont in St St, working another dec rnd every 16 (16, 12, 12, 10) (10, 8, 8, 5, 6)th rnd, 2 (2, 3, 3, 4) (4, 5, 5, 7, 6) times. [44 (48, 48, 52, 52) (56, 56, 60, 60, 64) sts]

Cont in St St until the sleeve measures 12.25" / 31 cm or 2.75" / 7 cm less than desired length from underarm to cuff.

Cuff

Change to US 9 / 5.5 mm needles.
K 1 rnd.

Cont, working Basketweave patt as foll:

Rnd 1: *2/2 RC* to end.

Rnd 2: K to end.

Rnd 3: Move the BOR m to the right as foll: remove BOR m, sl 2 sts from RHN to CN and hold in front of the work, replace BOR m on RHN. K2 from LHN, k2 from CN, *2/2 LC* to end.

Rnd 4: K to end.

Rnd 5: Move the BOR m to the left as foll: remove BOR m, sl 2 sts from LHN to RHN and replace BOR m, pass yarn behind the 2 slipped sts, *2/2 RC* to end.

Rnd 6: K to end.

Rep rnds 3–6 twice more.

K 1 rnd.

Using US 8 / 5 mm needles, BO all sts.

FINISHING

Weave in ends. Wet block to measurements.

Jaime Dorfman

07 Chloe

The Chloe sweater by Jaime Dorfman (the designer behind Jaime Creates) is a cosy yet elegant winter staple. A lace pattern is worked across the yoke.

SIZES

1 (2, 3, 4, 5) (6, 7, 8, 9)

Recommended ease: 10.25–14.5" / 26–37 cm of positive ease.

FINISHED MEASUREMENTS

Chest Circumference: 41.25 (44.25, 50.25, 53.5, 56.25) (62.5, 65.5, 68.5, 74.5)" / 104.5 (112.5, 127.5, 135.5, 143) (158.5, 166, 174, 189) cm.
Length from Shoulder to Hem: 21.75 (22, 22.25, 22.75, 22.75) (23, 23, 23.5, 23.5)" / 55 (56, 56.5, 57.5, 58) (58.5, 58.5, 60, 60) cm.
Length from Underarm to Hem: 13.75 (14.25, 13.5, 13.75, 13) (13.5, 12.5, 13, 12)" / 35 (36, 34, 35, 33) (34, 31, 33, 30.5) cm.
Sleeve Length: 15.75 (16.25, 16.25, 16.75, 16.75) (17.25, 17.25, 17.75, 17.75)" / 40 (41, 41, 42.5, 42.5) (43.5, 43.5, 45, 45) cm.
Upper Arm Circumference: 13.5 (14, 15.75, 17, 17.5) (18.75, 20, 20.75, 22)" / 34 (35.5, 40, 43, 44.5) (47.5, 51, 52.5, 55.5) cm.

MATERIALS

Yarn: 7 (8, 9, 9, 10) (11, 11, 12, 13) skeins of Chunky Merino by Wool and Works (100% sw merino, 110 yds / 100 m – 100 g), colourway Flat Feet.

Or approx. 745 (810, 885, 940, 1010) (1130, 1190, 1260, 1400) yds / 680 (740, 810, 860, 920) (1030, 1090, 1150, 1280) m of bulky-weight yarn. Alternative yarn suggestions are for example Drops Design Andes, Lionbrand Hue + Me and Wool and the Gang Alpachino Merino.

Needles: 10 / 6 mm and US 10.5 / 7 mm 16" / 40 cm and 32–40" / 80–100 cm circular needles.

Notions: Stitch markers, stitch holders or waste yarn.

GAUGE

13 sts x 20 rnds to 4" / 10 cm on US 10.5 / 7 mm needles in St St in the rnd, after blocking.

13 sts x 17 rows to 4" / 10 cm on US 10.5 / 7 mm needles in Open Twisted Rib St, worked flat, after blocking.

13 sts x 18 rows to 4" / 10 cm on US 10 / 6 mm needles in Half Twisted Rib St in the rnd, after blocking.

STITCH PATTERNS

Half Twisted Rib Stitch

In the rnd, over a multiple of 2 sts.
Rnd 1: *K1tbl, p1* to end.

Open Twisted Rib Stitch

Worked flat, over a multiple of 5+3 sts.

Set-Up Row 1 (RS): *P1, k1tbl, p1, k2*, rep *–* to 3 sts bef end, p1, k1tbl, p1.
Set-Up Row 2 (WS): K1, p1tbl, k1, *p2, k1, p1tbl, k1*, rep *–* to end.
Row 1: *P1, k1tbl, p1, k1, yo, k1*, rep *–* to 3 sts bef end, p1, k1tbl, p1.
Row 2: K1, p1tbl, k1, *p3, k1, p1tbl, k1*, rep *–* to end.
Row 3: *P1, k1tbl, p1, k3, pass 3rd st on RHN over 1st 2 sts on RHN*, rep *–* to 3 sts bef end, p1, k1tbl, p1.
Row 4: K1, p1tbl, k1, *p2, k1, p1tbl, k1*, rep *–* to end.
Rep rows 1–4.

CONSTRUCTION

This sweater is worked seamlessly from the top down. It features a turtleneck and dropped shoulders. The top section is worked flat in an Open Twisted Rib Stitch. The back shoulders are worked separately before joining them to work the remainder of the top back piece as one. Stitches are then picked along each of the back shoulder edges to work the front shoulders separately before joining them to work the remainder of the front piece as one. The front and back pieces are joined to work the body in the round in Stockinette Stitch. The hem is knitted in Half Twisted Rib. The neck trim and sleeves are both worked in the round by picking up stitches along the neckline and armhole edges.

DIRECTIONS

Note! When counting sts, note that each rep of the Open Twisted Rib St patt has a yo on row 1 of the st patt, and a matching dec on every row 3 of the st patt. These yo's and dec's are not included in the st counts, except at the end of the front shoulders.

BACK LEFT SHOULDER

Using US 10.5 / 7 mm needles, CO 21 (23, 26, 28, 30) (32, 37, 39, 44) sts with preferred CO method.

Est the Open Twisted Rib St, while inc at the neck edge as foll:

Sizes 1 and 3 only
Row 1 (RS): *P1, k1tbl, p1, k2*, rep *–* to st, k1.
Row 2 (WS): P1, *p2, k1, p1tbl, k1*, rep *–* to end.
Row 3 (Inc): *P1, k1tbl, p1, k1, yo, k1*, rep *–* to 1 st bef end, m1r(p), k1. (1 st inc'd)
Row 4: P1, k1, *p3, k1, p1tbl, k1*, rep *–* to end.
Row 5 (Inc): *P1, k1tbl, p1, k3, pass 3rd st on RHN over 1st 2 sts on RHN*, rep *–* to 2 sts bef end, p1, m1r, k1. (1 st inc'd) [23 (–, 28, –, –) (–, –, –, –) sts]

Sizes 2 and 4 only
Row 1 (RS): *P1, k1tbl, p1, k2*, rep *–* to 3 sts bef end, p1, k1tbl, k1.
Row 2 (WS): P1, p1tbl, k1, *p2, k1, p1tbl, k1*, rep *–* to end.
Row 3 (Inc): *P1, k1tbl, p1, k1, yo, k1*, rep *–* to 3 sts bef end, p1, k1tbl, m1r(p), k1. (1 st inc'd)
Row 4: P1, k1, p1tbl, k1, *p3, k1, p1tbl, k1*, rep *–* to end.
Row 5 (Inc): *P1, k1tbl, p1, k3, pass 3rd st on RHN over 1st 2 sts on RHN*, rep *–* to 4 sts bef end, p1, k1tbl, p1, m1r, k1. (1 st inc'd) [– (25, –, 30, –) (–, –, –, –) sts]

Size 5 only
Row 1 (RS): *P1, k1tbl, p1, k2*, rep *–* to end.
Row 2 (WS): *P2, k1, p1tbl, k1*, rep *–* to end.
Row 3 (Inc): *P1, k1tbl, p1, k1, yo, k1*, rep *–* to 5 sts bef end, p1, k1tbl, p1, k1, yo, m1r, k1. (1 st inc'd)
Row 4: P1, *p3, k1, p1tbl, k1*, rep *–* to end.
Row 5 (Inc): *P1, k1tbl, p1, k3, pass 3rd st on RHN over 1st 2 sts on RHN*, rep *–* to 1 st bef end, m1r(p), k1. (1 st inc'd) [– (–, –, –, 32) (–, –, –, –) sts]

Sizes 6 and 7 only
Row 1 (RS): *P1, k1tbl, p1, k2*, rep *–* to 2 sts bef end, p1, k1.
Row 2 (WS): P1, k1, *p2, k1, p1tbl, k1*, rep *–* to end.
Row 3 (Inc): *P1, k1tbl, p1, k1, yo, k1*, rep *–* to 2 sts bef end, p1, m1r, k1. (1 st inc'd)
Row 4: P1, p1tbl, k1, *p3, k1, p1tbl, k1*, rep *–* to end.
Row 5 (Inc): *P1, k1tbl, p1, k3, pass 3rd st on RHN over 1st 2 sts on RHN*, rep *–* to 3 sts bef end, p1, k1tbl, m1r(p), k1. (1 st inc'd) [– (–, –, –, –) (34, 39, –, –) sts]

Sizes 8 and 9 only
Row 1 (RS): *P1, k1tbl, p1, k2*, rep *–* to 4 sts bef end, p1, k1tbl, p1, k1.
Row 2 (WS): P1, k1, p1tbl, k1, *p2, k1, p1tbl, k1*, rep *–* to end.
Row 3 (Inc): *P1, k1tbl, p1, k1, yo, k1*, rep *–* to 4 sts bef end, p1, k1tbl, p1, m1r, k1. (1 st inc'd)
Row 4: P2, k1, p1tbl, k1, *p3, k1, p1tbl, k1*, rep *–* to end.
Row 5 (Inc): *P1, k1tbl, p1, k3, pass 3rd st on RHN over 1st 2 sts on RHN*, rep *–* to 5 sts bef end, p1, k1tbl, p1, k1, m1r, k1. (1 st inc'd) [– (–, –, –, –) (–, –, 41, 46) sts]

[23 (25, 28, 30, 32) (34, 39, 41, 46) sts] Cut yarn and pl these sts on hold.

BACK RIGHT SHOULDER

Using US 10.5 / 7 mm needles, CO 21 (23, 26, 28, 30) (32, 37, 39, 44) sts with preferred CO method.

Sizes 1 and 3 only

Row 1 (RS): K1, *k2, p1, k1tbl, p1*, rep *–* to end.

Row 2 (WS): *K1, p1tbl, k1, p2*, rep *–* to 1 st bef end, p1.

Row 3 (Inc): K1, m1l(p), *k1, yo, k1, p1, k1tbl, p1*, rep *–* to end. (1 st inc'd)

Row 4: *K1, p1tbl, k1, p3*, rep *–* to 2 sts bef end, k1, p1.

Row 5 (Inc): K1, m1l, p1, *k3, pass 3rd st on RHN over 1st 2 sts on RHN, p1, k1tbl, p1*, rep *–* to end. (1 st inc'd) [23 (–, 28, –, –) (–, –, –, –) sts]

Sizes 2 and 4 only

Row 1 (RS): K1, k1tbl, p1, *k2, p1, k1tbl, p1*, rep *–* to 5 sts bef end, k2, p1, k1tbl, p1.

Row 2 (WS): *K1, p1tbl, k1, p2*, rep *–* to 3 sts bef end, k1, p1tbl, p1.

Row 3 (Inc): K1, m1l(p), k1tbl, p1, *k1, yo, k1, p1, k1tbl, p1*, rep *–* to end. (1 st inc'd)

Row 4: *K1, p1tbl, k1, p3*, rep *–* to 4 sts bef end, k1, p1tbl, k1, p1.

Row 5 (Inc): K1, m1l, *p1, k1tbl, p1, k3, pass 3rd st on RHN over 1st 2 sts on RHN*, rep *–* until 3 sts bef end, p1, k1tbl, p1. (1 st inc'd) [– (25, –, 30, –) (–, –, –, –) sts]

Size 5 only

Row 1 (RS): *K2, p1, k1tbl, p1*, rep *–* to end.

Row 2 (WS): *K1, p1tbl, k1, p2*, rep *–* to end.

Row 3 (Inc): K1, m1l, yo, k1, *p1, k1tbl, p1, k1, yo, k1*, rep *–* to 3 sts bef end, p1, k1tbl, p1. (1 st inc'd)

Row 4: *K1, p1tbl, k1, p3*, rep *–* to 1 st bef end, p1.

Row 5 (Inc): K1, m1l(p), *k3, pass 3rd st on RHN over 1st 2 sts on RHN, p1, k1tbl, p1*, rep *–* to end. (1 st inc'd) [– (–, –, –, 32) (–, –, –, –) sts]

Sizes 6 and 7 only

Row 1 (RS): K1, p1, *k2, p1, k1tbl, p1*, rep *–* to end.

Row 2 (WS): *K1, p1tbl, k1, p2*, rep *–* to 2 sts bef end, k1, p1.

Row 3 (Inc): K1, m1l, p1, *k1, yo, k1, p1, k1tbl, p1*, rep *–* to end. (1 st inc'd)

Row 4: *K1, p1tbl, k1, p3*, rep *–* to 3 sts bef end, k1, p1tbl, p1.

Row 5 (Inc): K1, m1l(p), k1tbl, p1, *k3, pass 3rd st on RHN over 1st 2 sts on RHN, p1, k1tbl, p1*, rep *–* to end. (1 st inc'd) [– (–, –, –, –) (34, 39, –, –) sts]

Sizes 8 and 9 only

Row 1 (RS): K1, *p1, k1tbl, p1, k2*, rep *–* to 3 sts bef end, p1, k1tbl, p1.

Row 2 (WS): *K1, p1tbl, k1, p2*, rep *–* to 4 sts bef end, k1, p1tbl, k1, p1.

Row 3 (Inc): K1, m1l, *p1, k1tbl, p1, k1, yo, k1*, rep *–* to 3 sts bef end, p1, k1tbl, p1. (1 st inc'd)

Row 4: *K1, p1tbl, k1, p3*, rep *–* to 5 sts bef end, k1, p1tbl, k1, p2.

Row 5 (Inc): K1, m1l, k1, *p1, k1tbl, p1, k3, pass 3rd st on RHN over 1st 2 sts on RHN*, rep *–* to 3 sts bef end, p1, k1tbl, p1. (1 st inc'd) [– (–, –, –, –) (–, –, 41, 46) sts]

[23 (25, 28, 30, 32) (34, 39, 41, 46) sts] Do not cut yarn.

JOIN BACK SHOULDERS

Pl the 23 (25, 28, 30, 32) (34, 39, 41, 46) sts on hold for the back left shoulder onto the working needles with the WS facing. In the next row, join the shoulders by working across the back right shoulder sts, then CO additional sts to make up the back panel bef working across the sts for the back left shoulder.

Sizes 1 and 3 only

Next Row (WS): *K1, p1tbl, k1, p2*, rep *–* to last 3 sts, k1, p1tbl, k1, PM, CO 22 (–, 27, –, –) (–, –, –, –) sts using the Backwards Loop CO, PM, *k1, p1tbl, k1, p2*, rep *–* to 3 sts bef end, k1, p1tbl, k1. [68 (–, 83, –, –) (–, –, –, –) sts]

Next Row (RS): *P1, k1tbl, p1, k1, yo, k1*, rep *–* to 3 sts bef m, p1, k1tbl, p1, RM, *k1, yo, k1, p1, k1, p1*, rep *–* to 2 sts bef m, k1, yo, k1, RM, *p1, k1tbl, p1, k1, yo, k1*, rep *–* to 3 sts bef end, p1, k1tbl, p1.

Sizes 2 and 4 only

Next Row (WS): *K1, p1tbl, k1, p2*, rep *–* to end, PM, CO – (23, –, 28, –) (–, –, –, –) sts using the Backwards Loop CO, PM, *p2, k1, p1tbl, k1*, rep *–* to end. [– (73, –, 88, –) (–, –, –, –) sts]

Next Row (RS): *P1, k1tbl, p1, k1, yo, k1*, rep *–* to m, RM, *p1, k1, p1, k1, yo, k1*, rep *–* to 3 sts bef m, p1, k1, p1, RM, *k1, yo, k1, p1, k1tbl, p1*, rep *–* to end.

Size 5 only

Next Row (WS): *K1, p1tbl, k1, p2*, rep *–* to 2 sts bef end, k1, p1tbl, PM, CO 29 sts using the Backwards Loop CO, PM, p1tbl, k1, *p2, k1, p1tbl, k1*, rep *–* to end. (93 sts)

Next Row (RS): *P1, k1tbl, p1, k1, yo, k1*, rep *–* to 2 sts bef m, p1, k1tbl, RM, p1, *k1, yo, k1, p1, k1, p1*, rep *–* to 3 sts bef m, k1, yo, k1, p1, RM, k1tbl, p1, *k1, yo, k1, p1, k1tbl, p1*, rep *–* to end.

Sizes 6 and 7 only

Next Row (WS): *K1, p1tbl, k1, p2*, rep *–* to last 4 sts, k1, p1tbl, k1, p1, PM, CO – (–, –, –, –) (35, 30, –, –) sts using the Backwards Loop CO, PM, p1, *k1, p1tbl, k1, p2*, rep *–* to 3 sts bef end, k1, p1tbl, k1. [– (–, –, –, –) (103, 108, –, –) sts]

Next Row (RS): *P1, k1tbl, p1, k1, yo, k1*, rep *–* to 4 sts bef m, p1, k1tbl, p1, k1, RM, yo, k1, *p1, k1, p1, k1, yo, k1*, rep *–* to 4 sts bef m, p1, k1, p1, k1, RM, yo, k1, *p1, k1tbl, p1, k1, yo, k1*, rep *–* to 3 sts bef end, p1, k1tbl, p1.

Sizes 8 and 9 only

Next Row (WS): *K1, p1tbl, k1, p2*, rep *–* to last st, k1, PM, CO 31 sts using

the Backwards Loop CO, PM, k1, *p2, k1, p1tbl, k1*, rep *–* to end. [– (–, –, –, –) (–, –, 113, 123) sts]
Next Row (RS): *P1, k1tbl, p1, k1, yo, k1*, rep *–* to 1 st bef m, p1, RM, k1, p1, *k1, yo, k1, p1, k1, p1*, rep *–* to 4 sts bef m, k1, yo, k1, p1, k1, RM, p1, *k1, yo, k1, p1, k1tbl, p1*, rep *–* to end.

[68 (73, 83, 88 93) (103, 108, 113, 123) sts]

BACK

Next, work in Open Twisted Rib St across the whole back, starting with a row 2 (a WS row) of the 4-row patt as foll:
Next Row (WS, row 2 of patt): K1, p1tbl, k1, *p3, k1, p1tbl, k1*, rep *–* to end.

Now cont in Open Twisted Rib St as set for another 26 (26, 30, 30, 34) (34, 38, 38, 42) rows, or until piece measures as near as possible to 8 (8, 9, 9, 9.75) (9.75, 10.75, 10.75, 11.75)" / 20 (20, 22.5, 22.5, 24.5) (24.5, 27, 27, 29.5) cm from the Shoulder CO edge, making sure to end after a row 4 (a WS row).

Cut yarn and pl these 68 (73, 83, 88, 93) (103, 108, 113, 123) sts on hold.

FRONT RIGHT SHOULDER

Using US 10.5 / 7 mm circular needles with RS facing start at right edge of back right shoulder CO sts and pick up, without knitting, 21 (23, 26, 28, 30) (32, 37, 39, 44) sts. Slide sts along the cable until they are on the LHN. Attach yarn on the RS.

Sizes 1 and 3 only
Work rows 1–5 as on the back left shoulder. [23 (–, 28, –, –) (–, –, –, –) sts]
Row 6: *K1, p1tbl, k1, p2*, rep *–* to 3 sts bef end, k1, p1tbl, k1.
Row 7: *P1, k1tbl, p1, k1, yo, k1*, rep *–* to 3 sts bef end, p1, k1tbl, p1.
[27 (–, 33, –, –) (–, –, –, –) sts]
St count includes eyelets.

Sizes 2 and 4 only
Work rows 1–5 as on the back left shoulder. [– (25, –, 30, –) (–, –, –, –) sts]
Row 6: *P2, k1, p1tbl, k1*, rep *–* to end.
Row 7: *P1, k1tbl, p1, k1, yo, k1*, rep *–* to end.
[– (30, –, 36, –) (–, –, –, –) sts]
St counts includes eyelets.

Size 5 only
Work rows 1–5 as on the back left shoulder. [– (–, –, –, 32) (–, –, –, –) sts]
Row 6: P1, k1, *p2, k1, p1tbl, k1*, rep *–* to end.
Row 7: *P1, k1tbl, p1, k1, yo, k1*, rep *–* to 2 sts bef end, p1, k1.
[– (–, –, –, 38) (–, –, –, –) sts]
St count includes eyelets.

Sizes 6 and 7 only
Work rows 1–5 as on the back left shoulder. [– (–, –, –, –) (34, 39, –, –) sts]
Row 6: P1, *k1, p1tbl, k1, p2*, rep *–* to 3 sts bef end, k1, p1tbl, k1.
Row 7: *P1, k1tbl, p1, k1, yo, k1*, rep *–* to 4 sts bef end, p1, k1tbl, p1, k1.
[– (–, –, –, –) (40, 46, –, –) sts]
St count includes eyelets.

Sizes 8 and 9 only
Work rows 1–5 as on the back left shoulder. [– (–, –, –, –) (–, –, 41, 46) sts]
Row 6: P1, *p2, k1, p1tbl, k1*, rep *–* to end.
Row 7: *P1, k1tbl, p1, k1, yo, k1*, rep *–* to 1 st bef end, k1.
[– (–, –, –, –) (–, –, 49, 55) sts]
St count includes eyelets.

[27 (30, 33, 36, 38) (40, 46, 49, 55) sts]
Cut yarn and pl these sts on hold, being very careful to keep all the yo's in place.

FRONT LEFT SHOULDER

Using US 10.5 / 7 mm 32–40" / 80–100 cm circular needles, with RS facing, start at left edge of back left shoulder CO sts and use LHN to pick up, without knitting, 21 (23, 26, 28, 30) (32, 37, 39, 44) sts. Attach yarn on the RS.

Sizes 1 and 3 only
Work as for rows 1–5 of back right shoulder. [23 (–, 28, –, –) (–, –, –, –) sts]
Row 6: *K1, p1tbl, k1, p2*, rep *–* to 3 sts bef end, k1, p1tbl, p1.
Row 7: K1, k1tbl, p1 *k1, yo, k1, p1, k1tbl, p1*, rep *–* to end.
[27 (–, 33, –, –) (–, –, –, –) sts]
St count includes eyelets.

Sizes 2 and 4 only
Work as for rows 1–5 of back right shoulder. [– (25, –, 30, –) (–, –, –, –) sts]
Row 6: *K1, p1tbl, k1, p2*, rep *–* to end.
Row 7: *K1, yo, k1, p1, k1tbl, p1*, rep *–* to end.
[– (30, –, 36, –) (–, –, –, –) sts]
St count includes eyelets.

Size 5 only
Work as for rows 1–5 of back right shoulder. [– (–, –, –, 32) (–, –, –, –) sts]
Row 6: *K1, p1tbl, k1, p2*, rep *–* to 2 sts bef end, k1, p1.
Row 7: K1, p1, *k1, yo, k1, p1, k1tbl, p1*, rep *–* to end.
(38 sts) St count includes eyelets.

Sizes 6 and 7 only
Work as for rows 1–5 of back right shoulder. [– (–, –, –, –) (34, 39, –, –) sts]
Row 6: *K1, p1tbl, k1, p2*, rep *–* to 4 sts bef end, k1, p1tbl, k1, p1.
Row 7: K1, *p1, k1tbl, p1, k1, yo, k1*, rep *–* to 3 sts bef end, p1, k1tbl, p1.
[– (–, –, –, –) (40, 46, –, –) sts] St count includes eyelets.

Sizes 8 and 9 only
Work as for rows 1–5 of back right shoulder. [– (–, –, –, –) (–, –, 41, 46) sts]

Row 6: *K1, p1tbl, k1, p2*, rep *–* to 1 st bef end, p1.
Row 7: K1, *k1, yo, k1, p1, k1tbl, p1*, rep *–* to end.
[- (-, -, -, -) (-, -, 49, 55) sts] St count include the eyelets.

[27 (30, 33, 36, 38) (40, 46, 49, 55) sts] Do not cut yarn.

JOIN FRONT SHOULDERS

Pl the 27 (30, 33, 36, 38) (40, 46, 49, 55) sts (including the eyelets) prev put on hold for the front right shoulder onto the working needles with the WS facing, being careful not to lose any yo's. On the next row, join the shoulders as for the back and CO sts at centre front. The next row is row 2 (a WS row) of the patt.

Sizes 1 and 3 only
Next Row (WS): *K1, p1tbl, k1, p3*, rep *–* to 3 sts bef end, k1, p1tbl, k1, PM, CO 22 (–, 27, –, –) (–, –, –, –) sts using the Backwards Loop CO, PM. *K1, p1tbl, k1, p3*, rep *–* to 3 sts bef end, k1, p1tbl, k1. [76 (–, 93, –, –) (–, –, –, –) sts]
Next Row (RS): *P1, k1tbl, p1, k3, pass 3rd st on RHN over 1st 2 sts on RHN*, rep *–* to 3 sts bef m, p1, k1tbl, p1, RM, *k2, p1, k1tbl, p1*, rep *–* to 2 sts bef m, k2, RM, *p1, k1tbl, p1, k3, pass 3rd st on RHN over 1st 2 sts on RHN*, rep *–* to 3 sts bef end, p1, k1tbl, p1. [68 (–, 83, –, –) (–, –, –, –) sts]

Sizes 2 and 4 only
Next Row (WS): *K1, p1tbl, k1, p3*, rep *–* to end, PM, BLCO – (23, –, 28, –) (–, –, –, –) sts, PM, *p3, k1, p1tbl, k1*, rep *–* to end. [– (83, –, 100, –) (–, –, –, –) sts]
Next Row (RS): *P1, k1tbl, p1, k3, pass 3rd st on RHN over 1st 2 sts on RHN*, rep *–* to m, RM, *p1, k1, p1, k2*, rep *–* to 3 sts bef m, p1, k1, p1, RM. *K3, pass 3rd st on RHN over 1st 2 sts on RHN, p1, k1tbl, p1*, rep *–* to end. [– (73, –, 88, –) (–, –, –, –) sts]

Size 5 only
Next Row (WS): *K1, p1tbl, k1, p3*, rep *–* to last 2 sts, k1, p1tbl, PM, CO 29 sts using the Backwards Loop CO, PM, p1tbl, k1, *p3, k1, p1tbl, k1*, rep *–* to end. (105 sts)
Next Row (RS): *P1, k1tbl, p1, k3, pass 3rd st on RHN over 1st 2 sts on RHN*, rep *–* to 2 sts bef m, p1, k1tbl, RM, p1, *k2, p1, k1tbl, p1*, rep *–* to 3 sts bef m, k2, p1, RM, k1tbl, p1, *k3, pass 3rd st on RHN over 1st 2 sts on RHN, p1, k1tbl, p1*, rep *–* to end. (93 sts)

Sizes 6 and 7 only
Next Row (WS): *K1, p1tbl, k1, p3*, rep *–* to last 4 sts, k1, p1tbl, k1, p1, PM, CO – (–, –, –, –) (35, 30, –, –) sts using the Backwards Loop CO, PM, p1, *k1, p1tbl, k1, p3*, rep *–* to last 3 sts, k1, p1tbl, k1. [– (–, –, –, –) (115, 122, –, –) sts total].
Next Row (RS): *P1, k1tbl, p1, k3, pass 3rd st on RHN over 1st 2 sts on RHN*, rep *–* to 4 sts bef m, p1, k1tbl, p1, k1, RM, k1, *P1, k1tbl, p1, k2*, rep *–* to 4 sts bef m, p1, k1tbl, p1, k1, RM, k1, *p1, k1tbl, p1, k3, pass 3rd st on RHN over 1st 2 sts on RHN*, rep *–* to last 3 sts, p1, k1tbl, p1. [– (–, –, –, –) (103, 108, –, –) sts]

Sizes 8 and 9 only
Next Row (WS): *K1, p1tbl, k1, p3*, rep *–* to last st, k1, PM, CO 31 sts using the Backwards Loop CO, PM, k1, *p3, k1, p1tbl, k1*, rep *–* to end. [– (–, –, –, –) (–, –, 129, 141) sts]
Next Row (RS): *P1, k1tbl, p1, k3, pass 3rd st on RHN over 1st 2 sts on RHN*, rep *–* to 1 st bef m, p1, RM, k1tbl, p1, *k2, p1, k1tbl, p1*, rep *–* to 4 sts bef m, k2, p1, k1tbl, RM, p1, *k3, pass 3rd st on RHN over 1st 2 sts on RHN, p1, k1tbl, p1*, rep *–* to end. [– (–, –, –, –) (–, –, 113, 123) sts]

[68 (73, 83, 88, 93) (103, 108, 113, 123) sts]

FRONT

Work in patt (next row is a row 4, a WS row) for 25 (25, 29, 29, 33) (33, 37, 37, 41) rows, or until piece measures exactly or as close as you can to 8 (8, 9, 9, 9.75) (9.75, 10.75, 10.75, 11.75)" / 20 (20, 22.5, 22.5, 24.5) (24.5, 27, 27, 29.5) cm from the Shoulder CO edge, ending after a row 4.

BODY

Next, join the front and back sts to work in the rnd, working in St St. Leaving the front sts on the RHN, pl the 68 (73, 83, 88, 93) (103, 108, 113, 123) sts prev put on hold for the back onto the LHN with RS facing.

Next Rnd (RS): K across the 68 (73, 83, 88, 93) (103, 108, 113, 123) front sts, then k across the 68 (73, 83, 88, 93) (103, 108, 113, 123) back sts. PM for BOR. [136 (146, 166, 176, 186) (206, 216, 226, 246) sts]

Work in St St in the rnd until 58 (60, 56, 58, 54) (56, 51, 54, 49) rnds in St St have been worked, or until the piece measures 19.25 (19.75, 20, 20.25, 20.5) (20.75, 20.75, 21.25, 21.25)" / 49 (50, 50.5, 51.5, 52) (52.5, 52.5, 54, 54) cm from shoulder CO edge, or preferred length. The rib will add approx. 2.5" / 6 cm.

Rib

Change to US 10 / 6 mm 32–40" / 80–100 cm circular needles.

Work 10 rnds in 1 x 1 Half Twisted Rib, or until rib measures 2.25" / 5.5 cm.

Next Rnd: *K1tbl, sl1wyif* to end.
Next Rnd: *Sl1 pwise tbl wyib, p1*, rep *–* to end.

The k sts should now all be twisted. This will ensure that the BO edge looks consistent with the Half Twisted Rib St. BO all sts using the Italian BO method.

NECK TRIM

Using US 10 / 6 mm 16" / 40 cm circular needles, start at the back right shoulder and pick up and k 64 (66, 72, 74, 76) (78, 78, 80, 80) sts around the neckline as foll:
5 (5, 5, 5, 5) (3, 5, 5, 5) sts down the back right neck edge, 22 (23, 27, 28, 29) (35, 30, 31, 31) sts (1 st in every st, excl. the eyelets) along the back neck edge, 5 (5, 5, 5, 5) (3, 5, 5, 5) sts up the back left neck edge, 7 (7, 7, 7, 7) (5, 7, 7, 7) sts down the front left neck edge, 17 (18, 21, 22, 23) (28, 24, 24, 24) sts along the front neck edge (approx. 4 sts for every 5 sts) and 7 (7, 7, 7, 7) (5, 7, 7, 7) sts up the front right neck edge.

PM for BOR.

Work in 1 x 1 Half Twisted Rib St for 9 rnds or 2" / 5 cm.
Note! If a crew neck fit rather than a mock turtleneck is preferred, work 4 rnds or 1" / 2.5 cm instead.

Next Rnd: *K1tbl, sl1wyif* to end.
Next Rnd: *Sl1 pwise tbl wyib, p1*, rep *–* to end.

BO all sts using the Italian BO method.

SLEEVES

Using US 10.5 / 7 mm 16" / 40 cm circular needles, starting at the underarm point, pick up and k 44 (46, 52, 56, 58) (62, 66, 68, 72) sts evenly spaced around the armhole. PM for BOR.

Work 68 (70, 70, 73, 73) (75, 75, 78, 78) rnds in St St, or until sleeve measures 13.5 (13.75, 13.75, 14.25, 14.25) (14.75, 14.75, 15.25, 15.25)" / 34 (35, 35, 36.5, 36.5) (37.5, 37.5, 39, 39) cm, or to preferred length. The rib will add approx. 2.25" / 5.5 cm.

Rib

Switch to US 10 / 6 mm 16" / 40 cm circular needles.

Work in 1 x 1 Half Twisted Rib St for 10 rnds or 2.25" / 5.5 cm.

Next Rnd: *K1tbl, sl1wyif* to end.
Next Rnd: *Sl1 pwise tbl wyib, p1*, rep *–* to end.

BO all sts using the Italian BO method.

FINISHING

Weave in ends. Wet block to measurements.

Marie Régnier

08 Berlingot

This top-down cable dress was inspired by a French candy. It is a quick knit featuring a fully reversible design with a bubbly motif when worn one way out and diamond shapes when reversed.

SIZES

1 (2, 3, 4, 5) (6, 7, 8)

Recommended ease: 6–8" / 15–20.5 cm of positive ease.

FINISHED MEASUREMENTS

Bust Circumference: 36.5 (41.25, 45.75, 50.25, 59.5) (64, 68.5, 73.25)" / 91.5 (103, 114.5, 125.5, 148.5) (160, 171.5, 183) cm.
Upper Arm Circumference: 16 (16, 16, 16, 18.25) (18.25, 18.25, 18.25)" / 40 (40, 40, 40, 45.5) (45.5, 45.5, 45.5) cm.
Body Length from the Underarm to Hem: 31.5" / 80 cm.
Total Sleeve Length: 17.75" / 45 cm.
Yoke Depth: 9.75 (9.75, 9.75, 9.75, 12.75) (12.75, 12.75, 12.75)" / 24.5 (24.5, 24.5, 24.5, 32) (32, 32, 32) cm.
Neckband Circumference: 22.75 (22.75, 32, 32, 41.25) (41.25, 50.25, 50.25)" / 57 (57, 80, 80, 103) (103, 125.5, 125.5) cm.

MATERIALS

Yarn: 9 (9, 10, 11, 11) (14, 15, 15) skeins of Tundra by The Fibre Co (60% alpaca, 30% wool, 10% silk), 120 yds / 109 m – 100 g), colourway Amber Burn.

Or approx. 1050 (1060, 1200, 1270, 1320) (1650, 1710, 1760) yds / 960 (969, 1097, 1161, 1207) (1509, 1564, 1609) m of bulky-weight yarn. Alternative yarn suggestions are for example Wool and the Gang Alpachino Merino, Berroco Ultra Alpaca Chunky and We are Knitters The Squishy Yarn.

Needles: US 6 / 4 mm and US 10.5 / 6.5 mm 32" / 80 cm circular needles.

Notions: Stitch markers, cable needle, waste yarn, elastic thread (optional).

GAUGE

14 sts x 11 rnds to 4" / 10 cm on US 10.5 / 6.5 mm needles in Berlingo St patt worked in the rnd, after blocking.

SPECIAL ABBREVIATIONS

1/2 LPC: 1 over 2 left purl cross. Sl 1 st to CN and hold in front, p2, k1 from CN.

1/2 RPC: 1 over 2 right purl cross. Sl 2 p sts to CN and hold in back, k1, p2 from CN.

SPECIAL TECHNIQUES

TSP (Twin stitches purlwise): Sl the next st pwise to the RHN, with LHN lift the left leg of the st below the slipped st. P it and slip both sts on your LHN. Two sts are coming out of the same p st.

NOTES

You can adjust the length to your preference, whether a full dress or a cropped sweater. The dress has a wide collar. If using a softer yarn or wanting a tighter fit at the neck, feel free to sew an elastic thread to the WS of the neckband to tighten it.

The dress is photographed together with the Ingrid cowl (see page 205). Find more photos of the dress at lainepublishing.com.

CONSTRUCTION

This dress is worked from the top down starting with the Alternating Cable Cast-On for 2 x 2 ribbing. The neckband is knitted in 2 x 2 ribbing, with short rows at the back to raise this part of the garment. Then, increases are worked to shape the yoke. When separating the body from the sleeves, a Provisional CO is worked at the underarm to have a seamless and reversible garment. All the hems use a 2 x 2 ribbing and a sewn bind-off.

DIRECTIONS

NECKBAND

With US 6 / 4 mm needles, and the Alternating Cable CO for 2 x 2 Ribbing method, CO 80 (80, 112, 112, 144) (144, 176, 176) sts. Join to work in the rnd and PM for BOR.

Rib Rnd 1: *P2, k2*, rep to end. Work in est 2 x 2 rib until the neckband measures approx 4.75" / 12 cm.

Back Neck Short Row Shaping

Short Row 1 (RS): *P2, k2*, rep *–* 4 (4, 6, 6, 8) (8, 10, 10) more times, TSP, tw.
Short Row 2 (WS): *P2, k2*, rep *–* to m, SM, *p2, k2*, rep *–* 4 (4, 6, 6, 8) (8, 10, 10) more times, TSP, tw.
Short Row 3: *P2, k2*, rep *–* to m, SM, *p2, k2*, rep *–* to 4 sts bef the prev TSP, TSP, tw.
Short Row 4: *P2, k2*, rep *–* to m, SM, *p2, k2*, rep *–* to 4 sts bef the prev TSP, TSP, tw.

Rep short rows 3–4 2 (2, 2, 3, 3) (3, 3, 3) more times.

Next Rnd (RS): *P2, k2*, rep *–* to m, SM, *p2, k2* to the end of rnd and resolve all TSP by p2tog.

YOKE

Change to US 10.5 / 6.5 mm needles.
Set-Up Rnd: *P2, k2*, rep *–* 2 (2, 4, 4, 6) (6, 8, 8) more times, PM (new BOR), p2, PM, *k2, p2* twice, k2, PM, p2, PM, *k2, p2*, rep 5 (5, 9, 9, 13) (13, 17, 17) more times, k2, PM, p2, PM, *k2, p2* twice, k2, PM, p2, PM, *k2, p2*, rep *–* to 2 sts bef end, k2.

Rnd 1 (Inc): *P2, SM, m1r(p), [k2, p2] to 2 sts bef m, k2, m1l(p), SM*, rep *–* 3 more times. (8 sts inc'd) [88 (88, 120, 120, 152) (152, 184, 184) sts]
Rnd 2: *P2, SM, p1, [k2, p2] to 3 sts bef m, k2, p1, SM*, rep *–* 3 more times.
Rnd 3 (Inc): *P2, SM, m1r(p), p1, [k2, p2] to 3 sts bef m, k2, p1, m1l(p), SM*, rep *–* 3 more times.
Rnd 4: *P2, SM, [1/2 RPC, 1/2 LPC, k2] to 6 sts bef m, [1/2 RPC, 1/2 LPC], SM*, rep *–* 3 more times.
Rnd 5 (Inc): *P2, SM, m1r, k1, [p4, k4] to 5 sts bef m, p4, k1, m1l, SM*, rep *–* 3 more times.
Rnd 6: *P2, SM, k2, [p4, k4] to 6 sts bef m, p4, k2, SM*, rep *–* 3 more times.
Rnd 7 (Inc): *P2, SM, m1r, k2, [p4, k4] to 6 sts bef m, p4, k2, m1l, SM*, rep *–* 3 more times.
Rnd 8: *P2, SM, k2, [1/2 LPC, 1/2 RPC, k2] to m, SM*, rep *–* 3 more times.
Rnd 9 (Inc): *P2, SM, m1r(p), [k2, p2] to 2 sts bef m, k2, m1l(p), SM*, rep *–* 3 more times.
Rnd 10: *P2, SM, p1, [k2, p2] to 3 sts bef m, k2, p1, SM*, rep *–* 3 more times.
Rnd 11 (Inc): *P2, SM, m1r(p), p1, [k2, p2] to 3 sts bef m, k2, p1, m1l(p), SM*, rep *–* 3 more times.
Rnd 12: *P2, SM, [1/2 RPC, 1/2 LPC, k2] to 6 sts bef m, [1/2 RPC, 1/2 LPC], SM*, rep *–* 3 more times.
Rnd 13 (Inc): *P2, SM, m1r, k1, [p4, k4] to 5 sts bef m, p4, k1, m1l, SM* rep *–* 3 more times.
Rnd 14: *P2, SM, k2, [p4, k4] to 6 sts bef m, p4, k2, SM*, rep *–* 3 more times.
Rnd 15 (Inc): *P2, SM, m1r, k2, [p4, k4] to 6 sts bef m, p4, k2, m1l, SM*, rep *–* 3 more times.
Rnd 16: *P2, SM, k2, [1/2 LPC, 1/2 RPC, k2] to m, SM*, rep *–* 3 more times.

[26 (26, 26, 26, 26) (26, 26, 26) sts for each sleeve, 42 (42, 58, 58, 74) (74, 90, 90) sts for front and back and 2 sts for each raglan seam]

Sizes 1, 2, 3 and 4 only
Rep rnds 1–11 once more. [192 (192, 224, 224, –) (–, –, –) sts. 38 (38, 38, 38, –) (–, –, –) sts for each sleeve, 54 (54, 70, 70, –) (–, –, –) sts for front and back and 2 sts for each raglan seam]

Sizes 5, 6, 7 and 8 only
Rep rnds 1–16 once more, then rep rnds 1–3 once more. [– (–, –, –, 288) (288, 320, 320) sts. – (–, –, –, 46) (46, 46, 46) sts for each sleeve, – (–, –, –, 94) (94, 110, 110) sts for front and back and 2 sts for each raglan seam]

BODY

Separating Body and Sleeves

Set-Up Rnd 1: (Removing m as you go), *sl 42 (42, 42, 42, 50) (50, 50, 50) sts on hold on a piece of scrap yarn for the first sleeve, using a Provisional CO method, CO 10 (18, 10, 18, 10) (18, 10, 18) sts, [1/2 RPC, 1/2 LPC, k2] to 6 sts bef m, 1/2 RPC, 1/2 LPC*, rep *–* once. [128 (144, 160, 176, 208) (224, 240, 256) sts for the body]

Set-Up Rnd 2: RM, sl 1st st from RHN to LHN, PM (new BOR), sl st back from LHN to RHN, k1, *p4, k4*, rep *–* to 6 sts bef m, p4, k2.

Sizes 1, 2, 3 and 4 only
Work rnds 3–16 of chart, then keep working rnds 1–16 until the body measures approx. 28.75" / 73 cm from the underarm, or until desired length. End on a rnd 5 or 13 of chart.

Sizes 5, 6, 7 and 8 only
Work rnds 11–16 of chart, then keep working rnds 1–16 until the body measures approx. 28.75" / 73 cm from the underarm, or until desired length. End on a rnd 5 or 13 of chart.

Hem

Rnd 1: *K2, p2*, rep *–* to end.
Rep rnd 1 until the hem ribbing measures approx. 2.75" / 7 cm, or until desired length.

SLEEVES

Set-Up Rnd: Pl 42 (42, 42, 42, 50) (50, 50, 50) sleeve sts back on the needles, PM (for BOR) and unravel the Provisional CO and pl 10 (18, 10, 18, 10) (18, 10, 18) sts on the needles, rejoin yarn, p2, [1/2 RPC, 1/2 LPC, k2] to 8 sts bef m, 1/2 RPC, 1/2 LPC, p2. [52 (60, 52, 60, 60) (68, 60, 68) sts]

Sizes 1, 3, 5 and 7 only
Set-Up Rnd 1 (Inc): M1l, k10, m1r, p2, k1, *p4, k4*, rep *–* to 7 sts bef end, p4, k1, p2. (2 sts inc'd) [54 (–, 54, –, 62) (–, 62, –) sts]
Set-Up Rnd 2: K12, p2, k1, *p4, k4*, rep *–* to 7 sts bef end, p4, k1, p2.
Set-Up Rnd 3 (inc): M1l, k12, m1r, p2, k1, *p4, k4*, rep *–* to 7 sts bef end, p4, k1, p2.
Set- Up Rnd 4: K14, p2, *1/2 LPC, 1/2 RPC, k2*, rep *–* to 8 sts bef end, 1/2 LPC, 1/2 RPC, p2.

Sizes 2, 4, 6 and 8 only
Set-Up Rnd 1 (Dec): K2tog, k14, k2tog, p2, k1, *p4, k4*, rep *–* to 7 sts bef end, p4, k1, p2. (2 sts dec'd) [– (58, –, 58, –) (66, –, 66) sts]
Set- Up Rnd 2: K16, p2, k1, *p4, k4*, rep *–* to 7 sts bef end, p4, k1, p2.
Set- Up Rnd 3 (Dec): K2tog, k12, k2tog, p2, k1, *p4, k4*, rep *–* to 7 sts bef end, p4, k1, p2.
Set-Up Rnd 4: K14, p2, *1/2 LPC, 1/2 RPC, k2*, rep *–* to 8 sts bef end, 1/2 LPC, 1/2 RPC, p2.

All sizes
Next Rnd: RM, sl 1st st from RHN to LHN, PM (new BOR), sl st back from LHN to RHN, *p2, k2*, rep to 3 sts bef end, p2, k1.

Work rnds 7–16 of chart, then keep working rnds 1–16 until the sleeve is approx. 15" / 38 cm from the underarm, or until 2.75" / 7 cm from the desired length. End on a rnd 5 or 13 of chart.

HEM

Set-Up Rnd (Dec): *K2tog*, rep *–* to end. [28 (28, 28, 28, 32) (32, 32, 32) sts dec'd] [28 (28, 28, 28, 32) (32, 32, 32) sts]

Rib Rnd 1: *K2, p2*, rep *–* to end. Work in est 2 x 2 rib until the hem measures approx. 2.75" / 7 cm from the set-up rnd. BO using the 2/2 Tubular BO method.

FINISHING

Weave in ends. Gently block to measurements.

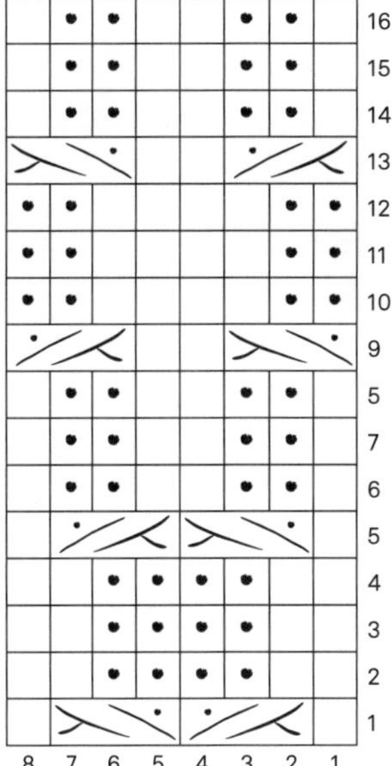

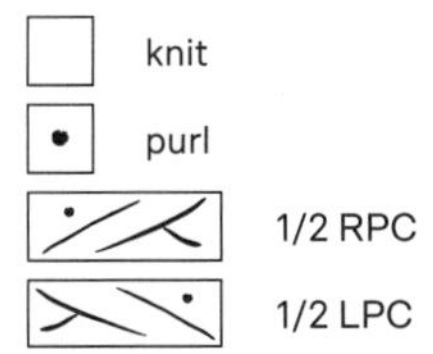

Brenda Lam

09 Snow and Tell

Snow and Tell features an easy-to-memorise textured mosaic pattern. Made with super-chunky yarn, this drop-shoulder jumper will be ready in no time!

SIZES

1 (2, 3, 4, 5) (6, 7, 8, 9)

Recommended ease: 6–9.25" / 15.5–23.5 cm of positive ease.

FINISHED MEASUREMENTS

Bust Circumference: 37.25 (40, 45.25, 48, 53.25, 56) (61.25, 64, 69.25)" / 94.5 (101.5, 115, 122, 135, 142) (155.5, 162.5, 176) cm.
Length from Shoulder to Hem: 16.5 (17, 17.5, 19, 19.5, 20) (21.5, 22, 22.5)" / 42 (43, 44.5, 48, 49.5, 51) (54.5, 56, 57) cm.
Length from Underarm to Hem: 10.5 (10.5, 10.5, 11.5, 11.5, 11.5) (12.5, 12.5, 12.5)" / 26.5 (26.5, 26.5, 29, 29, 29) (32, 32, 32) cm.
Sleeve Circumference: 18.75 (18.75, 18.75, 21.25, 21.25, 21.25) (24, 24, 24)" / 47.5 (47.5, 47.5, 54, 54, 54) (61, 61, 61) cm.
Sleeve Length (Adjustable): 17.5" / 44.5 cm.

MATERIALS

Yarn: Softy by Yarnalia (100% merino, 49 yds / 45 m – 100 g).
Colour A: 2 (2, 2, 2, 2) (2, 2, 3, 3) balls of colourway Medallion.
Colour B: 4 (5, 5, 6, 6) (6, 7, 8, 8) balls of colourway Cloudy Day.
Colour C: 4 (5, 5, 6, 6) (6, 7, 8, 8) balls of colourway Creamy Oats.

Or approx. 60 (65, 70, 75, 85) (90, 95, 100, 105) yds / 55 (60, 65, 70, 80) (85, 90, 90, 95) m (in Colour A), 195 (205, 225, 260, 280) (295, 340, 355, 380) yds / 180 (190, 205, 240, 255) (270, 310, 325, 350) m (in Colour B) and 195 (205, 225, 260, 280) (295, 340, 355, 380) yds / 180 (190, 205, 240, 255) (270, 310, 325, 350) m (in Colour C) of a super-bulky-weight yarn. Alternative yarn options are for example Wool and the Gang Crazy Sexy Wool, We Are Knitters The Wool and Bettaknit Cool Wool.

Needles: US 15 / 10 mm (for rib, collar and cuffs) and US 19 / 15 mm (for body) 32" / 80 cm circular needles and an extra US 19 / 15 mm needle (for 3-Needle BO).

Notions: Stitch marker, stitch holders or waste yarn.

GAUGE

9 sts x 16 rows to 4" / 10 cm on US 19 / 15 mm needles in Dotted Ladder Mosaic patt, after blocking.

12 sts x 14 rows to 4" / 10 cm on US 15 / 10 mm needles in 1 x 1 rib, after blocking.

STITCH PATTERNS

Dotted Ladder Mosaic Pattern

In the rnd, multiples of 6 sts.
Set-Up Rnd: With Colour B, p to end.
Rnd 1: With Colour C, *sl1, k1, sl1, k3*, rep *–* to end.
Rnd 2: *Sl1, p1, sl1, k3*, rep *–* to end.
Rnd 3: With B, *k3, sl1, k1, sl1*, rep *–* to end.
Rnd 4: *K3, sl1, p1, sl1*, rep *–* to end.
Rep rnds 1–4 for patt.

Dotted Ladder Mosaic Pattern
Worked flat, multiples of 6 sts.
Set-Up Row (WS): With Colour B, p to end.
Row 1 (RS): With Colour C, *sl1, k1, sl1, k3*, rep *–* to end.
Row 2: *P3, sl1, k1, sl1*, rep *–* to end.
Row 3: With B, *k3, sl1, k1, sl1*, rep *–* to end.
Row 4: *Sl1, k1, sl1, p3*, rep *–* to end.
Rep rows 1–4 for patt.

NOTES

Colour A is used for the ribbing. Colours B and C are used in the mosaic pattern.

Slip stitches with yarn in back on RS rows and yarn in front on WS rows.

CONSTRUCTION

This jumper features an all-over textured mosaic pattern. The body is knitted from the bottom up in one piece working in the round to the armholes and then flat. The shoulders are joined with a 3-Needle BO. The sleeves are picked up from the body and worked in the round, with decreases just before the cuff ribbing. The collar is picked up from the neckline and worked in ribbing in the round.

DIRECTIONS

HEM

With US 15 / 10 mm circular needles and Colour A, CO 84 (90, 102, 108, 120, 126) (138, 144, 156) sts using the Long-Tail CO method. Join in the rnd and PM for BOR.

Rib Rnd: *K1, p1* to end.
Work in est in 1 x 1 Rib for 6 rnds in total.

BODY

Change to US 19 / 15 mm needles.

Set-Up Rnd: With B, k to end.

Work rnds 1–4 of the Dotted Mosaic Ladder St, 8 (8, 8, 9, 9) (9, 10, 10, 10) times. [33 (33, 33, 37, 37) (37, 41, 41, 41) rnds worked since start of body]

Rep rnds 1 and 2 once.

FRONT UPPER BODY

Next, work flat over half of the sts to create the front upper body.
PM after 42 (45, 51, 54, 60, 63) (69, 72, 78) sts to mark the end of front sts. After working row 1 to m, tw and leave rem 42 (45, 51, 54, 60, 63) (69, 72, 78) sts on the cable or a stitch holder for later.

Sizes 1, 4, 5, 8 and 9 only
Row 1 (RS): With B, k3, *sl1, k1, sl1, k3*, rep *–* to last 3 sts, sl1, k1, sl1.
Row 2 (WS): K2, sl1, *p3, sl1, k1, sl1*, rep *–* to last 3 sts, p2, sl1.
Row 3: With C, k2, sl1, *k3, sl1, k1, sl1*, rep *–* to last 3 sts, k2, sl1.
Row 4: K1, p2, *sl1, k1, sl1, p3*, rep *–* to last 3 sts, sl1, k1, sl1.

Rows 5 to 16 (–, –, 24, 24) (–, –, 28, 32): Rep prev rows 1–4 another 3 (–, –, 5, 5) (–, –, 6, 7) times.

Sizes 2, 3, 6 and 7 only
Row 1 (RS): With B, *k3, sl1, k1, sl1*, rep *–* to last 3 sts, k2, sl1.
Row 2 (WS): K1, p1, *p1, sl1, k1, sl1, p2*, rep *–* to last st, sl1.
Row 3: With C, k2, *sl1, k3, sl1, k1*, rep *–* to last st, sl1.
Row 4: K2, *sl1, p3, sl1, k1*, rep *–* to last st, sl1.
Rows 5 to – (20, 20, –, –) (24, 28, –, –): Rep rows 1–4 above another – (4, 4, –, –) (5, 6, –, –) times.

Sizes 1, 3, 6 and 8 only
Rows 17–18 (–, 21–22, –, –) (25–26, –, 29–30, –): Rep rows 1 and 2 once more.

All sizes
Work according to size to finish the front and work the shoulders.

Size 1 only
Row 19 (RS): With C, k2, sl1, *k3, sl1, k1, sl1* twice, k1, BO 10 sts, (first sl1 of patt is already on RHN) k3, sl1, k1, sl1, k3, sl1, k1, sl1, k2, sl1.

Work across rem 16 sts to shape right shoulder:
Row 20 (WS): K1, p2, *sl1, k1, sl1, p3* twice, sl1.
Row 21 (RS) (Dec): With B, ssk, k1, *sl1, k3, sl1, k1* twice, sl1. (1 st dec'd)
Row 22: K2, *sl1, p3, sl1, k1* twice, sl1.
Row 23 (Dec): With C, ssk, *k1, sl1, k1, sl1, k2* twice, sl1. (1 st dec'd)
Row 24: K1, p1, *p1, sl1, k1, sl1, p2* twice.

Cut yarn and pl rem 14 sts on a spare needle or scrap yarn.

With WS facing, rejoin C to rem 16 front sts for left shoulder.
Row 20 (WS): P1, sl1, k1, *sl1, p3, sl1, k1* twice, sl1.

Row 21 (RS) (Dec): With B, *k3, sl1, k1, sl1* twice, k2, k2tog. (1 st dec'd)
Row 22: *P3, sl1, k1, sl1* twice, p2, sl1.
Row 23 (Dec): With C, k1, *k1, sl1, k3, sl1* twice, k2tog. (1 st dec'd)
Row 24: K1, sl1, *p3, sl1, k1, sl1* twice.
Cut yarn and pl the 14 sts on a spare needle or scrap yarn.

Size 2 only
Row 21 (RS): With B, *k3, sl1, k1, sl1* twice, k3, sl1, k1, BO 11 sts, (first k1 of patt is already on RHN) sl1, k3, sl1, k1, sl1, k3, sl1, k1, sl1, k2, sl1.

Work across rem 17 sts to shape right shoulder:
Row 22 (WS): K1, p2, *sl1, k1, sl1, p3* twice, sl1, k1.
Row 23 (RS) (Dec): With C, ssk, *sl1, k1, sl1, k3* twice, sl1, k1, sl1. (1 st dec'd)
Row 24: K2, sl1, *p3, sl1, k1, sl1* twice, p1.
Row 25 (Dec): With B, ssk, k1, *k1, sl1, k1, sl1, k2* twice, sl1. (1 st dec'd)
Row 26: K1, p2, *sl1, k1, sl1, p3* twice.
Cut yarn and pl the 15 sts on a spare needle or scrap yarn.

With WS facing, rejoin B to rem 17 front sts for left shoulder.
Row 22 (WS): K1, sl1, *p3, sl1, k1, sl1* twice, p2, sl1.
Row 23 (RS) (Dec): With C, k2, sl1, *k3, sl1, k1, sl1* twice, k2tog. (1 st dec'd)
Row 24: P1, *sl1, k1, sl1, p3* twice, sl1, k1, sl1.
Row 25 (Dec): With B, *k3, sl1, k1, sl1* twice, k2, k2tog. (1 st dec'd)
Row 26: *P3, sl1, k1, sl1* twice, p2, sl1.
Cut yarn and pl the 15 sts on a spare needle or scrap yarn.

Size 3 only
Row 23: With C, k1, *k1, sl1, k3, sl1* 3 times, BO 13 sts, (first k1 of patt is already on RHN) sl1, k3, sl1, *k1, sl1, k3, sl1* twice, sl1.

Work across rem 19 sts to shape right shoulder:
Row 24 (WS): K1, *k1, sl1, p3, sl1* 3 times.
Row 25 (RS) (Dec): With B, ssk, k1, sl1, *k3, sl1, k1, sl1* twice, k2, sl1. (1 st dec'd)
Row 26: K1, p2, *sl1, k1, sl1, p3* twice, sl1, k1, sl1.
Row 27 (Dec): With C, ssk, k1, *sl1, k1, sl1, k3* twice, sl1, k1, sl1. (1 st dec'd)
Row 28: K2, *sl1, p3, sl1, k1* twice, sl1, p2.
Cut yarn and pl the 17 sts on a spare needle or scrap yarn.

With WS facing, rejoin C to rem 19 front sts for left shoulder.
Row 24 (WS): *Sl1, p3, sl1, k1* 3 times, sl1.
Row 25 (RS) (Dec): With B, *k3, sl1, k1, sl1* twice, k3, sl1, k1, k2tog. (1 st dec'd)
Row 26: *Sl1, k1, sl1, p3* twice, sl1, k1, sl1, p2, sl1.
Row 27 (Dec): With C, k2, *sl1, k3, sl1, k1* twice, sl1, k1, k2tog. (1 st dec'd)
Row 28: P2, *sl1, k1, sl1, p3* twice, sl1, k1, sl1.
Cut yarn and pl the 17 sts on a spare needle or scrap yarn.

Size 4 only
Row 25 (RS): With B, *k3, sl1, k1, sl1* 3 times, k2, BO 14 sts, (first k1 of patt is already on the RHN) sl1, k3, sl1, *k1, sl1, k3, sl1* twice, k1, sl1.

Work across rem 20 sts to shape right shoulder:
Row 26 (WS): K2, *sl1, p3, sl1, k1* 3 times.
Row 27 (RS) (Dec): With C, ssk, *sl1, k1, sl1, k3* twice, sl1, k1, sl1, k2, sl1. (1 st dec'd)
Row 28: K1, *p2, sl1, k1, sl1, p1* 3 times.
Row 29 (Dec): With B, ssk, k2, *sl1, k1, sl1, k3* twice, sl1, k1, sl1. (1 st dec'd)
Row 30: K2, sl1, *p3, sl1, k1, sl1* twice, p3.
Cut yarn and pl the 18 sts on a spare needle or scrap yarn.

With WS facing, rejoin B to rem 20 front sts for left shoulder.
Row 26 (WS): *P2, sl1, k1, sl1, p1* 3 times, p1, sl1.
Row 27 (RS) (Dec): With C, k2, *sl1, k3, sl1, k1* twice, sl1, k3, k2tog. (1 st dec'd)
Row 28: Sl1, *p3, sl1, k1, sl1* 3 times.
Row 29 (Dec): With B, *k3, sl1, k1, sl1* twice, k3, sl1, k1, k2tog. (1 st dec'd)
Row 30: *Sl1, k1, sl1, p3* twice, sl1, k1, sl1, p2, sl1.
Cut yarn and pl the 18 sts on a spare needle or scrap yarn.

Size 5 only
Row 25 (RS): With B, *k3, sl1, k1, sl1* 3 times, k3, sl1, k1, BO 14 sts, (first k st of right front is already on RHN) k1, *sl1, k1, sl1, k3* 3 times, sl1, k1, sl1.

Work across rem 23 sts to shape right shoulder:
Row 26 (WS): K2, sl1, *p3, sl1, k1, sl1* 3 times, p2.
Row 27 (RS) (Dec): With C, ssk, *k3, sl1, k1, sl1* 3 times, k2, sl1. (1 st dec'd)
Row 28: K1, p2, *sl1, k1, sl1, p3* 3 times, sl1.
Row 29 (Dec): With B, ssk, *k1, sl1, k3, sl1* 3 times, k1, sl1. (1 st dec'd)
Row 30: K2, sl1, *p3, sl1, k1, sl1* 3 times.
Row 31 (Dec): With C, ssk, *k1, sl1, k1, sl1, k2* 3 times, sl1. (1 st dec'd)
Row 32: K1, *p2, sl1, k1, sl1, p1* 3 times, p1.
Cut yarn and pl the 20 sts on a spare needle or scrap yarn.

With WS facing, rejoin B to rem 23 front sts for left shoulder.
Row 26 (WS): *K1, sl1, p3, sl1* 3 times, k1, sl1, p2, sl1.
Row 27 (RS) (Dec): With C, k2, *sl1, k3, sl1, k1* 3 times, sl1, k2tog. (1 st dec'd)
Row 28: P1, *sl1, k1, sl1, p3* 3 times, sl1, k1, sl1.
Row 29 (Dec): With B, *k3, sl1, k1, sl1* 3 times, k2, k2tog. (1 st dec'd)
Row 30: *P3, sl1, k1, sl1* 3 times, p2, sl1.

Row 31 (Dec): With C, k1, *k1, sl1, k3, sl1* 3 times, k2tog. (1 st dec'd)
Row 32: K1, sl1, *p3, sl1, k1, sl1* 3 times.
Cut yarn and pl the 20 sts on a spare needle or scrap yarn.

Size 6 only
Row 27 (RS): With C, k1, *k1, sl1, k3, sl1* 3 times, k1, sl1, k3, BO 15 sts, (first k st of patt is already on RHN) k2, sl1, k1, sl1, *k3, sl1, k1, sl1* twice, k3, sl1, k1, sl1.

Work across rem 24 sts to shape the right shoulder:
Row 28 (WS): K2, *sl1, p3, sl1, k1* 3 times, sl1, p3.
Row 29 (RS) (Dec): With B, ssk, sl1, *k3, sl1, k1, sl1* 3 times, k2, sl1. (1 st dec'd)
Row 30: K1, p2, *sl1, k1, sl1, p3* 3 times, sl1, k1.
Row 31 (Dec): With C, ssk, *sl1, k1, sl1, k3* 3 times, sl1, k1, sl1. (1 st dec'd)
Row 32: K2, *sl1, p3, sl1, k1* 3 times, sl1, p1.
Row 33 (Dec): With B, ssk, *k2, sl1, k1, sl1, k1* 3 times, k1, sl1. (1 st dec'd)
Row 34: K1, p2, *sl1, k1, sl1, p3* 3 times.
Cut yarn and pl the 21 sts on a spare needle or scrap yarn.

With WS facing, rejoin C to rem 24 front sts for left shoulder.
Row 28 (WS): *P3, sl1, k1, sl1* 4 times.
Row 29 (RS) (Dec): With B, *k3, sl1, k1, sl1* 3 times, k3, sl1, k2tog. (1 st dec'd)
Row 30: *K1, sl1, p3, sl1* 3 times, k1, sl1, p2, sl1.
Row 31 (Dec): With C, k2, sl1, *k3, sl1, k1, sl1* 3 times, k2tog. (1 st dec'd)
Row 32: P1, *sl1, k1, sl1, p3* 3 times, sl1, K1, sl1.
Row 33 (Dec): With B, *k3, sl1, k1, sl1* 3 times, k2, k2tog. (1 st dec'd)
Row 34: *P3, sl1, k1, sl1* 3 times, p2, sl1.
Cut yarn and pl the 21 sts on a spare needle or scrap yarn.

Size 7 only
Row 29 (RS): With B, *k3, sl1, k1, sl1* 4 times, k2, BO 17 sts, (first k st of patt is already on RHN) k1, sl1, k1, sl1, *k2, sl1, k1, sl1* 4 times, k1, sl1.
Work across rem 26 sts to shape the right shoulder:
Row 30 (WS): K1, *p2, sl1, k1, sl1, p1* 4 times, p1.
Row 31 (RS) (Dec): With C, ssk, *k3, sl1, k1, sl1* 3 times, k3, sl1, k1, sl1. (1 st dec'd)
Row 32: K1, *k1, sl1, p3, sl1* 4 times.
Row 33 (Dec): With B, ssk, *k1, sl1, k3, sl1* twice, k1, sl1, k2, sl1. (1 st dec'd)
Row 34: K1, p2, *sl1, k1, sl1, p3* 3 times, sl1, k1, sl1.
Row 35 (Dec): With C, ssk, k1, *sl1, k1, sl1, k3* 3 times, sl1, k1, sl1. (1 st dec'd)
Row 36: K2, sl1, *p3, sl1, k1, sl1* 3 times, p2.
Cut yarn and pl the 23 sts on a spare needle or scrap yarn.

With WS facing, rejoin B to rem 26 front sts for left shoulder.
Row 30 (WS): *P2, sl1, k1, sl1, p1* 3 times, p1, sl1.
Row 31 (RS) (Dec): With C, k2, sl1, *k3, sl1, k1, sl1* 3 times, k3, k2tog. (1 st dec'd)
Row 32: Sl1, *p3, sl1, k1, sl1* 4 times.
Row 33 (Dec): With B, *k3, sl1, k1, sl1* 3 times, k3, sl1, k1, k2tog. (1 st dec'd)
Row 34: *Sl1, k1, sl1, p3* 3 times, sl1, k1, sl1, p2, sl1.
Row 35 (Dec): With C, k2, sl1, *k3, sl1, k1, sl1* 3 times, k1, k2tog.(1 st dec'd)
Row 36: P2, *sl1, k1, sl1, p3* 3 times, sl1, k1, sl1.
Cut yarn and pl the 23 sts on a spare needle or scrap yarn.

Size 8 only
Row 31: With C, k2, sl1, *k3, sl1, k1, sl1* 4 times, BO 18 sts, (first k st of patt is already on RHN) k2, sl1, k1, sl1, *k3, sl1, k1, sl1* 3 times, k2, sl1.

Work across rem 27 sts to shape the right shoulder:
Row 32 (WS): K1, p2, *sl1, k1, sl1, p3* 4 times.
Row 33 (RS) (Dec): With B, ssk, *sl1, k3, sl1, k1* 4 times, sl1. (1 st dec'd)
Row 34: K2, *sl1, p3, sl1, k1* 4 times.
Row 35 (Dec): With C, ssk, *sl1, k1, sl1, k3* 3 times, sl1, k1, sl1, k2, sl1. (1 st dec'd)
Row 36: K1, *p2, sl1, k1, sl1, p1* 4 times.
Row 37 (Dec): With B, ssk, *k2, sl1, k1, sl1, k1* 3 times, k2, sl1, k1, sl1. (1 st dec'd)
Row 38: K2, *sl1, p3, sl1, k1* 3 times, sl1, p3.
Cut yarn and pl the 24 sts on a spare needle or scrap yarn.

With WS facing, rejoin C to rem 27 front sts for left shoulder.
Row 32 (WS): *Sl1, k1, sl1, p3* 3 times, sl1, k1, sl1.
Row 33 (RS): With B, *k3, sl1, k1, sl1* 4 times, k1, k2tog. (1 st dec'd)
Row 34: *P2, sl1, k1, sl1, p1* 4 times, p1, sl1.
Row 35 (Dec): With C, k2, sl1, *k3, sl1, k1, sl1* 3 times, k3, k2tog. (1 st dec'd)
Row 36: *Sl1, p3, sl1, k1* 4 times, sl1.
Row 37 (Dec): With B, *k3, sl1, k1, sl1* 3 times, k3, sl1, k1, k2tog. (1 st dec'd)
Row 38: *Sl1, k1, sl1, p3* 3 times, sl1, k1, sl1, p2, sl1.
Cut yarn and pl the 24 sts on a spare needle or scrap yarn.

Size 9 only
Row 33 (RS): With B, *k3, sl1, k1, sl1* 5 times, BO 18 sts, (first k st of patt is already on RHN) k2, sl1, k1, sl1, *k3, sl1, k1, sl1* 3 times, k3, sl1, k1, s1.

Work across rem 30 sts to shape the right shoulder:
Row 34 (WS): K2, *sl1, p3, sl1, k1* 4 times, sl1, p3.
Row 35 (RS) (Dec): With C, ssk, *sl1, k3, sl1, k1* 4 times, sl1, k2, sl1. (1 st dec'd)
Row 36: K1, p2, *sl1, k1, sl1, p3* 4 times, sl1, k1.
Row 37 (Dec): With B, ssk, *sl1, k1, sl1, k3* 4 times, sl1, k1, sl1. (1 st dec'd)
Row 38: K2, *sl1, p3, sl1, k1* twice, sl1, p1.

Row 39 (Dec): With C, ssk, *k2, sl1, k1, sl1, k1* 4 times, k1, sl1. (1 st dec'd)
Row 40: K1, p2, *sl1, k1, sl1, p3* 4 times.
Cut yarn and pl the 27 sts on a spare needle or scrap yarn.

With WS facing, rejoin B to rem 30 front sts for left shoulder.
Row 34 (WS): *Sl1, k1, sl1, p3* 4 times, sl1, k1, sl1, p2, sl1.
Row 35 (RS) (Dec): With C, k2, sl1, *k3, sl1, k1, sl1* 4 times, k1, k2tog. (1 st dec'd)
Row 36: P2, *sl1, k1, sl1, p3* 4 times, sl1, k1, sl1.
Row 37 (Dec): With B, *k3, sl1, k1, sl1* 4 times, k3, k2tog. (1 st dec'd)
Row 38: *Sl1, p3, sl1, k1* 4 times, sl1, p2, sl1.
Row 39 (Dec): With C, k2, *sl1, k3, sl1, k1* 4 times, k2tog. (1 st dec'd)
Row 40: *Sl1, k1, sl1, p3* 4 times, sl1, k1, sl1.
Cut yarn and pl the 27 sts on a spare needle or scrap yarn.

All sizes
14 (15, 17, 18, 20, 21) (23, 24, 27) sts on hold for each shoulder, and 14 (15, 17, 18, 20, 21) (23, 24, 24) on hold for front neck. Next, the upper back will be worked.

BACK UPPER BODY

Pl the 42 (45, 51, 54, 60, 63) (69, 72, 78) sts for the back on US 19 / 15 mm needles and prepare to work a RS row with B.

Sizes 1, 4, 5, 8 and 9 only
Row 1 (RS): With B, *k3, sl1, k1, sl1*, rep *–* to last 6 sts, k3, sl1, k1, sl1.
Row 2 (WS): K2, sl1, *p3, sl1, k1, sl1*, rep *–* to last 3 sts, p2, sl1.
Row 3: With C, k2, sl1, *k3, sl1, k1, sl1*, rep *–* to last 3 sts, k2, sl1.
Row 4: K1, p2, *sl1, k1, sl1, p3*, rep *–* to last 3 sts, sl1, k1, sl1.
Rows 5 to 24 (28, 32, 36, 40): Rep rows 1–4 another 5 (–, –, 6, 7) (–, –, 8, 9) times.

Sizes 4 and 8 only
Rows – (–, –, 29 and 30, –) (–, – 37 and 38, –): Rep rows 1 and 2 once more.

Sizes 2, 3, 6 and 7 only
Row 1 (RS): With B, k2, *sl1, k3, sl1, k1*, rep *–* to last st, sl1.
Row 2 (WS): K2, sl1, *p3, sl1, k1, sl1*, rep *–* to end.
Row 3: With C, *k3, sl1, k1, sl1*, rep *–* to last 3 sts, k2, sl1.
Row 4: K1, *p2, sl1, k1, sl1, p1*, rep *–* to last 3 sts, p1, sl1.
Rows 5 to – (24, 28, –, –) (32, 36, –, –): Rep rows 1–4 another – (5, 6, –, –) (7, 8, –, –) times.

Sizes 2 and 6 only
Rows – (25 and 26, –, –, –) (33 and 34, –, –, –): Rep rows 1 and 2 once more.

All sizes
Next, the shoulders will be seamed.

SHOULDERS

Pl the front right shoulder and back sections tog with the RSs facing each other. Starting from the armhole edge of both pieces, use the 3-Needle BO method to BO all 14 (15, 17, 18, 20, 21) (23, 24, 27) sts from both the front and back sections.

BO the next 14 (15, 17, 18, 20, 21) (23, 24, 24) sts from the back neck.

Pl the front left shoulder and back sections tog with RSs facing each other. Starting from the neck edge of both pieces and using st rem after BO, use the 3-Needle BO method to BO all 14 (15, 17, 18, 20, 21) (23, 24, 27) sts from both the front and back sections.

Cut yarn and secure last st.

COLLAR

With US 15 / 10 mm circular needles and A, start at the left shoulder seam and pick up, without knitting, 1 st at the seam, 5 (5, 5, 5, 7) (7, 7, 7, 7) sts down left front neck, 10 (11, 13, 14, 14) (15, 17, 18, 18) across front neck, 5 (5, 5, 5, 7) (7, 7, 7, 7) sts up right front, 1 st at the seam, 14 (15, 17, 18, 20) (21, 23, 24, 24) across back neck. [36 (38, 42, 44, 50) (52, 56, 58, 58) sts]
PM and beg working in the rnd.

Rib Rnd: *K1, p1* to end.
Work in est 1 x 1 rib for 5 rnds in total.

BO in patt.

SLEEVES

With US 19 / 15 mm circular needles and B, pick up 42 (42, 42, 48, 48, 48) (54, 54, 54) sts evenly spaced along the armhole, starting at the underarm. PM for BOR.

Work rnds 1–4 of Dotted Ladder Mosaic St, 15 times (60 rnds in total) or to desired length. The cuff adds approx. 2" / 5 cm. Cut B and C.

Next Rnd (Dec):
Sizes 1 and 2 only: *K2tog, k1* 6 times, *k2tog* 2 times, *k2tog, k1* 6 times, k2tog. (15 sts dec'd)
Size 3 only: K1, *k2tog, k2* 3 times, *k2tog, k1* 5 times, *k2tog, k2* 3 times, k2tog. (12 sts dec'd)
Size 4 only: K1, *k2tog* 3 times, *k2tog, k1* 11 times, *k2tog* 4 times. (18 sts dec'd)
Sizes 5 and 6 only: K1, *k2tog, k1* 6 times, *k2tog, k2* twice, *k2tog, k1* 7 times. (15 sts dec'd)
Sizes 7, 8 and 9 only: *K1, k2tog* 18 times. (18 sts dec'd)

[27 (27, 30, 30, 33, 33) (36, 36, 36) sts]

Cuff

Next Rnd (Dec): With US 15 / 10 mm needles and A, *k1, p2tog* to end. [9 (9, 10, 10, 11, 11) (12, 12, 12) sts dec'd] [18 (18, 20, 20, 22, 22) (24, 24, 24) sts]

Rib Rnd: *K1, p1* to end.
Work in est 1 x 1 rib for 5 rnds in total.

BO in patt.

Work other sleeve alike.

FINISHING

Weave in ends. Wet block to measurements.

DOTTED LADDER MOSAIC PATTERN (IN THE ROUND)

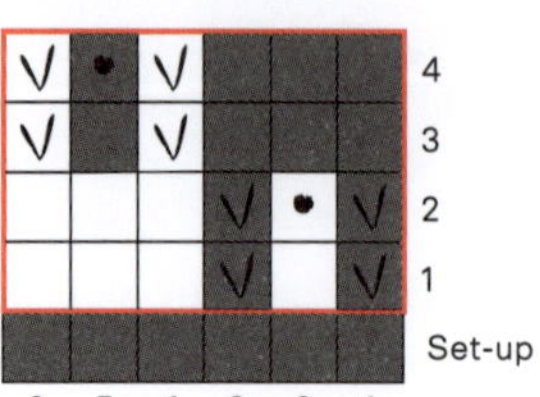

- RS: knit / WS: purl
- RS: purl / WS: knit
- sl1
- Colour B
- Colour C
- pattern repeat

Esti Juango

10 Festa

A geometrical, lacy pattern is worked on the body of this colourful drop-shoulder sweater, with decreases and yarnovers. Festa will make any day one to celebrate!

SIZES

1 (2, 3, 4, 5) (6, 7, 8, 9)

Recommended ease: 6–8" / 15–20 cm of positive ease.

FINISHED MEASUREMENTS

Chest Circumference: 40 (44.5, 49.25, 51.5, 56) (60.5, 65.25, 67.5, 72)" / 100 (111.5, 123, 128.5, 140) (151.5, 163, 168.5, 180) cm.
Length from Underarm to Hem: 12.5" / 32 cm.
Sleeve Length: 17 (16.75, 16.25, 15.75, 15.5) (15, 15, 14.75, 14.25)" / 43 (42, 41, 40, 39) (38, 38, 37, 36) cm.
Upper Arm Circumference: 16 (17.25, 18.5, 19.5, 20.5) (21.5, 22.75, 24, 25.25)" / 40 (43, 46, 49, 51) (54, 57, 60, 63) cm.

MATERIALS

Yarn: 5 (5, 6, 6, 7) (7, 8, 8, 9) skeins of The Wool by We are Knitters (100% wool, 87 yds / 80 m - 200 g), colourway Neon Marshmallow.

Or approx. 383 (438, 465, 520, 547) (574, 629, 657, 711) yds / 350 (400, 425, 475, 500) (525, 575, 600, 650) m of super bulky-weight yarn. Alternative yarn suggestions are for example Wool and the Gang Heal the Wool, Katia Love Wool and Drops Design Drops Polaris.

Needles: US 15 / 10 mm 32" / 80 cm (for the body and sleeves) and US 13 / 9 mm 32" / 40 cm circular needles (for the collar and cuffs).

Notions: Stitch markers, stitch holders or waste yarn.

GAUGE

7 sts x 10 rnds to 4" / 10 cm on US 15 / 10 mm needles in St St, after blocking.

7 sts x 10 rnds to 4" / 10 cm on US 15 / 10 mm needles in Lace patt, after blocking.

STITCH PATTERN

Lace Pattern

Rows 1–2: K to end.
Row 3: K3, yo, *k3togtbl, yo, k7, yo*, rep *–* to 6 sts bef end, k3togtbl, yo, k3.
Row 4: K2, yo, ssk, *k1, k2tog, yo, k5, yo ssk*, rep *–* to 5 sts bef end, k1, k2tog, yo, k2.
Row 5: K1, yo, ssk, yo, *k3togtbl, yo. k2tog, yo, k3, yo, ssk, yo*, rep *–* to 6 sts bef end, k3togtbl, yo, k2tog, yo, k1.
Row 6: K2, yo, ssk, *k1, k2tog, yo, k5, yo, ssk*, rep *–* to 5 sts bef end, k1, k2tog, yo, k2.
Row 7: K3, yo, *k3togtbl, yo, k2, yo, k3togtbl, yo, k2, yo*, rep *–* to 6 sts bef end, k3togtbl, yo, k3.
Row 8: K4, *k3, yo, ssk, k1, k2tog, yo, k2*, rep *–* to 5 sts bef end, k5.
Row 9: K4, *k2, yo, ssk, yo, k3togtbl, yo, k2tog, yo, k1*, rep *–* to 5 sts bef end, k5.
Row 10: K4, *k3, yo, ssk, k1, k2tog, yo, k2*, rep *–* to 5 sts bef end, k5.
Row 11: K3, yo, *k3togtbl, yo, k2, yo, k3togtbl, yo, k2, yo*, rep *–* to 6 sts bef end, k3togtbl, yo, k3.
Row 12: K2, yo, ssk, *k1, k2tog, yo, k5,

yo, ssk*, rep *–* to 5 sts bef end, k1, k2tog, yo, k2.
Row 13: K1, yo, ssk, yo, *k3togtbl, yo, k2tog, yo, k3, yo, ssk, yo*, rep *–* to 6 sts bef end, k3togtbl, yo, k2tog, yo, k1.
Row 14: K2, yo, ssk, *k1, k2tog, yo, k5, yo, ssk*, rep *–* to 5 sts bef end, k1, k2tog, yo, k2.
Rep rows 7–14 for patt.

NOTES

Work pattern repeat outlined in the chart with blue (rows 1–6) once only, as you begin the Lace pattern. Then, work the pattern repeat outlined with red (rows 7–14) for the remainder of the sweater.

CONSTRUCTION

This all-over lace sweater is worked from bottom up, in the round up to the armholes. After that the back and front are worked flat. Lastly, stitches are picked up for the sleeves and worked in the round up to the cuff.

DIRECTIONS

CAST-ON

With US 15 / 10 mm needles, CO 70 (78, 86, 90, 98) (106, 114, 118, 126) sts using the Long-Tail CO method. Join to work in the rnd and PM for BOR.

Rib Rnd: *K1, p1* to end.
Work in 1 x 1 rib as est until the hem measures 3.25" / 8 cm.

Start working from the chart. PM to divide front and back as foll:
Rnd 1: *K3 (0, 2, 3, 0) (2, 4, 0, 2), work from the chart working the 10-st patt rep 2 (3, 3, 3, 4) (4, 4, 5, 5) times, k3 (0, 2, 3, 0) (2, 4, 0, 2)*, PM, rep *–* once more.
Rnd 2: *K3 (0, 2, 3, 0) (2, 4, 0, 2), work from the chart working the 10-st patt rep 2 (3, 3, 3, 4) (4, 4, 5, 5) times, k3 (0, 2, 3, 0) (2, 4, 0, 2)*, SM, rep *–* once more.

Cont working in patt until the piece measures 12.5" / 32 cm from the CO edge, or until desired length. End after an even-numbered chart row.

BACK

Next, separate the front and back and start working flat, maintaining edge sts:
Row 1 (RS): Work the first 35 (39, 43, 45, 49) (53, 57, 59, 63) sts following the chart, leave the next 35 (39, 43, 45, 49) (53, 57, 59, 63) sts on hold for the front.
Row 2 (WS): Work next row of chart on WS. *Note!* Remember to read the chart from left to right.
Rep rows 1–2 until the back measures 8 (8.5, 9, 9.75, 10) (10.75, 11.25, 11.75, 12.5)" / 20 (21.5, 23, 24.5, 25.5) (27, 28.5, 30, 31.5) cm from the front and back separation. End after an even-numbered row of the chart and make a note of the row number.

Shaping Shoulder

Next, German Short Rows are worked to shape the shoulder.
Row 1 (RS): Work chart until 3 (4, 4, 4, 5) (5, 6, 6, 6) sts rem, tw.
Row 2 (WS): MDS, work in patt until 3 (4, 4, 4, 5) (5, 6, 6, 6) sts rem, tw.
Row 3: MDS, work in patt until 2 (2, 3, 3, 4) (4, 4, 5, 5) sts rem bef prev DS, tw.
Row 4: MDS, work in patt until 2 (2, 3, 3, 4) (4, 4, 5, 5) sts rem bef prev DS, tw.

Next, central sts of the neckline are BO and right and left sides are separated.
Row 5 (RS): MDS, work in patt until there are 11 (13, 15, 16, 18) (19, 21, 22, 24) sts on your RHN (be careful to count DS as 1 st), tw.

Leave the next 13 (13, 13, 13, 13) (15, 15, 15, 15) sts on hold for the neckline and the next 11 (13, 15, 16, 18) (19, 21, 22, 24) sts on hold for the left shoulder.

Back Right Shoulder

Row 6 (WS): Work in patt to 2 (2, 3, 3, 3) (4, 4, 4, 5) sts bef prev DS, tw.
Row 7 (RS): MDS, k to end.

During the next row, work DSs as 1 st.
Row 8: P to end.
Row 9: K to end.
Leave the sts on hold and cut the yarn.

Back Left Shoulder

Join yarn on RS. [11 (13, 15, 16, 18) (19, 21, 22, 24) sts for left shoulder]

Row 5 (RS): Work in patt to 2 (2, 3, 3, 3) (4, 4, 4, 5) sts bef prev DS, tw.
Row 6 (WS): MDS, work in patt to end.

During the next row, work DSs as 1 st.
Row 7: K to end.
Row 8: P to end.
Row 9: K to end.

Leave the sts on hold and cut the yarn.

FRONT

Pl the 35 (39, 43, 45, 49) (53, 57, 59, 63) front sts back onto the US 15 / 10 mm needles and start working flat as foll, maintaining edge sts:
Row 1 (RS): Work next RS row of patt.
Row 2 (WS): Work next WS of patt.
Rep rows 1–2 until the front measures 0.75" / 2 cm less than the back to start of shoulder shaping.
Note! End after an even-numbered chart row, 2 rows bef the row you noted earlier for the back.

Shaping Neckline

Row 1 (RS): Work in patt for the first 13 (15, 17, 18, 20) (21, 23, 24, 26) sts, tw. Leave next 9 (9, 9, 9, 9) (11, 11, 11, 11) sts on hold for the collar and the next 13 (15, 17, 18, 20) (21, 23, 24, 26) sts on hold for the right shoulder.

Front Left Shoulder

Row 2 (WS): BO 2 sts, work in patt to end. (2 sts dec'd) [11 (13, 15, 16, 18) (19, 21, 22, 24) sts]

Next, German Short Rows are worked to shape the shoulder.
Row 3 (RS): Work in patt to end.
Row 4: Work in patt until 3 (4, 4, 4, 5) (5, 6, 6, 6) sts rem, tw.
Row 5: MDS, work in patt to end.
Row 6: Work in patt until 2 (2, 3, 3, 4) (4, 4, 5, 5) sts rem bef prev DS, tw.
Row 7: MDS, work in patt to end.
Row 8: Work in patt until 2 (2, 3, 3, 3) (4, 4, 4, 5) sts rem bef prev DS, tw.
Row 9: MDS, work in patt to end.

During the next row, work DSs as 1 st.
Row 10: P to end.
Row 11: K to end.
Leave the sts on hold and break yarn, leaving a long tail for sewing up.

Front Right Shoulder

Join yarn on RS. [13 (15, 17, 18, 20) (21, 23, 24, 26) sts for right shoulder]

Row 1 (RS): Work in patt to end.
Row 2 (WS): Work in patt to end.
Row 3: BO 2 sts, work in patt until 3 (4, 4, 4, 5) (5, 6, 6, 6) sts rem, tw. (2 sts dec'd). [11 (13, 15, 16, 18) (19, 21, 22, 24) sts]
Row 4: MDS, work in patt to end.
Row 5: Work in patt until 2 (2, 3, 3, 4) (4, 4, 5, 5) sts bef last DS, tw.
Row 6: MDS, work in patt to end.
Row 7: Work in patt until 2 (2, 3, 3, 3) (4, 4, 4, 5) sts bef last DS, tw.
Row 8: MDS, work in patt to end.

During the next row, work DSs as 1 st.
Row 9 (RS): K to end.
Row 10 (WS): P to end.
Row 11: K to end.

Leave the sts on hold and cut the yarn.

With WS tog, graft the shoulder seams together. You can also use a 3-Needle BO.

SLEEVES

With US 15 / 10 mm needles and starting at the underarm, pick up and k 28 (30, 32, 34, 36) (38, 40, 42, 44) sts around the armhole (approx. 2 sts per 3 rows). PM for BOR.

K 2 rnds.

Row	19	18	17	16	15	14	13	12	11	10	9	8	7	6	5	4	3	2	1
14			O	/		\	O						O	/		\	O		
13		O	/	O	Λ	O	\	O				O	/	O	Λ	O	\	O	
12			O	/		\	O						O	/		\	O		
11				O	Λ	O			O	Λ	O			O	Λ	O			
10								O	/		\	O							
9							O	/	O	Λ	O	\	O						
8								O	/		\	O							
7				O	Λ	O			O	Λ	O			O	Λ	O			
6			O	/		\	O						O	/		\	O		
5		O	/	O	Λ	O	\	O				O	/	O	Λ	O	\	O	
4			O	/		\	O						O	/		\	O		
3				O	Λ	O								O	Λ	O			
2																			
1																			

- (blank) RS: knit / WS: purl
- \ RS: ssk / WS: ssp
- / RS: k2tog / WS: p2tog
- Λ k3tog tbl
- O yo
- (red box) repeat rows 7–14
- (blue box) work rows 1–6 once

Sleeve Decreases

K5 (4, 3, 2, 2) (2, 2, 1, 1) rnd(s).

Dec Rnd: K1, k2tog, k to last 3 sts, ssk, k1. (2 sts dec'd)

Rep last 6 (5, 4, 3, 3) (3, 3, 2, 2) rnds 4 (5, 6, 7, 7) (8, 8, 9, 10) more times. [8 (10, 12, 14, 14) (16, 16, 18, 20) sts dec'd] [18 (18, 18, 18, 20) (20, 22, 22, 22) sts]

Work straight in St St until the sleeve measures 13.75 (13.5, 13, 12.5, 12.25) (11.75, 11.75, 11.5, 11)" / 35 (34, 33, 32, 31) (30, 30, 29, 28) cm, or 3.25" / 8 cm less than desired length.

Change to US 13 / 9 mm needles and work 1 x 1 rib for 3.25" / 8 cm.

BO all sts with the Tubular BO method.

NECKLINE

With US 13 / 9 mm needles and starting at right shoulder seam, pick up and k 3 sts down right back neck, move the held back neckline sts to LHN then k them, pick up and k 3 sts up left back neck, 8 sts down the left front, move the held centre front sts to LHN then knit them, pick up and k 8 sts up the right front. [44 (44, 44, 44, 44) (48, 48, 48, 48) sts]

Work in 1 x 1 rib until the neckline rib measures 2.25" / 5.5 cm.

BO all sts with the Tubular BO method.

FINISHING

Weave in ends. Steam or wet block to measurements.

Bernice Lim

11 Crossing

Drop-stitch cables and stripes are combined fascinatingly in this yoked sweater by Bernice Lim, also known as Yamagara. Fluffy brushed alpaca and silk mohair create a super cosy fabric.

SIZES

1 (2, 3, 4) (5, 6, 7, 8)

Recommended ease: 6–12" / 15–30.5 cm of positive ease.

FINISHED MEASUREMENTS

Chest Circumference: 36.5 (42.25, 49.25, 56) (59.5, 67.5, 73.25, 76.5)" / 91.5 (105.5, 123, 140) (148.5, 168.5, 183, 191.5) cm.
Neck Circumference: 14.5 (15.5, 16.5, 17.5) (17.5, 19.5, 20.25, 20.25)" / 36.5 (39, 41, 43.5) (43.5, 48.5, 51, 51) cm.
Front Yoke (from CO): 9.25 (9.25, 9.5, 9.5) (10, 10, 10.25, 10.25)" / 23 (23, 23.5, 23.5) (25, 25, 26, 26) cm.
Length from Underarm to Hem: 11.25 (11.25, 11.25, 11.25) (12, 12, 12, 12)" / 28.5 (28.5, 28.5, 28.5) (30, 30, 30, 30) cm.
Sleeve Length: 16.5" / 42 cm.
Upper Arm Circumference: 12.5 (14.25, 14.25, 14.25) (17.75, 17.75, 20.5, 22.25)" / 31.5 (35.5, 35.5, 35.5) (44.5, 44.5, 51.5, 55.5) cm.
Cuff Circumference: 9.25 (10.25, 10.25, 10.25) (11.5, 12, 12.5, 13.75)" / 23 (25.5, 25.5, 25.5) (28.5, 30, 31.5, 34.5) cm.

MATERIALS

Yarn: MC: 4 (5, 5, 6) (7, 7, 8, 8) skeins of Børstet Alpakka by Sandnes Garn (96% brushed alpaca, 4% nylon), 120 yds / 110 m – 50 g, colourway 6046.

Or approx. 455 (525, 585, 640) (725, 795, 895, 935) yds / 415 (480, 535, 585) (665, 725, 820, 855) m of similar yarn. *Note!* Even though Børstet Alpakka is categorised as a bulky-weight yarn, it is rather light and airy.

CC: 1 skein of Mohair Silk by La Bien Aimée (70% mohair, 30% mulberry silk, 546 yds / 500 m – 50 g), colourway Confetti Cake.

Or approx. 165 (190, 210, 230) (260, 285, 320, 335) yds / 150 (175, 190, 210) (240, 260, 295, 305) m of lace-weight yarn.

Alternative yarn suggestions are for example Rico Design Fashion Light Luxury or Rauma Tjukk Mohair (for MC) and Isager Silk Mohair or CaMaRose Midnatssol (for CC).

Needles: US 8 / 5 mm and US 10 / 6 mm 32" / 80 cm circular needles and preferred needle(s) for small circumference knitting.

Notions: 15–23 stitch markers for the st patt, 1 unique stitch marker for BOR, waste yarn or stitch holder, cable needles.

GAUGE

14 sts x 20 rnds to 4" / 10 cm on US 10 / 6 mm needles in St St, after blocking.

14 sts x 22 rnds to 4" / 10 cm on US 10 / 6 mm needles in Texture and Stripe patt, after blocking.

16.5 sts x 10 rnds to 4" / 10 cm on US 8 / 5 mm needles in rib, after blocking.

SPECIAL ABBREVIATIONS

LSC: Left Slip Cross. Sl 1 st to CN and hold in front, k1, sl1 from CN.

RSC: Right Slip Cross. Sl 1 st to CN and hold in back, sl1, k1 from CN.

kyo3: K1 with triple yo. K1, wrapping yarn 3 times around RHN instead of once, bef pulling yarn through the st. This makes a long st after the yo's are unwrapped.

1/1/1 LC: Sl 1 long st to CN1 and hold in front, sl 1 st to CN2 and hold in back, k long st, k1 from CN2, k long st from CN1.

STITCH PATTERN FOR SWATCHING

Texture and Stripe Pattern

24-round repeat.

The st patt is worked in the rnd. Use 1 strand of MC and 2 strands of CC throughout the work. Until instructed in the patt, carry unused MC and CC up the WS of the work instead of cutting them at the end of each stripe.

To make a swatch, with MC and using US 10 / 6 mm needles, CO sts in multiples of 12 for swatching in the rnd.

Set-Up Rnd: *K12, PM* to end, PM for BOR and join to work in the rnd.
Next Rnd: *K12, SM* to end.
With MC:
Rnd 1: *K7, LSC, k1, RSC, SM*, rep *–* to end.
Rnd 2: *K8, kyo3, k1, kyo3, k1, SM*, rep *–* to end. Join CC.
With CC:
Rnd 3: *K8, [sl to unwrap triple yo to make a long st], k1, rep [ ], k1, SM*, rep *–* to end.
Rnds 4–5: *K8, slip the long st, k1, sl the long st, k1, SM*, rep *–* to end.
With MC:
Rnd 6: *K8, sl the long st, k1, sl the long st, k1, SM*, rep *–* to end.
Rnd 7: *K8, work 1/1/1 LC with the pair of long sts, k1, SM*, rep *–* to end.
Rnds 8–12: K to end.
Rnd 13: *K1, LSC, k1, RSC, k6, SM*, rep *–* to end.
Rnd 14: *K2, kyo3, k1, kyo3, k7, SM*, rep *–* to end.
With CC:
Rnd 15: *K2, [sl to unwrap triple yo to make a long st], k1, rep [ ], k7, SM*, rep *–* to end.
Rnds 16–17: *K2, sl the long st, k1, slip the long st, k7, SM*, rep *–* to end. Break CC.
With MC:
Rnd 18: *K2, sl the long st, k1, slip the long st, k7, SM*, rep *–* to end.
Rnd 19: *K2, work 1/1/1 LC with the pair of long sts, k7, SM*, rep *–* to end.
Rnds 20–24: Remove patt m's, k to end.

BO. Break MC.

CONSTRUCTION

This sweater is knitted from the top down in the round. Short rows are used to shape the back. Increases are worked around the yoke with gradually widening stitch pattern repeats. The sweater has plenty of positive ease, fully featuring the light fluffiness of the yarn combination. The sheer stripes are knitted with two strands of lace weight yarn, while a single strand of the main yarn layers long crossed stitches rhythmically over parts of the stripes.

DIRECTIONS

NECK

With MC and US 8 / 5 mm needles, CO 64 (64, 68, 72) (72, 80, 84, 88) sts with the Long-Tail CO method. PM and join to work in the rnd.

Rib Rnd: *K1tbl, p1* to end.
Work in est rib until it measures 2 (2, 2.25, 2.25) (2.25, 2.25, 2.5, 2.5)" / 5 (5, 5.5, 5.5) (5.5, 5.5, 6.5, 6.5) cm.

Change US 10 / 6 mm needles.

Sizes 1, 2, 5 and 6 only
K 2 rnds.

Sizes 3, 4, 7 and 8 only
K 1 rnd.
Next Rnd: *K– (–, 17, 9) (–, –, 7, 11), m1l*, rep *–* to end. [– (–, 4, 8) (–, –, 12, 8) sts inc'd] [– (–, 72, 80) (–, –, 96, 96) sts]

Shape Back Neck

German Short Rows are used to shape the back.
Short Row 1 (RS): K5 (5, 6, 6) (6, 6, 7, 7), tw.
Short Row 2 (WS): MDS, p to m, SM, p5 (5, 6, 6) (6, 6, 7, 7), tw.
Short Row 3: MDS, k to m, SM, k to DS, kDS, k5 (5, 6, 6) (6, 6, 7, 7), tw.
Short Row 4: MDS, p to m, SM, p to DS, pDS, p5 (5, 6, 6) (6, 6, 7, 7), tw.
Short Rows 5–8: Rep Short rows 3 and 4, 2 more times.
Short Row 9: MDS, k to m.
Next Rnd: K to end, working each DS as 1 st as you come across it.

YOKE

Part 1

Rnd 1: RM (BOR), sl1, PM (new BOR), *k1, m1l, k3, m1r, PM (patt m)*, rep *–* to the last 4 sts, k1, m1l, k3, m1r.

[32 (32, 36, 40) (36, 40, 48, 48) sts inc'd] [96 (96, 108, 120) (108, 120, 144, 144) sts] [16 (16, 18, 20) (18, 20, 24, 24) groups of 6 sts between patt m's]
Rnd 2: K to end.
Rnd 3: *K1, LSC, k1, RSC, SM*, rep *–* to end.
Rnd 4: *K2, kyo3, k1, kyo3, k1, SM*, rep *–* to end.
Join CC. With CC:
Rnd 5: *K2, [slip to unwrap triple yo to make a long st], k1, rep [ ], k1, SM*, rep *–* to end.
Rnd 6: *K2, slip the long st, k1, slip the long st, k1, SM*, rep *–* to end.
Rnd 7: Rep rnd 6.
With MC:
Rnd 8: Rep rnd 6.
Rnd 9: *K2, 1/1/1 LC, k1, SM*, rep *–* to end.

Sizes 1, 2, 3 and 4 only
K 3 rnds.

Sizes 5, 6, 7 and 8 only
K 4 rnds.

Part 2

With MC:
Rnd 1: *M1l, k3, m1r, k3, SM*, rep *–* to end. [32 (32, 36, 40) (36, 40, 48, 48) sts inc'd] [128 (128, 144, 160) (144, 160, 192, 192) sts] [8 sts between m's]
Rnd 2: K to end.
Rnd 3: *LSC, k1, RSC, k3, SM*, rep *–* to end.
Rnd 4: *K1, kyo3, k1, kyo3, k4, SM*, rep *–* to end.
***With CC:*
Rnd 5: K to end while slipping and unwrapping each st with triple yo's to make a long st.
Rnds 6–7: K to end while slipping long sts.
With MC:
Rnd 8: K to end while slipping long sts.
Rnd 9: K to end, working 1/1/1 LC with each pair of long sts.

Sizes 1, 2, 3 and 4 only
K 3 rnds.

Sizes 5, 6, 7 and 8 only
K 4 rnds.**

Part 3

Sizes 1, 2, 3 and 4 only
With MC:
Rnd 1: *K5, m1l, k3, m1r, SM*, rep *–* to end. [32 (32, 36, 40) (–, –, –, –) sts inc'd] [160 (160, 180, 200) (–, –, –, –) sts. 10 sts between m's]
Rnd 2: K to end.
Rnd 3: *K5, LSC, k1, RSC, SM*, rep *–* to end.
Rnd 4: *K6, kyo3, k1, kyo3, k1, SM*, rep *–* to end.
Rnds 5–12: Rep **–** of Yoke Part 2.

Size 1 only
Rnd 13: K to end.

Sizes 2, 3 and 4 only
Rnd 13: *K1, m1l, k3, m1r, k6*, rep *–* to end. [– (32, 36, 40) (–, –, –, –) sts inc'd] [– (192, 216, 240) (–, –, –, –) sts. 12 sts between m's]
The front yoke measures approx 9.25 (9.25, 9.5, 9.5) (–, –, –, –)" / 23 (23, 23.5, 23.5) (–, –, –, –) cm from CO. Proceed to Divide Body and Sleeves.

Sizes 5, 6, 7 and 8 only
Cont with MC:
Rnd 1: *K1, m1l, k3, m1r, k1, m1l, k3, m1r, SM*, rep *–* to end. [– (–, –, –) (72, 80, 96, 96) sts inc'd] [– (–, –, –) (216, 240, 288, 288) sts. 12 sts between m's]
Rnd 2: K to end.
Rnd 3: *K7, LSC, k1, RSC, SM*, rep *–* to end.
Rnd 4: *K8, kyo3, k1, kyo3, k1, SM*, rep *–* to end.
Rnds 5–13: Rep **–** of Yoke Part 2.
Rnd 14: *K2, m1l, k3, m1r, k7, SM*, rep *–* to end. [– (–, –, –) (36, 40, 48, 48) sts inc'd] [– (–, –, –) (252, 280, 336, 336) sts. 14 sts between m's]
The front yoke measures approx. – (–, –, –) (10, 10, 10.25, 10.25)" / (25, 25, 26, 26) cm from CO. Proceed to Divide Body and Sleeves.

DIVIDE BODY AND SLEEVES

Keeping all m's including BOR m in place, k 23 (28, 34, 40) (42, 47, 54, 54) sts across (right back), pl next 30 (36, 36, 36) (42, 42, 56, 56) sts (right sleeve) on waste yarn, using the Cable CO method, CO 14 (14, 14, 14) (20, 20, 16, 22) sts (underarm), k 50 (60, 72, 84) (84, 98, 112, 112) sts (front), pl next 30 (36, 36, 36) (42, 42, 56, 56) sts (left sleeve) on waste yarn, using the Cable CO method, CO 14 (14, 14, 14) (20, 20, 16, 22) sts (underarm), k 27 (32, 38, 44) (42, 51, 58, 58) sts (left back). [128 (148, 172, 196) (208, 236, 256, 268) sts on the needles for body]

BODY

Part 1

Rnd 1: *K– (1, 1, 1) (2, 2, 2, 2), LSC, k1, RSC, k5 (6, 6, 6) (7, 7, 7, 7), SM (see note below)*, rep *–* 1 (1, 2, 2) (2, 2, 3, 3) more time(s), [k– (1, 2, 1) (5, 5, 3, 6), LSC, k1, RSC, k9 (8, 7, 8) (10, 10, 8, 11), PM (see note)], rep *–* 5 (5, 6, 7) (6, 7, 8, 8) more times, rep [–] once more, rep *–* 3 (3, 3, 4) (3, 4, 4, 4) more times. *Note!* PM if m is not there. SM if m is already in place.
Rnd 2: *K1 (2, 2, 2) (3, 3, 3, 3), kyo3, k1, kyo3, k6 (7, 7, 7) (8, 8, 8, 8), SM*, rep *–* 1 (1, 2, 2) (2, 2, 3, 3) more time(s), [k1 (2, 3, 2) (6, 6, 4, 7), kyo3, k1, kyo3, k10 (9, 8, 9) (11, 11, 9, 12), SM], rep *–* 5 (5, 6, 7) (6, 7, 8, 8) more times, rep [–] one more time, rep *–* 3 (3, 3, 4) (3, 4, 4, 4) more times.
***With CC:*
Rnd 3: K to end while slipping and unwrapping each st with triple yo's to make a long st.
Rnds 4–5: K to end while slipping long sts.
With MC:
Rnd 6: K to end while slipping long sts.
Rnd 7: K to end, working 1/1/1 LC with each pair of long sts.

Sizes 1, 2, 3 and 4 only
K 5 rnds.

Sizes 5, 6, 7 and 8 only
K 6 rnds.**

Part 2

With MC:
Rnd 1: *K5 (7, 7, 7) (9, 9, 9, 9), LSC, k1, RSC, SM*, rep *–* 1 (1, 2, 2) (2, 2, 3, 3) more time(s), [k7 (8, 8, 8) (12, 12, 10, 13), LSC, k1, RSC, k2 (1, 1, 1) (3, 3, 1, 4), SM], rep *–* 5 (5, 6, 7) (6, 7, 8, 8) more times, rep [–] once more, rep *–* 3 (3, 3, 4) (3, 4, 4, 4) more times.
Rnd 2: *K6 (8, 8, 8) (10, 10, 10, 10), kyo3, k1, kyo3, k1, SM*, rep *–* 1 (1, 2, 2) (2, 2, 3, 3) more time(s), [k8 (9, 9, 9) (13, 13, 11, 14), kyo3, k1, kyo3, k3 (2, 2, 2) (4, 4, 2, 5), SM], rep *–* 5 (5, 6, 7) (6, 7, 8, 8) more times, rep [–] once more, rep *–* 3 (3, 3, 4) (3, 4, 4, 4) more times.

Rep **–** of Body Part 1.
Rep Part 1 and Part 2 of Body once more. Break CC after the last rep of CC rnds. The body measures approx. 8.75 (8.75, 8.75, 8.75) (9.5, 9.5, 9.5, 9.5)" / 22 (22, 22, 22) (23.5, 23.5, 23.5, 23.5) cm measured from underarm.
If you would like your sweater to be longer, work a few more rnds in St St until body is 2.5" / 6.5 cm shorter than desired length from underarm.

Hem Rib

Change to US 8 / 5 mm needles and work the next rnd, removing all m's except for BOR m.

Rib Rnd: *K1tbl, p1* to end.
Work in est 1 x 1 twisted rib until the hem measures 2.5" / 6.5 cm.

BO all sts in patt. Break yarn.

SLEEVES

Transfer the 30 (36, 36, 36) (42, 42, 56, 56) sleeve sts to US 10 / 6 mm needles.

Part 1

Sizes 1, 2, 4 and 6 only
Rnd 1: With RS facing, join MC at the 12th (11th, –, 11th) (–, 16th, –, –) st of the underarm CO. Pick up and k 3 (4, –, 4) (–, 5, –, –) sts along underarm, k 7 (8, –, 8) (–, 9, –, –) sleeve sts to m, SM, *k to m, SM* twice, k3 (4, –, 4) (–, 5, –, –) sleeve sts, pick up and k 11 (10, –, 10) (–, 15, –, –) sts along underarm, PM (BOR m) and join in the rnd.

Sizes 3, 5, 7 and 8 only
Rnd 1: With RS facing, sl the first 2 sleeve sts, RM, join MC, *k to m, SM*, rep *–* – (–, 1, –) (1, –, 2, 2) more time(s), k – (–, 10, –) (12, –, 12, 12) sleeve sts, pick up and knit 2 sts along underarm, PM, pick up and k – (–, 12, –) (18, –, 14, 20) sts along underarm, k2 (slipped sleeve sts) PM (BOR m) and join in the rnd. [44 (50, 50, 50) (62, 62, 72, 78) sts]
Rnd 2: *K– (1, 1, 1) (2, 2, 2, 2), LSC, k1, RSC, k5 (6, 6, 6) (7, 7, 7, 7), SM*, rep *–* to last patt m (m bef BOR m), SM, k– (1, 2, 1) (5, 5, 3, 6), LSC, k1, RSC, k to end.
Rnd 3: *K1 (2, 2, 2) (3, 3, 3, 3), kyo3, k1, kyo3, k6 (7, 7, 7) (8, 8, 8, 8), SM*, rep *–* to last patt m (m bef BOR m), SM, k1 (2, 3, 2) (6, 6, 4, 7), kyo3, k1, kyo3, k to end.

***With CC:*
Rnd 4: K to end while slipping and unwrapping each st with triple yo's to make a long st.
Rnds 5–6: K to end while slipping long sts.
With MC:
Rnd 7: K to end while slipping long sts.
Rnd 8: K to end, working 1/1/1 LC with each pair of long sts.
Rnds 9–10: K to end.**
Rnd 11: K to last patt m, SM, k2tog, k to 2 sts bef BOR m, k2tog. (2 sts dec'd) [42 (48, 48, 48) (60, 60, 70, 76) sts]
Rnds 12–13: K to end.

Part 2

With MC:
Rnd 1: *K5 (7, 7, 7) (9, 9, 9, 9), LSC, k1, RSC, SM*, rep *–* to last patt m, SM, k6 (7, 7, 7) (11, 11, 9, 12), LSC, k1, RSC, k1 (–, –, –) (2, 2, –, 3).
Rnd 2: *K6 (8, 8, 8) (10, 10, 10, 10), kyo3, k1, kyo3, k1, SM*, rep *–* to last patt m, SM, k7 (8, 8, 8) (12, 12, 10, 13), kyo3, k1, kyo3, k to end.
Rnds 3–9: Rep **–** of Sleeve Part 1.

Rnd 10:
Sizes 1, 5, and 6 only
K to last patt m, SM, k2tog, k to 2 sts bef BOR m, k2tog. (2 sts dec'd)

Sizes 2, 3 and 4 only
K2tog, k to m, SM, rep *–* to end. (4 sts dec'd)

Size 7 only
K2tog, k to m, SM, rep *–* to end. (5 sts dec'd)

Size 8 only
K2tog, k to m, SM, rep *–* to last patt m, SM, k2tog, k8, k2tog, k8. (6 sts dec'd)

All sizes
[40 (44, 44, 44) (58, 58, 65, 70) sts]

Rnds 11–12: K to end.

Part 3

With MC:
Rnd 1:
Sizes 1, 2, 3 and 4 only
LSC, k1, RSC, k5 (6, 6, 6), SM, rep *–* to end.

Sizes 5 and 6 only
K2, LSC, k1, RSC, k7, SM, rep *–* to last patt m, k3, LSC, k1, RSC, k8.

Size 7 only
K1, LSC, k1, RSC, k7, SM, rep *–* to end.

Size 8 only
K1, LSC, k1, RSC, k7, SM, rep *–* to last patt m, k4, LSC, k1, RSC, k9.

All sizes
Rnd 2: *K1 (1, 1, 1) (3, 3, 2, 2), kyo3, k1, kyo3, k6 (7, 7, 7) (8, 8, 8, 8), SM*, rep *–* to last patt m, SM, k1 (1, 1, 1) (4, 4, 2, 5), kyo3, k1, kyo3, k to end.
Rnds 3–9: Rep **–** of Sleeve Part 1.

Rnd 10:
Sizes 1–7 only
K to 2 sts bef m, k2tog, SM, rep *–* to end. [4 (4, 4, 4) (4, 4, 5, –) sts dec'd]

Size 8 only
K to 2 sts bef m, k2tog, SM, rep *–* to last patt m, k7, k2tog, k7, k2tog. (6 sts dec'd) [36 (40, 40, 40) (54, 54, 60, 64) sts]
Rnds 11–12: K to end.

Part 4

With MC:
Rnd 1:
Sizes 1, 2, 3, 4 and 7 only
K4 (5, 5, 5) (–, –, 7, –), LSC, k1, RSC, SM, rep *–* to end.

Sizes 5 and 6 only
K8, LSC, k1, RSC, SM, rep *–* to last patt m, k9, LSC, k1, RSC, k1.

Size 8 only
K7, LSC, k1, RSC, SM, rep *–* to last patt m, k9, LSC, k1, RSC, k2.
Rnd 2: *K5 (6, 6, 6) (9, 9, 8, 8), kyo3, k1, kyo3, k1, SM*, rep *–* to last patt m, SM, k5 (6, 6, 6) (10, 10, 8, 10), kyo3, k1, kyo3, k to end.
Rnds 3–9: Rep **–** of Sleeve Part 1.

Rnd 10:
Sizes 1–7 only
K2tog, k to m, SM, rep *–* to end. [4 (4, 4, 4) (4, 4, 5, –) sts dec'd]

Size 8 only
K2tog, k to m, SM, rep *–* to last patt m, k2tog, k6, k2tog, k6. (6 sts dec'd)

All sizes
[32 (36, 36, 36) (50, 50, 55, 58) sts]

Rnds 11–12: K to end.

Part 5

With MC:
Rnd 1:
Sizes 1, 2, 3, 4 and 7 only
LSC, k1, RSC, k3 (4, 4, 4) (–, –, 6, –), SM, rep *–* to end.

Sizes 5 and 6 only
K1, LSC, k1, RSC, k6, SM, rep *–* to last patt m, k2, LSC, k1, RSC, k7.

Size 8 only
LSC, k1, RSC, k6, SM, rep *–* to last patt m, k2, LSC, k1, RSC, k7.
Rnd 2: *K1 (1, 1, 1) (2, 2, 1, 1), kyo3, k1, kyo3, k4 (5, 5, 5) (7, 7, 7, 7), SM*, rep *–* to last patt m, k1 (1, 1, 1) (3, 3, 1, 3), kyo3, k1, kyo3, k to end.
Rnds 3–9: Rep **–** of Sleeve Part 1. Break CC after the last rep of CC rnds.

Rnd 10:
Sizes 5, 6 and 7 only
K to 2 sts bef m, k2tog, SM, rep *–* to end. [– (–, –, –) (4, 4, 5, –) sts dec'd]

Size 8 only
K to 2 sts bef m, k2tog, SM, rep *–* to last patt m, k5, k2tog, k5, k2tog. (6 sts dec'd)

All sizes
[32 (36, 36, 36) (46, 46, 50, 52) sts]

Removing all patt markers, work in St St until sleeve measures approx. 13.5" / 34.5 cm from underarm, or 3" / 7.5 cm less than desired length.

Sizes 1, 2, 3 and 4 only
K 2 more rnds.

Sizes 5, 6, 7 and 8 only
Dec Rnd: *K – (–, –, –) (5, 9, 6, 11), k2tog*, rep *–*, – (–, –, –) (5, 3, 5, 3) more times, k2tog, k to end. [– (–, –, –) (6, 4, 6, 4) sts dec'd] [– (–, –, –, –) (40, 42, 44, 48) sts]
Next Rnd: K to end.

Cuff

Change to US 8 / 5 mm needles.

Rib Rnd: *K1tbl, p1* to end.
Work in est 1 x 1 twisted rib until cuff measures 2.5" / 6.5 cm.

BO all sts in patt. Break yarn.

FINISHING

Weave in all ends. Wet block to measurements.

Arianna Frasca

12 Victorine

This sweater is designed to reflect the details and refined beauty of the Victorian era, with the modern twist of puffy bishop sleeves and big cables.

SIZES

1 (2, 3, 4, 5) (6, 7, 8, 9)

Recommended ease: 2" / 5 cm of positive ease.

FINISHED MEASUREMENTS

Bust Circumference: 34.75 (38.75, 44, 46, 50.75) (53.25, 58.75, 61.25, 64)" / 88.5 (98.5, 112, 117, 129) (135.5, 149, 155.5, 162.5) cm.
Sleeve Circumference at Underarm: 13 (13.75, 14.25, 15, 16.25) (17, 18.25, 18.25, 19)" / 33 (35, 36, 38, 41.5) (43, 46.5, 46.5, 48.5) cm.
Yoke Depth: 8.25 (9, 10.5, 10.75, 11.5) (12.5, 13.25, 14, 14.5)" / 21 (23, 26.5, 27.5, 29) (32, 33.5, 35.5, 37) cm.
Sleeve Length: 18.75" / 47.5 cm.
Length from Underarm to Hem Edge: 9" / 23 cm.

MATERIALS

Yarn: 6 (7, 8, 9, 10) (10, 11, 11, 12) skeins of Blizzard Bulky by The Frosted Stitch (80% sw merino, 20% nylon, 76 yds / 70 m – 100 g), colourway Stacks.

Or approx. 450 (505, 560, 615, 670) (725, 780, 835, 890) yds / 412 (462, 512, 562, 613) (663, 713, 763, 814) m of chunky-weight yarn. Alternative yarn suggestions are for example The Fibre Co. Tundra and Malabrigo Noventa.

Needles: US 10 / 6 mm and US 10.5 / 6.5 mm 32" / 80 cm circular needles.

Notions: Stitch markers, stitch holders or waste yarn, cable needle.

GAUGE

12 sts x 18 rnds to 4" / 10 cm on US 10.5 / 6.5 mm needles in St St, after blocking.

11 sts x 18 rnds to 4" / 10 cm on US 10.5 / 6.5 mm needles in cable patt, after blocking.

13 sts x 18 rnds to 4" / 10 cm on US 10 / 6 mm needles in 2 x 2 rib, after blocking.

SPECIAL ABBREVIATIONS

C8F: Cable 8 front (left-leaning)
In the rnd and on RS rows.
Pl 4 sts on CN and hold in front of work, k next 4 sts and then k 4 sts from CN.

On WS rows.
Pl 4 sts on CN and hold in front of work, p next 4 sts and then p 4 sts from CN.

C8B: Cable 8 back (right-leaning)
In the rnd and on RS rows.
Pl 4 sts on CN and hold in back of work, k next 4 sts and then k 4 sts from CN.

On WS rows.
Pl 4 sts on CN and hold in back of work, p next 4 sts and then p 4 sts from CN.

NOTES

When working the Cable Chart flat, work RS rows from right to left and WS rows from left to right.

CONSTRUCTION

This cropped, V-neck raglan sweater is worked from the top down. A cable is worked for the body and sleeves. The hem, cuffs and neckline feature a 2 x 2 ribbing.

DIRECTIONS

NECK

With US 10.5 / 6.5 mm needles, CO 44 (46, 50, 50, 56) (58, 58, 58, 60) sts.

Set-Up Row (WS): P1, PM, p3, PM, p6 (6, 7, 6, 7) (8, 7, 7, 7), PM, p3, PM, p18 (20, 22, 24, 28) (28, 30, 30, 32), PM, p3, PM, p6 (6, 7, 6, 7) (8, 7, 7, 7), PM, p3, PM, p1.

[44 (46, 50, 50, 56) (58, 58, 58, 60) sts: 1 st for each front, 6 (6, 7, 6, 7) (8, 7, 7, 7) sts for each sleeve, 18 (20, 22, 24, 28) (28, 30, 30, 32) sts for the back, 3 sts for each of the 4 raglan lines]

SHOULDER AND NECK SHAPING

Row 1 (RS) (Inc): K to m, *m1r, SM, k3, SM, m1l, k to m*, rep *–* twice more, m1r, SM, k3, SM, m1l, k to end. (8 sts inc'd)
Row 2: P to end.
Row 3 (Inc): K1, m1l, k to m, *m1r, SM, k3, SM, m1l, k to m*, rep *–* twice more, m1r, SM, k3, SM, m1l, k to 1 st bef end, m1r, k1. (10 sts inc'd)
Row 4: P to end.
Rows 5–16: Rep rows 1–4, 3 more times. (54 sts inc'd)

[116 (118, 122, 122, 128) (130, 130, 130, 132) sts: 13 sts for each front, 22 (22, 23, 22, 23) (24, 23, 23, 23) sts for each sleeve, 34 (36, 38, 40, 44) (44, 46, 46, 48) sts for the back, 12 raglan sts]

The next row will est the cable on the top of each sleeve. Refer to cable chart worked flat.
Row 17 (RS, Inc): K1, *m1l, k to m, m1r, SM, k3, SM, m1l, k5 (5, 5, 5, 5) (6, 5, 5, 5), PM, work row 1 of Cable Chart, PM, k to m, m1r, SM, k3, SM*, rep *–* once more, m1l, k to 1 st bef end, m1r, k1. (10 sts inc'd)
Row 18 (WS): P to end, working next row of Cable Chart row.
Row 19 (Inc): K1, *m1l, k to m, m1r, SM, k3, SM, m1l, k to m, SM, work next row of Cable Chart, SM, k to m, m1r, SM, k3, SM*, rep *–* once more, m1l, k to 1 st bef end, m1r, k1. (10 sts inc'd)
Row 20: P to end, working next row of Cable Chart.
Rep rows 19–20, 1 (3, 3, 5, 6) (7, 9, 10, 11) more time(s), always working next row of Cable Chart. [10 (30, 30, 50, 60) (70, 90, 100, 110) sts inc'd]

Rep row 19 once more. (10 sts inc'd)

[156 (178, 182, 202, 218) (230, 250, 260, 272) sts: 21 (25, 25, 29, 31) (33, 37, 39, 41) for each front, 30 (34, 35, 38, 41) (44, 47, 49, 51) sts for each sleeve, 42 (48, 50, 56, 62) (64, 70, 72, 76) sts for the back, 12 raglan sts]

Join to work in the rnd and PM for BOR. Refer to cable chart worked in the rnd.

Rnd 1: K to end.
Rnd 2: *K to m, m1r, SM, k3, SM, k to m, SM, work next row of Cable Chart, SM, k to m, SM, k3, SM, m1l*, rep *–* once more, k to end. (4 sts inc'd)
Rep rnds 1–2, 0 (0, 3, 2, 2) (3, 3, 4, 4) more times. [0 (0, 12, 8, 8) (12, 12, 16, 16) sts inc'd]

[160 (182, 198, 214, 230) (246, 266, 280, 292) sts: 22 (26, 29, 32, 34) (37, 41, 44, 46) for each front, 30 (34, 35, 38, 41) (44, 47, 49, 51) sts for each sleeve, 44 (50, 58, 62, 68) (72, 78, 82, 86) sts for the back, 12 raglan sts]

Divide for Body and Sleeves

Next Rnd: K6, PM, k to m, RM, k3, RM, pl next 30 (34, 35, 38, 41) (44, 47, 49, 51) sts (and both m's) on hold for left sleeve, RM, CO 2 (1, 2, 1, 2) (1, 2, 1, 1) st(s), k3, RM, k to m, RM, k3, RM, pl the next 30 (34, 35, 38, 41) (44, 47, 49, 51) sts (and both m's) on hold for right sleeve, RM, CO 2 (1, 2, 1,) (1, 2, 1, 1) st(s), PM (new BOR), k3, RM, k to 6 sts bef prev BOR, PM, k6, remove prev BOR m.

[104 (116, 132, 140, 152) (160, 176, 184, 192) sts on needles] [30 (34, 35, 38, 41) (44, 47, 49, 51) sts on hold for each sleeve]

BODY

Next Rnd: K to end.

The next rnd will est the cable at centre front.
Rnd 1: K to m, SM, work row 1 of Cable Chart, SM, k to end.
Rnd 2: K to m, SM, work next row of Cable Chart, SM, k to end.
Rep rnd 2, always working next row of Cable Chart, until work measures 6.5" / 16.5 cm from the armhole or 2.5" / 6.5 cm less than desired length, ending after rows 1–3 or 5–7 of the Chart Chart.

HEM

Change to US 10 / 6 mm needles.

Rnd 1: *K2, p2* to m, RM, rep *–* to m, RM, rep *–* to end.
Work in 2 x 2 rib as est until hem measures 2.25" / 5.5 cm.

BO all sts in patt.

SLEEVES

Starting at the centre of the armhole, with US 10.5 / 6.5 mm needles pick up and k 3 (2, 3, 2, 2) (2, 2, 2, 2) sts from CO sts. K the 30 (34, 35, 38, 41) (44, 47, 49, 51) sts you had on hold for the sleeve, working next Cable Chart row. Pick up and k 3 (2, 2, 2, 3) (2, 3, 1, 1) st(s) from rem CO sts, reaching the centre of the armhole again. PM and join to work in the rnd. [36 (38, 40, 42, 46) (48, 52, 52, 54) sts]
Rnd 1 (Inc): K to m, m1l, SM, work next row of Cable Chart, SM, m1r, k to end.

(2 sts inc'd) [38 (40, 42, 44, 48) (50, 54, 54, 56) sts]

Rnd 2: K to m, SM, work next row of Cable Chart, SM, k to end.
Rep rnd 2, always working next Cable Chart row, until the sleeve measures 16.5" / 42 cm or 2.25" / 5.5 cm less than desired length, ending after rows 1–3 or 5–7 of the Cable Chart.

Cuff

Next Rnd: Dec according to size and remove all markers except BOR m.
Size 1: K1, *k2tog* 2 times, *k2tog, k1* 9 times, *k2tog* 3 times. (14 sts dec'd)
Size 2: K1, *k2tog* 4 times, *k2tog, k1* 7 times, *k2tog* 5 times. (16 sts dec'd)
Size 3: K1, *k2tog, k1* 13 times, k2tog. (14 sts dec'd)
Size 4: K1, *k2tog* 2 times, *k2tog, k1* 11 times, *k2tog* 3 times. (16 sts dec'd)
Size 5: K1, *k2tog* 6 times, *k2tog, k1* 7 times, *k2tog* 7 times. (20 sts dec'd)
Size 6: K1, *k2tog* 8 times, *k2tog, k1* 5 times, *k2tog* 9 times. (22 sts dec'd)
Sizes 7 and 8: K1, *k2tog* 6 times, *k2tog, k1* 9 times, *k2tog* 7 times. (22 sts dec'd)
Size 9: K1, *k2tog* 8 times, *k2tog, k1* 7 times, *k2tog* 9 times. (24 sts dec'd)
[24 (24, 28, 28, 28) (28, 32, 32, 32) sts]

Change to US 10 / 6 mm needles.

Rib Rnd: *K2, p2* to end.
Work in est 2 x 2 rib until cuff measures 2.25" / 5.5 cm.

BO all sts in patt.

Make second sleeve alike.

NECKBAND

With US 10 / 6 mm needles and starting at the centre of the back neck, pick up and k 22 (23, 25, 25, 28) (29, 29, 29, 30) sts along the left back neck and left raglan sleeve, pick up and k 10 (11, 11, 13, 14) (15, 15, 15, 16) sts along the left side of the V-neck, PM, pick up and k 10 (11, 11, 13, 14) (15, 15, 15, 16) sts along the right side of the V-neck, pick up and k 22 (23, 25, 25, 28) (29, 29, 29, 30) sts from the right raglan sleeve and the right half of the back neck. PM and join to work in the rnd. [64 (68, 72, 76, 84) (88, 88, 88, 92) sts]

Rnd 1: *K2, p2* to end.
Rnd 2: Work in est 2 x 2 rib to 2 sts bef m, k2tog, SM, ssk, work in est 2 x 2 rib as est to end. (2 sts dec'd)
Rep rnd 2 twice more. [58 (62, 66, 70, 78) (72, 82, 82, 86) sts]

BO all sts in patt.

FINISHING

Weave in ends. Block to measurements.

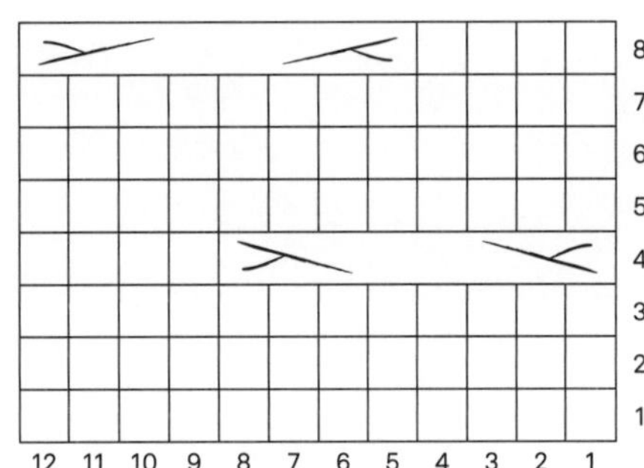

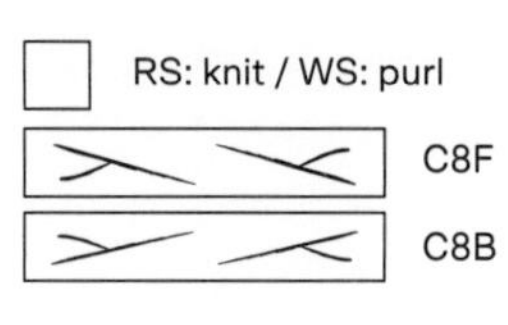

13

Cardigans

Marie Régnier — Yukie Onodera — Gina Rockenwagner

Anna Daku — Eliza Hinkes — Veranika Barel — Sasha Hyre

Marie Régnier

13 Petit Palais

Featuring a cropped hem and sleeves, this cosy open cardigan is the perfect layering piece. The multi-coloured yarn creates a striking fabric.

SIZES

1 (2, 3, 4, 5) (6, 7, 8, 9, 10)

Recommended ease: 4–8" / 10–20 cm of positive ease.

FINISHED MEASUREMENTS

Chest Circumference (Back Width x 2): 43 (43.75, 44.75, 50.75, 61.25) (62.25, 63, 63.75, 73.5, 74.5)" / 109 (111, 113.5, 129, 155.5) (158, 160, 162, 186.5, 189) cm.
Upper Arm Circumference: 18.25 (21, 21, 21, 23.5) (23.5, 23.5, 23.5, 26.25, 26.25)" / 46.5 (53.5, 53.5, 53.5, 60) (60, 60, 60, 66.5, 66.5) cm.
Hem Length: 1.5" / 4 cm.
Body Length from Underarm: 8.5" / 22 cm.
Sleeve Length from Underarm: 11" / 28 cm.
Yoke Depth: 8.75 (9, 9.75, 10.25, 10.25) (10.75, 11, 11.5, 11.75, 12.25)" / 22 (23, 25, 26, 26) (27, 28, 29, 30, 31) cm.
Neckband Width: 3.25" / 8 cm.
Total Length: 17.5 (17.75, 18.5, 19, 19) (19.25, 19.75, 20, 20.5, 21)" / 44 (45, 47, 48, 48) (49, 50, 51, 52, 53) cm.

MATERIALS

Yarn: 5 (6, 6, 7, 8) (8, 9, 10, 11, 12) skeins of Plump by Spincycle Yarns (100% sw American wool, 100 yds / 91 m – approx. 100 g), colourway Deep Bump.

Or approx. 460, (495, 505, 580, 695) (720, 740, 755, 885, 910) yds / 420 (450, 460, 530, 635) (660, 675, 690, 810, 830) m of a bulky-weight yarn. Alternative yarn suggestions are for example Katia Wow Chunky, Drops Snow and Wool and the Gang Alpachino Merino.

Needles: US 11 / 8 mm 32" / 80 cm and 47" / 120 cm circular needles, and needles to work small circumferences.

Notions: Stitch markers and waste yarn or stitch holders.

GAUGE

9 sts x 13 rows to 4" / 10 cm on US 11 / 8 mm needles in Open Rib St patt worked flat, after blocking.

STITCH PATTERNS

Open Rib

Flat (worked on 6 + 2 sts).
Row 1 (RS): *P2, yo, ssk, k2tog, yo*, rep *–* to 2 sts bef end, p2.
Row 2 (WS): *K2, p4* to 2 sts bef end, k2.
Row 3: *P2, yo, k2tog, ssk, yo*, rep *–* to 2 sts bef end, p2.
Row 4: Rep row 2.

In the rnd (worked on 6 sts).
Rnd 1: *P2, yo, ssk, k2tog, yo*, rep *–* to end.
Rnd 2: *P2, k4* to end.
Rnd 3: *P2, yo, k2tog, ssk, yo*, rep *–* to end.
Rnd 4: Rep rnd 2.

NOTES

The yarn used for the sample is bulky-weight. However, correct gauge can be achieved by combining leftover yarns of different weights. The right thickness for needed gauge is around 7 WPI (wraps per inch).

Yardage cannot be estimated for this option as it would differ for every combination (mix of fingering, lace, DK, etc.). The idea is to work this cardigan as a granny square blanket, adding length and mixing yarns according to the leftover stash.

CONSTRUCTION

This cardigan is worked flat in a lace pattern from the top down, starting with a Provisional Cast-On at the shoulders for the back and front panels. A 3-Needle Bind-Off is worked at the shoulders to give more structure to the knit. Stitches are then cast on for the underarms and the body is completed. After the body is finished, stitches are picked up at the armhole and the sleeves are worked in lace pattern in the round. Finally, stitches are picked up around the neckband and worked flat. The body hem and the neckband are worked in 2 x 2 rib.

DIRECTIONS

RIGHT BACK SHOULDER

With US 11 / 8 mm needles and using a Provisional CO method, CO 14 (14, 14, 14, 20) (20, 20, 20, 26, 26) sts.

Next Row (RS): K to end.
Set-Up Row (WS): *K2, p4* to 2 sts bef end, k2.
Row 1 (RS): P2, *yo, ssk, k2tog, yo, p2*, rep *–* to end.
Row 2: *K2, p4* to 2 sts bef end, k2.
Row 3 (Inc): P1, m1l(p), p1, *yo, k2tog, ssk, yo, p2*, rep *–* to end. (1 st inc'd)
Row 4: *K2, p4* to 3 sts bef end, k3.
Row 5 (Inc): P1, m1l, p2, *yo, ssk, k2tog, yo, p2*, rep *–* to end. (1 st inc'd)
Row 6: *K2, p4* to 4 sts bef end, k2, p1, k1.
Row 7 (Inc): P1, m1l, k1, p2, *yo, k2tog, ssk, yo, p2*, rep *–* to end. (1 st inc'd)
Row 8: *K2, p4* to 5 sts bef end, k2, p2, k1.
[17 (17, 17, 17, 23) (23, 23, 23, 29, 29) sts]

Sizes 1–3 only
Break yarn and leave the sts on hold on a st holder or waste yarn.

Sizes 4–10 only
Row 9 (RS) (Inc): P1, m1l, k2, p2, *yo, ssk, k2tog, yo, p2*, rep *–* to end. (1 st inc'd)
Row 10 (WS): *K2, p4* to 6 sts bef end, k2, p3, k1.
Row 11 (Inc): P1, m1l, k3, p2, *yo, k2tog, ssk, yo, p2*, rep *–* to end. (1 st inc'd)
Row 12: *K2, p4* to 7 sts bef end, k2, p4, k1.
[- (–, –, 19, 25) (25, 25, 25, 31, 31) sts]

Break yarn and leave the sts on hold on a stitch holder or waste yarn.

LEFT BACK SHOULDER

With US 11 / 8 mm needles and using a Provisional CO method, CO 14 (14, 14, 14, 20) (20, 20, 20, 26, 26) sts.

Next Row (RS): K to end.
Set-Up Row (WS): *K2, p4* to 2 sts bef end, k2.
Row 1: *P2, yo, ssk, k2tog, yo*, rep *–* to 2 sts bef end, p2.
Row 2: *K2, p4* to 2 sts bef end, k2.
Row 3 (Inc): *P2, yo, k2tog, ssk, yo*, rep *–* to 2 sts bef end, p1, m1r(p), p1. (1 st inc'd)
Row 4: K3, *p4, k2* to end.
Row 5 (Inc): *P2, yo, ssk, k2tog, yo*, rep *–* to 3 sts bef end, p2, m1r, p1. (1 st inc'd)
Row 6: K1, p1, k2, *p4, k2* to end.
Row 7 (Inc): *P2, yo, k2tog, ssk, yo*, rep *–* to 4 sts bef end, p2, k1, m1r, p1. (1 st inc'd)
Row 8: K1, p2, k2, *p4, k2* to end.
[17 (17, 17, 17, 23) (23, 23, 23, 29, 29) sts]

Sizes 1–3 only
Do not break yarn. Move to the Back Panel section.

Sizes 4–10 only
Row 9 (RS) (Inc): *P2, yo, ssk, k2tog, yo*, rep to 5 sts bef end, p2, k2, m1r, p1. (1 st inc'd)
Row 10 (WS): K1, p3, k2, *p4, k2* to end.
Row 11 (Inc): *P2, yo, k2tog, ssk, yo*, rep to 6 sts bef end, p2, k3, m1r, p1. (1 st inc'd)
Row 12: K1, p4, k2, *p4, k2* to end.
[- (–, –, 19, 25) (25, 25, 25, 31, 31) sts]

Do not break yarn.

BACK PANEL

Sizes 1–3 only
Set-Up Row (RS): With RS facing, work left back shoulder sts in patt to 3 sts bef end, k3, PM, using the Backwards Loop CO method, CO 10 (10, 10–, –) (–, –, –, –, –) sts, PM, with RS facing k3 from right back shoulder and work in patt to

end. [44 (44, 44, –, –) (–, –, –, –, –) sts]
Next Row (WS): Work in patt to 3 sts bef m, p3, RM, p1, k2, p4, k2, p1, RM, p3, *k2, p4* to 2 sts bef end, k2.

Sizes 4–10 only
Set-Up Row (RS): With the RS facing, work left back shoulder sts in patt to 5 sts bef end, k4, p1, PM, using the Backwards Loop CO method, CO – (–, –, 12, 12) (12, 12, 12, 12, 12) sts, PM, with RS facing p1, k4 from right back shoulder, and work in patt to end. [– (–, –, 50, 62) (62, 62, 62, 74, 74) sts]
Next Row (WS): Work in patt to 5 sts bef m, p4, k1, RM, k1, p4, k2, p4, k1, RM, k1, *p4, k2* to end.

All sizes
Work in patt and rep rows 1–4 of the chart until the back panel measures 8.75 (9, 9.75, 10.25, 10.25) (10.75, 11, 11.5, 11.75, 12.25)" / 22 (23, 25, 26, 26) (27, 28, 29, 30, 31) cm, or until desired length from the shoulder CO edge, ending after a WS row.
Break yarn and put the sts on hold on stitch holders or waste yarn.

Note! Make a note of the last WS row for the back panel (chart row 2 or 4) in order to have a matching patt at the front when joining the body.

RIGHT FRONT

With US 11 / 8 mm needles, and using Provisional CO method, CO 14 (14, 14, 14, 20) (20, 20, 20, 26, 26) sts.

Next Row (RS): K to end.
Set-Up Row (WS): K2, *p4, k2* to end.
Row 1 (RS): P2, *yo, ssk, k2tog, yo, p2*, rep *–* to end.
Row 2: *K2, p4* to 2 sts bef end, k2.
Row 3 (Inc): *P2, yo, k2tog, ssk, yo*, rep *–* to 2 sts bef end, p1, m1r(p), p1. (1 st inc'd)
Row 4: K3, *p4, k2* to end.
Row 5 (Inc): *P2, yo, ssk, k2tog, yo*, rep *–* to 3 sts bef end, p2, m1r, p1. (1 st inc'd)
Row 6: K1, p1, k2, *p4, k2* to end.
Row 7 (Inc): *P2, yo, k2tog, ssk, yo*, rep *–* to 4 sts bef end, p2, k1, m1r, p1. (1 st inc'd)
Row 8: K1, p2, k2, *p4, k2* to end.
Row 9 (Inc): *P2, yo, ssk, k2tog, yo*, rep *–* to 5 sts bef end, p2, k2, m1r, p1. (1 st inc'd)
Row 10: K1, p3, k2, *p4, k2* to end.
Row 11 (Inc): *P2, yo, k2tog, ssk, yo*, rep *–* to 6 sts bef end, p2, k3, m1r, p1. (1 st inc'd)
Row 12: K1, *p4, k2* to end.
Row 13 (Inc): *P2, yo, ssk, k2tog, yo*, rep *–* to 1 st bef end, m1r(p), p1. (1 st inc'd)
Row 14: K2, *p4, k2* to end.
[20 (20, 20, 20, 26) (26, 26, 26, 32, 32) sts]

Sizes 1, 2, 3, 4, 6 and 9 only
Work rows 3–14 once more and then rows 3 and 4 once more.
[27 (27, 27, 27, –) (33, –, –, 39, –) sts]

Size 5 only
Work rows 3–12 once more. [– (–, –, –, 31) (–, –, –, –, –) sts]

Size 7 only
Rep rows 3–14 once more. Then work rows 3–12 once more. (37 sts)

Size 8 only
Rep rows 3–14 twice more. (38 sts)

Size 10 only
Rep rows 3–14 twice more. Then work rows 3 and 4 once more. (45 sts)

All sizes
Set-Up Row (RS): Work in patt to 3 (3, 3, 3, 1) (3, 1, 2, 3, 3) sts bef end, p to end.
Next Row (WS): Work in patt to 3 (3, 3, 3, 1) (3, 1, 2, 3, 3) sts bef end, k to end.

Work sts as est until the front measures 8.75 (9, 9.75, 10.25, 10.25) (10.75, 11, 11.5, 11.75, 12.25)" / 22 (23, 25, 26, 26) (27, 28, 29, 30, 31) cm from the shoulder CO edge.

Note! Make sure to end the front panel on the same WS row (row 2 or 4) as the back.
Break yarn and put sts on hold.

LEFT FRONT

With US 11 / 8 mm needles, and using a Provisional CO method, CO 14 (14, 14, 14, 20) (20, 20, 20, 26, 26) sts.

Next Row (RS): K to end.
Set-Up Row (WS): *K2, p4* to 2 sts bef end, k2.
Row 1: P2, *yo, ssk, k2tog, yo, p2*, rep *–* to end.
Row 2: *K2, p4* to 2 sts bef end, k2.
Row 3 (Inc): P1, m1l(p), p1, *yo, k2tog, ssk, yo, p2*, rep *–* to end. (1 st inc'd)
Row 4: *K2, p4* to 3 sts bef end, k3.
Row 5 (Inc): P1, m1l, p2, *yo, ssk, k2tog, yo, p2*, rep *–* to end. (1 st inc'd)
Row 6: *K2, p4* to 4 sts bef end, k2, p1, k1.
Row 7 (Inc): P1, m1l, k1, p2, *yo, k2tog, ssk, yo, p2*, rep *–* to end. (1 st inc'd)
Row 8: *K2, p4* to 5 sts bef end, k2, p2, k1.
Row 9 (Inc): P1, m1l, k2, p2, *yo, ssk, k2tog, yo, p2*, rep *–* to end. (1 st inc'd)
Row 10: *K2, p4* to 6 sts bef end, k2, p3, k1.
Row 11 (Inc): P1, m1l, k3, p2, *yo, k2tog, ssk, yo, p2*, rep *–* to end. (1 st inc'd)
Row 12: *K2, p4* to 1 st bef end, k1.
Row 13 (Inc): P1, m1l(p), *yo, ssk, k2tog, yo, p2*, rep *–* to end. (1 st inc'd)
Row 14: *K2, p4* to 2 sts bef end, k2.
[20 (20, 20, 20, 26) (26, 26, 26, 32, 32) sts]

Sizes 1, 2, 3, 4, 6 and 9 only
Work rows 3–14 once more. Then work rows 3 and 4 once more. [27 (27, 27, 27, –) (33, –, –, 39, –) sts]

Size 5 only
Work rows 3–12 once more. (31 sts)

Size 7 only
Rep rows 3–14 once more. Then work rows 3–12 once more. (37 sts)

Size 8 only
Rep rows 3–14 twice more. (38 sts)

Size 10 only
Rep rows 3–14 twice more. Then work rows 3 and 4 once more. (45 sts)

All sizes
Set-Up Row (RS): P3 (3, 3, 3, 1) (3, 1, 2, 3, 3), work in patt to end.
Next Row (WS): Work in patt to 3 (3, 3, 3, 1) (3, 1, 2, 3, 3) sts bef end, k to end.

Work sts as est until the front measures 8.75 (9, 9.75, 10.25, 10.25) (10.75, 11, 11.5, 11.75, 12.25)" / 22 (23, 25, 26, 26) (27, 28, 29, 30, 31) cm from the shoulder CO edge.

Note! Make sure to end the front panel on the same WS row (row 2 or 4) as the back.

Do not break yarn.

SHOULDERS

Unravel the Provisional CO and move the left back shoulder sts to US 11 / 8 mm needles. Pl the left front shoulder sts on another US 11 / 8 mm needle.

With the RS facing each other, use the 3-Needle BO method to BO all the shoulder sts.

Rep to join the right back and right front shoulders together.

BODY

Set-Up Row (RS): Rejoin yarn, work the left front sts in patt, PM, using the Backwards Loop CO method CO 5 (6, 7, 8, 8) (9, 10,11, 10, 11) sts, PM, put the back panel sts back onto LH needle and work as est, PM, CO 5 (6, 7, 8, 8) (9, 10, 11, 10, 11) sts, PM, work the right front in patt. [108 (110, 112, 120) (140, 146, 156) (160, 172, 186) sts]

Next Row (WS): *Work in patt to m, SM, p1, k3 (4, 5, 6, 6) (7, 8, 9, 8, 9), p1, SM*, rep *–* once more, patt to end.

Row 1 (RS): *Work in patt to m, SM, k1, p3 (4, 5, 6, 6) (7, 8, 9, 8, 9), k1, SM*, rep *–* once more, work in patt to end.
Row 2 (WS): *Work in patt to m, SM, p1, k3 (4, 5, 6, 6) (7, 8, 9, 8, 9), p1, SM*, rep *–* once more, work in patt to end.
Rep rows 1–2 until the body from underarm measures 7" / 18 cm, or 1.5" / 4 cm shorter than the desired length. End after an RS row.

HEM

Sizes 1, 3, 4, 5, 7, 8 and 9 only
Set-Up Row (WS): P2, m1r, p to 2 sts bef end, m1l, p2. (2 sts inc'd) [110 (–, 114, 122, 142) (–, 158, 162, 174, –) sts]

Sizes 2, 6, and 10 only
Set-Up Row (WS): P to end.

All sizes
Rib Row 1 (RS): *K2, p2* to 2 sts bef end, k2.
Rib Row 2 (WS): *P2, k2* to 2 sts bef end, p2.

Rep rows 1–2 for 2 x 2 rib until the hem rib measures 1.5" / 4 cm.

BO using the Italian BO method.

SLEEVES

Set-Up Rnd: With the RS facing, and starting at the underarm CO, use US 11 / 8 mm needle for small circumferences to pick up and k 42 (48, 48, 48, 54) (54, 54, 54, 60, 60) sts around the armhole (1 st for every CO st, and approx. 4 sts in every 5 rows), PM for BOR.

Rnd 1: *P2, yo, ssk, k2tog, yo*, rep *–* to end.
Rnd 2: *P2, k4* to end.
Rnd 3: *P2, yo, k2tog, ssk, yo*, rep *–* to end.
Rnd 4: *P2, k4* to end.
Rep rnds 1–4 until sleeve measures 11" / 28 cm, ending after a rnd 2 or 4.

BO in patt.

NECKBAND

Set-Up Row (RS): With RS facing, using longer US 11 / 8 mm needles, pick up and k 110 (110, 110, 114, 114) (134, 134, 134, 150, 150) sts evenly (approx 1 st in every st) along the front edges and back neck.
Next Row (WS): P to end.

Rib Row 1: *K2, p2* to 2 sts bef end, k2.
Rib Row 2: *P2, k2* to 2 sts bef end, p2.
Rep rows 1–2 for 2 x 2 rib until neckband measures 3.25" / 8 cm, or until desired length.

Using the Italian BO method or a stretchy BO of your liking, BO all sts.

FINISHING

Weave in ends. Block to measurements.

OPEN RIB CHART (WORKED FLAT)

8	7	6	5	4	3	2	1	
•	•					•	•	4
•	•	O	\	/	O	•	•	3
•	•					•	•	2
•	•	O	/	\	O	•	•	1

OPEN RIB CHART (WORKED IN THE RND)

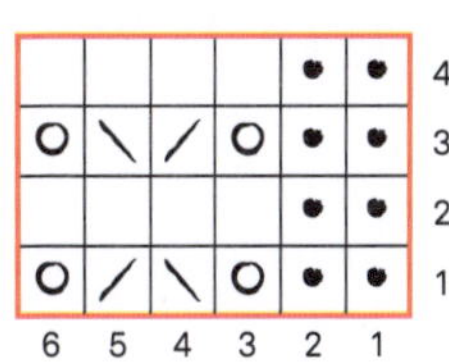

- ☐ RS: knit / WS: purl
- • RS: purl / WS: knit
- O yo
- \ RS: ssk / WS: ssp
- / RS: k2tog / WS: p2tog
- ☐ (orange) pattern repeat

Yukie Onodera

14 Butter

With its loose fit and cropped length, the Butter cardigan has a light and airy vibe. Its silhouette reminded the designer of a traditional butter dish – hence the name!

SIZES

1 (2, 3, 4) (5, 6, 7) (8, 9, 10, 11)

Recommended ease: 8–11.75" / 20–30 cm of positive ease.

FINISHED MEASUREMENTS

Chest Circumference (Worn Open): 38.25 (41, 44.75, 47.5) (51.5, 54.25, 58) (61.5, 64.5, 68.5, 71.25)" / 97.5 (104, 114, 121) (131, 137.5, 147.5) (156, 164, 174, 181) cm.
Back Width: 18.75 (20, 21.25, 22.75) (24.5, 26, 28) (29, 31, 32, 33)" / 47.5 (51, 54, 57.5) (62.5, 66, 71) (74, 79, 81, 84) cm.
Body Length from Back Neck Rib to Hem: 14.25 (14.5, 15, 15.75) (16.75, 17.5, 18.25) (19, 20, 20.5, 21.25)" / 36 (37, 38, 40) (42.5, 44.5, 46.5) (48.5, 51, 52, 54) cm.
Length from Underarm to Hem: 4.25" / 10.5 cm.
Yoke Depth: 10 (10.5, 10.75, 11.5) (12.5, 13.25, 14.25) (15, 16.25, 16.25, 17)" / 25.5 (26.5, 27.5, 29.5) (32, 34, 36) (38, 40.5, 41.5, 43.5) cm.
Upper Arm Circumference: 13.25 (13.75, 14.25, 15.25) (15.75, 17, 19) (21, 23, 24.25, 25)" / 33.5 (35, 36.5, 38.5) (40, 43.5, 48.5) (53.5, 58.5, 61.5, 63.5) cm.
Sleeve Length: 13" / 33 cm.

MATERIALS

Yarn: 4 (4, 4, 5) (5, 5, 6) (7, 7, 8, 8) skeins of Bun by Bread & Butter (100% US merino, 130 yds / 118 m – 100 g), colourway Yucca Blossom.

Or approx. 423 (463, 491, 535) (577, 638, 723) (798, 884, 946, 1004) yds / 387 (424, 449, 489) (528, 583, 661) (730, 808, 865, 918) m of bulky-weight yarn. Alternative yarn suggestions are for example Brooklyn Tweed Quarry, Quince & Co. Puffin and Woolfolk Luft.

Needles: US 10.5 / 6.5 mm circular needles 16" / 40 cm (for the neck rib), 16–48" / 40–120 cm (for the body) and 32" / 80 cm (for the sleeves, using Magic Loop).

Notions: 8 stitch markers, waste yarn.

GAUGE

12 sts × 19 rows to 4" / 10 cm in St St, after blocking.

SPECIAL TECHNIQUES

Long-Tail Cast-On Purlwise
Place both strands of yarn in the left hand in the same way as when working a basic Long-Tail CO. The working yarn runs over the index finger and the yarn end over the thumb. Take the needle under the strand of yarn that is over the index finger and pick the yarn up. Next, take the needle under the yarn that is over the thumb, catch the yarn and pull it through the loop around your index finger. Release the yarn tail and tighten the stitch.

CONSTRUCTION

This cardigan is worked flat from the top down until stitches are put on hold for the sleeves and the body is shaped with decreases. The sleeves are later worked in the round. The neckline, hem and cuffs feature a 1 x 1 ribbing.

DIRECTIONS

NECK RIB

With US 10.5 / 6.5 mm needles, CO 53 (59, 63, 63) (69, 69, 73) (73, 75, 79, 79) sts as foll:
CO 2 sts using the Long-Tail CO method, *CO 1 st Long-Tail CO Purlwise, CO 1 st using the Long-Tail CO method*, rep *–* until all but final 3 of required number of sts have been CO, CO 1 st using the Long-Tail CO Purlwise, CO 2 sts using the Long-Tail CO.

Row 1 (WS): Sl1 pwise wyif, *p1, k1* to 2 sts bef end, p2.
Row 2 (RS): Sl1 kwise wyib, *k1, p1* to 2 sts bef end, k2.
Rep rows 1–2 until the rib measures approx. 2" / 5 cm, ending after an RS row.

Next, PM for the raglan as foll:
Row 1 (WS): Sl1 pwise wyif, p 7 (8, 9, 9) (10, 10, 11) (11, 11, 12, 12) sts for right front, PM, p1, PM, p 8 (9, 9, 9) (10, 10, 10) (10, 10, 11, 11) sts for right sleeve, PM, p1, PM, p 17 (19, 21, 21) (23, 23, 25) (25, 27, 27, 27) sts for back, PM, p1, PM, p 8 (9, 9, 9) (10, 10, 10) (10, 10, 11, 11) sts for left sleeve, PM, p1, PM, p 8 (9, 10, 10) (11, 11, 12) (12, 12, 13, 13) sts for left front.
Row 2 (RS) (Inc): Sl1 kwise wyib, *k to m, m1l, SM, k1, SM, m1r*, rep *–* 3 more times, k to end.
(8 sts inc'd)

[51 (56, 60, 60) (65, 65, 69) (69, 71, 74, 74) sts: 9 (10, 11, 11) (12, 12, 13) (13, 13, 14, 14) sts per front, 19 (21, 23, 23) (25, 25, 27) (27, 29, 29, 29) sts for back, 10 (11, 11, 11) (12, 12, 12) (12, 12, 13, 13) sts per sleeve, 4 raglan sts]

Row 3 (WS): Sl1 pwise wyif, p to end.

SHORT ROW SHAPING FOR NECK

Next, German Short Rows are worked to add length to the back neck, at the same time as continuing to inc around the raglan sts as foll:
Short Row 1 (RS) (Inc): Sl1 kwise wyib, *k to m, m1l, SM, k1, SM, m1r*, rep *–* 3 more times, k1, tw. (8 sts inc'd)
Short Row 2 (WS): MDS, *p to m, SM, p1, SM*, rep *–* to 3 more times, p2, tw.

Short Row 3 (RS) (Inc): MDS, *k to m, m1l, SM, k1, SM, m1r*, rep *–* to 3 more times, k to DS, kDS, k1, tw. (8 sts inc'd)
Short Row 4 (WS): MDS, *p to m, SM, p1, SM*, rep *–* to 3 more times, p to DS, pDS, p1, tw.
Rep last 2 rows 3 more times. (24 sts inc'd)

Short Row 11 (RS) (Inc): MDS, *k to m, m1l, SM, k1, SM, m1r*, rep *–* 3 more times, k to DS, kDS, k to end. (8 sts inc'd)
Row 12 (WS): Sl1 pwise wyif, *p to m, SM, p1, SM*, rep *–* to 3 more times, p to DS, pDS, p to end.

[87 (92, 96, 96) (101, 101, 105) (105, 107, 110, 110) sts: 15 (16, 17, 17) (18, 18, 19) (19, 19, 20, 20) sts per front, 31 (33, 35, 35) (37, 37, 39) (39, 41, 41, 41) sts for back, 22 (23, 23, 23) (24, 24, 24) (24, 24, 25, 25) sts per sleeve, 4 raglan sts]

YOKE SHAPING

Full Raglan Increases

Row 1 (RS) (Inc): Sl1 kwise wyib, *k to m, m1l, SM, k1, SM, m1r*, rep *–* to 3 more times, k to end. (8 sts inc'd)
Row 2 (WS): Sl1 pwise wyif, p to end.
Rep rows 1–2 another 2 (1, 0, 0) (0, 2, 6) (8, 12, 11, 11) time(s).

[105 (104, 102, 102) (107, 119, 147) (159, 185, 182, 182) sts: (18 (18, 18, 18) (19, 21, 26) (28, 32, 32, 32) sts per front, 37 (37, 37, 37) (39, 43, 53) (57, 67, 65, 65) sts for back, 28 (27, 25, 25) (26, 30, 38) (42, 50, 49, 49) sts per sleeve, 4 raglan sts]

Body Raglan Increases

Row 1 (RS) (Inc): Sl1 kwise wyib, *k to m, m1l, SM, k1, SM, m1r*, rep *–* to 3 more times, k to end. (8 sts inc'd)
Row 2 (WS): Sl1 pwise wyif, p to end.
Row 3 (Body-Only Inc): Sl1 kwise wyib, *k to m, m1l, SM, k1, SM, k to m, SM, k1, SM, m1r*, rep *–* once more, k to end. (4 sts inc'd)
Row 4: Sl1 pwise wyif, p to end.
Rep rows 1–4 another 3 (4, 5, 6) (7, 7, 6) (6, 5, 6, 7) times. Then rep rows 1 and 2 once more.

[151 (160, 168, 178) (193, 205, 223) (235, 251, 258, 268) sts: 27 (29, 31, 33) (36, 38, 41) (43, 45, 47, 49) sts per front, 55 (59, 63, 67) (73, 77, 83) (87, 93, 95, 99) sts for back, 38 (39, 39, 41) (44, 48, 54) (58, 64, 65, 67) sts per sleeve, 4 raglan sts]

SEPARATE BODY AND SLEEVES

Next Row (RS): Sl1 kwise wyib, *k to m, RM, k1, RM, pl next 38 (39, 39, 41) (44, 48, 54) (58, 64, 65, 67) sts on hold, RM, CO 2 (2, 4, 4) (4, 4, 4) (5, 5, 8, 8) sts using the Backwards Loop CO method, k1, RM*, rep *–* once more, k to end. [117 (125, 137, 145) (157, 165, 177) (187, 197, 209, 217) sts]

BODY

Next, PM at the underarms for the decreases as foll:
Set-Up Row (WS): Sl1 pwise wyif, p 28 (30, 33, 35) (38, 40, 43) (45, 47, 51, 53) sts for right front, PM, p 59 (63, 69, 73) (79, 83, 89) (95, 101, 105, 109) sts, PM, p 29 (31, 34, 36) (39, 41, 44) (46, 48, 52, 54) sts to end of left front.
Row 1 (RS) (Dec): Sl1 kwise wyib, *k to 2 sts bef m, ssk, SM, k2tog*, rep *–* to

once more, k to end. (4 sts dec'd)
Row 2: Sl1 pwise wyif, p to end.
Row 3: Sl1 kwise wyib, k to end.
Row 4: Rep row 2.
Rep rows 1–4 another 2 times. (8 sts dec'd)

[105 (113, 125, 133) (145, 153, 165) (175, 185, 197, 205) sts: 26 (28, 31, 33) (36, 38, 41) (43, 45, 49, 51) sts per front, 53 (57, 63, 67) (73, 77, 83) (89, 95, 99, 103) sts for back]

Hem Rib

Remove all m's on the first row.
Row 1 (RS): Sl1 kwise wyib, *k1, p1* to 2 sts bef end, k2.
Row 2 (WS): Sl1 pwise wyif, *p1, k1* to 2 sts bef end, p2.
Rep rows 1–2 until rib measures 1.25" / 3 cm.

BO all sts loosely in patt.

SLEEVES

Move the sleeve sts back onto the needles. [38 (39, 39, 41) (44, 48, 54) (58, 64, 65, 67) sts]

Sizes 2, 3, 4, 8, 9, 10 and 11 only
Note that you will pick up 1 more st than the number of underarm CO sts.

Beg from the middle of the underarm CO, pick up and k 1 (2, 3, 3) (2, 2, 2) (3, 3, 5, 5) st(s), k to end of 38 (39, 39, 41) (44, 48, 54) (58, 64, 65, 67) sleeve sts, pick up and k 1 (1, 2, 2) (2, 2, 2) (3, 3, 4, 4) st(s) from the underarm, PM for BOR. [40 (42, 44, 46) (48, 52, 58) (64, 70, 74, 76) sts]

Work in St St in the rnd until the sleeve measures 7.5" / 19 cm from the underarm CO, or until 5.5" / 14 cm shorter than your desired length.

Sleeve Decreases

Sizes 1, 2, 3, 4, 5, 6, 7 and 8 only
Rnd 1 (Dec): K2tog, k to 2 sts bef end, ssk. (2 sts dec'd)
Rnd 2: K to end.
Rnd 3: K to end.
Rnd 4: K to end.
Rep rnds 1–4 another 4 times. (8 sts dec'd)

[30 (32, 34, 36) (38, 42, 48) (54, –, –, –) sts]

Size 9 only
Rnd 1 (Dec): K2tog, k to 2 sts bef end, ssk. (2 sts dec'd)
Rnd 2: K to end.
Rnd 3: K2tog, k to 2 sts bef end, ssk. (2 sts dec'd)
Rnds 4 and 5: K to end.
Rep rnds 1–5 another 3 times. (12 sts dec'd)

[– (–, –, –) (–, –, –) (–, 54, –, –) sts]

Sizes 10 and 11 only
Rnd 1 (Dec): K2tog, k to 2 sts bef end, ssk. (2 sts dec'd)
Rnd 2: K to end.
Rep rnds 1–2 another 9 times. (18 sts dec'd)

[– (–, –, –) (–, –, –) (–, –, 54, 56) sts]

Cuff

Rib Rnd (RS): *K1, p1* to end.
Work in est 1 x 1 rib until rib measures 1.25" / 3 cm.

BO all sts loosely in patt.

FINISHING

Weave in ends. Wet block to measurements.

Gina Rockenwagner

15 Willa

This open cardigan features gently sloping cables on the front, back and sleeves. A neat slipped-stitch edge is worked along the garter-stitch fronts.

SIZES

1 (2, 3, 4, 5) (6, 7, 8)

Recommended ease: 8" / 20.5 cm of positive ease.

FINISHED MEASUREMENTS

Chest Circumference (Worn Open): 44 (48, 52, 56, 60) (64, 68, 72)" / 112 (122, 132, 142, 152.5) (162.5, 172.5, 183) cm.
Front Body Length from Shoulder to Bottom Edge: 21.5 (21.5, 21.5, 22, 22) (22, 22.5, 22.5)" / 54.5 (54.5, 54.5, 56, 56) (56, 57, 57) cm.
Length from Underarm to Hem: 15" / 38 cm.
Upper Arm Circumference: 16 (16, 16, 17.25, 17.25) (17.25, 18.75, 18.5)" / 40.5 (40.5, 40.5, 44, 44) (44, 47.5, 47.5) cm.
Sleeve Length from Shoulder to Cuff: 16.5" / 42 cm.

MATERIALS

Yarn: 8 (8, 9, 9, 10) (10, 10, 10) skeins of Bread and Butter Bun by A Verb for Keeping Warm (100% US merino wool, 130 yds / 118 m – 100 g), colourway Lantana.

Or approx. 1000 (1040, 1085, 1130, 1175) (1215, 1260, 1300) yds / 915 (950, 995, 1035, 1075) (1115, 1155, 1190) m of chunky-weight yarn. Alternative yarn suggestions are for example Berroco Ultra Alpaca Chunky, Brown Sheep Lamb's Pride Bulky and Malabrigo Mecha.

Needles: US 10.5 / 6.5 mm 16" / 40 cm and 32–40" / 80–100 cm circular needles, US 10.5 / 6.5 mm DPNs (optional).

Notions: Stitch markers, cable needle, stitch holders or waste yarn.

GAUGE

12 sts x 16 rows to 4" / 10 cm in St St, after blocking.

15-st cable chart = 3" / 7.5 cm.

SPECIAL ABBREVIATIONS

5/5 RC: Sl 5 sts to CN and hold in back, k5, k5 from CN.

5/5 LC: Sl 5 sts to CN and hold in front, k5, k5 from CN.

CONSTRUCTION

This open cardigan is knitted in one piece starting at the upper back shoulder. It features gently sloping cables on the front, back and sleeves and a slipped-stitch neckline. First, stitches are cast on for the back and then worked flat, first in Garter Stitch and then in a cable pattern with Reverse Stockinette Stitch for the background, until the underarm. Stitches are picked up for both fronts across the top edge, then a bind-off is worked for the centre stitches to separate the fronts and create the neckline. Each upper front is worked separately until the underarm, with a cable pattern and a slipped-stitch edge along the fronts. At the underarms, the fronts are joined to the back and stitches are cast on for the armholes. The body is continued flat, in one piece. Before the ribbing, decreases are worked to nip in the waist slightly. Sleeve stitches are picked up and worked in the round in the cable pattern, with ribbing at the upper sleeve for a smooth line and ending with a ribbed cuff.

DIRECTIONS

BACK

With US 10.5 / 6.5 mm 32–40" / 80–100 cm needles, CO 78 (84, 90, 96, 102) (108, 114, 120) sts with the Long-Tail CO method.

K 3 (3, 3, 5, 5) (5, 7, 7) rows.

Beg working Cable Charts A and B with Rev St St on each side, as foll:
Row 1 (RS): P6 (9, 12, 15, 18) (21, 24, 27), work Cable Chart A starting at row 1, p36, work Cable Chart B starting at row 1, p6 (9, 12, 15, 18) (21, 24, 27).
Row 2 (WS): K6 (9, 12, 15, 18) (21, 24, 27), work Cable Chart B, k36, work Cable Chart A, k6 (9, 12, 15, 18) (21, 24, 27).
These 2 rows set the patt. Cont in patt as est, working the next row of the Cable Chart on each subsequent row, until the completion of row 6.

Begin sloping cables in towards centre back, without changing the st count, as foll:
Row 7 (RS): P to the first set of cable sts, m1l(p), k 14 Cable Chart A sts, ssk (last cable st with next p st), p to last p st bef second set of cable sts, k2tog (last p st with the first cable st), k 14 Cable Chart B sts, m1r(p), p to end. [7 (10, 13, 16, 19) (22, 25, 28) p sts on each side of the cable, 34 p sts between 15-st cables]
Row 8 (WS): K to first set of cable sts, work Cable Chart B, k to next set of cable sts, work Cable Chart A, k to end.
Row 9: P to first set of cable sts, work Cable Chart A, p to next set of cable sts, work Cable Chart B, p to end.
Rows 10–13: Rep rows 8 and 9, twice.
Row 14: Rep row 8.
Row 15: P to the first set of cable sts, m1l(p), k 14 Cable Chart A sts, ssk, p to last p st bef 2nd set of cable sts, k2tog, k 14 Cable Chart B sts, m1r(p), p to end. [8 (11, 14, 17, 20) (23, 26, 29) p sts on each side of the cable, 32 p sts between 15-st cables]
Row 16: Rep row 8.
Rep rows 1–15 once more. [10 (13, 16, 19, 22) (25, 28, 31) p sts on each side of the cable, 28 p sts between 15-st cables]

Break yarn and pl all sts on a st holder or waste yarn.

FRONTS

With RS of back facing and US 10.5 / 6.5 mm 32–40" / 80–100 cm needles, pick up and k 78 (84, 90, 96, 102) (108, 114, 120) sts from the CO edge (1 st per CO st).

K 1 row.

Divide Left Front and Right Front

Next Row (RS): K36 (39, 42, 45, 48) (51, 54, 57), BO 6 sts, k to end.
Pl the 36 (39, 42, 45, 48) (51, 54, 57) sts worked bef the BO on a st holder or waste yarn for the right front. [36 (39, 42, 45, 48) (51, 54, 57) sts for the left front]

LEFT FRONT

Next Row (WS): K to end.

Sizes 4, 5, 6, 7 and 8 only
Next Row (RS): Sl2 wyif, k to end.
Next Row (WS): K to end.

Sizes 7 and 8 only
Rep the prev 2 rows once more.

All sizes
Beg working Cable Chart B framed by Rev St St, with an 8-st Garter Stitch strip and 2-st slipped-st edging at the neck, as foll:
Row 1 (RS): Sl2 wyif, k8, p5, work Cable Chart B starting at row 1, p6 (9, 12, 15, 18) (21, 24, 27).
Row 2 (WS): K6 (9, 12, 15, 18) (21, 24, 27), work Cable Chart B, k15.
These 2 rows set the patt. Cont in patt as est, working the next row of the cable chart on each subsequent row, until the completion of row 14.

Row 15 (RS, Inc): Sl2 wyif, k8, p5, work Cable Chart B row 15, m1r(p), p6 (9, 12, 15, 18) (21, 24, 27). (1 st inc'd) [37 (40, 43, 46, 49) (52, 55, 58) sts]
Row 16 (WS): K to cable sts, work Cable Chart B row 16, k15.

Work another 14 rows as foll:
Row 1 (RS): Sl2 wyif, k8, p5, work Cable Chart B row 1, p7 (10, 13, 16, 19) (22, 25, 28).
Row 2 (WS): K to cable sts, work Cable Chart B row 2, k15.
Cont as est working the next row of the cable st patt on each subsequent row, until the completion of row 14.

Row 15 (RS) (Inc): Sl2 wyif, k8, p5, work Cable Chart B row 15, m1r(p), p7 (10, 13, 16, 19) (22, 25, 28). (1 st inc'd) [38 (41, 44, 47, 50) (53, 56, 59) sts, with 8 (11, 14, 17, 20) (23, 26, 29) p sts after the cable sts]

Break yarn and pl left front sts on a st holder or waste yarn.

RIGHT FRONT

Pl 36 (39, 42, 45, 48) (51, 54, 57) right front sts back onto needles. Join yarn to WS of neckline of right front.

Set-Up Row (WS): Sl2 wyif, k to end.

Sizes 4, 5, 6, 7 and8 only
Next Row (RS): K to end.
Next Row (WS): Sl2 wyif, k to end.

Sizes 7 and 8 only
Rep the prev 2 rows once more.

All sizes
Beg working Cable Chart A framed by Rev St St, with an 8-st Garter St strip and 2-st slipped-st edging at the neck, as foll:
Row 1 (RS): P6 (9, 12, 15, 18) (21, 24, 27), work Cable Chart A starting at row 1, p5, k10.
Row 2 (WS): Sl 2 wyif, k13, work Cable Chart A row 2, k to end.
Cont in est st patt, working the next row of the cable patt on each subsequent row, until the completion of row 14.

Row 15 (RS) (Inc): P to cable sts, m1l(p), work Cable Chart A row 15, p5, k10. (1 st inc'd) [37 (40, 43, 46, 49) (52, 55, 58) sts]
Row 16 (WS): Sl 2 wyif, k13, work Cable Chart A row 16, k to end.

Work another 14 rows as foll:
Row 1 (RS): P7 (10, 13, 16, 19) (22, 25, 28), work Cable Chart A starting at row 1, p5, k10.
Row 2 (WS): Sl 2 wyif, k13, work Cable Chart A row 2, k to end.
Cont as est working the next row of the cable patt on each subsequent row until the completion of row 14.

Row 15 (RS) (Inc): P to cable sts, m1l(p), work Cable Chart A row 15, p5, k10. (1 st inc'd) [38 (41, 44, 47, 50) (53, 56, 59) sts, with 8 (11, 14, 17, 20) (23, 26, 29) p sts bef the cable sts]

JOIN FRONTS AND BACK

Beg at the right front neckline, ready to work a WS row.
Joining Row (WS): Sl 2 wyif, k13, work Cable Chart A row 16, k to end of right front, CO 2 sts, then cont across the back sts on WS as foll: k to first set of cable sts, work Cable Chart B row 16, k28 to next set of cable sts, work Cable Chart A row 16, k to end of back sts, CO 2 sts, cont across the left front sts as foll: k to cable sts, work Cable Chart B row 16, k15. [158 (170, 182, 194, 206) (218, 230, 242) sts]

BODY

Row 1 (RS): Sl 2 wyif, k8, p5, work Cable Chart B row 1, p9 (12, 15, 18, 21) (24, 27, 30), PM, p11 (14, 17, 20, 23) (26, 29, 32), work Cable Chart A row 1, p28 to next set of cable sts, work Cable Chart B row 1, p11 (14, 17, 20, 23) (26, 29, 32), PM, p9 (12, 15, 18, 21) (24, 27, 30), work Cable Chart A row 1, p5, k10.
There are now two m's marking the right and left side of the cardigan.

Row 2 (WS): Sl 2 wyif, k13, work Cable Chart A row 2, k to m, SM, k to next set of cable sts, work Cable Chart B row 2, k to next set of cable sts, work Cable Chart A row 2, k to m, SM, k to next set of cable sts, work Cable Chart B row 2, k15.
Row 3 (RS): Sl 2 wyif, k8, p5, work Cable Chart B row 3, p to m, SM, p to next set of cable sts, work Cable Chart A row 3, p to next set of cable sts, work Cable Chart B row 3, p to m, SM, p to next set of cable sts, work Cable Chart A, row 3, p5, k10.
Rows 2 and 3 set the patt. Cont as est working the next row of the cable patt on each subsequent row, until the completion of row 6.

The next row cont the sloping of the back cables.
Row 7 (RS): Sl 2 wyif, k8, p5, k15 cable sts, p to m, SM, p to next set of cable sts, m1l(p), k 14 cable sts, ssk, p to 1 p st bef next set of cable sts, k2tog, k 14 cable sts, m1r(p), p to m, SM, p to next set of cable sts, k 15 cable sts, p5, k10.
Rows 8–14: Cont as set by rows 2 and 3, working the next row of the cable patt on each subsequent row.

The next row cont the sloping of the back cables and adds 2 sts.
Row 15 (Inc) (RS): Sl 2 wyif, k8, p5, k15 cable sts, m1l(p), p to m, SM, p to next set of cable sts, m1l(p), k 14 cable sts, ssk, p to last p st bef next set of cable sts, k2tog, k 14 cable sts, m1r(p), p to m, SM, p to next set of cable sts, m1r(p), k 15 cable sts, p5, k10. (2 sts inc'd) [160 (172, 184, 196, 208) (220, 232, 244) sts]
Row 16 and Rows 17–22: Continue as est by rows 2 and 3, working the next row of the cable patt on each subsequent row.
Row 23 (RS): Rep row 7.
Rows 24–30: Cont as est by rows 2 and 3, working the next row of the cable patt on each subsequent row.
Row 31 (RS): Sl 2 wyif, k8, p5, k 15 cable sts, p to m, SM, p to next set of cable sts, m1l(p), k 14 cable sts, ssk, p to 1 p st bef next set of cable sts, k2tog, k 14 cable sts, m1r(p), p to m, SM, p to next set of cable sts, k 15 cable sts, p5, k10.
Row 32 and Rows 33–38: Cont as est by rows 2 and 3, working the next row of the cable patt on each subsequent row.
Row 39 (RS): Rep row 7.
Rows 40–46: Cont as set by rows 2 and 3, working the next row of the cable patt on each subsequent row.
Row 47 (Dec) (RS): Sl 2 wyif, k8, p5, k 14 cable sts, ssk, p to m, SM, p to next set of cable sts, k 14 cable sts, ssk, p to 1 st bef next set of cable sts, k2tog, k 14 cable sts, p to m, SM, p to 1 st bef next set of cable sts, k2tog, k 14 cable sts, p5, k10. (4 sts dec'd) [156 (168, 180, 192, 204) (216, 228, 240) sts]
Row 48 (WS): Rep row 2.

Hem

Row 1 (RS): Sl 2 wyif, k8, *p1, k1* to 10 sts bef end, k10.
Row 2 (WS): Rep row 1.
Rep rows 1–2 until the rib measures 3" / 7.5 cm, ending after a WS row.

BO in patt or work a Tubular BO.

SLEEVES

Right Sleeve

With 16" / 40 needles (or longer if using the Magic Loop method) and RS facing, work as foll: Pick up and k 54 (54, 54, 58, 58) (58, 62, 62) sts evenly spaced around the armhole edge (approx. 3 sts every 4 rows), starting from the centre of the underarm CO. PM for BOR.

Rib Rnd: *K1, p1* to end.
Work in 1 x 1 rib as est until rib measures 1.5" / 4 cm.
**

Establish the cable patt as foll:
Rnd 1: P20 (20, 20, 22, 22) (22, 24, 24), work Cable Chart B row 1, p19 (19, 19, 21, 21) (21, 23, 23).
Cont as est, working the foll row of the cable patt on each subsequent rnd, until 3 repeats of the cable chart have been completed. (48 cable rnds)
***

At this point, try on the cardigan to check the length of the sleeve, keeping in mind that the cuff will increase the length by 3" / 7.5 cm. To lengthen the sleeve, cont as set in the cable patt, ending after either a row 8 or row 16 of the Cable Chart.

Dec Rnd: *K2tog, p2tog* to 2 sts bef end, k1, p1. [28 (28, 28, 30, 30) (30, 32, 32) sts]

Cuff

Rib Rnd: *K1, p1* to end.
Work in 1 x 1 rib as est until rib measures 3" / 7.5 cm.

BO in patt using a stretchy BO method or work a Tubular BO.

Left Sleeve

Work as right sleeve until **.

Establish the cable patt as foll:
Rnd 1: P19 (19, 19, 21, 21) (21, 23, 23),

CHART A

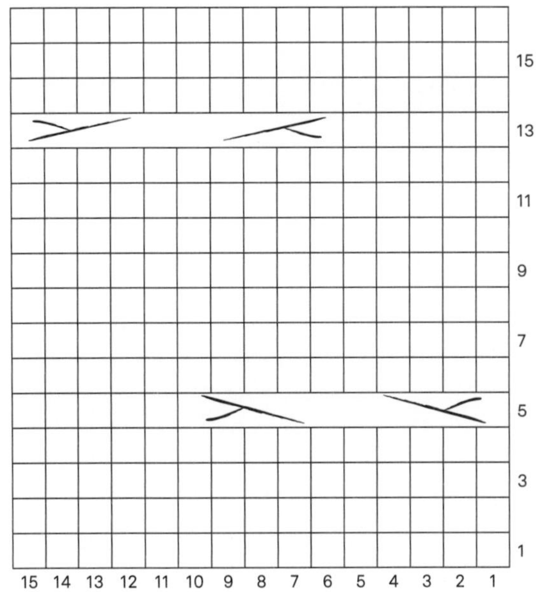

CHART B

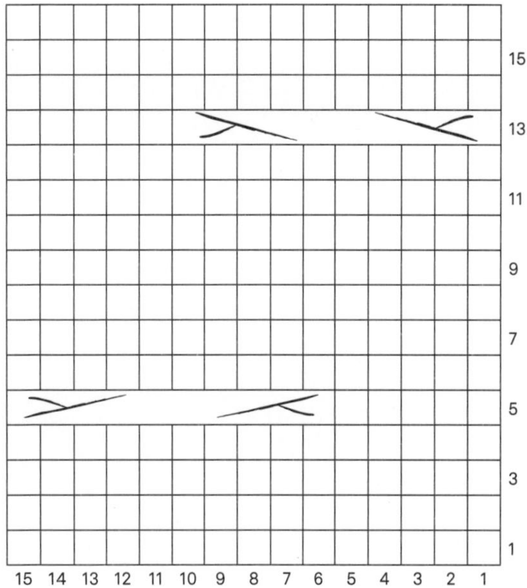

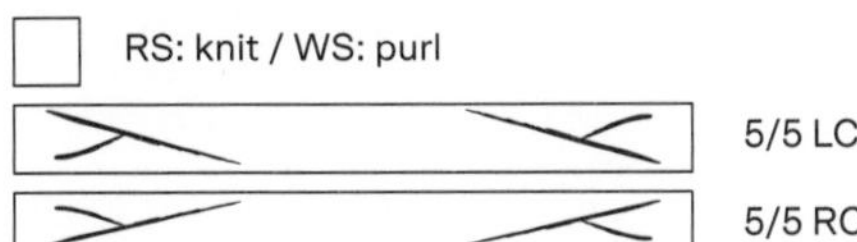

work Cable Chart A row 1, p20 (20, 20, 22, 22) (22, 24, 24).
Cont as est, working the foll row of the cable patt on each subsequent round, until 3 repeats of the cable chart have been completed. (48 cable rnds)
Work as right sleeve from *** to end.

FINISHING

Weave in ends. Block to measurements.

Anna Daku

16 Bud and Blossom

Bud and Blossom's fascinating tuck-stitch pattern mimics crochet but is entirely knitted! The pockets add a great element to this classic and interesting piece.

SIZES

1 (2, 3, 4) (5, 6, 7) (8, 9, 10)

Recommended ease: 6–8.75" / 15–22 cm of positive ease.

FINISHED MEASUREMENTS

Bust Circumference: 36.75 (40.75, 44.75, 48.75) (52.75, 56.75, 60.75) (64.75, 68.75, 72.75)" / 91.5 (101.5, 111.5, 121.5) (131.5, 141.5, 151.5) (161.5, 171.5, 181.5) cm.
Length from Underarm to Hem: 15.75 (15.25, 15, 14.75) (17.5, 16.75, 16.5) (15.75, 18.5, 18)" / 39 (38.5, 37.5, 37) (43.5, 42, 41) (39.5, 46.5, 44.5) cm.
Sleeve Length: 18.5 (18.5, 18.5, 18.5) (18, 18, 18) (17.5, 17.5, 17.5)" / 47 (47, 47, 47) (45.5, 45.5, 45.5) (44.5, 44.5, 44.5) cm.
Upper Arm Circumference: 14.25 (14.75, 15.5, 16) (16.5, 17.75, 18.5) (19.75, 20.25, 21.5)" / 35.5 (37, 38.5, 40) (41.5, 44.5, 46) (49, 51, 54) cm.

MATERIALS

Yarn: 8 (8, 9, 10) (11, 12, 12) (13, 15, 16) hanks of Mule Spinner 3 Ply by Custom Woolen Mills (100% wool, 141 yds / 129 m – 112 g), colourway 01.

Or approx. 1030 (1117, 1203, 1289) (1476, 1596, 1662) (1778, 2028, 2129) yds / 942 (1021, 1100, 1179) (1350, 1459, 1520) (1626, 1854, 1947) m of bulky-weight yarn. Alternative yarn suggestions are for example Briggs and Little Atlantic and Brooklyn Tweed Quarry.

Needles: US 10 / 6 mm and US 10.5 / 6.5 mm 32" / 80 cm circular needles.

Notions: Stitch markers, stitch holders or waste yarn, 6 pairs of extra large snaps (1 1/8" / 3 cm), 100% polyester sewing thread, sewing needle.

GAUGE

12 sts x 13.5 rows to 4" / 10 cm on US 10.5 / 6.5 mm needles in Bud St, after blocking.

13 sts x 26 rows/rnds to 4" / 10 cm on US 10.5 / 6.5 mm needles in Garter St, after blocking.

13 sts x 17 rows to 4" / 10 cm on US 10.5 / 6.5 mm needles in St St, after blocking.

SPECIAL ABBREVIATIONS

k4-below R: Wyib k through the yo below, pl loop on LHN and k, *wyib k through the next yo, pl loop on LHN and k*, rep *–* twice more (4 sts inc'd), k1. Pass first 4 sts over the last st worked (4 sts dec'd).

k4-below L: K1, wyib k through the yo below, pl loop on LHN and k, *wyib k through the next yo, pl loop on LHN and k*, rep *–* twice more (4 sts inc'd). Pass first 4 sts over the last st worked (4 sts dec'd).

Bud St: Wyib k through the right-most yo, pl loop on LHN and k, *wyib k through the next yo, place loop on LHN and k*, rep *–* twice more (4 sts inc'd), k1, *wyib k through the next

yo, place loop on LHN and k*, rep *–* 3 times (4 sts inc'd). Pass 8 sts on RHN over the last st worked (8 sts dec'd).

CONSTRUCTION

This dropped-shoulder cardigan is worked in pieces and features a tuck-stitch pattern on the body and Garter Stitch on the sleeves. The design is finished with pockets, button bands with snaps and a high, folded collar.

DIRECTIONS

BACK

With US 10 / 6 mm needles, CO 57 (63, 69, 75) (81, 87, 93) (99, 105, 111) sts.

Row 1 (RS): K1, *p1, k1* to end.
Row 2 (WS): P1, *k1, p1* to end.
Rep rows 1–2 until work measures 2" / 5 cm from CO.

Change to US 10.5 / 6.5 mm needles.
Row 1 (RS): K4 (1, 4, 1) (4, 1, 4) (1, 4, 1), PM, work Chart A to 4 (1, 4, 1) (4, 1, 4) (1, 4, 1) st(s) bef end, PM, k to end.
Row 2 (WS): P1, k to m, SM, work Chart A to m, SM, k to 1 st bef end, p1.
Rows 1 and 2 have est the Bud and Blossom St patt on the back with 1 St St selvage on each side, and garter edges for some sizes. Work in est patt for a total of 60 (60, 60, 60) (80, 80, 80) (80, 80, 80) rows, or 3 (3, 3, 3) (4, 4, 4) (4, 4, 4) total repeats of Chart A, then work another 10 (10, 10, 10) (0, 0, 0) (0, 10, 10) rows in patt.

Shoulder Shaping

Row 1 (RS): K2, ssk, k to 4 sts bef end, k2tog, k2. (2 sts dec'd)
Row 2 (WS): P2, ssk, k to 4 sts bef end, k2tog, p2. (2 sts dec'd)
Rep rows 1–2, 9 (9, 11, 12) (13, 14, 15) (16, 18, 19) times total, then row 1, 1 (0, 0, 0) (0, 1, 1) (1, 0, 0) more time(s). [21 (25, 25, 27) (29, 29, 31) (33, 33, 35) sts]

BO, break yarn and pull through.

LEFT FRONT

Hem

With US 10 / 6 mm needles, CO 30 (33, 36, 39) (42, 45, 48) (51, 54, 57) sts.

Row 1 (RS): K2 (1, 2, 1) (2, 1, 2) (1, 2, 1), *p1, k1* to end.
Row 2 (WS): *P1, k1* to 2 (1, 2, 1) (2, 1, 2) (1, 2, 1) st(s) bef end, p to end.
Rep rows 1–2 until work measures 2" / 5 cm from CO.

Body

Change to US 10.5 / 6.5 mm needles.

Row 1 (RS): K4 (1, 4, 1) (4, 1, 4) (1, 4, 1), PM, work Chart A (B, B, A) (A, B, B) (A, A, B) to 1 st bef end, PM, k1.
Row 2 (WS): P1, SM, work Chart A (B, B, A) (A, B, B) (A, A, B) to m, SM, k to 1 st bef end, p1.
Rows 1 and 2 have est the Bud and Blossom St patt on the left front with 1 St St selvage on side, and garter edge for some sizes. Work in est patt for a total of 19 rows.

To omit the pocket, proceed to Remainder of Left Front.

Row 20 (WS): P7, k1, p11 (11, 11, 11) (11, 11, 11) (23, 23, 23) sts, kfb, put rem 10 (13, 16, 19) (22, 25, 28) (19, 22, 25) sts on hold on stitch holder or waste yarn for side of pocket. [21 (21, 21, 21) (21, 21, 21) (33, 33, 33) sts]

Front of Pocket

Row 1 (RS): K1, work in est patt to end.
Row 2 (WS): Work in est patt to last st, p1.
Work in patt est in rows 1–2 for 18 more rows (20 rows total), ending after a WS row.

Pl sts on hold on st holder or waste yarn for front of pocket. Break yarn.

Pocket Liner and Side of Pocket

With US 10.5 / 6.5 mm needles, CO 20 (20, 20, 20) (20, 20, 20) (32, 32, 32) sts for pocket liner. Beg and end with a RS row and work in St St for 17 rows.

Next Row (WS): P to end. Keeping pocket liner sts on the RHN, PM, pl side of pocket sts on LHN with WS facing, join and work in est patt to end. [30 (33, 36, 39) (42, 45, 48) (51, 54, 57) sts]

Work another 19 rows in est patt, maintaining St St on pocket liner.

Row 20 (WS): BO all pocket liner sts to m, RM to BO last st, work in patt to end. [10 (13, 16, 19) (22, 25, 28) (19, 22, 25) sts]

Join Front and Side of Pocket

Next Row (RS): Work in est patt to last side of pocket st, sl1 from LHN to RHN, pl front of pocket sts on the LHN with RS facing, sl1 from RHN to LHN, k2tog last side of pocket st and first front of pocket st, thereby joining these pieces, work in est patt to end. [30 (33, 36, 39) (42, 45, 48) (51, 54, 57) sts]

Remainder of Left Front

Cont in est patt until a total of 3 (3, 3, 3) (4, 4, 4) (4, 4, 4) repeats of the Bud and Blossom St patt have been completed since CO, then work another 10 (10, 10, 10) (0, 0, 0) (0, 10, 10) rows in est patt.

Shoulder and Neckline Shaping

Row 1 (RS): K2, ssk, k to end. (1 st dec'd)
Row 2 (WS): P1, k to 4 sts bef end, k2tog, p2. (1 st dec'd)
Rep rows 1–2, 1 (2, 4, 5) (6, 6, 7) (8, 8, 9) more time(s). [26 (27, 26, 27) (28, 31, 32) (33, 36, 37) sts]

Row 3: Rep row 1. (1 st dec'd)
Row 4: BO 6 (7, 6, 7) (8, 8, 9) (10, 10, 11) sts pwise, k to 4 sts bef end, k2tog, p2. [18 (18, 18, 18) (18, 21, 21) (21, 24, 24) sts]
Row 5: K2, ssk, k to 3 sts bef end, k2tog, k1. (2 sts dec'd)
Row 6: Rep row 2. (1 st dec'd)
Rep rows 5–6, 3 (3, 3, 3) (3, 4, 4) (4, 5, 5) more times. (6 sts)

Row 7: Rep row 1. (5 sts)
Row 8: P1, k2tog, p2. (4 sts)
Row 9: K1, ssk, k1. (3 sts)

BO with WS facing.

RIGHT FRONT

Hem

Using 10 / 6 mm needles, CO 30 (33, 36, 39) (42, 45, 48) (51, 54, 57) sts.

Row 1 (RS): *K1, p1* to 2 (1, 2, 1) (2, 1, 2) (1, 2, 1) st(s) bef end, k to end.
Row 2 (WS): P2 (1, 2, 1) (2, 1, 2) (1, 2, 1), *k1, p1* to end.
Rep rows 1–2 until work measures 2" / 5 cm from CO.

Body

Change to 10.5 / 6.5 mm needles.

Row 1 (RS): K1, PM, work Chart A (C, C, A) (A, C, C) (A, A, C) to 4 (1, 4, 1) (4, 1, 4) (1, 4, 1) st(s) bef end, PM, k to end.
Row 2 (WS): P1, k to m, SM, work Chart A (C, C, A) (A, C, C) (A, A, C) to m, SM, p1.
Rows 1 and 2 have est the Bud and Blossom St patt on the right front with 1 St St selvage on side, and garter edge for some sizes. Work in est patt for a total of 19 rows.

To omit the pocket, proceed to Remainder of Right Front.

Row 20 (WS): Work in est patt for 10 (13, 16, 19) (22, 25, 28) (19, 22, 25) sts and put these sts on hold on stitch holder or waste yarn for side of pocket, kfb, p to end. [21 (21, 21, 21) (21, 21, 21) (33, 33, 33) sts]

Front of Pocket

Row 1 (RS): Work in est patt to last st, k1.
Row 2 (WS): P1, work in est patt to end.
Work in patt est in rows 1–2 for another 18 rows (20 rows total), ending after a WS row. Place sts on hold on stitch holder or waste yarn for front of pocket. Break yarn.

Pocket Liner and Side of Pocket

With US 10.5 / 6.5 mm needles, CO 20 (20, 20, 20) (20, 20, 20) (32, 32, 32) sts for pocket liner. Beg with a WS row and work in St St for 17 rows.

Row 1 (RS): K to end. Keeping pocket liner sts on RHN, PM, place side of pocket sts on LHN with RS facing, join and work in est patt to end. [30 (33, 36, 39) (42, 45, 48) (51, 54, 57) sts]

Work another 18 rows in est patt, maintaining St St on pocket liner.

Row 20 (WS): Work in patt to m, RM, BO all pocket liner sts to end.

Break yarn. [10 (13, 16, 19) (22, 25, 28) (19, 22, 25) sts]

Join Front and Side of Pocket

Pl front of pocket sts on LHN with RS facing, in front of side of pocket sts still on LHN.

Next Row (RS): Work in est patt to last front of pocket st, k2tog last front of pocket st and first side of pocket st, thereby joining these pieces, work in est patt to end. [30 (33, 36, 39) (42, 45, 48) (51, 54, 57) sts]

Remainder of Right Front

Cont in est patt until a total of 3 (3, 3, 3, 4) (4, 4, 4, 4, 4) repeats of the Bud and Blossom St patt have been completed since CO, then work another 10 (10, 10, 10, 0) (0, 0, 0, 10, 10) rows in est patt.

Shoulder and Neckline Shaping

Row 1 (RS): K to 4 sts bef end, k2tog, k2. (1 st dec'd)
Row 2 (WS): P2, ssk, k to last st, p1. (1 st dec'd)
Rep rows 1–2, 1 (2, 4, 5) (6, 6, 7) (8, 8, 9) more time(s). [26 (27, 26, 27) (28, 31, 32) (33, 36, 37) sts]

Row 3: BO 6 (7, 6, 7) (8, 8, 9) (10, 10, 11) sts, k to 4 sts bef end, k2tog, k2. [19 (19, 19, 19) (19, 22, 22) (22, 25, 25) sts]

Row 4: P2, ssk, k to last st, p1. (1 st dec'd)
Row 5: K1, ssk, k to 4 sts bef end, k2tog, k2. (2 sts dec'd)
Row 6: Rep row 2. (1 st dec'd)
Rep rows 5–6, 3 (3, 3, 3) (3, 4, 4) (4, 5, 5) more times. (6 sts)

Row 7: K to 4 sts bef end, k2tog, k2. (5 sts)
Row 8: P2, ssk, p1. (4 sts)
Row 9: Ssk, k2. (3 sts)

BO with WS facing.

Wash and block both front pieces and back piece to final measurements. Seam shoulders together with RS facing using Mattress St.

COLLAR

With US 10 / 6 mm needles and RS facing, beg at right front edge and pick up and k 11 (12, 12, 12) (13, 14, 15) (16, 17, 18) sts along right front BO and neckline edge, pick up and k 21 (25, 25, 27) (29, 29, 31) (33, 33, 35) sts along back neck, pick up and k 11 (12, 12, 12) (13, 14, 15) (16, 17, 18) sts along left front BO and neckline edge. [43 (49, 49, 51) (55, 57, 61) (65, 67, 71) sts]

Row 1 (WS): P1, *k1, p1* to end.
Row 2 (RS): K1, *p1, k1* to end.
Rep rows 1–2 until 1 x 1 rib measures 8" / 20.5 cm.

Seam live sts (or BO and seam BO edge) to WS of pick-up edge. Seam each collar fold to itself at front edges.

BUTTON BAND

With US 10.5 / 6.5 mm needles and RS facing, pick up and k approx. 76 (76, 76, 77) (84, 86, 87) (88, 96, 96) sts along the right front edge. Work in Garter St for 2" / 5 cm. BO, break yarn and pull through.

Rep button band instructions for left front.

POCKET EDGING

With US 10.5 / 6.5 mm needles and RS facing, pick up and k approx. 13 sts along the edge of the pocket opening. Work in Garter St for 9 rows. BO, break yarn and pull through.

Work second pocket alike.

SLEEVES

With US 10.5 / 6.5 mm needles, CO 48 (50, 52, 54) (56, 60, 62) (66, 68, 72) sts.

Row 1 (RS): K to end.
Row 2 (WS): P1, k to last st, p1.
Rep rows 1–2 until sleeve measures 16.5 (16.5, 16.5, 16.5) (16, 16, 16) (15.5, 15.5, 15.5)" / 42 (42, 42, 42) (40.5, 40.5, 40.5) (39.5, 39.5, 39.5) cm from CO, while, at the same time, working a dec row every 3rd (3rd, 3rd, 3rd) (3rd, 3rd, 3rd) (2nd, 2nd, 2nd) RS row a total of 14 (14, 14, 14) (15, 17, 17) (19, 19, 21) times as foll: K1, k2tog, k to 3 sts bef

end, ssk, k1. [20 (22, 24, 26) (26, 26, 28) (28, 30, 30) sts]

Change to US 10 / 6 mm needles. Work in 1 x 1 rib (*k1, p1*) for 2" / 5 cm.

BO using the Italian Sewn BO method or a stretchy BO method of choice.

FINISHING

Weave in ends. Block to measurements.

Seam the sides of the garment together, leaving an appropriate armhole depth opening. Seam the sleeve edges together. Seam the sleeves to the armholes. Seam the pocket liner edges to the inside of the cardigan. Seam the front pocket edgings in place.

Mark each button band with 6 equally-placed snap locations using removable stitch markers. Open the snaps, and sew one half to each button band in marked locations.

CHART A

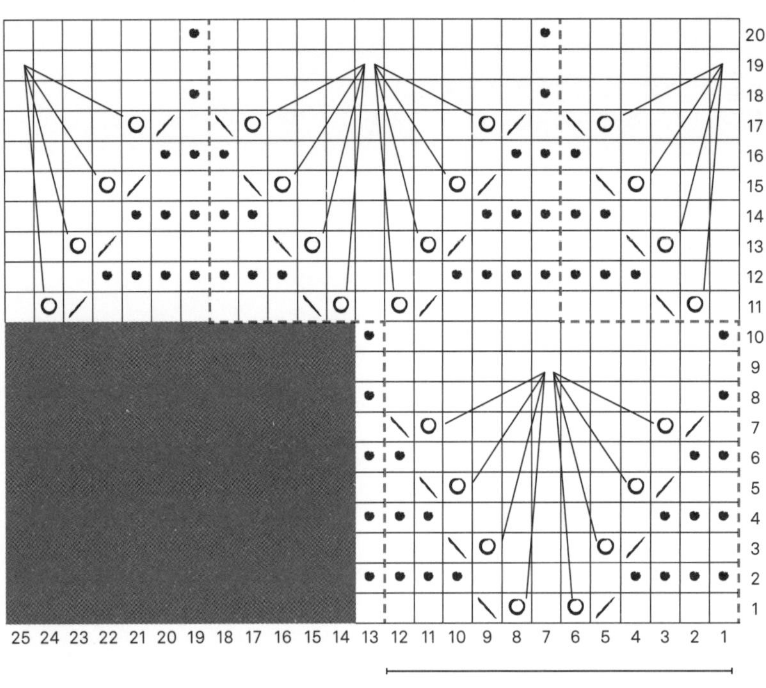

CHART B

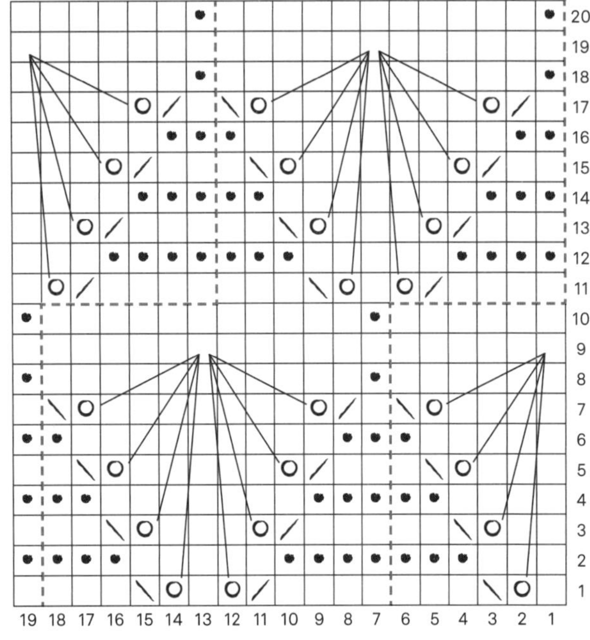

CHART C

20
19
18
17
16
15
14
13
12
11
10
9
8
7
6
5
4
3
2
1
19 18 17 16 15 14 13 12 11 10 9 8 7 6 5 4 3 2 1
12-st repeat

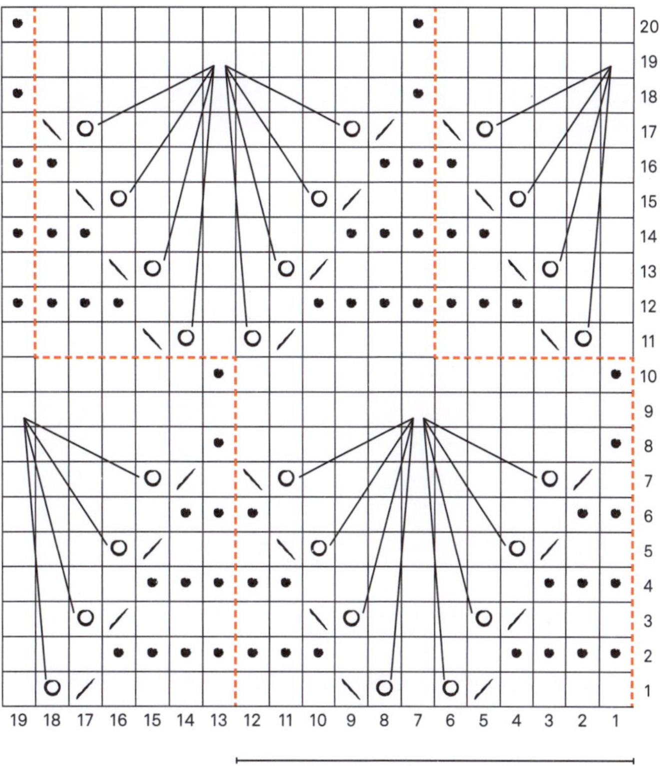

Eliza Hinkes

17 Ceto

Ceto is a roomy drop-shoulder cardigan in a zig-zag lace pattern that changes direction with each stripe. Minimal body shaping and straight sleeves keep the silhouette simple.

SIZES

1 (2, 3, 4, 5) (6, 7, 8, 9)

Recommended ease: 6–9" / 15–23 cm positive ease at chest.

FINISHED MEASUREMENTS

Chest Circumference (Worn Closed): 40.75 (45.5, 50, 52.75, 56.75) (60.75, 65.5, 68.75, 73.5)" / 101.5 (113.5, 123.5, 131.5, 141.5) (151.5, 163.5, 171.5, 183.5) cm.
Length from Underarm to Hem: 13 (12.25, 11.75, 11, 11) (10.5, 10, 9, 8.5)" / 33 (30.5, 29.5, 27, 27) (26, 25, 22.5, 21.5) cm.
Body Length (from Base of Back Neck): 20.75" / 52.5 cm.
Sleeve Length: 16" / 40 cm (3/4-length) or 18.75" / 47 cm (long).
Sleeve Circumference: 14.5 (15.25, 16, 17.5, 18.5) (19.25, 20.75, 22.5, 23.25)" / 36 (38, 40, 44, 46) (48, 52, 56, 58) cm.

MATERIALS

Yarn: Lana Grande by Cascade Yarns (100% Peruvian Highland wool, 88 yds / 80 m – 100 g).
MC: 5 (6, 6, 6, 7) (7, 7, 8, 8) skeins of colourway White.
CC: 3 (4, 4, 4, 4) (5, 5, 5 5) skeins of colourway Navy.

Or approx. 420 (450, 480, 510, 540) (570, 600, 625, 650) yds / 385 (410, 440, 465, 495) (520, 550, 570, 595) m (in MC) and 250 (275, 300, 320, 340) (355, 380, 400, 420) yds / 230 (250, 275, 295, 310) (325, 350, 365, 385) m (in CC) of super-bulky-weight yarn. Alternative yarn options are for example Rowan Big Wool and Katia Genuine Merino.

Needles: US 11 / 8 mm 40–60" / 80–150 cm circular needles (for body) and same size DPNs (for sleeves) (optional, depending on preference), US 10.5 / 6.5 mm 40–60" / 80–150 cm circular needles and same size DPNs (for sleeve cuffs) (optional, depending on preference).

Notions: Five 1.25" / 32 mm buttons, locking stitch markers, waste yarn/ extra circular needles to hold stitches, sewing needle, thread matching MC for buttons.

GAUGE

10 sts and 17.5 rows to 4" / 10 cm on US 11 / 8 mm needles in Lace Stripe patt, after blocking.

14 sts and 20 rows to 4" / 10 cm on US 10.5 / 6.5 mm needles in 1 x 1 rib, after blocking.

STITCH PATTERNS

Lace Stripe Pattern

Flat, for body, worked over multiples of 2 sts.
Beg with MC.
Row 1 (RS): *Yo, ssk* to end.
Row 2 (WS): P to end.
Row 3: K1, *yo, ssk* to last st, k1.
Row 4: P to end.
Rows 5–8: Rep rows 1–4.
Rows 9 and 10: Rep rows 1 and 2 once more.
Change to CC.
Row 11: *K1, sl1* to end. The sts you are slipping are above the dec's.
Row 12: P to end.
Row 13: *K2tog, yo* to end.
Row 14: P to end.
Row 15: K1, *k2tog, yo* to last st, k1.
Row 16: P to end.

Rows 17–20: Rep rows 13–16.
Rows 21 and 22: Rep rows 13 and 14 once more.
Change to MC.
Row 23: *Sl 1, k1* to end.
Row 24: P to end.

Lace Stripe Pattern
In the rnd, for sleeves.
Work as for body, but instead of purling every even-numbered row (WS rows), k every even-numbered row.

SPECIAL TECHNIQUES

One-Row Buttonhole (over 4 sts)
Bring yarn to front, sl 1 pw, bring yarn to back. *Sl 1 pwise, pass first slipped st over second*, rep *–* 3 more times. Pl last st back on LHN. (4 sts BO)
Tw. CO 5 sts using the Cable CO or Backwards Loop CO method.
Tw. Bring yarn to back. Sl first st on LHN onto RHN. Pass last CO st over the slipped st.

NOTES

The body and sleeve lengths are same for all sizes, owing to the large size of the stripes. It is important to check row gauge to be able to determine if the body or sleeve lengths will need to be modified. The ribbing sections can be easily made shorter or longer, if needed.

One 12-row stripe in the Lace Stripe pattern measures approx. 2.75" / 7 cm. If wanting to shorten or lengthen the body or sleeves by this amount, repeat the Lace Stripe pattern rows 23–24 and rows 1–10 (for another MC stripe) or rows 11–22 (for another CC stripe). It is also possible to keep the large stripes proportional by continuing the rib in the same colour as the last stripe.

Note that lengthening the cardigan's body or sleeves will increase the amount of yarn needed. In addition, buttonhole shaping may need to be modified.

There is a single-stitch garter selvage at the armholes, front neck edges and front edges to assist in picking up stitches.

CONSTRUCTION

This cardigan is worked from top down and in one piece. The body is started at the back neck. Once the upper back is worked flat, the back stitches are placed on hold while stitches for the fronts are picked up along the cast-on edge. Once the fronts are completed, the panels are joined and the body is worked flat to the hem, finished with ribbing. Stitches are picked up around the armholes for the sleeves which are worked in the round and finished with ribbing. The button bands are worked along the fronts, and finally, the neckband is worked. The shoulder seam sits behind the shoulder.

DIRECTIONS

UPPER BACK

Using MC and US 11 / 8 mm needles, CO 18 (18, 20, 20, 22) (24, 24, 24, 24) sts with the Long-Tail CO method.

Set-Up Row (WS): K1, p to last st, k1.
Row 1 (RS, Inc): K3, m1l, work row 1 of Lace Stripe patt to 3 sts bef end, m1r, k3. (2 sts inc'd)
Note! As you work the back, incorporate inc'd sts into Lace Stripe patt, working paired dec + yo once having 2 new sts.
Row 2 (WS, Inc): K1, p2, m1r(p), work row 2 of Lace Stripe patt to 3 sts bef end, m1l(p), p2, k1. (2 sts inc'd)
Row 3 (Inc): K3, m1l, cont in Lace Stripe patt to 3 sts bef end, m1r, k3. (2 sts inc'd)
Row 4 (Inc): K1, p2, m1r(p), cont in Lace Stripe patt to 3 sts bef end, m1l(p), p2, k1. (2 sts inc'd)
Rep rows 3–4, 6 (7, 8, 9, 9) (10, 11, 12, 13) more times. [24 (28, 32, 36, 36) (40, 44, 48, 52) sts inc'd] [50 (54, 60, 64, 66) (72, 76, 80, 84) sts]

Pl a locking m at the first and last sts of the last row to assist later in picking up sts for the fronts.

Row 5: K3, work in patt to 3 sts bef end, k3.
Row 6: K1, p2, work in patt to 3 sts bef end, p2, k1.
Rep rows 5–6 until a total of 32 (36, 38, 42, 42) (44, 46, 50, 52) rows have been worked after the set-up row, ending with a WS row. The work measures 7.25 (8.25, 8.75, 9.5, 9.5) (10, 10.5, 11.5, 12)" / 18 (20.5, 21.5, 24, 24) (25, 26.5, 28.5, 29.5) cm. Mark last worked row of Lace Stripe patt.

Cut yarn and pl sts on waste yarn or extra circular needles.

RIGHT FRONT

With CC and US 11 / 8 mm needles, with RS facing pick up and k 16 (18, 20, 22, 22) (24, 26, 28, 30) sts along the right shoulder, starting at the m and finishing bef the initial CO sts for the back neck. RM when finished.

Set-Up Row (WS): K1, p to last st, k1.
Row 1 (RS): K to end. Break yarn and change to MC.
Row 2: K1, p to last st, k1.
Row 3: K3, work row 1 of Lace Stripe patt to 3 sts bef end, k3.
Row 4: K1, p2, work row 2 of Lace Stripe patt to 3 sts bef end, p2, k1.
Row 5: K3, work in patt to 3 sts bef end, k3.
Row 6: K1, p2, work in patt to 3 sts bef end, p2, k1.
Rep rows 5–6, 1 (0, 0, 0, 0) (0, 0, 0, 0) more time(s).

Row 7 (Inc): K3, work in patt to last 3 sts, m1r, k3. (1 st inc'd)
Note! As you work the right front, incorporate inc'd sts into Lace Stripe patt.
Row 8: K1, p2, work in patt to 3 sts bef end, p2, k1.
Now rep rows 5–6 once more, then rep rows 7–8, 1 (3, 3, 3, 3) (3, 3, 3, 3) more time(s). [1 (3, 3, 3, 3) (3, 3, 3, 3) st(s) inc'd]

Row 9 (Inc): K3, work in patt to 3 sts bef end, m1r, k3. (1 st inc'd)
Row 10 (Inc): K1, p2, m1r(p), work in patt to 3 sts bef end, p2, k1. (1 st inc'd)
Rep rows 9–10, 1 (1, 1, 1, 2) (2, 2, 2, 2) more time(s). [2 (2, 2, 2, 4) (4, 4, 4, 4) sts inc'd] [22 (26, 28, 30, 32) (34, 36, 38, 40) sts]

Pl a locking m at the last st on this row at the edge of the neckline shaping to help with buttonhole band placement.

Cont as est in Lace Stripe patt until the same row as finished on at the back.

Cut yarn and move sts to waste yarn or extra circular needles.

LEFT FRONT

With CC and US 11 / 8 mm needles, with RS facing pick up and k 16 (18, 20, 22, 22) (24, 26, 28, 30) sts along left shoulder, starting after initial CO sts for the neck and finishing at m. RM when finished.

Set-Up Row (WS): K1, p to last st, k1.
Row 1 (RS): K to end. Break yarn and change to MC.
Row 2: K1, p to last st, k1.
Row 3: K3, work row 1 of Lace Stripe patt to 3 sts bef end, k3.
Row 4: K1, p2, work row 2 of Lace Stripe patt to 3 sts bef end, p2, k1.
Row 5: K3, work in patt to 3 sts bef end, k3.
Row 6: K1, p2, work in patt to 3 sts bef end, p2, k1.
Rep rows 5–6, 1 (0, 0, 0, 0) (0, 0, 0, 0) more time(s).

Row 7 (Inc): K3, m1l, work in patt to 3 sts bef end, k3. (1 st inc'd)
Note! As working the left front, incorporate inc'd sts into Lace Stripe patt.
Row 8: K1, p2, work in patt to 3 sts bef end, p2, k1.

Rep rows 5–6 once more, then rep rows 7–8, 1 (3, 3, 3, 3) (3, 3, 3, 3) more time(s).

[1 (3, 3, 3, 3) (3, 3, 3, 3) st(s) inc'd]

Row 9 (Inc): K3, m1l, work in patt to 3 sts bef end, k3. (1 st inc'd)
Row 10 (Inc): K1, p2, work in patt to 3 sts bef end, m1l(p), p2, k1. (1 st inc'd)
Rep rows 9–10, 1 (1, 1, 1, 2) (2, 2, 2, 2) more time(s). [2 (2, 2, 2, 3) (4, 4, 4, 4) sts inc'd]
[22 (26, 28, 30, 32) (34, 36, 38, 40) sts]

Pl a locking m at the last st on this row at the edge of the neckline shaping to help with button band placement.

Cont as est in Lace Stripe patt until reaching the same row as for the back and right front. Do not cut yarn.

JOIN FRONTS AND BACK

Transfer the back and right front sts from the waste yarn or extra circular needles onto the working needles, with the left front ready to work first.

Row 1 (RS): Starting with the left front, k3, work in Lace Stripe patt to last st on left front, k1, using the Cable CO or Backwards Loop CO method, CO 2 (2, 2, 2, 4) (4, 6, 6, 8) sts; k1, work in Lace Stripe patt across back to last st, k1, CO 2 (2, 2, 2, 4) (4, 6, 6, 8) sts as bef; k1, work in Lace Stripe patt across right front to last 3 sts, k3. [98 (110, 120, 128, 138) (148, 160, 168, 180) sts]
Row 2 (WS): K1, p2, work in patt to 3 sts bef end (incorporating the newly CO sts into Lace Stripe patt), p2, k1.
Row 3: K3, work in patt to 3 sts bef end, k3.
Row 4: K1, p2, work in patt to 3 sts bef end.
Rep rows 3–4 until about to work the last row of the third repeat of Lace Stripe patt. The work measures 16.75" / 42.5 cm from back neck CO edge.

Change to US 10.5 / 6.5 mm needles, then work the final row.

Hem Rib

Rib Row 1 (RS): K1, *k1, p1* to last st, k1.
Rib Row 2 (WS): K1, *k1, p1* to last st, k1.
Work rows 1–2 in est rib until the rib measures 4" / 10 cm.
Note! The 1 x 1 rib k sts should line up with the dec column sts of Lace Stripe patt. If the hem length has been modified, it's possible that the 1 x 1 rib needs to be worked in *p1, k1* instead.

BO using the Italian Tubular BO method or preferred BO method.

SLEEVES

3/4-Length Sleeve

With CC and US 11 / 8 mm circular needles (for the Magic Loop method) or DPNs, starting in the middle of the sts CO for the armhole, pick up and k 36 (38, 40, 44, 46) (48, 52, 56, 58) sts around the armhole (at a rate of approx. 2 sts per 3 rows). PM for BOR.

Set-Up Rnd: K to end.
Rnd 1: K1, work rnd 13 of Lace Stripe patt to 1 st bef end, k1.
Cont in Lace Stripe patt as est until half of the Lace Stripe patt rep (rnds 13–24) has been worked once, then work the entire Lace Stripe patt a total of 2 times, but stop bef working the final patt row on the final rep.

Change to US 10.5 / 6.5 mm needles and foll instructions beginning with Cuff Dec Rnd.

Full-Length Sleeve

With CC and US 11 / 8 mm circular needles (for the Magic Loop method) or DPNs, starting in the middle of the sts CO for the armhole, pick up and k 36 (38, 40, 44, 46) (48, 52, 56, 58) sts around the armhole (at a rate of approx. 2 st per 3 rows). PM for BOR.

Set-Up Rnd: K to end of rnd.
Rnd 1: K1, work rnd 1 of Lace Stripe patt to 1 st bef m, k1.
Cont in Lace Stripe patt as est until the entire Lace Stripe patt has been worked 3 times, but stop bef working the final patt row on final repeat.

Change to US 10.5 / 6.5 mm needles.

Cuff Dec Rnd: K1 (2, 0, 1, 1) (1, 1, 1, 1), k2tog 0 (0, 1, 2, 4) (3, 7, 8, 7) times, *k2tog, k1* 10 (11, 11, 10, 8) (10, 6, 6, 8) more times, k2tog 1 (0, 1, 3, 5) (4, 8, 9, 8) time(s). [24 (26, 26, 28, 28) (30, 30, 32, 34) sts]

Cuff

Rib Rnd: *K1, p1* to end.
Work in est 1 x 1 rib until the rib measures approx. 2" / 5 cm.

BO using the Italian Tubular BO method or your preferred BO method.

BUTTON BAND

Starting at the m on the left front and using US 10.5 / 6.5 mm needles with RS facing, pick up and k 55 sts along the left front to the end of the hem (at a rate of approx. 2 sts per 3 rows along the rib and 3 sts per 4 rows along the rest of the body).

Row 1 (WS): Sl1, *p1, k1* to end.
Row 2 (RS): K2, *p1, k1* to last st, k1.
Rep rows 1–2, 4 more times, then rep row 1 once more. Button band measures approx. 2.25" / 5.5 cm.

BO using the Italian Tubular BO method or your preferred BO method.

BUTTONHOLE BAND

Starting at the bottom edge of the right front and using US 10.5 / 6.5 mm needles, with RS facing pick up and k 55 st along the right front to the m at the neck edge (at a rate of approx. 2 sts per 3 rows along the ribbing and 3 sts per 4 rows along the rest of the body).

Row 1 (WS): *K1, p1* to last st, p1.
Row 2 (RS): Sl1, *k1, p1* to last 2 sts, k2.
Rep rows 1–2 once, then rep row 1 once more.

Buttonhole Row (RS): Work as est for 6 sts, work One-Row Buttonhole over next 4 sts, *work as est for 8 sts, work One-Row Buttonhole*, rep *–* twice more, work as est to end. (4 buttonholes created)

Rep rows 1 and 2 twice, then rep row 1 once. The buttonhole band measures approx. 2.25" / 5.5 cm.

BO using the Italian Tubular BO method or your preferred BO method.

COLLAR

Starting at the front edge of the buttonhole band and using US 10.5 / 6.5 mm needles, with RS facing pick up and k 2 sts per every 3 rows along the right front, 1 st for every st CO at back neck and 2 sts per every 3 rows along the left front and across the button band. The final number of sts picked up is unimportant, as long as you end up with an odd number and are happy with how the collar sits.

Row 1 (WS): Sl1, *p1, k1* to last 2 sts, p2.
Row 2 (RS): Sl1, *k1, p1* to last 2 sts, k2.
Rep rows 1–2 once, then rep row 1 once more.

Buttonhole Row (RS): Work as est for 3 sts, work One-Row Buttonhole, work as est to end. (1 buttonhole created)

Rep rows 1–2 twice, then rep row 1 once. The Collar measures approx. 2.25" / 5.5 cm.

BO using the Italian Tubular BO method or your preferred BO method.

FINISHING

Weave in ends. Block to measurements.

Sew buttons onto button band and collar, matching up their placement with the buttonholes.

LACE STRIPE PATTERN

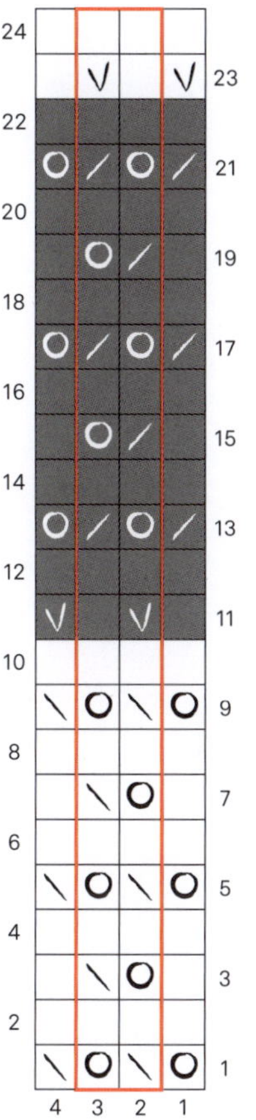

RS: knit / WS: purl
yo
ssk
k2tog
sl 1
MC
CC
lace pattern repeat

Veranika Barel

18 Of the Sea

Of the Sea is a timeless, slightly cropped cardigan. It is perfect for every season – either as a sturdy layer in winter or a coat for chilly weather.

SIZES

1 (2, 3, 4, 5) (6, 7, 8, 9)

Recommended ease: 6–8" / 15–20.5 cm of positive ease.

FINISHED MEASUREMENTS

Bust Circumference (Buttoned Up): 37 (42.75, 46, 49, 53) (56.25, 59.5, 66, 69)" / 93 (107, 115, 123, 133) (141, 149, 165, 173) cm.
Sleeve Length: 20.25" / 50.5 cm.
Upper Arm Circumference: 20 (20, 20.75, 20.75, 21.5) (21.5, 21.5, 22.5, 22.5)" / 50 (50, 52, 52, 54) (54, 54, 56, 56) cm.
Length (from Neckband to Hem): 21 (21.5, 22, 22, 22) (22.5, 22.5, 23, 23.5)" / 52.5 (53.5, 55, 55, 55) (56, 56, 57.5, 58.5) cm.

MATERIALS

Yarn: 11 (12, 13, 14, 15) (15, 16, 18, 18) skeins of Molto Bene by Mondial (80% merino, 20% microfibre, 55 yds / 50 m – 100 g), colourway Beige (676).

Or approx. 581 (651, 706, 735, 784) (824, 854, 941, 982) yds / 531 (595, 646, 672, 717) (753, 781, 860, 898) m of chunky-weight yarn. An alternative yarn option is for example Katia Love Wool.

Needles: US 13 / 9 mm (two pairs) and US 11 / 8 mm 32" / 80 cm circular needles.

Notions: Stitch markers, removable stitch markers, stitch holders or waste yarn, cable needle, 3 x 1" / 25 mm snaps.

GAUGE

8 sts x 14 rows to 4" / 10 cm on US 13 / 9 mm needles in St St, after blocking.

10 sts x 16 rows to 4" / 10 cm on US 13 / 9 mm needles in Slip-St patt, after blocking.

SPECIAL ABBREVIATIONS

sl2tog-k1-p2sso: Sl2, k1, pass 2 slipped sts over. (2 sts dec'd)

STITCH PATTERNS

Slip-Stitch Pattern
Worked flat.
Row 1 (RS): *Sl1 wyib, k1* to end.
Row 2 (WS): P to end.
Rep rows 1–2 for patt.

Worked in the rnd.
Rnd 1: *Sl1 wyib, k1* to end.
Rnd 2: K to end.
Rep rnds 1–2 for patt.

NOTES

While working wyib in Slip-St patt, be sure not to pull the yarn too much.

CONSTRUCTION

This cardigan is worked from the top down featuring a slip-stitch pattern and a button band with snaps. It is started at the neckband using the Double Knitting method. The upper back is worked back and forth. After the upper back is completed, stitches are picked up to shape the front edges and the button bands. These three parts are joined to make the body, which is worked flat. The button bands are knitted simultaneously with the body. Finally, stitches are picked up around the armholes and the sleeves are worked in the round. Both the sleeves and the body are finished with a neat 1 x 1 rib.

DIRECTIONS

NECKBAND

Using the two tips of the US 13 / 9 mm needles, CO 12 sts using Judy's Magic CO method. There should be 6 sts on each needle tip. Facing sts and needle tips looking right, sl the 6 sts from the bottom tip onto a st holder to leave them on hold.

Pull the wire of the circular needle out from the middle of the 6 sts (the same as when using the Magic Loop method) and distribute the 6 working sts so that there are 3 sts on each needle tip.

Pl the two tips of the circular needle on top of each other in parallel and work from both tips at the same time using an additional pair of US 13 / 9 mm needles for the set-up row as foll:
Set-Up Row (WS): *Sl1 wyif from the back needle, k1 from the front needle* to end. (6 sts)
The 6 sts are now joined on one needle and double knitting has been est.

Row 1 (RS): *Sl1 wyif, k1* to end.
Row 2 (WS): Rep row 1.
Work rows 1–2 a total of 17 (19, 19, 19, 21) (21, 21, 25, 25) times. Then, work row 1 once more. Now two ends of yarn are on the same side.

Let the 6 sts from the needle rest on a st holder, but do not break yarn. Sts for both ends of the front bands are left on hold while the back is worked from the side of the band just knitted.

BACK

Cont with the yarn just worked the neck edge with and US 13 / 9 mm circular needles, pick up and k 17 (19, 19, 19, 21) (21, 21, 25, 25) sts along the long side of the neckband where the working yarn end is (pick up at a ratio of 1:1).

Row 1 (WS): P to end.

Start to work in the Slip-St patt and shape the shoulders with inc's. Work inc's on every row.
Row 1 (RS): *K1, sl1 wyib* twice, m1l, *k1, sl1 wyib* to 5 sts bef end, k1, m1r, *sl1 wyib, k1* twice. (2 sts inc'd)
Row 2 (WS): P4, m1r(p), p to 4 sts bef end, m1l(p), p4. (2 sts inc'd)
Work rows 1–2 a total of 7 (8, 9, 10, 11) (12, 13, 14, 15) times. [45 (51, 55, 59, 65) (69, 73, 81, 85) sts]

To make picking up sts later easier, pl a removable m at each edge.

Cont to work flat as foll:
Row 1 (RS): K1, *sl1 wyib, k1* to end.
Row 2 (WS): P to end.
Work rows 1–2 a total of 9 (9, 9, 8, 8) (8, 8, 8, 8) times.

Break yarn. Transfer sts to a st holder.

RIGHT FRONT

The right front is worked back and forth in the Slip-St patt. The button band is worked at the same time in Double Knitting.

Before picking up sts, transfer the sts of the button band to the additional pair of US 13 / 9 mm needles and pull the needle cord in the middle. Pl the two tips of the circular needles on top of each other in parallel. The needle tips should both point towards the shoulder. Using a pair of US 13 / 9 mm needles, join a new yarn and pick up and k 15 (17, 19, 21, 23) (25, 27, 29, 31) sts along the slanting side at the back (pick up at a ratio of 1:1 along the entire slanting section of the back the armhole edge where the m is and towards the neck), PM.

Work sts for the button band as foll:
Set-Up Row (RS): *Sl1 wyif from the back needle, k1 from the front needle* to end. [21 (23, 25, 27, 29) (31, 33, 35, 37) sts]

Row 1 (WS): *Sl1 wyif, k1* to m, SM, p to end.
Row 2 (RS): K1, *sl1 wyib, k1* to m, SM, *sl1 wyif, k1* to end.
Work rows 1–2 a total of 14 (11, 13, 13, 14) (14, 15, 12, 12) times. Work row 1 once more.

Cont to work as est while, at the same time, working inc's on every 5th (RS) and 6th (WS) row as foll:
RS Rows: K1, *sl1 wyib, k1* to 2 sts bef m, m1r, sl1 wyib, k1, SM, *sl1 wyif, k1* to end. (1 st inc'd)
WS Rows: *Sl1 wyif, k1* to m, SM, p2, m1l(p), p to end. (1 st inc'd)
Work inc's 3 (4, 4, 4, 4) (4, 4, 5, 5) times. [27 (31, 33, 35, 37) (39, 41, 45, 47) sts]

Break yarn and transfer sts to a st holder while working the left front.

LEFT FRONT

The left front is worked like the right side but mirrored.

Before picking up sts, transfer the sts of the button band to the pair of US 13 / 9 mm needles. The needle tips should both point towards the shoulder, PM. Join new yarn and pick up and k 15 (17, 19, 21, 23) (25, 27, 29, 31) sts along the slanting side at the back (pick up at a ratio of 1:1 along the entire slanting section of the back from the neck towards the armhole edge where the m is). [21 (23, 25, 27, 29) (31, 33, 35, 37) sts]

Row 1 (WS): P to m, SM, *sl1 wyif, k1* to end.
Row 2 (RS): *Sl1 wyif, k1* to m, SM, *k1, sl1 wyib* to 1 st bef end, k1.
Work rows 1–2 a total of 14 (11, 13, 13, 14) (14, 15, 12, 12) times. Work row 1 once more.

Cont to work as est while, at the same time, working inc's on every 5th (RS) and 6th (WS) row as foll:
RS Rows: *Sl1 wyif, k1* to m, SM, k1, sl1 wyib, m1l, *k1, sl1 wyib* to 1 st bef end, k1. (1 st inc'd)
WS Rows: P to 2 sts bef m, m1r(p), p2, SM, *sl1 wyif, k1* to end. (1 st inc'd)

Work inc's 3 (4, 4, 4, 4) (4, 4, 5, 5) times. [27 (31, 33, 35, 37) (39, 41, 45, 47) sts]

Do not break yarn.

BODY

With US 13 / 9 mm needles and starting with the left front, work as foll:
Row 1 (RS): *Sl1 wyif, k1* to m, SM, work left front sts in est Slip-St patt, CO 1 st using the Backwards Loop CO method, work Slip-St patt as est across back, CO 1 st using the Backwards Loop CO method, work right front sts in est Slip-St patt, SM, *sl1 wyif, k1* to end. [101 (115, 123, 131, 141) (149, 157, 173, 181) sts]. Both fronts and the back piece are now joined.

Row 2 (WS): *Sl1 wyif, k1* to m, SM, p to m, SM, *sl1 wyif, k1* to end.

Cont to work back and forth:
Row 1 (RS): *Sl1 wyif, k1* to m, SM, *k1, sl1 wyib* to 1 st bef m, k1, SM, *sl1 wyif, k1* to end.
Row 2 (WS): *Sl1 wyif, k1* to m, SM, p to m, SM, *sl1 wyif, k1* to end.
Work rows 1–2 a total of 17 (17, 17, 17, 16) (16, 15, 15, 15) times.

Change to US 11 / 8 mm needles.

Work back and forth in 1 x 1 rib as foll while, at the same time, cont working bands in Double Knitting:
Row 1 (RS): *Sl1 wyif, k1* to m, SM, *p1, k1* to 1 st bef m, p1, SM, *sl1 wyif, k1* to end.
Row 2 (WS): *Sl1 wyif, k1* to m, SM, *k1, p1* to 1 st bef m, k1, SM, *sl1 wyif, k1* to end.
Work rows 1–2 a total of 3 (3, 3, 3, 3) (3, 3, 3, 3) times.

Work 2 rows of Double Knitting bef BO, while at the same time, re-arranging right band sts as foll:
Row 1 (RS): *Sl1 wyif, k1* to m, RM, *sl1 wyif, k1* to 1 st bef m, sl1 wyif, RM, *sl1 onto CN and hold in the back of the work, k1, sl1 wyif from CN* rep to end.
Row 2 (WS): *K1, sl1 wyif* to 1 st bef end, k1.

BO using the Italian BO method.

SLEEVES

The sleeves are worked in the Slip-St patt in the rnd.

With US 13 / 9 mm needles and RS facing, pick up and k 50 (50, 52, 52, 54) (54, 54, 56, 56) sts around armhole (picking up at an approx. ratio of 3:4) starting from above the Backwards Loop CO st, PM for BOR.

Start to work in the Slip-St patt:
Rnd 1: *Sl1 wyib, k1* to end.
Rnd 2: K to end.
Cont to work in est Slip-St patt while, at the same time, working dec's on every 6th rnd as foll: sl2tog-k1-p2sso, k to end. (2 sts dec'd) To make a centred dec, work all sts of 5th rnd in the Slip-St patt to the last one bef BOR, then complete dec: the first sl st will be always on top of sl2tog-k1-p2sso. (2 sts dec'd)

Cont working as est until 12 (12, 12, 12, 12) (12, 12, 12, 12) dec rnds have been worked. [26 (26, 28, 28, 30) (30, 30, 32, 32) sts]

Change to US 11 / 8 mm needles.

Rib Rnd: *K1, p1* to end.
Cont to work in est 1 x 1 rib for a total of 6 rnds.

Work 2 rnds of Double Knitting bef BO as foll:
Rnd 1: *K1, sl1 wyif* to end.
Rnd 2: *Sl1 wyib, p1* to end.

BO with the Italian Tubular BO method.

Work second sleeve alike.

SEWING SNAPS

Mark the positions for the button band snaps. Make sure the snaps are evenly spaced. Sew on three snaps both along the left and the right front placket – typically, the male snap part (with the prong) will be placed on the right side of the garment (as worn), and the female snap part (with the indentation) will be placed on the left side.

FINISHING

Weave in ends. Block to measurements.

Sasha Hyre

19 Laeticia

If you don't yet have a duster to snuggle up in, meet Laeticia! Knitted with a lightweight, super-chunky bouclé, it feels as light as a feather.

SIZES

1 (2, 3, 4, 5) (6, 7, 8, 9)

Recommended ease: 12–14" / 30.5–35.5 cm of positive ease.

FINISHED MEASUREMENTS

Chest Circumference (Worn Open): 46.25 (49.5, 55.75, 59, 62.25) (68.5, 71.75, 75, 78.25)" / 117.5 (125.5, 141.5, 150, 158) (174, 182, 190.5, 198.5) cm.
Shoulder Length: 8.5 (9, 9.5. 9.5, 10) (10.5, 11, 11.5, 12)" / 21.5 (22.5, 24, 24, 25.5) (26.5, 28, 29, 30.5) cm.
Armhole Depth: 10.5 (10.5, 11, 11.5, 12) (12, 12.5, 12.5, 12.5)" / 26.5 (26.5, 28, 29, 30.5) (30.5, 31.5, 31.5, 31.5) cm.
Length from Underarm to Hem: 15.5" / 39 cm.

MATERIALS

Yarn: Y1: 6 (6, 6, 7, 7) (7, 7, 8, 8) skeins of Lambkin by A Verb for Keeping Warm (70% highland wool, 30% superfine alpaca, 87 yds / 80 m – 100 g), colourway Apricot.

Or approx. 490 (505, 520, 535, 555) (575, 590, 615, 640) yds / 445 (460, 475, 490, 505) (525, 540, 560, 585) m of super-bulky bouclé yarn. Alternative yarn suggestions are for example Urth Yarns Lanalpaca, Pickles Teddy and Plymouth Yarn Baby Alpaca Ultimo.

Y2: 2 (2, 2, 3, 3) (3, 3, 3, 3) skeins of Horizon by A Verb for Keeping Warm (100% organic New Mexico Rambouillet wool, 160 yds / 146 m – 50 g), colourway Apricot.

Or approx. 260 (280, 305, 340, 365) (390, 420, 445, 480) yds / 240 (260, 275, 310, 335) (360, 380, 410, 435) m of DK or worsted-weight yarn for the rib (to be held double). Alternative yarn suggestions are for example Pickles Soft Merino, Knitting for Olive Heavy Merino and Woolfolk Tov DK, held double. It is possible to also choose a bulky-weight yarn rather than holding a DK or worsted-weight double.

Needles: US 9 / 5.5 mm (to for the ribbing), US 10 / 6 mm circular needles (for the body).

Notions: Scissors, stitch markers (some removable), waste yarn or stitch holders.

GAUGE

10 sts x 16 rows to 4" / 10 cm on US 10 / 6 mm needles in St St, after blocking in Y1.

12 sts x 18 rows to 4" / 10 cm on US 9 / 5.5 mm needles in 2 x 2 rib, after blocking in Y2.

NOTES

Take into consideration that pocket placement is affected if modifying length.

CONSTRUCTION

This duster is knitted from the top down. It starts at the neckline where stitches are increased on either side of the shoulder seam for the fronts and back. The two fronts and the back are worked separately until the chest dimensions are reached. Then, the work is rejoined and the body is worked to desired length. The rib is worked at the front opening and around the armhole at the end with short rows shaping around the collar. Pockets are added at the end.

DIRECTIONS

NECK

With US 10 / 6 mm needles, Y1 and the Long-Tail CO method, CO 26 (26, 28, 28, 28) (30, 30, 30, 30) sts.

Next Row (WS): P1, PM, k2, PM, p20 (20, 22, 22, 22) (24, 24, 24, 24), PM, k2, PM, p1.

Row 1 (RS): K1, m1r, SM, p2, SM, m1l, k to next m, m1r, SM, p2, SM, m1l, k1. (4 sts inc'd)
Row 2 (WS): *P to m, SM, k2, SM*, rep *–* once more, p to end.
Row 3: K1, *m1l, k to m, m1r, SM, p2, SM*, rep *–* once more, m1l, k to last st, m1r, k1. (6 sts inc'd)
Row 4: *P to m, SM, k2, SM*, rep *–* once more, p to end.
Work rows 3–4 a further 11 (12, 14, 15, 16) (18, 19, 20, 21) times. [102 (108, 122, 128, 134) (148, 154, 160, 166) sts on your needles: 26 (28, 32, 34, 36) (40, 42, 44, 46) for each front, 46 (48, 54, 56, 58) (64, 66, 68, 70) for the back and 2 sts for each shoulder]

Sizes 1–5 only
Cont to inc sts on the back only.
Row 5 (RS): K to m, SM, p2, SM, m1l, k to m, m1r, SM, p2, SM, k to end. (2 sts inc'd)
Row 6 (WS): *P to m, SM, k2, SM*, rep *–* once more, p to end.
Work rows 5–6 a further 2 (2, 1, 0, 0) (–, –, –, –) times. [108 (114, 126, 130, 136) (–, –, –, –) sts on needles, 26 (28, 32, 34, 36) (–, –, –, –) for each front, 52 (54, 58, 58, 60) (–, –, –, –) for the back and 2 sts for each shoulder]

All sizes
The shoulder length and the width of the fronts has now been achieved. Increases will be worked on the back only and the armhole opening will be worked.

LEFT FRONT

Pl a removable m at the beg of the row. This will serve as the m for the neckline shaping.

Row 1 (RS): K to m, SM, p1. Pl the rem 81 (85, 93, 95, 99) (107, 111, 115, 119) sts on a holder or waste yarn leaving m's in place. [27 (29, 33, 35, 37) (41, 43, 45, 47) sts]
Row 2 (WS): K1, SM, p to end.

Cont working in patt until the left front measures 10.5 (10.5, 11, 11.5, 12) (12, 12.5, 12.5, 12.5)" / 26.5 (26.5, 28, 29, 30.5) (30.5, 32, 32, 32) cm from shoulder separation. Make a note of the number of rows worked.

Cut yarn and pl sts on a holder or waste yarn, and leave the m in place.

BACK

Sl 1 shoulder st, the back sts and 1 more shoulder st from the holder onto the US 10 / 6 mm circular needles, leaving the rem 27 (29, 33, 35, 37) (41, 43, 45, 47) sts on a holder or waste yarn. With the RS facing you are ready to cont knitting. [54 (56, 60, 60, 62) (66, 68, 70, 72) sts]

All sizes except size 1
Row 1 (RS): P1, SM, m1l, k to m, m1r, SM, p1. (2 sts inc'd)
Row 2 (WS): K1, SM, p to m, SM, k1.
Work rows 1–2 a further – (0, 2, 4, 5) (7, 8, 9, 10) times. [54 (58, 66, 70, 74) (82, 86, 90, 94) sts]

All sizes
Cont working in patt until the back measures 10.5 (10.5, 11, 11.5, 12) (12, 12.5, 12.5, 12.5)" / 26.5 (26.5, 28, 29, 30.5) (30.5, 32, 32, 32) cm from shoulder separation. Match the number of rows worked for the left front.

Cut yarn and pl sts on a holder or waste yarn, and leave m's in place.

RIGHT FRONT

Slip rem 27 (29, 33, 35, 37) (41, 43, 45, 47) sts from the holder back onto US 10 / 6 mm needles, and with the RS facing prepare to continue your knitting. Pl a removable m at the neck edge. This will serve as the other m for the neckline shaping.

Row 1 (RS): P1, SM, k to end.
Row 2 (WS): P to m, SM, k1.
Cont working in patt until the right front measures 10.5 (10.5, 11, 11.5, 12) (12, 12.5, 12.5, 12.5)" / 26.5 (26.5, 28, 29, 30.5) (30.5, 32, 32, 32) cm from shoulder separation. Match the number of rows worked for the left front and the back.

Do not break yarn.

BODY

Rejoin the 54 (58, 66, 70, 74) (82, 86, 90, 94) back and 27 (29, 33, 35, 37) (41, 43, 45, 47) left front sts on needles, keeping m's in place and ready to work the body. The 2 shoulder sts now become the faux side seams for the remainder of the body. [108 (116, 132, 140, 148) (164, 172, 180, 188) sts]

First row will be a WS row.

Row 1 (WS): *P to m, SM, k2, SM*, rep *–* once more, p to end.
Row 2 (RS): *K to m, SM, p2, SM*, rep *–* once more, k to end.
Rep rows 1–2 until the body measures 14" / 35.5 cm from joining row, or 1.5" / 4 cm less than desired length, ending after a RS row.

HEM

Change to US 9 / 5.5 mm needles and Y2 to work the rib.

Set-Up Row (WS): *P to m, RM, p2tog, RM*, rep *–* once more, p to end. (2 sts dec'd) [106 (114, 130, 138, 146) (162, 170, 178, 186) sts]

Rib Row 1 (RS): *K2, p2* to 2 sts bef end, k2.
Rib Row 2 (WS): *P2, k2* to 2 sts bef end, p2
Cont to rep rows 1–2 for 2 x 2 rib until the hem rib measures 1.5" / 4 cm, or until desired length.

BO in patt.

ARMHOLE RIB

With US 9 / 5.5 mm needles, Y2 and the RS facing, pick up and k 3 out of 4 sts from the arm opening to work the rib, making sure the final st count is a multiple of 4. Join for working in the rnd. PM for BOR. [64 (64, 68, 68, 72) (72, 76, 76, 76) sts]

Rib Rnd: *K2, p2* to end.
Cont to work in est 2 x 2 rib until it measures 1" / 2.5 cm, or desired length.

BO in patt.

FRONT BAND

In this section, a rib is worked along the front opening and the neckline with Y2. Short row shaping is also worked around the neck.

Step 1: With US 9 / 5.5 mm needles, Y2 and the RS facing, and starting at the bottom right hem, pick up and k 3 out of every 4 sts evenly on the right front up to the marked stitch, making sure to have a multiple of 4 sts. [78 (78, 78, 82) (82, 82, 86) (86, 86, 86) sts]
Step 2: Remove the removable m and pl it on your needle, pick up and k 3 out of every 4 sts evenly around the neckline to the next marked st, making sure to have a multiple of 4 + 2 sts in this section. [90 (94, 102, 102, 106) (110, 114, 118, 122) sts]
Step 3: Remove the removable m and pl it on your needle, pick up and k 3 out of every 4 sts evenly on the left front to the end, making sure to have a multiple of 4 sts in this section. [78 (78, 78, 82) (82, 82, 86) (86, 86, 86) sts]

[246 (250, 258, 266, 270) (274, 286, 290, 292) sts]

Short Row 1 (WS): *P2, k2* to m, SM, *p2, k2*, rep *–* to 2 sts bef next m, p2, SM, w&t.
Short Row 2 (RS): SM, *k2, p2* to 2 sts bef next m, k2, SM, w&t.
Short Row 3: Cont in patt to 4 sts bef last w&t, w&t.
Short Row 4: Cont in patt to 4 sts bef last w&t, w&t.
Work rows 3–4 a further 2 (2, 2, 3, 3) (3, 4, 4, 4) times. [4 (4, 4, 5, 5) (5, 6, 6, 6) wrapped sts on either side of the neckline]

Next Row (WS): Work in patt and resolve the wrapped sts as you come to them to m, RM, *k2, p2* to end.
Next Row (RS): Work in patt and resolve the wrapped sts as you come to them to m, RM, work in patt to end.

Rib Row 1 (WS): *P2, k2* to 2 sts bef end, p2.
Rib Row 2 (RS): *K2, p2* to 2 sts bef end, k2.
Work rows 1–2 for 2 x 2 rib once more.

BO in patt.

POCKETS

With US 10 / 6 mm needles and Y1, CO 27 (29, 33, 35, 37) (41, 43, 45, 47) sts.

Work in St St until pocket measures 6" / 15 cm.

Right Pocket

Next Row (RS): K to last 2 sts, k2tog. (1 st dec'd)
Next Row (WS): P2tog, p to end. (1 st dec'd)
Rep the last 2 rows until 1 st rem. Cut yarn and pull tail through the last st.

Cont to Rib.

Left Pocket

With US 10 / 6 mm needles and Y1, CO 27 (29, 33, 35, 37) (41, 43, 45, 47) sts.

Work in St St until pocket measures 6" / 15 cm.

Next Row (RS): K2tog tbl, k to end. (1 st dec'd)
Next Row (WS): P to last 2 sts, p2tog. (1 st dec'd)
Rep the last 2 rows until 1 st rem. Cut yarn and pull tail through the last st.

Rib

With the WS facing and using Y2, switch to US 9 / 5.5 mm needles and pick up and k each st along the diagonal edge, making sure you have a multiple of 4 sts plus 2. [30 (30, 34, 38, 38) (42, 42, 46, 50) sts]

Rib Row 1 (RS): *K2, p2* to end.
Rib Row 2 (WS): *P2, k2* to end.
2 x 2 rib should measure 0.5" / 1 cm.

BO in patt. Cut yarn.

Attaching Pockets

See diagram for pocket placement.

Line up right pocket with right front, with the bottom edge approx. 3.75" / 9.5 cm above the hem, the shorter side next to the faux side seam and the long side next to the front band (see illustration). The short side is approx. 3.5" / 9 cm below the underarm.

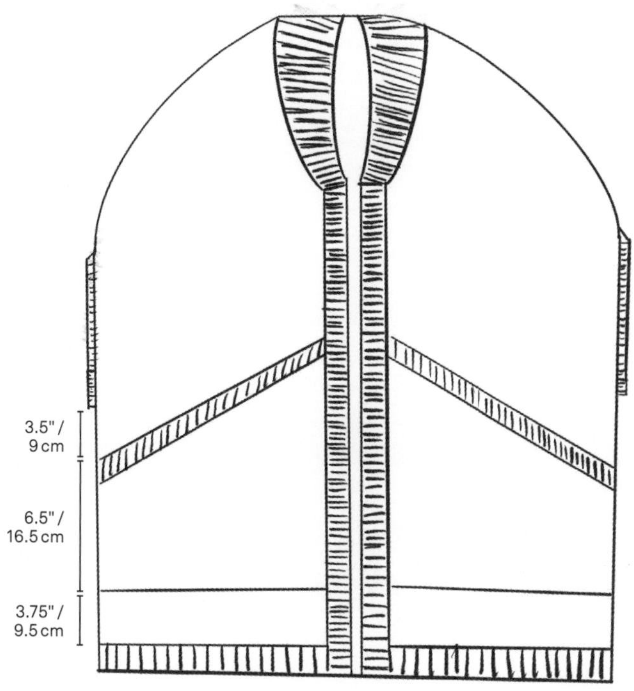

Ensure that you have a straight line across for the bottom of the pocket. With a tail of DK-weight yarn approx. twice the length of 3 sides of the pocket, begin seaming from the top point around to the lower point of the pocket opening.

Rep for the left pocket and the left front.

FINISHING

Weave in your ends. Wet or steam block to measurements.

20

Vests & Slipovers

Rastus Hsu — Thea Vesterby — Cata Rubke — Vivian Wei

Megumi Shinagawa — Kare Peacock — Sara Ottosson

Rastus Hsu

20 Jorvin

This bouclé slipover is inspired by city landscape and architecture. Stranded colourwork and 1/1 cables echo the lines of a building with large, steel-framed windows.

SIZES

1 (2, 3, 4, 5) (6, 7, 8)

Recommended ease: 8" / 20.5 cm of positive ease.

FINISHED MEASUREMENTS

Chest Circumference: 39.25 (44, 48.75, 53.5, 58) (63, 67.75, 72.5)" / 99.5 (112, 124, 136, 147.5) (160, 172, 184) cm.
Length from Underarm to Hem (not Including Armbands): 17.5" / 44.5 cm.
Armhole Depth: 8.25 (8.75, 9.25, 10, 10.5) (11, 11.75, 12.25)" / 20.5 (22, 23, 25, 26.5) (27.5, 29.5, 30.5) cm.

MATERIALS

Yarn: Flette Bulky by Woolfolk (100% Ovis 21 Ultimate Merino®, 131 yds / 120 m – 100 g).
MC: 3 (3, 3, 4, 4) (4, 5, 5) skeins of colourway FB14.
CC: 3 (3, 4, 4, 4) (5, 5, 6) skeins of colourway FB15.
Or approx. 286 (328, 373, 422, 471) (519, 576, 629) yds / 262 (300, 341, 387, 431) (476, 527, 576) m (in MC) and 353 (393, 437, 484, 527) (573, 625, 673) yds / 323 (360, 400, 443, 483) (525, 573, 616) m (in CC) of bulky-weight yarn. Alternative yarn suggestions are for example Daruma Loop and Gepard Garn Teddy Dear.

Needles: US 10 / 6 mm 16" / 40 cm and 32" / 80 cm circular needles, US 11 / 8 mm 32" / 80 cm circular needles.

Notions: Stitch markers.

GAUGE

13.5 sts x 13.5 rows to 4" / 10 cm on US 11 / 8 mm needles in charted patt, after blocking.

12 sts x 16 rows to 4" / 10 cm on US 10 / 6 mm needles in 1 x 1 rib, after blocking.

SPECIAL ABBREVIATION

2C-1/1 RC: Insert the RHN into the first 2 sts on the LHN as if to k2tog, with CC, wrap the yarn and k2tog without sliding them off, insert the RHN into the first st kwise, with MC, wrap the yarn to k it and remove both sts off the LHN.

2C-1/1 LC: Sl 2 sts kwise separately from LHN to RHN, return both sts to the LHN in the new orientation, working behind the first st on LHN insert the RHN into the second st of the LHN tbl, with MC, wrap the yarn to k it and leave this st on the needle, insert the RHN into the first 2 sts of the LHN tbl, with CC, wrap the yarn and k both sts tog, slide them off the LHN.

CONSTRUCTION

This textured slipover is knitted from the bottom up. It is worked flat, in pieces and features stranded colourwork and 1/1 cables. After seaming both sides and the shoulders, stitches are picked up for the neckband and armbands.

DIRECTIONS

BACK

With CC and US 10 / 6 mm 32" / 80 cm needles, using the Alternating CO method, CO 62 (68, 76, 84, 90) (98, 104, 112) sts as foll: K1, *k1, p1* to 1 st left to CO, k1.

Hem

Row 1 (WS): K1, *k1, p1* to 1 st bef end, k1.
Row 2 (RS): K1, *k1, p1* to 1 st bef end, k1.
Work rows 1–2, 6 times in total.

Change to US 11 / 8 mm 32" / 80 cm needles.

Inc row (WS): K1, *p10 (8, 9, 10, 8) (9, 8, 9), m1r(p)*, rep *–* 6 (6, 6, 6, 2) (4, 6, 10) times in total, *p – (9, 10, 11, 9) (10, 9, 10), m1r(p)*, rep *–* – (2, 2, 2, 8) (6, 6, 2) times in total, k1. [6 (8, 8, 8, 10) (10, 12, 12) sts inc'd] [68 (76, 84, 92, 100) (108, 116, 124) sts]

Body

Note! Knit the first and the last st of every row with CC for the garter selvage st.

Work the chart as foll:
Odd Rows (RS): K1, work the chart from right to left, k1.
Even Rows (WS): K1, work the chart from left to right, k1.
Work rows 1–16 of chart 3 times in total. (48 rows worked for all sizes)

Armhole BO

Note! Cont working in est patt while working on armholes and back neck shaping. Selvage sts and BOs are worked in CC.

BO 4 sts at beg of the next 2 rows. BO 3 sts at the beg of next 2 (2, 2, 2, 4) (4, 4, 6) rows. BO 2 sts at the beg of next 2 (2, 2, 4, 4) (4, 6, 6) rows. [50 (58, 66, 70, 72) (80, 84, 86) sts]

Armhole Shaping

Sizes 2, 3, 4, 5, 6, 7 and 8 only
Row 1 (RS): K1, k2tog, cont in est patt to 3 sts bef end, ssk, k1. (2 sts dec'd)
Row 2 (WS): K1, cont in est patt to 1 st bef end, k1.
Work rows 1–2, – (1, 5, 6, 6) (10, 9, 10) time(s) total. [50 (56, 56, 58, 60) (60, 66, 66) sts]

All sizes
Cont in est patt for another 16 (16, 10, 8, 8) (2, 4, 2) rows.

Back Neck BO

Row 1 (RS): K1, cont in est patt for 16 (18, 18, 18, 18) (18, 20, 20) sts. Using CC, BO 16 (18, 18, 20, 22) (22, 24, 24) sts. Join new ball of MC yarn, cont in est patt for 16 (18, 18, 18, 18) (18, 20, 20) sts, k1.

[17 (19, 19, 19, 19) (19, 21, 21) sts for each side of the shoulder.] Work each shoulder separately.

Left Neck Shaping

Row 2 (WS): K1, cont in est patt to 1 st bef end, k1.
Row 3: K1, ssk, cont in est patt to 1 st bef end, k1. (1 st dec'd) [16 (18, 18, 18, 18) (18, 20, 20) sts]
Rows 4–6: K1, cont in est patt to 1 st bef end, k1.

Cut MC. Using CC, BO all sts.

Right Neck Shaping

With WS facing, rejoin CC yarn.
Row 2 (WS): K1, cont in est patt to 1 st bef end, k1.
Row 3: K1, cont in est patt to 3 sts bef end, k2tog, k1. (1 st dec'd) [16 (18, 18, 18, 18) (18, 20, 20) sts]
Rows 4–6: K1, cont in est patt to 1 st bef end, k1.

Cut MC, using CC, BO all sts.

FRONT

Work as Back to Armhole Shaping. [50 (58, 66, 70, 72) (80, 84, 86) sts]

PM for neck placement after the 19th (23rd, 27th, 28th, 28th) (32nd, 34th, 35th) and 31st (35th, 39th, 42nd, 44th) (48th, 50th, 51st) st.

Armhole Shaping

Sizes 2, 3, 4, 5, 6, 7 and 8 only
Row 1 (RS): K1, k2tog, cont in est patt to 3 sts bef end, ssk, k1. (2 sts dec'd)
Row 2 (WS): K1, cont in est patt to 1 st bef end, k1.
Work rows 1–2, – (1, 5, 6, 6) (7, 8, 8) time(s) in total. [50 (56, 56, 58, 60) (66, 68, 70) sts]

Sizes 1, 2, 3, 4, 5, 6 only
Cont in est patt for another 10 (10, 2, 2, 2) (–, –, –) rows.

Sizes 7, 8, 9 only
Rep rows 1–2 of armhole shaping a further – (–, –, –, –) (3, 1, 2) time(s) AT THE SAME TIME proceeding to work Front Neck BO and shaping.

Front Neck BO

Row 1 (RS): K1, cont in est patt to the first m, RM, BO 12 (12, 12, 14, 16) (16, 16, 16) sts, RM, join new ball of MC, cont in est patt to 1 st bef end, k1.

Work each shoulder separately.

Front Right Neck Shaping

Row 2 (WS): K1, cont in est patt to the last st, k1.
Row 3 (RS): BO 2 st, cont in est patt to 1 st bef end, k1. (2 sts dec'd)
Row 4: K1, cont in est patt to 1 st bef end, k1.

Row 5: K1, ssk, cont in est patt to the last st, k1. (1 st dec'd)
Row 6: K1, cont in est patt to 1 st bef end, k1.

Work row 5–6, 1 (2, 2, 2, 2) (2, 3, 2) time(s) in total.

Cont in est patt for 6 (4, 6, 4, 4) (–, –, –) rows.

Cut MC. With CC, BO all sts.

Front Left Neck Shaping

With WS facing, join CC yarn.

Row 1 (WS): BO 2 sts, cont in est patt to 1 st bef end, k1. (2 sts dec'd)
Row 2 (RS): K1, cont in est patt to 1 st bef end, k1.
Row 3: K1, ssp, cont in est patt to the last st, k1. (1 st dec'd)
Row 4: K1, cont in est patt to the last st, k1.
Work rows 3–4, 1 (2, 2, 2, 2) (2, 3, 2) time(s) total.

Cont in est patt for 7 (5, 7, 5, 5) (1, 1, 1) row(s).

Cut MC. Using CC, BO all sts.

Block the front and back piece to measurements.

Seam sides and shoulders using mattress stitch.

ARMBANDS

With CC and US 10 / 6 mm 16" / 40 cm needles, RS facing and beg at underarm side seam, pick up and k 62 (66, 70, 76, 78) (82, 88, 92) sts around the armhole opening. PM for BOR.

Rnd 1: *K1, p1* to end.
Cont to work in est 1 x 1 rib for 6 rnds in total.

BO in patt.

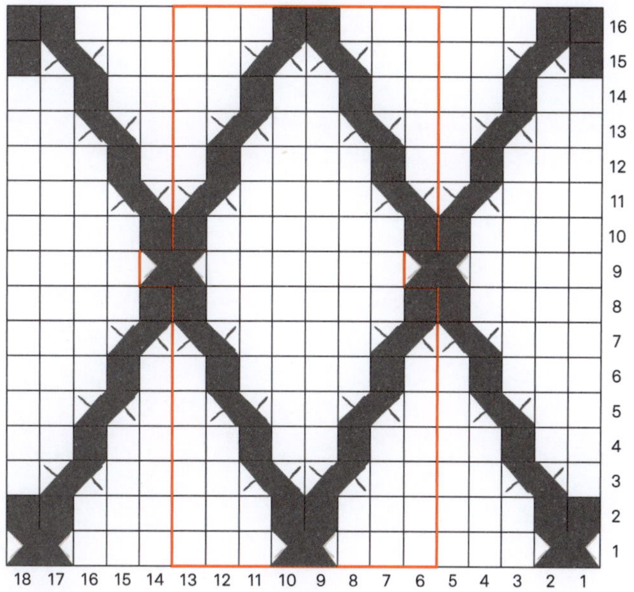

RS: knit with MC / WS: purl with MC

RS: knit with CC / WS: purl with CC

2C-1/1 LC

2C-1/1 RC

1/1 LC with CC

pattern repeat

NECKBAND

With RS facing and beg at the back right BO edge, using CC and US 10 / 6 mm 16" / 40 cm needles, pick up and k 17 (18, 19, 21, 22) (22, 23, 24) sts along back neck BO line, 7 sts along back left shoulder drop, 12 sts along the front left neckline, 9 (10, 11, 11, 12) (12, 13, 14) sts along front neck BO line, 12 sts along the front right neckline and 7 sts along back right shoulder drop. PM for BOR. [64 (66, 68, 70, 72) (72, 74, 76) sts]

Rib Rnd: *K1, p1* to end.
Cont to work in est 1 x 1 rib for 26 rnds in total.

BO in patt.

FINISHING

Weave in ends. Steam block the armbands and neckband.

Thea Vesterby

21 Cable Blur

Cable Blur is a warm slipover covered with elaborate texture. It features a centred cable pattern on the front and back, bordered by smaller cables.

SIZES

1 (2, 3, 4, 5) (6, 7, 8, 9, 10)

Recommended ease: 4–6" / 10–15 cm of positive ease.

FINISHED MEASUREMENTS

Chest Circumference: 30.75 (34, 39.5, 42.25, 45) (47.75, 50.5, 53.25, 56, 59)" / 78 (86.5, 100.5, 107.5, 114.5) (121.5, 128.5, 135.5, 142.5, 149.5) cm.
Length (from Back Neck, not incl. Collar): 19.75 (19.75, 19.75, 21.25, 23) (23.5, 23.5, 23.5, 23.5, 23.5)" / 50 (50, 50, 54, 58.5) (59.5, 59.5, 59.5, 59.5, 59.5) cm.
Back Width (incl. Armhole Rib): 17.25 (18.75, 20.75, 22, 24) (24.75, 25.5, 26.25, 27.5, 30.25)" / 44 (47.5, 52.5, 56, 61) (63, 64.5, 66.5, 70, 77) cm.
Length from Underarm: 11.25 (10.75, 10.25, 10.75, 12.25) (12.5, 12.5, 12.5, 12.25, 12.25)" / 29 (27.5, 26, 27.5, 31) (32, 32, 32, 31, 31) cm.
Armhole Depth: 8.25 (9, 9.5, 10.25, 10.75) (10.75, 10.75, 10.75, 11.5, 11.5)" / 21 (22.5, 24, 26, 27.5) (27.5, 27.5, 27.5, 29, 29) cm.

MATERIALS

Yarn: 5 (5, 6, 6, 7) (8, 8, 8, 9, 9) balls of WoolAddicts Fire by Lang Yarns (98% extrafine merino, 2% polyester, 82 yds / 75 m – 100 g), colourway 35.

Or approx. 345 (375, 425, 450, 575) (615, 635, 650, 680, 720) yds / 315 (345, 390, 410, 525) (560, 580, 595, 620, 650) m of super-bulky-weight yarn. Alternative yarn suggestions are for example We Are Knitters The Wool and Katia Big Merino.

Needles: US 11 / 8 mm (for body) and US 9 / 5.5 mm (for neckline and rib on body) 32–40" / 80–100 cm circular needles.

Notions: Stitch markers, waste yarn or stitch holders.

GAUGE

14 sts x 16 rows to 4" / 10 cm on US 11 / 8 mm needles in St St, after blocking.

11.5 sts x 16 rows or rnds to 4" / 10 cm on US 11 / 8 mm needles in Edge Cable, after blocking.

Main Cable (23 sts) = 6" / 15.5 cm.

SPECIAL ABBREVIATIONS

3/3 RC: Sl 3 sts to CN and hold in back, k3, k3 from CN.

3/3 LC: Sl 3 sts to CN and hold in front, k3, k3 from CN.

STITCH PATTERNS

Cable Pattern (Edge Chart)
Worked over multiples of 4 sts.
Row 1 (RS): *P2, yo, ssk* to end.
Row 2 (WS): *P2, k2* to end.
Row 3: *P2, k2tog, yo* to end.
Row 4: *P2, k2* to end.

NOTES

Always work edge stitches as knit stitches.

Cable Pattern

The slipover is worked with a cable pattern in the middle of the front and back pieces (Main Chart). Repeats of a smaller cable pattern (Edge Chart) are worked on both sides of the main cable pattern.

CONSTRUCTION

This slipover features a cable pattern at the centre front and back. The upper back and fronts are worked flat, with front stitches picked up from the back shoulders, and then joined. The body is worked in the round in a cable pattern with a large central cable at the back and front, and finished with a ribbed hem and a stretchy bind-off. Stitches are picked up at the armhole edge, briefly worked in the round in ribbing and finished with a neat, ribbed bind-off. Finally, stitches for the neckline are picked up, then worked in ribbing and finished with a stretchy bind-off.

DIRECTIONS

BACK

With US 11 / 8 mm needles and preferred CO method, CO 15 (17, 19, 21, 21) (21, 21, 21, 21, 21) sts.

Set-Up Row (WS): P3 (4, 5, 6, 6) (6, 6, 6, 6, 6), k2, p2, k1, p2, k2, p3 (4, 5, 6, 6) (6, 6, 6, 6, 6), CO 6 (7, 9, 9, 11) (12, 13, 14, 15, 19) sts using the Backwards Loop CO method. [21 (24, 28, 30, 32) (33, 34, 35, 36, 40) sts]
Row 1 (RS): K1, p0 (0, 0, 0, 0) (0, 0, 1, 0, 0), k0 (2, 1, 2, 0) (1, 2, 2, 0, 0), *p2, k2* 0 (0, 1, 1, 2) (2, 2, 2, 3, 4) times, PM, p2, k6, p2, k2, p1, k2, p2, k3 (4, 5, 6, 6) (6, 6, 6, 6, 6), PM, CO 6 (7, 9, 9, 11) (12, 13, 14, 15, 19) sts as bef. [27 (31, 37, 39, 43) (45, 47, 49, 51, 59) sts]
Row 2 (WS): K1, p0 (0, 1, 0, 0) (1, 0, 0, 0, 0), k2 (0, 2, 0, 2) (2, 0, 1, 2, 2), *p2, k2* 0 (1, 1, 2, 2) (2, 3, 3, 3, 4) times, SM, work row 2 of Chart 1 across next 23 sts, SM, *p2, k2* 0 (0, 1, 1, 2) (2, 2, 2, 3, 4) times, p0 (2, 1, 2, 0) (1, 2, 2, 0, 0), k0 (0, 0, 0, 0) (0, 0, 1, 0, 0), k1.
Row 3 (RS): K1, k0 (0, 1, 0, 0) (1, 2, 0, 0, 0), p0 (0, 0, 0, 0) (0, 0, 1, 0, 0), *k2tog, yo* 0 (1, 0, 1, 0) (0, 0, 1, 0, 0) times, *work row 3 of Edge Chart* 0 (0, 1, 1, 2) (2, 2, 2, 3, 4) times, SM, work row 3 of Main Chart, SM, *work row 3 of Edge Chart* 0 (1, 1, 2, 2) (2, 2, 3, 3, 4) times, p2 (0, 2, 0, 2) (2, 2, 1, 2, 2), k0 (0, 1, 0, 0) (1, 2, 0, 1, 0), k1.
Row 4 (WS): K1, p0 (0, 1, 0, 0) (1, 0, 0, 0, 0), k2 (0, 2, 0, 2) (2, 0, 1, 2, 2), *work row 4 of Edge Chart* 0 (1, 1, 2, 2) (2, 3, 3, 3, 4) times, SM, work row 4 of Main Chart, SM, *work row 4 of Edge Chart* 0 (0, 1, 1, 2) (2, 2, 2, 3, 4) times, p0 (2, 1, 2, 0) (0, 2, 2, 0, 0), k0 (0, 0, 0, 0) (0, 0, 1, 0, 0), k1.

[27 (31, 37, 39, 43) (45, 47, 49, 51, 59) sts]

It may be helpful to pl a m after every 4-st rep of the Edge Chart on either side of the 23 sts of Main Chart.

Work as set, with a k1 at each edge, rep any rows 1–4 of Edge Chart, and cont with Main Chart, for 6 (8, 10, 12, 12) (12, 12, 12, 12, 12) more rows, ending after a Main Chart row 10 (12, 14, 16, 16) (16, 16, 16, 16, 16).

BACK ARMHOLE SHAPING

Start to inc on every RS row as foll, inc 4 sts at each side over the 8 rows to add a full rep of the Edge Chart at each side:
Row 1 (RS) (Inc): K1, m1l, work as set to last st, m1r, k1. (2 sts inc'd)
Row 2 (WS): K1, k1, work as set to last 2 sts, k1, k1.
Row 3 (Inc): K1, m1l, p1, work as set to last 2 sts, p1, m1r, k1. (2 sts inc'd)
Row 4: K1, k2, work as set to last 3 sts, k2, k1.
Row 5 (Inc): K1, m1l, p2, work as set to last 3 sts, p2, m1r, k1. (2 sts inc'd)
Row 6: K1, p1, k2, work as set to last 4 sts, k2, p1, k1.
Row 7 (Inc): K1, m1l, k1, p2, work as set to last 4 sts, p2, k1, m1r, k1. (2 sts inc'd)
Row 8: K1, p2, k2, work as set to last 5 sts, k2, p2, k1.

[35 (39, 45, 49, 51) (53, 55, 57, 59, 67) sts]

Cont as est, with inc's on RS rows, for another 6 (4, 2, 0, 0) (0, 0, 0, 0, 0) rows. You have just worked row 24 of Main Chart. [6 (4, 2, 0, 0) (0, 0, 0, 0, 0) sts inc'd]

Cont as est, working inc's for another 10 (12, 14, 18, 20) (20, 20, 20, 22, 22) rows. [10 (12, 14, 18, 20) (20, 20, 20, 22, 22) sts inc'd]

All sizes
[51 (55, 61, 65, 71) (73, 75, 77, 81, 89) sts]
Row 10 (12, 14, 18, 20) (20, 20, 20, 22,

22) of Main Chart has just been worked. The back is now finished. Pl sts on hold and break yarn.

LEFT FRONT

With RS of back facing and the CO edge at the top, start at the left side and count 4 (6, 6, 8, 8) (10, 10, 12, 12, 16) sts towards the middle of the CO edge. PM after the last st. Using US 11 / 8 mm needles, pick up, without knitting, 4 (6, 6, 8, 8) (10, 10, 12, 12, 16) sts starting at the m and ending at the side edge.

Set-Up Row (WS): K1, p0 (0, 1, 0, 0) (1, 0, 0, 0, 0), k2 (0, 2, 0, 2) (2, 0, 1, 2, 2), *p2, k2* 0 (1, 0, 1, 1) (1, 2, 2, 2, 3) times, p0 (0, 1, 2, 0) (1, 0, 1, 0, 0), k1.
Row 1 (RS): K1, k0 (0, 1, 0, 0) (1, 0, 1, 0, 0), p2 (0, 2, 0, 0) (0, 0, 0, 0, 0), *yo, ssk* 0 (0, 0, 1, 0) (0, 0, 0, 0, 0) times, *work row 1 of Edge Chart* 0 (1, 0, 1, 1) (1, 2, 2, 2, 3) times, p0 (0, 0, 0, 2) (2, 0, 1, 2, 2), k0 (0, 1, 0, 0) (1, 0, 0, 0, 0), k1.
Row 2: K1, p0 (0, 1, 0, 0) (1, 0, 0, 0, 0), k2 (2, 2, 0, 2) (2, 0, 1, 2, 2), *work row 2 of Edge Chart* 0 (0, 0, 1, 1) (1, 2, 2, 2, 3) times, p0 (2, 1, 2, 0) (1, 0, 1, 0, 0), k1.
Row 3: K1, k0 (0, 1, 0, 0) (1, 0, 1, 0, 0), *k2tog, yo* 0 (0, 0, 1, 0) (0, 0, 0, 0, 0) times, *work row 3 of Edge Chart* 0 (1, 0, 1, 1) (1, 2, 2, 2, 3) times, p2 (0, 2, 0, 2) (2, 0, 1, 2, 2), k0 (0, 1, 0, 0) (1, 0, 0, 0, 0), k1.
Row 4: K1, p0 (0, 1, 0, 0) (1, 0, 0, 0, 0), k2 (2, 2, 0, 2) (2, 0, 1, 2, 2), *work row 4 of Edge Chart* 0 (0, 0, 1, 1) (1, 2, 2, 2, 3) times, p0 (2, 1, 2, 0) (1, 0, 1, 0, 0), k1.

Neckline Shaping

Next, work neckline inc's on every RS row.
Work as est working prev rows 1–4, and make an m1l inc after the first k1 edge st on every RS row, for 8 (8, 10, 10, 10) (10, 10, 10, 10, 10) rows. [4 (4, 5, 5, 5) (5, 5, 5, 5, 5) sts inc'd]

Note! Take sts into 4-st Edge Chart patt when able to work a full rep, as for the back.
[8 (10, 11, 13, 13) (15, 15, 17, 17, 21) sts]

Row 4 (4, 2, 2, 2) (2, 2, 2, 2, 2) of Edge Chart has just been worked.

Break yarn and pl sts on hold.

RIGHT FRONT

With RS of back facing and the CO edge at the top, start at the right side. With US 11 / 8 mm needles, pick up, without knitting, 4 (6, 6, 8, 8) (10, 10, 12, 12, 16) sts along the CO edge from the side towards the middle.

Set-Up Row (WS): K1, p0 (0, 1, 0, 0) (1, 0, 1, 0, 0), k2 (2, 2, 0, 2) (2, 2, 2, 0, 2), *p2, k2* 0 (0, 0, 1, 1) (1, 1, 1, 2, 3) times, p0 (2, 2, 2, 0) (1, 2, 2, 0, 0), k0 (0, 0, 0, 0) (0, 0, 1, 0, 0), k1.
Row 1 (RS): K1, p2 (0, 0, 0, 0) (0, 0, 1, 0, 0), k0 (0, 1, 0, 0) (1, 0, 0, 0, 2), *yo, ssk* 0 (1, 0, 1, 0) (0, 1, 1, 0, 0) times, *work row 1 of Edge Chart* 0 (0, 0, 1, 1) (1, 1, 1, 2, 3) times, p0 (2, 1, 0, 2) (2, 2, 2, 2, 2), k0 (0, 0, 0, 0) (1, 0, 1, 0, 0), k1.
Row 2: K1, p0 (0, 1, 0, 0) (1, 0, 1, 0, 0), k2 (2, 2, 0, 2) (2, 2, 2, 2, 2), *work row 2 of Edge Chart* 0 (0, 0, 1, 1) (1, 1, 1, 2, 3) times, p0 (2, 1, 2, 0) (1, 2, 2, 0, 0), k0 (0, 0, 0, 0) (0, 0, 1, 0, 0), k1.
Row 3: K1, p2 (0, 0, 0, 0) (0, 0, 1, 0, 0), k0 (0, 1, 0, 0) (1, 0, 0, 0, 0), *k2tog, yo* 0 (1, 0, 1, 0) (0, 1, 1, 0, 0) times, *work row 3 of Edge Chart* 0 (0, 0, 1, 1) (1, 1, 1, 2, 3) times, p0 (2, 2, 0, 2) (2, 2, 2, 2, 2), k0 (0, 1, 0, 0) (1, 0, 1, 0, 0), k1.
Row 4: K1, p0 (0, 1, 0, 0) (1, 0, 1, 0, 0), k2 (2, 2, 0, 2) (2, 2, 2, 2, 2), *work row 4 of Edge Chart* 0 (0, 0, 1, 1) (1, 1, 1, 2, 3) times, p0 (0, 0, 0, 0) (0, 0, 2, 0, 0), k0 (0, 0, 0, 0) (0, 2, 1, 0, 0), p0 (2, 1, 2, 0) (1, 0, 0, 0, 0), k1.

Neckline Shaping

Next, work inc's on every RS row to create the neckline.

Work as est working prev rows 1–4, and make an m1r increase before the final k1 edge st on every RS row, for 8 (8, 10, 10, 10) (10, 10, 10, 10, 10) rows. [4 (4, 5, 5, 5) (5, 5, 5, 5, 5) sts inc'd]

Note! Take sts into 4-st Edge Chart patt when able to work a full repeat.

[8 (10, 11, 13, 13) (15, 15, 17, 17, 21) sts] Row 4 (4, 2, 2, 2) (2, 2, 2, 2, 2) of Edge Chart has just been worked.

FRONT

Join the left and right fronts.

Start working across the right front: K1, work as set to end of right front, CO 11 (11, 15, 13, 17) (15, 17, 15, 17, 17) sts using the Backwards Loop CO method, cont across the left front piece as set, k1. [27 (31, 37, 39, 43) (45, 47, 49, 51, 59) sts]

Next Row (WS): K1, work as est to CO sts, p CO sts, work as est, k1.
Row 2 (2, 4, 4, 4) (4, 4, 4, 4, 4) of Edge Chart has just been worked.
Next Row (RS): K1, work 0 (2, 5, 6, 8) (9, 10, 11, 12, 16) sts, PM, work row 1 of Main Chart over next 23 sts, PM, work 2 (4, 7, 8, 10) (11, 12, 13, 14, 18) sts, k1.
Cont as est for 9 (11, 13, 15, 15) (15, 15, 15, 15, 15) more rows, ending after a WS row. Row 10 (12, 14, 16, 16) (16, 16, 16, 16, 16) of Main Chart and row 4 (2, 2, 4, 4) (4, 4, 4, 4, 4) of Edge Chart has just been worked.

FRONT ARMHOLE SHAPING

Work Armhole Shaping as for the back. [24 (24, 24, 26, 28) (28, 28, 28, 30, 30) sts inc'd] [51 (55, 61, 65, 71) (73, 75, 77, 81, 89) sts]
Row 10 (12, 14, 18, 20) (20, 20, 20, 22, 22) of Main Chart and row 4 (2, 2, 2, 4) (4, 4, 4, 2, 2) of Edge Chart has just been worked.

BODY

Next, the front and back pieces are joined. Work according to size as foll, using the Backwards Loop CO method to CO any sts:
Size 1: K1, pl BOR m, ** *work Edge Chart* 3 times, SM, work row 11 of Main Chart, SM, *work Edge Chart* 3 times, p2, k2tog (working last st of front with first st of back), yo**, rep **–** once more, (working last st of back with first st of front).
Size 2: **P1, yo, ssk, *work row 3 of Edge Chart* 3 times, SM, work row 13 of Main Chart, SM, *work row 3 of Edge Chart* 4 times**, p1, cont across the back, rep **–** once more, pl BOR m, p1.
Size 3: **K2tog, yo, *work row 3 of Edge Chart* 4 times, SM, work row 15 of Main Chart, SM, *work row 3 of Edge Chart* 5 times**, CO 2 sts, cont across the back and rep **–** once more, pl BOR m, CO 2 sts. (4 sts inc'd)
Size 4: ** *Work row 3 of Edge Chart* 5 times, SM, work row 19 of Main Chart, SM, *work row 3 of Edge Chart* 5 times, p2, CO 2 sts**, cont across the back piece and rep **–** once more, pl BOR M. (4 sts inc'd)
Size 5: **P1, yo, ssk, *work row 1 of Edge Chart* 5 times, SM, work row 21 of Main Chart, SM, *work row 1 of Edge Chart* 6 times, p1**, cont across the back piece and rep **–** once more, pl BOR m, p1.
Size 6: ** *Work row 1 of Edge Chart* 6 times, SM, work row 21 of Main Chart, SM, *work row 1 of Edge Chart* 6 times, p2, CO 2 sts**, cont across the back piece and rep **–** once more, pl BOR m. (4 sts inc'd)
Size 7: **K1, *work row 1 of Edge Chart* 6 times, SM, work row 21 of Main Chart, SM, *work row 1 of Edge Chart* 6 times, p2, k1**, CO 4 sts, cont across the back piece and rep **–** once more, CO 1 st, pl BOR m, CO 3 sts. (8 sts inc'd)
Size 8: **K2, *work row 1 of Edge Chart* 6 times, SM, work row 21 of

Main Chart SM, *work row 1 of Edge Chart* 7 times**, CO 6 sts, cont across the back piece and rep **–** once more, CO 4 sts, pl BOR m, CO 2 sts. (12 sts inc'd)
Size 9: ** *Work row 3 of Edge Chart* 7 times, SM, work row 23 of Main Chart, SM, *work row 3 of Edge Chart* 7 times, p2**, CO 6 sts, cont across the back piece and rep **–** once more, CO 2 sts, pl BOR m, CO 4 sts. (12 sts inc'd)
Size 10: ** *Work row 3 of Edge Chart* 8 times, SM, work row 23 of Main Chart, SM, *work row 3 of Edge Chart* 8 times, p2, CO 2 sts**, cont across the back piece and rep **–** once more, pl BOR M. (4 sts inc'd)

All sizes
[102 (110, 126, 134, 142) (150, 158, 166, 174, 182) sts]
The next row of Edge Chart is row 2 (4, 4, 4, 2) (2, 2, 2, 4, 4) and the next row of Main Chart is row 12 (14, 16, 20, 22) (22, 22, 22, 24, 24).
Body Rnd: ** *Work next row of Edge Chart* 3 (4, 5, 5, 6) (6, 7, 7, 8, 8) times, SM, work next row of Main Chart, SM, *work next row of Edge Chart* 4 (4, 5, 6, 6) (7, 7, 8, 8, 9) times, rep **–** once more.
Work as now est for another 11 (9, 7, 3, 1) (1, 1, 1, 0, 0) rnd(s), ending after row 24 of Main Chart.
Then work as est for another 24 rnds, ending after row 24 of Main Chart.

Size 4 only
Work as est for another 6 rnds, ending after row 6 of Main Chart.

Sizes 5, 6, 7, 8, 9 and 10 only
Work as est for another 12 rnds, ending after row 12 of Main Chart.

All sizes
Work the body longer if desired. Work until the body measures 2 (2, 2, 2, 2.5) (2.75, 2.75, 2.75, 2.75, 2.75)" / 5 (5, 5, 6, 6) (7, 7, 7, 7, 7) cm less than desired length.

HEM

Change to US 9 / 5.5 mm needles.

Rib Set-Up Rnd: ** *P2, k2*, rep *–* to central p1 in Main Chart, m1l(p), p1**, rep **–** once more, *k2, p2*, rep *–* to last 2 sts, k2. (2 sts inc'd) [102, 112, 128, 136, 144) (152, 152, 160, 168, 184) sts]

Rib Rnd: *P2, k2* to end.
Work in 2 x 2 rib as est until rib measures 2 (2, 2, 2, 2.5) (2.75, 2.75, 2.75, 2.75, 2.75)" / 5 (5, 5, 6, 6) (7, 7, 7, 7, 7) cm.

BO using a stretchy BO method.

SLEEVES

With US 9 / 5.5 mm needles, start at the centre of the underarm and pick up, without knitting, 80 (82, 84, 88, 90) (90, 92, 92, 94, 94) sts evenly around the armhole. Pl m for BOR.

Rib Rnd: *K1, p1* to end.
Cont in 1 x 1 rib as est until rib measures 0.75" / 2 cm.

BO as foll:
K1, *p1, move both sts back to LHN, pass the second st over the first st; k2tog*, rep *–* to end and fasten off.

Make second sleeve alike.

NECKLINE

With US 9 / 5.5 mm needles, starting at left shoulder with RS facing, pick up, without knitting, 56 (56, 70, 66, 74) (70, 74, 70, 74, 74) sts around the neckline (1 st in every st). PM for BOR.

Rib Rnd: *K1, p1* to end.
Cont in 1 x 1 rib as est until rib measures 1.25" / 3 cm.

BO as bef.

FINISHING

Weave in ends. Wet block to measurements.

MAIN CHART

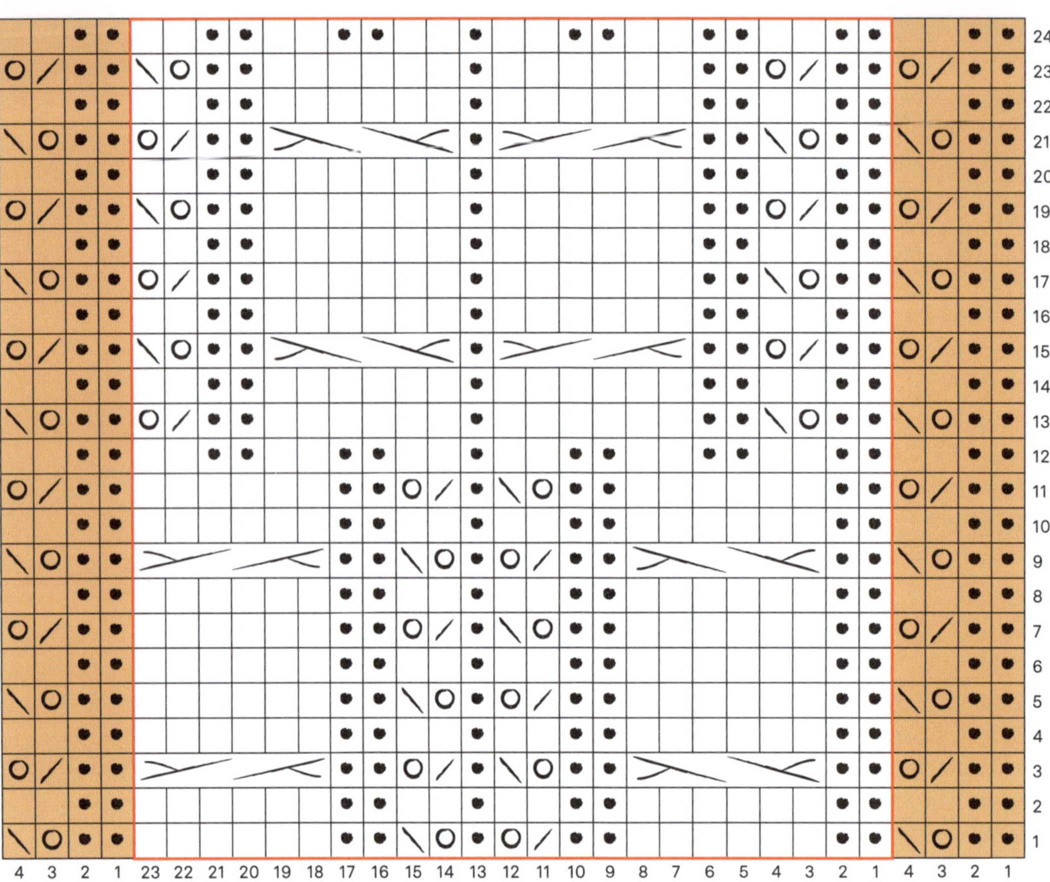

EDGE CHART

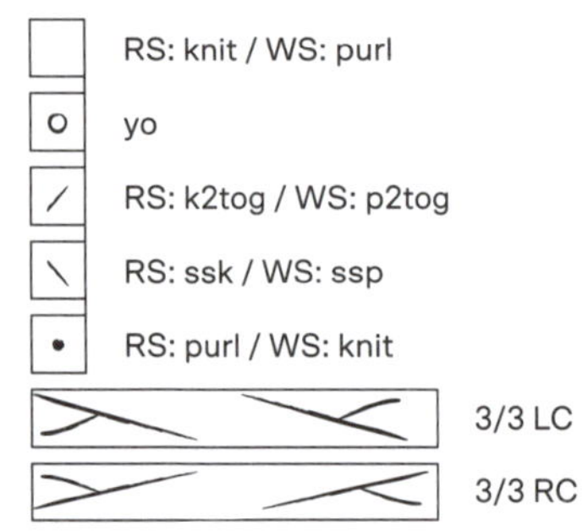

Note! The orange Edge Chart sts shown next to Main Chart are just for illustration. They show how these are worked in combination once working in the rnd.

- RS: knit / WS: purl
- yo
- RS: k2tog / WS: p2tog
- RS: ssk / WS: ssp
- RS: purl / WS: knit
- 3/3 LC
- 3/3 RC

Cata Rubke

22 Diana

Named after the Roman goddess of hunting, the moon and nature, this cabled slipover embodies timeless elegance. The relaxed fit makes for a beautiful drape on the body.

SIZES

1 (2, 3, 4, 5) (6, 7, 8, 9)

Recommended ease: 4–7.25" / 10–18 cm of positive ease.

FINISHED MEASUREMENTS

Chest Circumference: 34.5 (38.5, 42.5, 46.5, 50.5) (54.5, 58.5, 62.5, 66.5)" / 87.5 (97.5, 107.5, 117.5, 127.5) (137.5, 147.5, 157.5, 167.5) cm.
Shoulder to Shoulder (with Rib): 15.25 (15.25, 15.25, 16.5, 16.5) (17.25, 17.25, 18.5, 18.5)" / 38 (38, 38, 41, 41) (43, 43, 46, 46) cm.
Armhole Depth (with Rib): 10.5 (11, 11.5, 11.5, 12) (12.5, 13, 13, 13.5)" / 26.5 (27.5, 29, 29, 30) (31.5, 32.5, 32.5, 34) cm.
Length from Underarm (with Armhole Rib for Back Hem): 10 (10, 10, 10, 10) (10, 10, 10, 10)" / 25 (25, 25, 25, 25) (25, 25, 25, 25) cm.
Total Length: 20.5 (21, 21.5, 21.5, 22) (22.5, 23, 23, 23.5)" / 51.5 (52.5, 54, 54, 55) (56.5, 57.5, 57.5, 59) cm.

MATERIALS

Yarn: Yarn A: 3 (3, 3, 4, 4) (4, 5, 5, 5) balls of Organic Soft Merino by Kaos Yarn (100% merino, 246 yds / 225 m – 50 g), colourway 1001 Natural.

Or approx. 595 (665, 740, 805, 875) (945, 1010, 1085, 1150) yds / 545 (610, 675, 735, 800) (865, 925, 990, 1050) m of fingering-weight yarn. Alternative yarn suggestions are for example Knitting for Olive Merino, Sandnes Garn Sunday and Isager Tvinni.

Yarn B: 2 (2, 2, 2, 2) (2, 3, 3, 3) balls of Organic Brushed Alpaca by Kaos Yarn (100% brushed alpaca, 246 yds / 225 m – 25 g), colourway 2001 Natural.

Or approx. 300 (335, 365, 405, 435) (470, 510, 540, 575) yds / 275 (305, 335, 370, 400) (430, 465, 495, 525) m of lace-weight alpaca yarn. Alternative yarn suggestions are for example Knitting for Olive Soft Silk Mohair, Sandnes Garn Tynn Silk Mohair and Isager Soft Fine.

Needles: US 11 / 8 mm 32–40" / 80–100 cm circular needles (for body), US 10.5 / 6.5 mm 32–40" / 80–100 cm and 8" / 20 cm circular needles (for rib).

Notions: Stitch markers, stitch holders or waste yarn.

GAUGE

12 sts x 16 rows to 4" / 10 cm on US 11 / 8 mm needles (with 2 strands of Yarn A and 1 strand of Yarn B held tog) in St St, after blocking.

12 sts x 16 rows to 4" / 10 cm on US 11 / 8 mm needles (with 2 strands of Yarn A and 1 strand of Yarn B held tog) in Cable patt, after blocking.

14 sts x 22 rows to 4" / 10 cm on US 10.5 / 6.5 mm needles (with 2 strands of Yarn A and 2 strands of Yarn B held tog) in 1 x 1 rib, after blocking.

SPECIAL ABBREVIATIONS

3/3 LC: Left cross. Sl 3 sts onto CN and hold in front, k3, k3 from CN.

NOTES

Three strands of yarn are held together throughout (2 strands of Yarn A with 1 of Yarn B), except for the neckline and armhole ribbing, in which 4 strands are held together (2 strands of Yarn A with 2 of Yarn B).

CONSTRUCTION

This slipover is knitted from the top down. The upper back is worked first, followed by both fronts. The front is designed to be slightly longer than the back before the join, so that the cast-on edge falls slightly towards the back. The front and back are joined together at the underarms and the slipover is worked in the round until the split hem. Stitches are then picked up around the neckline and armholes and ribbings are worked to finish off the vest. A cable pattern is worked on the front, while the back is worked in stockinette stitch.

DIRECTIONS

BACK

With US 11 / 8 mm needles, and 2 strands of Yarn A and 1 strand of Yarn B held tog, use Judy's Magic CO and CO 40 (40, 40, 42, 42) (46, 46, 46, 46) sts on each needle; 80 (80, 80, 84, 84) (92, 92, 92, 92) sts in total. The back sts are on the top needle: pl the sts for the front on a st holder or leave on cable.

Row 1 (RS): K to end.
Row 2 (WS): P to end.
Rep rows 1–2 until work measures 9 (8.5, 8, 8, 7.5) (7.5, 7.5, 6.5, 6.5)" / 22.5 (21, 20, 20, 19) (19, 19, 16.5, 16.5) cm measured from CO edge, ending after a WS row.

Armhole Shaping

Row 1 (RS, Inc): K2, m1l, k until 2 sts rem, m1r, k2. (2 sts inc'd)
Row 2 (WS): P to end.
Work rows 1–2 a total of 3 (5, 6, 5, 6) (7, 7, 8, 8) times. [46 (50, 52, 52, 54) (60, 60, 62, 62) sts]

Sizes 3–9 only
Row 1 (RS, Inc): K2, m1l, k until 2 sts rem, m1r, k2. (2 sts inc'd)
Row 2 (WS, Inc): P2, m1r(p), p until 2 sts rem, m1l(p), p2. (2 sts inc'd)
Work rows 1–2 a total of – (–, 1, 2, 3) (3, 4, 5, 6) time(s). [– (–, 56, 60, 66) (72, 76, 82, 86) sts]

All sizes
The back should now measure approx. 10.5 (11, 11.5, 11.5, 12) (12.5, 13, 13, 13.5)" / 26.5 (27.5, 29, 29, 30) (31.5, 32.5, 32.5, 34) cm from CO edge. Cut yarns and pl sts on a st holder or waste yarn.

LEFT FRONT SHOULDER

With WS of back facing, move first 12 (12, 12, 12, 12) (14, 14, 14, 14) sts on hold back onto US 11 / 8 mm needles. Leave rem sts for the neck and right front shoulder on hold. First row is a WS row.

Sizes 1–5 only
Row 1 (WS): P2 (2, 2, 3, 3) (–, –, –, –), PM, k1, p6, k1, PM, p to end.
Row 2 (RS): K to m, SM, p1, k6, p1, SM, k to end.
Row 3: P to m, SM, k1, p6, k1, SM, p to end.
Row 4: K to m, SM, p1, 3/3 LC, p1, SM, k to end.
Row 5: Rep row 3.
Rows 6 and 7: Rep rows 2 and 3.
Row 8 (Inc): K1, m1l, k to m, SM, p1, k6, p1, SM, k to end. (1 st inc'd)
Rows 9–12: Rep rows 5–8. (1 st inc'd)
Rows 13–15: Rep rows 5–7.
Row 16 (Inc): K1, m1l, k to m, SM, p1, 3/3 LC, p1, SM, k to end. (1 inc'd)
Rows 17–24: Rep rows 5–8 twice. (2 sts inc'd)
Rows 25–27: Rep rows 5–7.
[17 (17, 17, 17, 17) (–, –, –, –) sts]

Sizes 6–9 only
Row 1 (WS): P– (–, –, –, –) (5, 5, 5, 5), PM, k1, p6, k1, PM, p to end.
Row 2 (RS): K to m, SM, p1, k6, p1, SM, k to end.
Row 3: P to m, SM, k1, p6, k1, SM, p to end.
Rows 4 and 5: Rep rows 2 and 3.
Row 6: K to m, SM, p1, 3/3 LC, p1, SM, k to end.
Row 7: Rep row 3.
Rows 8–13: Rep rows 2 and 3, 3 times.
Row 14 (Inc): K1, m1l, k to m, SM, p1, k6, p1, SM, k to end. (1 st inc'd)
Row 15: Rep row 3.
Rows 16 and 17: Rep rows 2 and 3.
Row 18 (Inc): K1, m1l, k to m, SM, p1, 3/3 LC, p1, SM, k to end. (1 st inc'd)
Row 19–21: Rep rows 15–17.
Row 22 (Inc): Rep row 14. (1 st inc'd)
Rows 23–26: Rep rows 19–22. (1 st inc'd)
Rows 27–29: Rep rows 19–21.
[– (–, –, –, –) (18, 18, 18, 18) sts]

All sizes
Cut yarns and pl sts on a stitch holder or waste yarn.

RIGHT FRONT SHOULDER

With RS of back facing, move the first 12 (12, 12, 12, 12) (14, 14, 14, 14) sts back onto US 11 / 8 mm needles. Leave rem 16 (16, 16, 18, 18) (18, 18, 18, 18) sts for neck on hold. First row is a WS row.

Sizes 1–5 only
Row 1 (WS): P2 (2, 2, 1, 1) (–, –, –, –), PM, k1, p6, k1, PM, p to end.
Row 2 (RS): K to m, SM, p1, k6, p1, SM, k to end.
Row 3: P to m, SM, k1, p6, k1, SM, p to end.
Row 4: K to m, SM, p1, 3/3 LC, p1, SM, k to end.
Row 5: Rep row 3.
Rows 6 and 7: Rep rows 2 and 3.
Row 8 (Inc): K to m, SM, p1, k6, p1, SM, k to 1 st bef end, m1r, k1. (1 st inc'd)
Rows 9–12: Rep rows 5–8. (1 st inc'd)
Rows 13–15: Rep rows 5–7.
Row 16 (Inc): K to m, SM, p1, 3/3 LC, p1, SM, k to 1 st bef end, m1r, k1. (1 st inc'd)
Rows 17–24: Rep rows 5–8 twice. (2 sts inc'd)
Rows 25–27: Rep rows 5–7.
[17 (17, 17, 17, 17) (–, –, –, –) sts]

Sizes 6–9 only
Row 1 (WS): P– (–, –, –, –) (1, 1, 1, 1), PM, k1, p6, k1, PM, p to end.
Row 2 (RS): K to m, SM, p1, k6, p1, SM, k to end.
Row 3: P to m, SM, k1, p6, k1, SM, p to end.
Rows 4 and 5: Rep rows 2 and 3.
Row 6: K to m, SM, p1, 3/3 LC, p1, SM, k to end.
Row 7: Rep row 3.
Rows 8–13: Rep rows 2 and 3, 3 times.
Row 14 (Inc): K to m, SM, p1, k6, p1, SM, k to 1 st bef end, m1r, k1. (1 st inc'd)
Row 15: Rep row 3.
Rows 16 and 17: Rep rows 2–3.
Row 18 (Inc): K to m, SM, p1, 3/3 LC, p1, SM, k to 1 st bef end, m1r, k1. (1 st inc'd)
Row 19: Rep rows 15–17.
Row 22 (Inc): Rep row 14. (1 st inc'd)
Rows 23–26: Rep rows 19–22. (1 st inc'd)
Rows 27–29: Rep rows 19–21.
[– (–, –, –, –) (18, 18, 18, 18) sts]

All sizes
Prepare left front shoulder sts for joining to the right front shoulder on the next row.

Next Row (RS): Starting with right shoulder, k to m, SM, p1, 3/3 LC, p1, RM, k to end, CO 6 (6, 6, 8, 8) (10, 10, 10, 10) sts using the Backwards Loop CO method, cont with RS of left shoulder and k to m, RM, p1, 3/3 LC, p1, SM, k to end.
Next Row (WS): P to m, SM, *k1, p6* a total of 5 times, k1, SM, p to end.

[40 (40, 40, 42, 42) (46, 46, 46, 46) sts for front]

FRONT

The 36 sts between the cable panel m's are going to be worked repeating rows 1–12 of the Cable Chart while the rem sts are in St St. Make sure to pay close attention to the cable row you are on during the armhole inc's.

Row 1 (RS): K to m, SM, work from Cable Chart, SM, k to end.
Row 2 (WS): P to m, SM, work from Cable Chart, SM, p to end.
Work rows 1–2 a total of 7 (6, 5, 5, 4) (3, 3, 1, 1) time(s) or until work measures approx. 10.5 (10, 9.5, 9.5, 9) (9, 9, 8, 8)" / 26.5 (25, 24, 24, 22.5) (22.5, 22.5, 20, 20) cm from CO edge, ending after a WS row.

Armhole Shaping

Row 1 (RS): K2, m1l, k to m (if not already there), SM, work from Cable Chart, SM, k to 2 sts bef end (if not already there), m1r, k2. (2 sts inc'd)
Row 2 (WS): P to m, SM, work from Cable Chart, SM, p to end.
Work rows 1–2 a total of 3 (5, 6, 5, 6) (7, 7, 8, 8) times. [46 (50, 52, 52, 54) (60, 60, 62, 62) sts]

Sizes 3–9 only
Row 1 (RS): K2, m1l, k to 2 sts bef end, m1r, k2. (2 sts inc'd)
Row 2 (WS): P2, m1r(p), p to 2 sts bef end, m1l(p), p2. (2 sts inc'd)
Work rows 1–2 a total of – (–, 1, 2, 3) (3, 4, 5, 6) time(s). [– (–, 56, 60, 66) (72, 76, 82, 86) sts]

BODY

Join the front and back on the next row as foll, keeping track of what cable row you are on:
Next Row (RS): Starting with the front sts, k to m, SM, work from Cable Chart, SM, k to end, CO 6 (8, 8, 10, 10) (10, 12, 12, 14) sts using the Backwards Loop CO method, cont with the back sts and k to end, CO 3 (4, 4, 5, 5) (5, 6, 6, 7) sts, PM, CO 3 (4, 4, 5, 5) (5, 6, 6, 7) sts. Join to work the body in the rnd. [104 (116, 128, 140, 152) (164, 176, 188, 200) sts]

Body Rnd: K to m, SM, work from Cable Chart, SM, k to end.
Rep body rnd until work measures 5.5" / 14 cm from underarm CO edge, or until 3.5" / 9 cm less than desired length at back. End after either row 2, 3, 8 or 9 of the Cable Chart.

Change to US 10.5 / 6.5 mm needles. Work 1 more body rnd to 1 st bef BOR m, sl1 wyib.

SPLIT HEM

The hem is worked flat. The longer back hem is worked first.

Back Hem

Set-Up Row 1 (RS): With RS facing, RM, sl first st on LHN onto CN and hold in front, sl first st on RHN to LHN, k the st on CN, tw.

Set-Up Row 2 (WS): With WS facing, sl1 wyif, *p1, k1* a total of 12 (14, 15, 17, 18) (20, 21, 23, 24) times, p1, m1l, *p1, k1* a total of 12 (13, 15, 16, 18) (19, 21, 22, 24) times, p1, sl1 wyif, tw. (1 st inc'd)

Now, with RS facing, sl first st on LHN onto CN and hold in back, sl first st on RHN to LHN, and sl the st on CN to RHN. The rem 52 (58, 64, 70, 76) (82, 88, 94, 100) front sts can rem on the cable or on a st holder or waste yarn. [53 (59, 65, 71, 77) (83, 89, 95, 101) sts]

Row 1 (RS): K1, k1, *p1, k1* to 1 st bef end, k1.

Row 2 (WS): Sl1 wyif, p1, *k1, p1* to 1 st bef end, sl1 wyif.

Rep rows 1–2 until hem measures 3.5" / 9 cm.

BO all sts using the Italian Sewn BO method. Sew the selvage st tog with the st next to it, as if they were a single st.

Front Hem

With WS facing, put all 52 (58, 64, 70, 76) (82, 88, 94, 100) sts back on US 10.5 / 6.5 mm needles and join yarn to work the front hem. In the first row, remove cable markers.

Set-Up Row (WS): Sl1 wyif, *p1, k1* a total of 12 (14, 15, 17, 18) (20, 21, 23, 24) times, p1, m1l, *p1, k1* a total of 12 (13, 15, 16, 18) (19, 21, 21, 24) times, p1, sl1 wyif. (1 st inc'd) [53 (59, 65, 71, 77) (83, 89, 95, 101) sts]

Rep rows 1 and 2 as for the back until front hem measures 2.5" / 6 cm.

BO all sts using the Italian Sewn BO method. Sew the selvage st tog with the st next to it, as if they were a single st.

NECKLINE

With RS facing, move rem 16 (16, 16, 18, 18) (18, 18, 18, 18) back neck sts onto

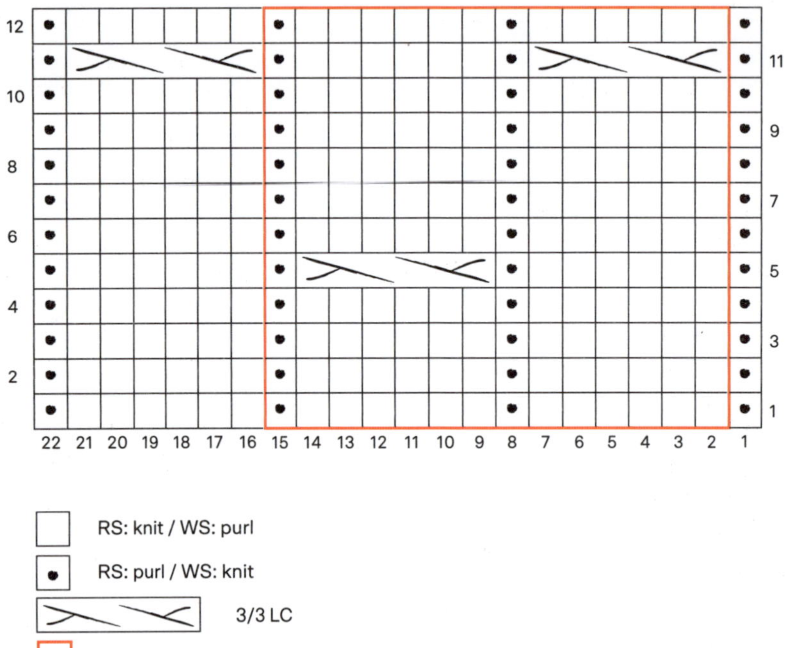

US 10.5 / 6.5 mm needles. Then, with 2 strands of Yarn A and 2 strands of Yarn B held tog, pick up and k approx. 21 (21, 21, 21, 21) (23, 23, 23, 23) sts (3 sts per every 4 rows) down the left front to just bef the front CO sts. Pick up and k 6 (6, 6, 8, 8) (10, 10, 10, 10) sts from front CO sts. Cont up the right front, picking up and k the same number of sts as on the left front, PM. [Approx. 64 (64, 64, 68, 68) (74, 74, 74, 74) sts] Make sure the number of sts is a multiple of 2.

Rib Rnd: *K1, p1* to end.
Work in est 1 x 1 rib until the rib measures 0.75" / 2 cm.

BO all sts using the Italian Sewn BO method.

ARMHOLES

With US 10.5 / 6.5 mm needles, the RS facing and with 2 strands of Yarn A and 2 of Yarn B held tog, beg from the centre of the armhole CO and pick up and k 3 (4, 4, 5, 5) (5, 6, 6, 7) sts, then pick up and k approx. 68 (70, 74, 74, 76) (80, 82, 82, 86) sts around armhole (3 sts per every 4 rows), pick up and k 3 (4, 4, 5, 5) (5, 6, 6, 7) sts from rem CO sts, PM. [Approx. 74 (78, 82, 84, 86) (90, 94, 94, 100) sts] Make sure the number of sts is a multiple of 2.

Rib Rnd: *K1, p1* to end.
Work in est 1 x 1 rib until the rib measures 0.75" / 2 cm.

BO all sts using the Italian Sewn BO.

FINISHING

Weave in ends. Wet block gently.

Vivian Wei

23 Semilla

Semilla is decorated with subtle details: a wave pattern on the armscyes and simple braids at the neckline and hem. The slipover was named after the designer's coffee shop in Tianjin, China.

SIZES

1 (2, 3, 4, 5) (6, 7, 8, 9)

Recommended ease: Approx. 8" / 20 cm of positive ease.

FINISHED MEASUREMENTS

Chest Circumference: 39.5 (43.5, 47.25, 51.25, 55) (59, 63, 67, 71)" / 100 (110, 120, 130, 140) (150, 160, 170, 180) cm.
Length from Shoulder to Front Hem: 21.5 (21.5, 21.5, 22.25, 22.25) (22.25, 23.25, 23.25, 24)" / 54 (54, 54, 56.5, 56.5) (56.5, 59, 59, 61) cm.
Length from Shoulder to Back Hem: 22 (22, 22, 23, 23) (23, 24, 24, 25)" / 56 (56, 56, 58.5, 58.5) (58.5, 61, 61, 63) cm.
Front Hem Length: 2.5" / 6 cm.
Back Hem Length: 3" / 8 cm.
Armhole Depth: 11.75 (11.75, 11.75, 12.5, 12.5) (12.5, 13.75, 13.75, 14.5)" / 30 (30, 30, 32, 32) (32, 35, 35, 37) cm.
Width from Shoulder to Shoulder: 14.5 (15.25, 15.25, 15.75, 16) (17, 17, 17.75, 18.5)" / 37 (38.5, 38.5, 40, 41) (43.5, 43.5, 45, 47) cm.

MATERIALS

Yarn: 2 (2, 3, 3, 3) (3, 3, 4, 4) skeins of 220 Grande by Cascade (100% Peruvian Highland wool, 220 yds / 200 m – 200 g), colourway 8401 Silver Grey.

Or approx. 320 (347, 375, 421, 448) (476, 521, 558, 604) yds / 350 (380, 410, 460, 490) (520, 570, 610, 660) m of bulky-weight yarn. Alternative yarn suggestions are for example Knit Picks Wool of the Andes Bulky, Juniper Moon Farm La Pampa and Malabrigo Yarn Chunky.

Needles: US 10.75 / 7 mm 16–24" / 40–60 cm and US 11 / 8 mm 32–47" / 80–120 cm circular needles.

Notions: Stitch marker, stitch holders or waste yarn, cable needle.

GAUGE

12 sts x 17 rows to 4" / 10 cm on US 11 / 8 mm needles in Reverse St St, after blocking.

SPECIAL ABBREVIATIONS

2/1 LPC: Left Purl Cross. Sl next 2 sts onto CN and hold in front of work, p1, then k2 from CN.

2/1 RPC: Right Purl Cross. Sl next st onto CN and hold in back of work, k2, then p1 from CN.

STITCH PATTERN

Wave Cable Pattern
Row 1 (RS): K2, p3, 2/1 RPC, p to 8 sts bef end, 2/1 LPC, p3, sl2.
Row 2 (WS): P2, k3, p2, k to 7 sts bef end, p2, k3, sl2.
Row 3: K2, p2, 2/1 RPC, p to 7 sts bef end, 2/1 LPC, p2, sl2.
Row 4: P2, k2, p2, k to 6 sts bef end, p2, k2, sl2.
Row 5: K2, p1, 2/1 RPC, p to 6 sts bef end, 2/1 LPC, p1, sl2.
Row 6: P2, k1, p2, k to 5 sts bef end, p2, k1, sl2.
Row 7: K2, p1, 2/1 LPC, p to 6 sts bef end, 2/1 RPC, p1, sl2.
Row 8: P2, k2, p2, k to 6 sts bef end,

p2, k2, sl2.
Row 9: K2, p2, 2/1 LPC, p to 7 sts bef end, 2/1 RPC, p2, sl2.
Row 10: P2, k3, p2, k to 7 sts bef end, p2, k3, sl2.
Row 11: K2, p3, 2/1 LPC, p to 8 sts bef end, 2/1 RPC, p3, sl2.
Row 12: P2, k4, p2, k to 8 sts bef end, p2, k4, sl2.

CONSTRUCTION

This slipover is worked from the bottom up. It features a split hem with a slightly longer back, a wave pattern on the armscye sides, a neat i-cord around the armholes and a simple braid detail around the neckline and hem. The knit is started with a Provisional Cast-On and first knitted in the round without increases with the inside out to enable working only knit stitches. Then, the back and front are separated and worked flat while shaping the armholes and neckline. A horizontal braid is worked around the neck before working in 1 x 1 ribbing and finishing by binding off knitwise to mimic the look of the horizontal braid. Lastly, the Provisional Cast-On is unravelled and the front and back hem are worked separately, flat, in 1 x 1 ribbing.

DIRECTIONS

BODY

Using the Provisional CO method and US 11 / 8 mm needles, CO 120 (132, 144, 156, 168) (180, 192, 204, 216) sts. Join to work in the rnd being careful not to twist sts. PM for BOR. The side facing you is now the WS of the work.

Work 28 rnds in St St (k all sts), or until work measures approx. 6.5" / 16.5 cm, or desired body length.

SEPARATE BACK AND FRONT

Turn the work inside out, so that the purl side (RS of the work) is now facing you. Beg to work the back.

The first 61 (67, 73, 79, 85) (91, 97, 103, 109) sts are for the back. Pl rem 59 (65, 71, 77, 83) (89, 95, 101, 107) sts (for the front) on a st holder or waste yarn.

Beg to work flat with the 61 (67, 73, 79, 85) (91, 97, 103, 109) back sts. A Wave Cable patt is worked at each side and an i-cord edge is worked at the armholes.

Set-Up

Row 1 (RS): K2, p1, k2, p to 5 sts bef end, k2, p1, sl2.
Row 2 (WS): P2, k1, p2, k to 5 sts bef end, p2, k1, sl2.

Decrease

Row 3 (RS): K2, p1, 2/1 LPC, ssp, p to 8 sts bef end, p2tog, 2/1 RPC, p1, sl2. (2 sts dec'd)
Row 4 (WS): P2, k2, p2, k to 6 sts bef end, p2, k2, sl2.
Row 5: K2, p2, 2/1 LPC, ssp, p to 9 sts bef end, p2tog, 2/1 RPC, p2, sl2. (2 sts dec'd)
Row 6: P2, k3, p2, k to 7 sts bef end, p2, k3, sl2.
Row 7: K2, p3, 2/1 LPC, ssp, p to 10 sts bef end, p2tog, 2/1 RPC, p3, sl2. (2 sts dec'd)
Row 8: P2, k4, p2, k to 8 sts bef end, p2, k4, sl2.
Row 9: K2, p3, 2/1 RPC, ssp, p to 10 sts bef end, p2tog, 2/1 LPC, p3, sl2. (2 sts dec'd)
Row 10: P2, k3, p2, k to 7 sts bef end, p2, k3, sl2.
Row 11: K2, p2, 2/1 RPC, ssp, p to 9 sts bef end, p2tog, 2/1 LPC, p2, sl2. (2 sts dec'd)
Row 12: P2, k2, p2, k to 6 sts bef end, p2, k2, sl2.
Row 13: K2, p1, 2/1 RPC, ssp, p to 8 sts bef end, p2tog, 2/1 LPC, p1, sl2. (2 sts dec'd)
Row 14: P2, k1, p2, k to 5 sts bef end, p2, k1, sl2.

Size 1 only
Work rows 3–6 once.

Size 2 only
Work rows 3–8 once.

Size 3 only
Work rows 3–14 once.

Size 4 only
Work rows 3–14 once, then rows 3–6 once again.

Size 5 only
Work rows 3–14 once, then rows 3–10 once again.

Size 6 only
Work rows 3–14 twice.

Size 7 only
Work rows 3–14 twice, then rows 3–8 once more.

Size 8 only
Work rows 3–14 twice, then rows 3–12 once.

Size 9 only
Work rows 3–14, 3 times, then rows 3–4 once.

[45 (49, 49, 51, 53) (55, 55, 57, 59) sts for the back]

Knit without Decreases

Beg with row 11 (1, 7, 11, 3) (7, 1, 5, 9), work 30 (28, 22, 22, 18) (14, 12, 8, 8) rows in Wave Cable patt. You will end on a row 4 (4, 4, 8, 8) (8, 12, 12, 4) of patt.

Shape Back Neck

Right Back

Row 1 (RS): Work next row of Wave Cable patt for 11 (12, 12, 13, 13) (14, 14, 15, 15) sts. Turn, leaving rem sts unworked.
Row 2 (WS): Work next row of est patt.
Row 3: Work next row of est patt to last 3 sts, ssp, p1. (1 st dec'd)
Row 4: Work next row of est patt.
Rows 5 and 6: Rep rows 3 and 4. (1 st dec'd)

Cut yarn and pl 9 (10, 10, 11, 11) (12, 12, 13, 13) right shoulder sts on a st holder or waste yarn.

Click here to enter text. With RS facing, pl the next 23 (25, 25, 25, 27) (27, 27, 27, 29) sts on waste yarn for neck and beg to work the left back with the rem 11 (12, 12, 13, 13) (14, 14, 15, 15) sts.

Left Back

Row 1 (RS): Work next row of est patt.
Row 2 (WS): Work next row of est patt.
Row 3: P1, p2tog, work in est patt to end. (1 st dec'd)
Row 4: Work next row of est patt.
Rows 5 and 6: Rep rows 3 and 4. (1 st dec'd)

Cut yarn and pl rem 9 (10, 10, 11, 11) (12, 12, 13, 13) left shoulder sts on a st holder or waste yarn.

FRONT

Pl 59 (65, 71, 77, 83) (89, 95, 101, 107) front sts from holder onto the needles.

Work the Set-Up and Decrease sections as for Back. [43 (47, 47, 49, 51) (53, 53, 55, 57) sts]

Knit without Decreases

Sizes 1–7 only

Beg with row 11 (1, 7, 11, 3) (7, 1, –, –), work 22 (20, 14, 14, 10) (6, 4, –, –) rows in same 12-row patt as given for Back. You will end on a row 8 (8, 8, 12, 12) (12, 4, –, –) of patt.

Sizes 8 and 9 only

Proceed to Left Front.

Shape Front Neck

Left Front

Row 1 (RS): Work next row of est patt for 12 (13, 13, 14, 14) (15, 15, 16, 16) sts. Turn, leaving rem sts unworked.
Row 2 (WS): Work next row of est patt.
Row 3: Work next row of est patt to last 3 sts, ssp, p1. (1 st dec'd)
Rows 4–6: Work next row of est patt.
Rep rows 3–6 twice more. [9 (10, 10, 11, 11) (12, 12, 13, 13) sts]

Do not cut yarn. With WS facing and using the 3-Needle BO method, join left front and left back shoulder sts.

With RS facing, pl the next 19 (21, 21, 21, 23) (23, 23, 23, 25) neck sts on a st holder or waste yarn and beg to work the right front with the rem 12 (13, 13, 14, 14) (15, 15, 16, 16) sts.

Right Front

Row 1 (RS): Work next row of est patt.
Row 2 (WS): Work next row of est patt.
Row 3: P1, p2tog, work next row of est patt to end. (1 st dec'd)
Rows 4–6: Work next row of est patt.
Rep rows 3–6 twice more. [9 (10, 10, 11, 11) (12, 12, 13, 13) sts]

Do not cut yarn. With WS facing and using the 3-Needle BO method, join the right back and right front shoulder sts.

NECKLINE

With RS facing, US 10.75 / 7 mm circular needles, and beg at back right shoulder seam, pick up and k7 sts along the right back neck, k23 (25, 25, 25, 27) (27, 27, 27, 29) sts from st holder or waste yarn for back neck. Pick up and k 7 sts along the left back neck, pick up and k 10 sts along the left front neck, k 19 (21, 21, 21, 23) (23, 23, 23, 25) sts from st holder or waste yarn for front neck, pick up and k 10 sts along the right front neck, PM for BOR and join to work in the rnd. [76 (80, 80, 80, 84) (84, 84, 84, 88) sts]

Rnd 1 (Horizontal Braid): *Working behind the 1st st on LHN, k1tbl the 2nd st and do not drop off the needle, k the 1st st on the LHN and drop both sts from the LHN, sl 1st st from the RHN back onto the LHN*, rep *–* to end.
Rnd 2: *K1, p1* to end.
Rep rnd 2, 4 more times.

BO kwise.

HEM

Note! Hem is worked in the opposite direction from the body, top-down from the Provisional CO edge with the WS facing.

With RS facing, pl the 120 (132, 144, 156, 168) (180, 192, 204, 216) body sts from Provisional CO onto US 10.75 / 7 mm needles. PM for BOR.

Work Horizonal Braid rnd as given for rnd 1 of Neckline.

The first the 59 (65, 71, 77, 83) (89, 95, 101, 107) sts are for the front hem. Pl rem 61 (67, 73, 79, 85) (91, 97, 103, 109) sts for back hem on a st holder or waste yarn.

Front Hem

Beg to work flat with the 59 (65, 71, 77, 83) (89, 95, 101, 107) sts for front hem.

Row 1 (RS): K1, *p1, k1* to end.
Row 2 (WS): P1, *k1, p1* to end.
Rep rows 1–2, 4 more times.

BO kwise.

Back Hem

With RS facing, pl rem 61 (67, 73, 79, 85) (91, 97, 103, 109) sts for back hem onto US 10.75 / 7 mm needles. Work as front hem but rep rows 1–2, 6 more times.

FINISHING

Weave in ends. Wet block to measurements.

Megumi Shinagawa

24 Cinnamon Roll

Lightweight yet warm, the Cinnamon Roll vest is perfect for layering. The soft, variegated yarn used for the sample creates a lively, marled fabric.

SIZES

1 (2, 3, 4, 5) (6, 7, 8, 9)

Recommended ease: 2.75–11.5" / 7–29 cm of positive ease.

FINISHED MEASUREMENTS

Chest Circumference: 38.5 (43.75, 47.75, 51.75, 55.75) (61, 65, 69, 74.5)" / 96 (109.5, 119.5, 129.5, 139.5) (152.5, 162.5, 172.5, 186) cm.
Yoke Depth: 9.75 (10.75, 10.75, 12, 12) (12.75, 13.25, 14, 14)" / 25 (27, 27, 30.5, 30.5) (32.5, 34, 36, 36) cm.
Armhole Circumference after I-Cord BO: 16 (17.25, 17.25, 20.5, 20.5) (21.25, 22.5, 24, 24.75)" / 40 (43.5, 43.5, 51.5, 51.5) (53.5, 56, 60, 62) cm.
Length From Underarm to Hem: 9" / 23 cm.

MATERIALS

Yarn: 2 (2, 2, 2, 3) (3, 3, 3, 3) skeins of Domitilla by Colori Naturali (90% baby suri alpaca, 10% mulberry silk, 246 yds / 225 m – 100 g), colourway Viaggiatori Incauti.

Or approx. 355 (406, 435, 479, 529) (580, 629, 681, 722) yds / 325 (371, 398, 438, 484) (530, 575, 623, 660) m of DK, worsted or bulky-weight yarn. Pay attention to gauge, so make sure to swatch. Alternative yarn suggestions are for example Lana Grossa Avio or Woolkfolk Tåge, or two strands of Isager Silk Mohair held together with one strand of Isager Bouclé.

Needles: US 9 / 5.5 mm 24" / 60 cm circular needles (for neck and hem), US 10 / 6 mm 32" / 80 cm circular needles (for body and armholes), US 8 / 5 mm DPNs (for i-cord BO).

Notions: 8 stitch markers, cable needle, stitch holders or waste yarn, spare needles, 7 (7, 7, 8, 8) (8, 8, 9, 9) buttons (approx. 1 3/16" / 30 mm in diameter).

GAUGE

12 sts x 17 rows to 4" / 10 cm on US 10 / 6 mm needles in St St, after blocking.

15 sts x 17 rows to 4" / 10 cm on US 10 / 6 mm needles in 1 x 1 rib, after blocking.

12 sts x 10 rows to 3.15" x 2.15" / 8 cm x 5.5 cm on US 10 / 6 mm needles in first 12 sts of Chart A or last 12 sts of Chart B, after blocking.

18 sts x 20 rows to 4.75" x 4.25" / 12 cm x 11 cm on US 10 / 6 mm needles in Chart A or Chart B, after blocking.

SPECIAL ABBREVIATIONS

C3L: Cable 3 Left. Sl 1 st onto CN and hold in front, k2 from LHN, k1 from CN.

C3R: Cable 3 Right. Sl 2 sts onto CN and hold in back, k1 from LHN, k2 from CN.

NOTES

Chart B yarnovers are used as buttonholes. The buttons are placed on purl stitches (stitch number 7) on row 5 of Chart A.

If wanting to make the body longer, knit 10 more rows before the hem. As a result, the length from underarm to hem increases by approx. 2.25" / 5.5 cm.

Be careful not to knit too tight when working increase stitches.

If the i-cord BO for armholes became loose, use US 7 / 4.5 mm DPNs instead of US 8 / 5 mm DPNs for it.

CONSTRUCTION

This vest features a cable pattern on both sides of the button band and a rib-stitch at the shoulders as well as a symmetrical rib-stitch at the centre back. It is knitted top down, flat with saddle shoulders. Short rows are worked not only for the neck but also for the shoulders to add length. The vest is started with the neck and shoulder line which are worked in Stockinette Stitch and German Short Rows. The fronts and back are then joined at the underarms and the vest is worked from underarm to hem. Sleeve stitches are picked up from the armhole and worked in the round with an I-Cord Bind-Off.

DIRECTIONS

NECK

With US 9 / 5.5 mm needles, *CO 36 (36, 38, 38, 40) (40, 42, 44, 46) sts using the Long-Tail CO method*, PM for the centre of the back, rep *–* once more. [72 (72, 76, 76, 80) (80, 84, 88, 92) sts]

Row 1 (RS): Sl1 kwise wyib, k1, *p1, k1* to m, SM, *k1, p1* to end.
Row 2: Sl1 pwise wyif, p1, *k1, p1* to m, SM, *p1, k1* to end.
Rows 3-6: Rep rows 1–2 twice more.

GERMAN SHORT ROWS FOR NECK & SHOULDERS

Change to US 10 / 6 mm needles.

Sizes 1, 2, 3, 4 and 5 only
Note! Inc sts are worked to make the shoulders wider.
Set-Up Row 1 (RS): Sl1 kwise wyib, k17 (17, 17, 17, 18) (–, –, –, –) for left front, PM, m1r, *p1, k1* 3 (3, 4, 4, 4) (–, –, –, –) times, m1l(p) for the saddle shoulder, PM, k3 (3, 3, 3, 4) (–, –, –, –), PM, *k1, p1* 3 times, PM, k3, RM, k3, PM, *p1, k1* 3 times, PM, k3 (3, 3, 3, 4) (–, –, –, –) for the back, PM, m1r(p), *k1, p1* 3 (3, 4, 4, 4) (–, –, –, –) times, m1l for the saddle shoulder, PM, k18 (18, 18, 18, 19) (–, –, –, –) for right front. (4 sts inc'd)
Set-Up Row 2 (WS): Sl1 pwise wyif, p to m, SM, m1l, *p1, k1* to m, m1r(p), SM, p to m, SM, *p1, k1* to m, SM, p to m, SM, *k1, p1* to m, SM, p to m, SM, m1l(p), *k1, p1* to m, m1r, SM, p to end. (4 sts inc'd)

Sizes 6, 7, 8 and 9 only
Note! Body inc's are started from here.
Set-Up Row 1 (RS): Sl1 kwise wyib, k– (–, –, –, –) (16, 17, 17, 17), m1r for left front, PM, *p1, k1* – (–, –, –, –) (6, 6, 7, 8) times for the saddle shoulder, PM, m1l, k– (–, –, –, –) (2, 3, 3, 3), PM, *k1, p1* 3 times, PM, k3, RM, k3, PM, *p1, k1* 3 times, PM, k– (–, –, –, –) (2, 3, 3, 3), m1r for the back, PM, *k1, p1* – (–, –, –, –) (6, 6, 7, 8) times for the saddle shoulder, PM, m1l, k– (–, –, –, –) (17, 18, 18, 18) for right front. (4 sts inc'd)
Set-Up Row 2 (WS): Sl1 pwise wyif, p to m, m1l(p), SM, *k1, p1* to m, SM, m1r(p), p to m, SM, *p1, k1* to m, SM, p to M, SM, *k1, p1* to m, SM, p to m, m1l(p), SM, *p1, k1* to m, SM, m1r(p), p to end. (4 sts inc'd)

[80 (80, 84, 84, 88) (88, 92, 96, 100) sts: 18 (18, 18, 18, 19) (19, 20, 20, 20) sts for each front, 10 (10, 12, 12, 12) (12, 12, 14, 16) sts for each saddle shoulders, 24 (24, 24, 24, 26) (26, 28, 28, 28) sts for the back]

All sizes
Start working short rows to shape the neck and back as foll:
Row 1 (RS): Sl1 kwise wyib, k1, p1, C3R, k1, C3L, p1, k to m, m1r, SM, *p1, k1* to m, SM, m1l, k to m, SM, *k1, p1* to m, SM, k to m, SM, *p1, k1* to m, SM, k to m, m1r, SM, *k1, p1* to m, SM, m1l, k2, tw. (4 sts inc'd)
Row 2 (WS): MDS, p to m, m1l(p), SM, *k1, p1* to m, SM, m1r(p), p to m, SM, *p1, k1* to m, SM, p to m, SM, *k1, p1* to m, SM, p to m, m1l(p), SM, *p1, k1* to m, SM, m1r(p), p3, tw. (4 sts inc'd) [88 (88, 92, 92, 96) (96, 100, 104, 108) sts]

Start German Short Rows for saddle shoulders. To get length for the saddle shoulder, short rows are worked not only for the neck but also for the shoulders.
Row 3: MDS, k to 2 sts bef m, m1r, k2, m1r, SM, *p1, k1* to m, tw.
Row 4: MDS, k1, *p1, k1* to m, tw.
Row 5: MDS, *k1, p1* to DS, kDS, SM, m1l, k2, m1l, k to m, SM, *k1, p1* to m, SM, k to m, SM, *p1, k1* to m, SM, k to 2 sts bef m, m1r, k2, m1r, SM, *k1, p1* to m, tw.
Row 6: MDS, p1, *k1, p1* to m, tw.

Row 7: MDS, *p1, k1* to DS, pDS, SM, m1l, k2, m1l, k to DS, kDS, k1, tw. (8 sts inc'd)
Row 8: MDS, p to m, m1l(p), SM, *k1, p1* to 2 sts bef m, k1, pDS, SM, m1r(p), p to m, SM, *p1, k1* to m, SM, p to m, SM, *k1, p1* to m, SM, p to m, m1l(p), SM, *p1, k1* to 2 sts bef m, p1, kDS, SM, m1r(p), p to DS, pDS, p1, tw. (4 sts inc'd)
Row 9: MDS, k to m, m1r, SM, *p1, k1* to m, SM, m1l, k to m, SM, *k1, p1* to m, SM, k to m, SM, *p1, k1* to m, SM, k to m, m1r, SM, *k1, p1* to m, SM, m1l, k to DS, kDS, k1, tw. (4 sts inc'd)
Row 10: MDS, p to m, m1l(p), SM, *k1, p1* to m, SM, m1r(p), p to m, SM, *p1, k1* to m, SM, p to m, SM, *k1, p1* to m, SM, p to m, m1l(p), SM, *p1, k1* to m, SM, m1r(p), p to DS, pDS, p1, tw. (4 sts inc'd)

[108 (108, 112, 112, 116) (116, 120, 124, 128) sts]

Sizes 5, 6, 7, 8 and 9 only
Rows 11–18: Rep rows 3–10 once more. (20 sts inc'd) [– (–, –, –, 136) (136, 140, 144, 148) sts]

All sizes
Row 11 (11, 11, 11, 19) (19, 19, 19, 19) (RS): MDS, k to 2 sts bef m, m1r, k2, m1r, SM, *p1, k1* to m, tw.
Row 12 (12, 12, 12, 20) (20, 20, 20, 20) (WS): MDS, k1, *p1, k1* to m, tw.
Row 13 (13, 13, 13, 21) (21, 21, 21, 21): MDS, *k1, p1* to DS, kDS, SM, m1l, k2, m1l, k to m, SM, *k1, p1* to m, SM, k to m, SM, *p1, k1* to m, SM, k to 2 sts bef m, m1r, k2, m1r, SM, *k1, p1* to m, tw.
Row 14 (14, 14, 14, 22) (22, 22, 22, 22): MDS, p1, *k1, p1* to m, tw.
Row 15 (15, 15, 15, 23) (23, 23, 23, 23): MDS, *p1, k1* to DS, pDS, SM, m1l, k2, m1l, k to DS, kDS, k2, tw. (8 sts inc'd)
Row 16 (16, 16, 16, 24) (24, 24, 24, 24): MDS, p to m, m1l(p), SM, *k1, p1* to 2 sts bef m, k1, pDS, SM, m1r(p), p to m, SM, *p1, k1* to m, SM, p to m, SM, *k1, p1* to m, SM, p to m, m1l(p), SM, *p1, k1* to 2 sts bef m, p1, kDS, SM, m1r(p), p to DS, pDS, p2, tw. (4 sts inc'd)

[120 (120, 124, 124, 148) (148, 152, 156, 160) sts]

Start to work from the charts.
Note! KDS or pDS as you reach DS on rows 1–2.
Row 1 (RS): MDS, k to m, m1r, SM, *p1, k1* to m, SM, m1l, k to m, SM, *k1, p1* to m, SM, k to m, SM, *p1, k1* to m, SM, k to m, m1r, SM, *k1, p1* to m, SM, m1l, k to 12 sts bef end, k1, p1, C3R, k1, C3L, p1, k2. (4 sts inc'd)
Row 2 (WS): Work row 2 of Chart B, p to m, m1l(p), SM, *k1, p1* to m, SM, m1r(p), p to m, SM, *p1, k1* to m, SM, p to m, SM, *k1, p1* to m, SM, p to m, m1l(p), SM, *p1, k1* to m, SM, m1r(p), p to 18 sts bef end, work row 2 of Chart A. (4 sts inc'd)
Row 3: Work row 3 of Chart A, k to 2 sts bef m, m1r, k2, m1r, SM, *p1, k1* to m, tw.
Row 4: MDS, k1, *p1, k1* to m, tw.
Row 5: MDS, *k1, p1* to DS, kDS, SM, m1l, k2, m1l, k to m, SM, *k1, p1* to m, SM, k to m, SM, *p1, k1* to m, SM, k to 2 sts bef m, m1r, k2, m1r, SM, *k1, p1* to m, tw.
Row 6: MDS, p1, *k1, p1* to m, tw.
Row 7: MDS, *p1, k1* to DS, pDS, SM, m1l, k2, m1l, k to 18 sts bef end, work row 3 of Chart B. (8 sts inc'd)
Row 8: Work row 4 of Chart B, p to m, m1l(p), SM, *k1, p1* to 2 sts bef m, k1, pDS, SM, m1r(p), p to m, SM, *p1, k1* to m, SM, p to m, SM, *k1, p1* to m, SM, p to m, m1l(p), SM, *p1, k1* to 2 sts bef m, p1, kDS, SM, m1r(p), p to 18 sts bef end, work row 4 of Chart A. (4 sts inc'd)

[140 (140, 144, 144, 168) (168, 172, 176, 180) sts]

Size 1 only
Proceed to Left Front.

Sizes 2, 3, 4, 5, 6, 7, 8 and 9 only
Row 9: Work row 5 of Chart A, k to m, m1r, SM, *p1, k1* to m, SM, m1l, k to m, SM, *k1, p1* to m, SM, k to m, SM, *p1, k1* to m, SM, k to m, m1r, SM, *k1, p1* to m, SM, m1l, k to 18 sts bef end, work row 5 of Chart B. (4 sts inc'd)
Row 10: Work row 6 of Chart B, p to m, m1l(p), SM, *k1, p1* to m, SM, m1r(p), p to m, SM, *p1, k1* to m, SM, p to m, SM, *k1, p1* to m, SM, p to m, m1l(p), SM, *p1, k1* to m, SM, m1r(p), p to 18 sts bef end, work row 6 of Chart A. (4 sts inc'd)

Sizes 2 and 5 only
Proceed to Left Front.

Sizes 3, 4, and 6 only
Rows 11–16: Rep rows 3–8 once more working rows 7–8 of the charts. (12 sts inc'd)
Proceed to Left Front.

Sizes 7 only
Rows 11–18: Rep rows 3–10 once more working rows 7–10 of the charts. (20 sts inc'd)
Proceed to Left Front.

Sizes 8 only
Rows 11–18: Rep rows 3–10 once more working rows 7–10 of the charts. (20 sts inc'd)
Row 19: Rep row 9 once more working row 1 of the charts. (4 sts inc'd)
Row 20: Work row 2 of Chart B, p to m, SM, *k1, p1* to m, SM, p to m, SM, *p1, k1* to m, SM, p to m, SM, *k1, p1* to m, SM, p to m, SM, *p1, k1* to m, SM, p to 18 sts bef end, work row 2 of Chart A.
Proceed to Left Front.

Size 9 only
Rows 11–18: Rep rows 3–10 once more working rows 7–10 of the charts. (20 sts inc'd)
Rows 19–24: Rep rows 3–8 once more working rows 1–2 of the charts. (12 sts inc'd)

LEFT FRONT

You should have 140 (148, 164, 164, 176) (188, 200, 208, 220) sts in total: 33 (35, 38, 38, 41) (44, 47, 48, 50) sts for each front, 10 (10, 12, 12, 12) (12, 12, 14, 16) sts for each saddle shoulder and 54 (58, 64, 64, 70) (76, 82, 84, 88) sts for the back.

Set-Up Row 1 (RS): Work row 5 (7, 9, 9, 7) (9, 1, 3, 3) of Chart A, PM, k to m, RM, *pl next 10 (10, 12, 12, 12) (12, 12, 14, 16) sts for the saddle shoulder onto scrap yarn*, RM, pl next 54 (58, 64, 64, 70) (76, 82, 84, 88) sts for the back onto scrap yarn, RM, rep *–* once more, RM, pl next 33 (35, 38, 38, 41) (44, 47, 48, 50) sts onto scrap yarn for right front.

[33 (35, 38, 38, 41) (44, 47, 48, 50) sts for left front on working needles]

Set-Up Row 2 (WS): P to m, SM, work next row of Chart A.
Row 1 (RS): Work next row of Chart A, SM, k to end.
Row 2 (WS): P to m, SM, work next row of Chart A.
Rep rows 1–2, 14 (14, 13, 14, 15) (16, 16, 16, 13) more times.
Last worked row is row 6 (8, 8, 10, 10) (4, 6, 8, 2) of Chart A.

Armhole Shaping

Row 1 (RS): Work next row of Chart A, SM, k to 2 sts bef end, m1r, k to end. (1 st inc'd)
Row 2 (WS): P to m, SM, work next row of Chart A.

Size 1 only
Row 3: Rep row 1 once more. (1 st inc'd)
(35 sts for left front)

Sizes 2, 3, 4, 5, 6, and 7 only
Rows 3 to – (4, 4, 8, 8) (8, 8, –, –): Rep rows 1–2, – (1, 1, 3, 3) (3, 3, –, –) times.
[– (1, 1, 3, 3) (3, 3, –, –) sts inc'd]
Row – (5, 5, 9, 9) (9, 9, –, –): Rep row 1 once more. (1 st inc'd)
[– (38, 41, 43, 46) (49, 52, –, –) sts for left front]

Size 8 only
Row 3: Work next row of Chart A, SM, k to end.
Row 4: P to m, SM, work next row of Chart A.
Rows 5–10: Rep rows 1–2. (3 sts inc'd)
Row 11: Rep row 1 once more. (1 st inc'd)
(53 sts for left front)

Size 9 only
Row 3: Work next row of Chart A, SM, k to end.
Row 4: P to m, SM, work row 6 of Chart A.
Rows 5–8: Rep rows 1–4. (1 st inc'd)
Rows 9–16: Rep rows 1–2. (4 sts inc'd)
Row 17: Rep row 1 once more. (1 st inc'd)
(57 sts for left front)

All sizes
Cut yarn. Pl all left front sts on spare needles.

BACK

Pl the back sts from the scrap yarn back onto the working needles. [54 (58, 64, 64, 70) (76, 82, 84, 88) sts]

Join yarn.

Row 1 (RS): K to m, SM, *k1, p1* to m, SM, k to m, SM, *p1, k1* to m, SM, k to end.
Row 2 (WS): P to m, SM, *p1, k1* to m, SM, p to m, SM, *k1, p1* to m, SM, p to end.
Rep rows 1–2, 15 (15, 14, 15, 16) (17, 17, 17, 14) more times.

Armhole Shaping

Row 1 (RS): K2, m1l, k to m, SM, *k1, p1* to m, SM, k to m, SM, *p1, k1* to m, SM, k to 2 sts bef end, m1r, k to end. (2 sts inc'd)
Row 2 (WS): P to m, SM, *p1, k1* to m, SM, p to m, SM, *k1, p1* to m, SM, p to end.

Size 1 only
Row 3: Rep row 1 once more. (2 sts inc'd)
[58 sts for back]

Sizes 2, 3, 4, 5, 6, and 7 only
Rows 3 to – (4, 4, 8, 8) (8, 8, –, –): Rep rows 1–2, – (1, 1, 3, 3) (3, 3, –, –) times.
[– (2, 2, 6, 6) (6, 6, –, –) sts inc'd]
Row – (5, 5, 9, 9) (9, 9, –, –): Rep row 1 once more. (2 sts inc'd)
[– (64, 70, 74, 80) (86, 92, –, –) sts for back]

Sizes 8 and 9 only
Row 3: K to m, SM, *k1, p1* to m, SM, k to m, SM, *p1, k1* to m, SM, k to end.
Row 4: Rep row 2.

Size 8 only
Rows 5–10: Rep rows 1–2. (6 sts inc'd)
Row 11: Rep row 1 once more. (2 sts inc'd)
(94 sts for back)

Size 9 only
Rows 5–8: Rep rows 1–4. (2 sts inc'd)
Rows 9–16: Rep rows 1–2. (8 sts inc'd)
Row 17: Rep row 1 once more. (2 sts inc'd)
(102 sts for back)

All sizes
Cut yarn.

Pl all back sts on spare needles.

RIGHT FRONT

Pl the right front sts from the scrap yarn back onto the working needles. [33 (35, 38, 38, 41) (44, 47, 48, 50) sts]

Join yarn.

Set-Up Row 1 (RS): K to 18 sts bef end, PM, work row 5 (7, 9, 9, 7) (9, 1, 3, 3) of Chart B.
Set-Up Row 2 (WS): Work next row of Chart B, SM, p to end.

Row 1 (RS): K to m, SM, work next row of Chart B.
Row 2 (WS): Work next row of Chart B, SM, p to end.
Rep rows 1–2, 14 (14, 13, 14, 15) (16, 16, 16, 13) times.

On the last row, you worked row 6 (8, 8, 10, 10) (4, 6, 8, 2) of Chart B.

Armhole Shaping

Row 1 (RS): K2, m1l, k to m, SM, work next row of Chart B. (1 st inc'd)
Row 2 (WS): Work next row of Chart B, SM, p to end.

Size 1 only
Row 3 (RS): Rep row 1. (1 st inc'd)
(35 sts for right front)

Sizes 2, 3, 4, 5, 6 and 7 only
Note! Cont working Chart B according to your size.
Rows 3 to – (4, 4, 8, 8) (8, 10, –, –): Rep rows 1–2, – (1, 1, 3, 3) (3, 3, –, –) times.
[– (1, 1, 3, 3) (3, 3, –, –) sts inc'd]
Row – (5, 5, 9, 9) (9, 11, –, –): Rep row 1 once more. (1 st inc'd)
[– (38, 41, 43, 46) (49, 52, –, –) sts for right front]

Size 8 only
Row 3: K to m, SM, work next row of Chart B.
Row 4: Work next row of Chart B, SM, p to end.
Rows 5–10: Rep rows 1–2. (3 sts inc'd)
Row 11: Rep row 1 once more. (1 sts inc'd)
(53 sts for right front)

Size 9 only
Row 3: K to m, SM, work next row of Chart B.
Row 4: Work next row of Chart B, SM, p to end.
Rows 5–8: Rep rows 1–4. (1 st inc'd)
Rows 9–16: Rep rows 1–2. (4 sts inc'd)
Row 17: Rep row 1 once more. (1 st inc'd)
(57 sts for right front)

JOIN FRONT AND BACK

Row 1 (WS): Work next row of Chart B, SM, p to end of right front, CO 1 (2, 3, 4, 4) (4, 4, 6, 7) st(s) using Backwards Loop CO method, PM, CO 1 (2, 2, 3, 3) (4, 4, 6, 6) st(s) using Backwards Loop CO method, p to m, SM, *p1, k1* to m, SM, p to m, SM, *k1, p1* to m, SM, p to end of the back, CO 1 (2, 2, 3, 3) (4, 4, 6, 6) st(s) using Backwards Loop CO method, PM, CO 1 (2, 3, 4, 4) (4, 4, 6, 7) st(s), p to m, SM, work next row of Chart A.

[132 (148, 162, 174, 186) (200, 212, 224, 242) sts]

LOWER BODY

Sizes 1, 4, 5, 8 and 9 only
Row 1 (RS): Work next row of Chart A, SM, *k to m, SM* twice, *k1, p1* to m, SM, k to m, SM, *p1, k1* to m, SM, *k to m, SM* twice, work next row of Chart B.
Row 2 (WS): Work next row of Chart B, SM, *p to m, SM* twice, *p1, k1* to m, SM, p to m, SM, *k1, p1* to m, SM, *p to m, SM* twice, work next row of Chart A.
Rows 3–4: Rep rows 1–2.
Start German Short Rows for lower body:
Row 5: Work next row of Chart A, SM, *k to m, SM* twice, *k1, p1* to m, SM, k to m, SM, *p1, k1* to m, *SM, k to m* twice, tw.
Row 6: MDS, *p to m, SM* twice, *p1, k1* to m, SM, p to m, SM, *k1, p1* to m, *SM, p to m* twice, tw.
Row 7: MDS, *k to m, SM* twice, *k1, p1* to m, SM, k to m, SM, *p1, k1* to m, SM, k to m, SM, k to DS, kDS, SM, work next row of Chart B.
Row 8: Rep row 2 once, pDS as you reach it.
Rows 9–12: Rep rows 1–2, twice.
Rows 13–22: Rep rows 1–2, 5 times
Rows 23–34: Rep rows 1–12 once more.

Note! If wanting to make the piece longer, rep rows 13–22 once more.

Sizes 2, 3, 6 and 7 only
Start German Short Rows for lower body:
Row 1 (RS): Work next row of Chart A, SM, *k to m, SM* twice, *k1, p1* to m, SM, k to m, SM, *p1, k1* to m, *SM, k to m* twice, tw.
Row 2 (WS): MDS, *p to m, SM* twice, *p1, k1* to m, SM, p to m, SM, *k1, p1* to m, *SM, p to m* twice, tw.
Row 3: MDS, *k to m, SM* twice, *k1, p1* to m, SM, k to m, SM, *p1, k1* to m, SM, k to m, SM, k to DS, kDS, SM, work next row of Chart B.
Row 4: Work next row of Chart B, SM, *p to m, SM* twice, *p1, k1* to m, SM, p to m, SM, *k1, p1* to m, SM, p to m, SM, p to DS, pDS, SM, work next row of Chart A.
Row 5: Work next row of Chart A, SM, *k to m, SM* twice, *k1, p1* to m, SM, k to m, SM, *p1, k1* to m, SM, *k to m, SM* twice, work next row of Chart B.
Row 6: Work next row of Chart B, SM, *p to m, SM* twice, *p1, k1* to m, SM, p to m, SM, *k1, p1* to m, SM, *p to m, SM* twice, work next row of Chart A.
Rows 7–12: Rep rows 5–6, 3 times.
Rows 13–22: Rep rows 5–6, 5 times.
Rows 23–34: Rep rows 1–12 once more.
Note! Size 7 only: For the last yo, work as k instead of making a yo.

Note! If wanting to make the piece longer, rep rows 13–22 once more.

HEM

Change to US 9 / 5.5 mm needles.

Sizes 1, 2, 6, 7 and 8 only
Set-Up Row 1 (RS): Sl1 kwise wyib, *k to m, RM* twice, k to m, SM, *k1, p1* to m, SM, k to m, SM, *p1, k1* to m, SM, *k to m, RM* twice, k to end.

Sizes 3, 4, 5 and 9 only

Set-Up Row 1 (RS): Sl1 kwise wyib, k to m, RM, k to 2 sts bef m, k2tog, RM, k to m, SM, *k1, p1* to m, SM, k to m, SM, *p1, k1* to m, SM, k to m, RM, k2tog, k to m, RM, k to end. (2 sts dec'd) [– (–, 160, 172, 184) (–, –, –, 240) sts]

All sizes

Set-Up Row 2 (WS): Sl1 pwise wyif, p to m, SM, *p1, k1* to m, SM, p to m, SM, *k1, p1* to m, SM, p to end.
Row 1 (RS): Sl1 kwise wyib, *k1, p1* to m, RM, *k1, p1* to m, RM, k1, p1, k1, PM, k1, p1, k1, RM, *p1, k1* to m, RM, *p1, k1* to last st bef end, p1.
Row 2 (WS): Sl1 pwise wyif, p1, *k1, p1* to m, SM, *p1, k1* to end.
Row 3: Sl1 kwise wyib, k1, *p1, k1* to m, SM, *k1, p1* to end.
Rows 4–7: Rep rows 2–3, twice more.

BO all sts kwise loosely. RM as you reach it.

I-CORD BO FOR ARMHOLES

With US 10 / 6 mm needles.

Right Armhole

Move 10 (10, 12, 12, 12) (12, 12, 14, 16) sts from right shoulder onto a spare needle. Join yarn.
Set-Up Rnd: Starting from middle of underarm, pick up and k 1 (3, 3, 4, 4) (4, 6, 6, 7) st(s) from the CO edge, pick up and k 24 (25, 24, 29, 29) (30, 30, 32, 32) sts (approx. 2 sts for every 3 rows) along armhole edge, *k1, p1* 5 (5, 6, 6, 6) (6, 6, 7, 8) times from spare needle, pick up and k 24 (25, 24, 29, 29) (30, 30, 32, 32) sts along armhole edge, pick up and k 1 (2, 2, 3, 3) (4, 6, 6, 6) st(s) from CO edge, PM. [60 (65, 65, 77, 77) (80, 84, 90, 93) sts]

The armhole circumference is now 20 (21.75, 21.75, 25.75, 25.75) (26.75, 28, 30, 31)" / 50 (54, 54, 64, 64) (66.5, 70, 75, 77.5) cm. The circumference will decrease when working the i-cord BO.

Rnd 1: K to end, RM.

I-Cord BO (3 sts)

With US 8 / 5 mm DPNs and using the Cable Cast-On method, CO 3 sts.
K2, k2tog tbl, slip 3 sts back to LHN, rep *–* to last st, cut yarn leaving approx. 8" / 20 cm tail.

Using a tapestry needle, graft rem sts. Cut yarn.

Left Armhole

Move 10 (10, 12, 12, 12) (12, 12, 14, 16) sts from left shoulder onto a spare needle. Join yarn.

Set-Up Rnd: Starting from middle of underarm, pick up and k 1 (2, 2, 3, 3) (4, 6, 6, 6) st(s) from the CO edge, pick up and k 24 (25, 24, 29, 29) (30, 30, 32, 32) sts (approx. 2 sts for every 3 rows) along armhole edge, *p1, k1* 5 (5, 6, 6, 6) (6, 6, 7, 8) times from spare needle, pick up and k 24 (25, 24, 29, 29) (30, 30, 32, 32) sts along armhole edge, pick up and k 1 (3, 3, 4, 4) (4, 6, 6, 7) st(s) from CO edge, PM. [60 (65, 65, 77, 77) (80, 84, 90, 93) sts]

Work same as right armhole about rnd 1 and i-cord BO (3 sts).

FINISHING

Weave in ends. Wet block to measurements.

If attaching buttons, sew buttons on the 7th stitch of row 5 (which is a purl st) in Chart A, opposite yo of Chart B, which is buttonhole. If attaching buttons on each point opposite all buttonholes, 7 (7, 7, 8, 8) (8, 8, 9, 9) buttons are needed. For the sample, a button is attached for every other buttonhole.

CHART A

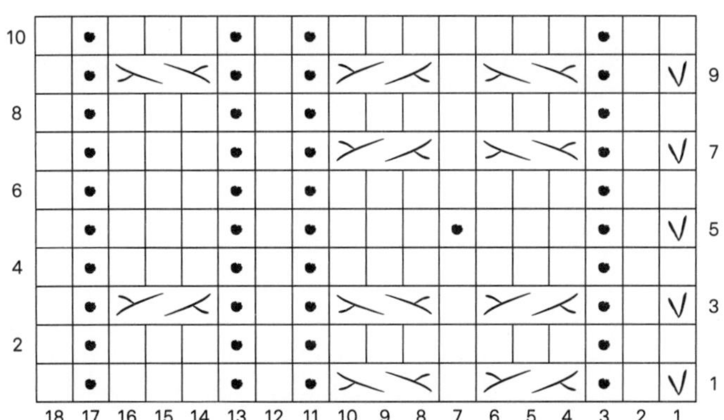

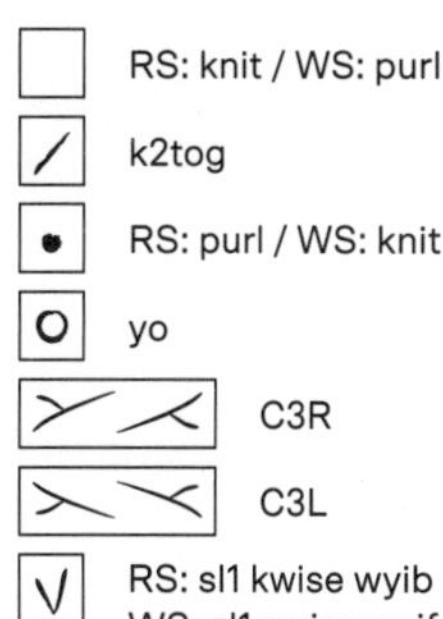

CHART B

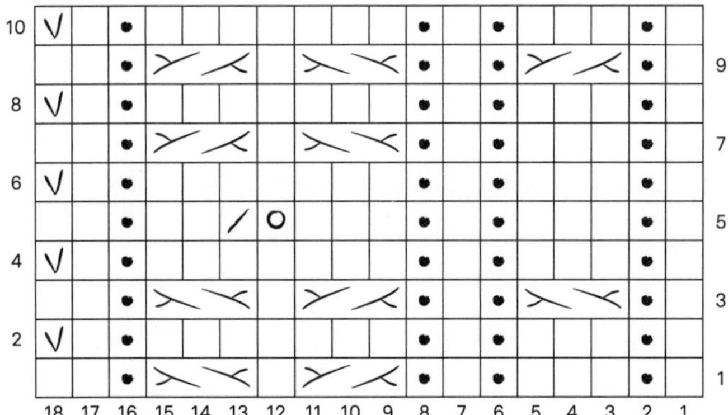

Kare Peacock

25 Synergy

This cropped, reversible crochet vest feels like a vintage wool blanket. The pattern and colours used for it are inspired by California's beautiful fields.

SIZES

1 (2, 3, 4, 5) (6, 7, 8, 9)

Recommended ease: 0–4" / 0–10 cm of negative ease.

FINISHED MEASUREMENTS

Bust Circumference: 31.75 (34.25, 36.5, 41.5, 46.5) (51.5, 56.25, 61.25, 66.25)" / 80.5 (87, 93, 105.5, 118) (130.5, 143, 155.5, 168) cm.
Length from Back Hem to Armhole: 9" / 23 cm.
Length from Back Hem to Back Neck: 18 (18.5, 19, 19.5, 20.5) (20.5, 21, 21.5, 21.5)" / 45.5 (47, 48.5, 50, 52) (52, 53.5, 55, 55) cm.
Armhole Depth: 9.75 (10.5, 11, 11.75, 12.25) (12.25, 13, 13.5, 13.5)" / 25 (26.5, 28, 29.5, 31.5) (31.5, 33, 34.5, 34.5) cm.

MATERIALS

Yarn: Bun by Bread & Butter (100% US merino, 130 yds / 118 m – 100 g).
C1: 2 (2, 2, 3, 3) (3, 3, 3, 3) skeins of colourway Elote.
C2: 1 (1, 1, 1, 1) (1, 1, 2, 2) skein(s) of colourway Lantana.
C3: 2 (2, 2, 2, 2) (3, 3, 3, 3) skeins of colourway Coastal Redwood.
C4: 2 (2, 2, 2, 2) (2, 3, 3, 3) skeins of colourway Baby Frog.

Or approx. the foll amounts of chunky-weight yarn:
C1: 185 (210, 235, 270, 295) (310, 340, 365, 385) yds / 165 (190, 215, 245, 270) (285, 310, 335, 355) m.
C2: 70 (80, 90, 105, 110) (120, 130, 140, 150) yds / 65 (75, 80, 95, 105) (110, 120, 130, 135) m.
C3: 175 (190, 210, 235, 255) (265, 285, 310, 325) yds / 160 (175, 190, 215, 230) (245, 265, 280, 295) m.
C4: 150 (175, 195, 225, 245) (260, 280, 305, 320) yds / 140 (160, 180, 205, 225) (235, 255, 280, 295) m.

An alternative yarn suggestion is for example Berroco Lanas Quick.

Crochet hook: US H-8 / 5 mm and US J-10 / 6 mm crochet hook.

Notions: Stitch marker.

GAUGE

13 sts x 13 rows to 4" / 10 cm on US J-10 / 6 mm hook in main patt with surface slip sts added, unblocked.

SPECIAL ABBREVIATIONS

ch: Chain.
sc: Single crochet.
sk: Skip.
sp: Space.
sc2tog: Single crochet 2 together. (1 st dec'd)
yoh: Yarn over hook.

NOTES

This pattern uses US crochet terminology.

For the background fabric, work according to the foll colour sequence:
5 rows of C1.

2 rows of C2.
2 rows of C3.
4 rows of C4.

For the vertical stripes, work according to the following colour sequence: the patt is reversible so the maker can choose whether to wear the raised chain side or the flat side.
3 rows of C1.
1 row of C2.
1 row of C3.
2 rows of C4.

The rib is worked after weaving in the ends.

CONSTRUCTION

This vest is crocheted from the bottom up in one piece to the armholes. The fronts and back are then worked separately before being seamed at the shoulders. The vest is worked in single crochet and chain stitches in a 4-colour sequence over 13 rows, then vertical rows of slip-stitches are crocheted in the open spaces in a 4-colour sequence over 7 rows to create the plaid pattern. Lastly, the armholes, neckline and hem are finished with a single crochet ribbed edge.

DIRECTIONS

BODY

Using US J-10 / 6 mm hook and C1, ch 104 (112, 120, 136, 152) (168, 184, 200, 216).

Row 1: Sc in 2nd ch from hook, *ch 1, sk next ch, sc in next ch*, rep *–* across, tw. [103 (111, 119, 135, 151) (167, 183, 199, 215) sts]
Row 2: Ch 1 (does not count as a st throughout), sc in first sc, ch 1, sk next ch-1 sp, *sc in next sc, ch 1, sk next ch-1 sp*, rep *–* across, sc in last sc, tw.
Rows 3–5: Rep row 2, break yarn and change to C2.
Rows 6–7: Rep row 2, break yarn and change to C3.
Rows 8–9: Rep row 2, break yarn and change to C4.
Rows 10–13: Rep row 2, break yarn and change to C1.
Cont in same colour sequence to end.

Cont in est 13-row patt changing yarn as indicated until piece measures 7" / 18 cm from edge, ending with a WS row.

FIRST FRONT

Armhole Shaping

Cont in est patt while changing yarn as required and beg to shape armholes as foll:
Row 1 (RS): Work 21 (23, 25, 27, 27) (29, 31, 33, 35) sts as est, tw.
Dec Row 1: Ch 1, sk first sc, sc in next ch-1 sp, sc in next sc, cont in patt across, tw. (1 st dec'd)
Dec Row 2: Work in patt to last 2 sc, sc2tog, tw. (1 st dec'd)
Rep dec rows 1–2 another 2 (2, 2, 2, 2) (3, 4, 5, 6) times. [15 (17, 19, 21, 21) (21, 21, 21, 21) sts]

Work straight until piece measures 5.75 (6.5, 7, 7.75, 8.25) (8.25, 9, 9.5, 9.5)" / 14.5 (16.5, 18, 19.5, 21) (21, 23, 24, 24) cm from beg of armhole, ending after a WS row.

Neck Shaping

Work dec rows 1–2 another 5 times. [5 (7, 9, 11, 11) (11, 11, 11, 11) sts]

Work straight until piece measures 9.75 (10.5, 11, 11.75, 12.25) (12.25, 13, 13.5, 13.5)" / 25 (26.5, 28, 30, 31) (31, 33, 34.5, 34.5) cm from beg of armhole. Break yarn.

BACK

Maintain colour sequence from body.

Row 1 (RS): Beg at end of row 1 of front armhole, sk 7 (7, 7, 11, 19) (23, 27, 31, 35) body sts, join yarn with sl st in next sc, work 47 (51, 55, 59, 59) (63, 67, 71, 75) sts as est, tw.
Dec Row 1: Ch 1, sk first sc, sc in next ch-1 sp, sc in next sc, cont in patt across to last 2 sts, sc in ch-1 sp, sk last sc, tw. (2 sts dec'd)
Dec Row 2: Ch 1, sc2tog, cont in patt across to last 2 sts, sc2tog, tw. (2 sts dec'd)
Rep dec rows 1–2 another 2 (2, 2, 2, 2) (3, 4, 5, 6) times. [35 (39, 43, 47, 47) (47, 47, 47, 47) sts]

Work straight until the piece measures 8.25 (9, 9.5, 10.25, 10.75) (10.75, 11.5, 12, 12)" / 21 (23, 24, 26, 27.5) (27.5, 29, 30.5, 30.5) cm from beg of armhole.

Back Neck Shaping

First Side
Row 1: Work 9 (11, 13, 15, 15) (15, 15, 15, 15) sts as est, tw.
Work front dec rows 1–2 twice more. [5 (7, 9, 11, 11) (11, 11, 11, 11) sts]

Break yarn.

Second Side
Join yarn with sl st in first st at opposite armhole edge. Rep first side neck shaping.

SECOND FRONT

Armhole Shaping

Maintain colour sequence from body. With WS facing, join yarn in first unworked body st at front edge.

Work as for first front.

VERTICAL STRIPES

Lay the piece flat. Begin at the front corner, and working all stripes from bottom edge up, work stripes of surface slip-sts in colour sequence in notes as follows: Make a slip knot and place it on the hook. With the hook in front of the piece and working yarn behind, insert the hook in first ch-sp at bottom edge, yoh and pull loop through ch-sp and loop on the hook, creating a slip-stitch. Insert the hook in ch-sp directly above, yoh and pull loop through ch-sp and loop on the hook. Continue up, working in each ch-sp. If running out of ch-sp due to decreases, keep going until you reach the edge of the garment by working through the sc.

FINISHING

Weave in ends.

With RSs facing each other, seam shoulders tog using Whip St.

RIBBED EDGE

The ribbed edge is crocheted in turned rnds. Join with a slip-st at end of each rnd, then tw to crochet in the opposite direction.

Using US H-8 / 5 mm hook and C3, join yarn at base of armhole.

Rnd 1: Ch 1, sc in same st, sc in each st and row end around, join with a slip-st in 1st st of rnd, tw.
Rep rnd 1 twice more. Break yarn.

Make second armhole alike.

Join yarn at back neck and rep rib instructions, working across back neckline, down front edge, around hemline and up other front edge.

Weave in rem ends. Wet block to measurements, if desired.

Sara Ottosson

26 Stratocumulus

Stratocumulus features some charming retro details! The plaid pattern of this zipped vest combines intarsia, marling and a variation of fisherman's rib.

SIZES

1 (2, 3, 4, 5) (6, 7, 8, 9)

Recommended ease: 4" / 10 cm of positive ease.

FINISHED MEASUREMENTS

Bust Circumference: 35.5 (39.25, 43.25, 47.25, 51.25) (55, 59, 63, 67)" / 90 (100, 110, 120, 130) (140, 150, 160, 170) cm.
Length from Underarm to Hem: 12.5 (12.25, 11.5, 12.75, 12.5) (11.75, 13.25, 12.5, 12.25)" / 31.5 (31, 29, 32.5, 31.5) (30, 33.5, 31.5, 31) cm.
Armhole Depth: 7.75 (8.25, 9, 9.5, 9.75) (10.5, 10.75, 11.5, 11.75)" / 20 (21, 23, 24, 25) (26.5, 27.5, 29.5, 30) cm.
Cross Back: 14.25 (15.25, 16.25, 17.25, 17.25) (18.25, 18.25, 19.25, 19.25)" / 36.5 (39, 41.5, 44, 44) (46.5, 46.5, 49, 49) cm.
Full Length (from Shoulder Top to Hem): 21.75 (21.75, 21.75, 23.5, 23.5) (23.5, 25.5, 25.5, 25.5)" / 55.5 (55.5, 55.5, 60, 60) (60, 64.5, 64.5, 64.5) cm.
Collar Height: 4.5 (4.5, 4.5, 4.5, 5.5) (5.5, 5.5, 5.5, 5.5)" / 11.5 (11.5, 11.5, 11.5, 14) (14, 14, 14, 14) cm.

MATERIALS

Yarn: Fritidsgarn by Sandnes Garn (100% Norwegian wool, 76 yds / 70 m - 50 g).
Yarn A: 3 (3, 3, 3, 4) (4, 4, 4, 4) balls of colourway 3326 Orange.
Yarn B: 4 (4, 5, 5, 5) (6, 6, 6, 6) balls of colourway 1012 Nature.
Yarn C: 4 (4, 5, 5, 6) (6, 7, 8, 8) balls of colourway 4023 Dusty Pink.

The yarns are held double throughout the pattern.

Or approx. 185 (200, 210, 225, 245) (260, 275, 285, 290) yds / 170 (185, 190, 205, 225) (240, 250, 260, 265) m (in Yarn A), 275 (300, 315, 365, 385) (405, 440, 445, 445) yds / 255 (275, 290, 335, 350) (370, 400, 405, 405) m (in Yarn B) and 285 (300, 345, 385, 400) (430, 520, 555, 575) yds / 260 (275, 315, 350, 365) (395, 475, 505, 525) m (in Yarn C) of bulky-weight yarn. Alternative yarn suggestions are for example Drops Alaska and Rauma Garn Vams (both held double).

Needles: US 10.5 / 7 mm 32–60" / 80–150 cm circular needles (for ribbing) and an extra needle for the 3-Needle BO. US 11 / 8 mm 32" / 80 cm circular needles (for main body). Two US 13 / 9 mm DPNs (for attached i-cord).

Notions: Stitch markers, stitch holder or waste yarn, zip 20 (20, 20, 21.5, 21.5) (21.5, 23, 23, 23)" / 50 (50, 50, 55, 55) (55, 60, 60, 60) cm long, sewing needle, sewing thread in the same colour as the zipper, row counter (optional but recommended).

GAUGE

10.5 sts x 14 rows to 4" / 10 cm on US 11 / 8 mm needles in St St worked flat with yarn held double, after blocking.

8 sts x 22 rows to 4" / 10 cm on US 11 / 8 mm needles in Fisherman's Rib worked flat with yarn held double, after blocking.

11 sts x 16 rows to 4" / 10 cm on US 10.5 / 7 mm needles in 1 x 1 rib worked flat with yarn held double, after blocking.

SPECIAL ABBREVIATIONS

K1b: K one st below.

STITCH PATTERNS

Fisherman's Rib Variation

Worked flat, over multiples of 2 sts, plus 1.
Row 1 (RS): *K1b, k1* to last st, k1b.
Row 2 (WS): K to end.
Rep rows 1–2 for patt.

SPECIAL TECHNIQUES

Marled Intarsia

In marled intarsia, marling is combined with intarsia to create a pattern where colours weave in and out of each other – in this case a plaid pattern. This is achieved by holding two strands of yarn together throughout: one strand is worked across the entire row(s) and the other changes according to the pattern, using intarsia to attach the separate colours. In intarsia, when changing colour, always pick up the new colour from underneath the old, regardless of which side you are on.

NOTES

The different balls of yarn will be referred to with both colours, A–C, and number to keep track of which ball is used in which part of the intarsia pattern. To prepare, you need the following balls in the specific weights:
A: Divide the yarn into 2 equal balls to have 2 strands to work with.
B1: 90 (95, 105, 135, 140) (145, 155, 160, 165) g. Mark this B ball with a marker (optional).
B2 and B3: 45 (50, 50, 60, 55) (60, 65, 65, 60) g.
C1 and C3: 25 (25, 30, 35, 35) (40, 45, 50, 50) g.
C2: 45 (50, 60, 70, 75) (80, 95, 100, 110) g.
C4: 90 (95, 105, 110, 115) (120, 155, 160, 165) g. Mark this C ball with a marker (optional).

Note! If using a yarn with a different yardage to Sandnes Fritidsgarn (76 yds / 70 m – 50 g), the specific weights given before don't match. Add more yarn to the ball later if running out.

Stitch counts include selvage stitches.

CONSTRUCTION

This vest is worked flat in two strands of yarn held together from the bottom up. First, a section of 1 x 1 ribbing is worked after which a variation of the classic Fisherman's Rib is knitted throughout the vest. The body is worked in marled intarsia using two strands of yarn: one strand is worked throughout the row and the other changes using intarsia to create a plaid pattern. The plaid pattern expands through the sizes. At the armholes, the vest is divided into two front pieces and a back piece that are worked separately and joined at the shoulders with a 3-Needle Bind-Off. Stitches are then picked up along the neckline to work the ribbed collar. Lastly, the fronts and armholes are finished with an i-cord. After blocking, a zipper is sewn to the front.

DIRECTIONS

HEM

With US 10.5 / 7 mm needles, Yarn A held double, and the Italian Tubular CO method, CO 71 (79, 87, 95, 103) (111, 119, 127, 135) sts (including the slip knot).

Row 1 (WS): K1tbl, *sl1 wyif, k1* to end.
Row 2 (RS): Sl1 wyif, *k1, sl1 wyif* to end.

The first and last st of each row is a selvage st and is worked as foll throughout unless otherwise stated:
RS Rows: Sl1 wyif, cont according to patt to last st, sl1 wyif.
WS Rows: K first and last st.
Note! When changing colour, work the selvage st and then change to the new colour with the yarn held in back.

Rib Row 1 (WS): K1, *p1, k1* to end.
Rib Row 2 (RS): Sl1 wyif, *k1, p1* to last 2 sts, k1, sl1 wyif.
Work as set for another 3 rows (end after a WS row).

Without cutting Yarn A, change to Yarn B held double and work 2 rows in rib.
Cut Yarn B and change back to Yarn A. Work another 5 rows of rib, ending after a RS row.

On the next row, pl 4 markers as foll:
Next Row (WS): Work 8 (9, 10, 11, 12) (13, 14, 15, 16) sts in rib, PM, work 19 (21, 23, 25, 27) (29, 31, 33, 35) sts in rib, PM, work 17 (19, 21, 23, 25) (27, 29, 31, 33) sts in rib, PM, work 19 (21, 23, 25, 27) (29, 31, 33, 35) sts in rib, PM, work in rib to end.

Cut Yarn A.

BODY

The body is worked flat in the Fisherman's Rib Variation patt and marled intarsia using Yarns B and C to create the plaid pattern. Selvage sts are worked as bef throughout the body. Slip m's as you reach them.

Beg with B1 + C1. B1 is used throughout the set-up rows (and the rest of Plaid A).
Set-Up Row (RS): Using B1 and C1, k to m, change C1 to B2, k to m, change B2 to C2, k to m, change C2 to B3, k to m, change B3 to C3, k to end using B1 and C3.

Change to US 11 / 8 mm needles.

Set-Up Row (WS): Using B1 and C3, k to m, change C3 to B3 and k to m, change B3 to C2 and k to m, change C2 to B2 and k to m, change B2 to C1 and k to end using C1 and B1.

Plaid A

Row 1 (RS): Working Fisherman's Rib Variation patt throughout, using B1 and C1 work in patt to m, change C1 to B2, work in patt to m, change B2 to C2, work in patt to m, change C2 to B3, work in patt to m, change B3 to C3, work in patt to end using B1 and C3.
Row 2 (WS): Working Fisherman's Rib Variation patt throughout, using B1 and C3 work in patt to m, change C3 to B3, work in patt to m, change B3 to C2, work in patt to m, change C2 to B2, work in patt to m, change B2 to C1, work in patt to end using B1 and C1.
Rep rows 1–2 a further 3 times. A total of 10 rows of Plaid A patt (including the 2 set-up rows) have been worked.

Plaid B

Cut B1. Change to C4.
Rep row 1–2, 5 times, using C4 in place of B1. A total of 10 rows of Plaid B patt have been worked.

Work Plaid A (changing back to B1) for 10 rows, then Plaid B (changing back to C4) for 10 rows.
A total number of 4 stripes and 2 sets of Plaids A + B have been worked.

Throughout the rest of the work, alternate between Plaid A and Plaid B stripes (10 rows each) at the same time as working in the Fisherman's Rib Variation patt. When body is finished, there will be 10 (10, 10, 11, 11) (11, 12, 12, 12) stripes in total, counting from the bottom hem to the top of the shoulders.

From this point on, you will need to keep careful count of the rows (use a row counter or preferred method).

Work 10 (8, 4, 12, 10) (6, 14, 10, 8) rows in patt, ending after a WS row.
Last row worked is row 10 (8, 4, 2, 10) (6, 4, 10, 8) of Plaid A (A, A, B, A) (A, B, A, A).

Divide for Fronts and Back

Next Row (RS): Work 16 (18, 19, 21, 22) (24, 25, 27, 28) sts in patt for right front, BO next 3 (3, 5, 5, 7) (7, 9, 9, 11) sts in patt, work in patt until there are 33 (37, 39, 43, 45) (49, 51, 55, 57) sts on RHN for the back, BO next 3 (3, 5, 5, 7) (7, 9, 9, 11) sts in patt, work in patt to end. [65 (73, 77, 85, 89) (97, 101, 109, 113) sts: 16 (18, 19, 21, 22) (24, 25, 27, 28) sts for each front and 33 (37, 39, 43, 45) (49, 51, 55, 57) sts for the back]

Do not cut yarns.

Either keep all sts on the needles, or pl back sts and right front sts on a stitch holder or scrap yarn, leaving 16 (18, 19, 21, 22) (24, 25, 27, 28) sts for left front.

LEFT FRONT

Selvage sts are worked as set at both ends of each row unless otherwise stated. Cont with Plaids A + B and Fisherman's Rib Variation patt.

Cont where the working yarn is.
Next row will be row 2 (10, 6, 4, 2) (8, 6, 2, 10) of Plaid B (A, A, B, B) (A, B, B, A).

Note! When changing colour while shaping the armhole, use the previous colour to work the first 2 sts of the new row (the slipped selvage st and the p st) then cut the yarn and change colour.

Armhole Shaping

Sizes 5–9 only
Row 1 (WS): Work in patt to 2 sts bef end, sl2 wyib.
Row 2 (RS): Sl1 wyif, p1, pass slipped st over p st to BO, work in patt to end. (1 st dec'd)
Rep rows 1–2 a further – (–, –, –, 0) (1, 2, 3, 4) time(s). [– (–, –, –, 21) (22, 22, 23, 23) sts]

All sizes
Row 1 (WS): Work in patt to 2 sts bef end, sl2 wyib.
Row 2 (RS): Sl1 wyif, p1, BO slipped st over p st, work in patt to end. (1 st dec'd)
Row 3: Work in patt.
Row 4: Work in patt.
Rep rows 1–4 a further 1 (2, 2, 3, 3) (3, 3, 3, 3) time(s). [14 (15, 16, 17, 17) (18, 18, 19, 19) sts]

Last worked row is row 9 (1, 7, 9, 9) (7, 7, 5, 5) of Plaid B (A, B, A, A) (A, B, B, B).

Work 22 (20, 24, 22, 20) (22, 22, 24, 24) rows in patt, ending after an RS row. Last worked row is row 1 (1, 1, 1, 9) (9, 9, 9, 9) of Plaid A (A, A, B, A) (A, B, B, B).

Neckline Shaping

Next Row (WS): BO 3 (3, 4, 4, 4) (4, 4, 4, 4) sts pwise (k selvage st), work in patt to end. [11 (12, 12, 13, 13) (14, 14, 15, 15) sts]
Row 1 (RS): Work in patt to 2 sts bef end, sl2 wyib. *Note!* If the first st of the last 2 sts is supposed to be a k1b, sl it pwise together with the st below.
Row 2: Sl1 wyif, p1, BO sl st over p st, work in patt to end. (1 st dec'd)
Rep rows 1–2 once more. [9 (10, 10, 11, 11) (12, 12, 13, 13) sts]

Work 2 rows in patt without shaping, RS and WS.
Then, work rows 1 and 2 once more. [8 (9, 9, 10, 10) (11, 11, 12, 12) sts]
Last worked row is row 10 (10, 10, 10, 8) (8, 8, 8, 8) of Plaid A (A, A, B, B) (B, A, A, A).

Work 7 (7, 7, 7, 9) (9, 9, 9, 9) rows in patt, ending after an RS row.
Last worked row is row 7 of Plaid B (B, B, A, A) (A, B, B, B).

Shoulder Shaping

When shaping the shoulders with short rows, you don't change colours of the yarn regardless of if you have a few extra rows on that stripe.
Row 1 (WS): Work 5 (5, 6, 6, 6) (6, 6, 6, 6) sts in patt, tw.
Row 2 (RS): MDS, work in patt to end.
Row 3: Work in patt to DS, kDS, work in patt to end.
Row 4: RM as you come to it, work in patt to end.

Cut yarns. Either keep all sts on the needles, or pl shoulder sts on a st holder or scrap yarn.

BACK

Selvage sts are worked as bef on both sides, unless otherwise stated. Cont in Plaid and Fisherman's Rib Variation patt.

Note! As bef, when changing colour while shaping the armhole, use the prev colour to work the first 2 sts of the new row (the slipped selvage st and the p st), then cut the yarn and change colour.

Put the 33 (37, 39, 43, 45) (49, 51, 55, 57) sts for the back on US 11 / 8 mm 32" / 80 cm needles.

Beg at WS with C4+B3 (B1+B3, B1+B3, C4+B3, C4+B3) (B1+B3, C4+B3, C4+B3, B1+B3) and row 2 (10, 6, 4, 2) (8, 6, 2, 10) of Plaid B (A, A, B, B) (A, B, B, A).

Armhole Shaping

Sizes 5–9 only
Row 1 (WS): Sl1 wyif, p1, pass slipped st over p st to BO, work in patt to 2 sts bef end, sl2 wyib. (1 st dec'd)
Row 2 (RS): Sl1 wyif, p1, pass slipped st over p st to BO, work in patt to 2 sts bef end, sl2 wyib. (1 st dec'd)
Rep rows 1–2 a further – (–, –, –, 0) (1, 2, 3, 4) time(s). [– (–, –, –, 43) (45, 45, 47, 47) sts]

All sizes
Row 1 (WS): Sl1 wyif, p1, pass slipped st over p st to BO, work in patt to 2 sts bef end, sl2 wyib. (1 st dec'd)
Row 2 (RS): Sl1 wyif, p1, pass slipped st over p st to BO, work in patt to end. (1 st dec'd)
Row 3: Work in patt.
Row 4: Work in patt to 2 sts bef end, sl2 wyib.
Rep rows 1–4 a further 1 (2, 2, 3, 3) (3, 3, 3, 3) time(s). *Note!* On the last row, don't slip the last 2 sts, work in patt to end. [29 (31, 33, 35, 35) (37, 37, 39, 39) sts]

Last row worked is row 9 (1, 7, 9, 9) (7, 7, 5, 5) of Plaid B (A, B, A, A) (A, B, B, B).

Work 35 (33, 37, 35, 35) (37, 37, 39, 39) rows in patt, ending after a WS row. Last row worked is row 4 of Plaid B (B, B, A, A) (A, B, B, B).

Neckline Shaping

Next Row (RS): Work 10 (11, 11, 12, 12) (13, 13, 14, 14) sts in patt, BO the next 9 (9, 11, 11, 11) (11, 11, 11, 11) sts in patt, work in patt to end. [10 (11, 11, 12, 12) (13, 13, 14, 14) sts for each shoulder]

Left Shoulder Shaping

When shaping the shoulders with short rows, you don't change colours of the yarn regardless of if you have a few extra rows on that stripe.

Row 1 (WS): Work in patt to 2 sts bef end, sl2 wyib.
Row 2 (RS): Sl1 wyif, p1, pass slipped st over p st to BO, work in patt to end. (1 st dec'd)
Row 3: Work in patt to 2 sts bef end, sl2 wyib.
Row 4: Sl1 wyif, p1, pass slipped st over p st to BO, work 3 (4, 4, 4, 4) (5, 5, 4, 4) sts in patt, tw. (1 st dec'd)
Row 5: MDS, work in patt to end.
Row 6: RM as you come to it, work in patt to DS, kDS, work in patt to end. [8 (9, 9, 10, 10) (11, 11, 12, 12) sts]

Cont with working yarn and join left back shoulder tog with left front piece using the 3-Needle BO method, WS facing out. Cut yarns.

Right Shoulder

10 (11, 11, 12, 12) (13, 13, 14, 14) sts on your needles.

Beg at WS using C4+C2 (C4+C2, C4+C2, B1+C2, B1+C2) (B1+C2, C4+C2, C4+C2, C4+C2) and row 6 of Plaid B (B, B, A, A) (A, B, B, B).

When finishing a Plaid stripe during the shoulder, do not change colours of the yarn regardless of if you have a few extra rows on that stripe.
Row 1 (WS): Sl1, p1, pass slipped st over p st to BO, work in patt to end. (1 st dec'd)
Row 2 (RS): Work in patt to 2 sts bef end, sl2 wyib. *Note!* If the first st of the last 2 sts is supposed to be a k1b, sl it pwise together with the st below.
Row 3: Sl1, p1, pass slipped st over p st to BO, work 4 (4, 5, 5, 5) (5, 5, 5, 5) sts in patt, tw. (1 st dec'd)
Row 4: MDS, work in patt to end.
Row 5: Work in patt to DS, kDS, work in patt to end.
Row 6: RM as you come to it, work in patt to end. [8 (9, 9, 10, 10) (11, 11, 12, 12) sts]

Cut yarns. Either keep all sts on the needles, or pl shoulder sts on a st holder or scrap yarn.

RIGHT FRONT

Selvage sts are worked as bef both in the front and at the armhole. Cont with the Plaid patt and the Fisherman's Rib Variation patt.

Put the 16 (18, 19, 21, 22) (24, 25, 27, 28) sts for the right front on US 11 / 8 mm needles.

Beg at WS using C4+B2 (B1+B2, B1+B2, C4+B2, C4+B2) (B1+B2, C4+B2, C4+B2, B1+B2) and row 2 (10, 6, 4, 2) (8, 6, 2, 10) of Plaid B (A, A, B, B) (A, B, B, A).

Armhole Shaping

Sizes 5–9 only
Row 1 (WS): Sl1 wyib, p1, pass slipped st over p st to BO, work in patt to end. (1 st dec'd)
Row 2 (RS): Work in patt to 2 sts bef end, sl2 wyib.
Rep rows 1–2 a further – (–, –, –, 0) (1, 2, 3, 3) time(s). [– (–, –, –, 21) (22, 22, 23, 23) sts]

All sizes
Row 1 (WS): Sl1 wyib, p1, pass slipped st over p st to BO, work in patt to end. (1 st dec'd)
Row 2 (RS): Work in patt.
Row 3: Work in patt.
Row 4: Work in patt to 2 sts bef end, sl2 wyib.
Rep rows 1–4 a further 1 (2, 2, 3, 3) (3, 3, 3, 3) time(s). *Note!* On the last row, don't slip the last 2 sts, work in patt to end. [14 (15, 16, 17, 17) (18, 18, 19, 19) sts]

Last row worked is row 9 (1, 7, 9, 9) (7, 7, 5, 5) of Plaid B (A, B, A, A) (A, B, B, B).

Work 21 (19, 23, 21 19) (21, 21, 23, 23) rows in patt, ending after a WS row. Last row worked is row 10 (10, 10, 10, 8) (8, 8, 8, 8) of Plaid B (B, B, A, A) (A, B, B, B).

Neckline Shaping

Next Row (RS): BO 3 (3, 4, 4, 4) (4, 4, 4, 4) sts in patt, work in patt to end. [11 (12, 12, 13, 13) (14, 14, 15, 15) sts]

Row 1 (WS): Work in patt to 2 sts bef end, sl2 wyib.
Row 2 (RS): Sl1 wyif, p1, pass slipped st over p st to BO, work in patt to end. (1 st dec'd)
Rep rows 1 and 2 once more. [9 (10, 10, 11, 11) (12, 12, 13, 13) sts]

Work 2 rows in patt.
Then, rep rows 1 and 2 once more. [8 (9, 9, 10, 10) (11, 11, 12, 12) sts]
Last row worked is row 9 (9, 9, 9, 7) (7, 7, 7, 7) of Plaid A (A, A, B, B) (B, A, A, A).

Work 9 (9, 9, 9, 11) (11, 11, 11, 11) rows in patt, ending after a WS row.
Last row worked is row 8 of Plaid B (B, B, A, A) (A, B, B, B).

Shoulder Shaping

If finishing a Plaid stripe during the shoulder, do not change colours of the yarn regardless of if you have a few extra rows on that stripe.

Row 1 (RS): Work 4 (5, 5, 5, 5) (6, 6, 5, 5) sts in patt, tw.
Row 2 (WS): MDS, work in patt to end.
Row 3: RM as you come to it, work in patt to DS, kDS, work in patt to end.

Cont with working yarn and join right back shoulder and right front piece using the 3-Needle BO method, WS facing out. Cut yarns.

COLLAR

With RS facing, using 2 strands of Yarn A and US 10.5 / 7 mm needles, pick up and k 47 (47, 51, 51, 53) (53, 53, 53, 53) sts around the neckline, beg at the right front neckline: pick up 1 st in every slipped selvage st, and pick up 1 extra st at each edge of the back neckline, next to the BO sts. At the front of the left front piece, pick up in the st below the selvage st, to match the right front piece.

Rib Row 1 (WS): K1, *p1, k1* to end.
Rib Row 2 (RS): Sl1 wyif, *k1, p1* to last 2 sts, k1, sl1 wyif.
Cont in rib and selvage sts as set for another 5 (5, 5, 5, 7) (7, 7, 7, 7) rows, ending after a WS row.

Without cutting Yarn A, change to Yarn B held double and work 2 rows in rib. Cut Yarn B and change back to Yarn A. Work another 6 (6, 6, 6, 8) (8, 8, 8, 8) rows in rib, ending after a WS row.

Next Row (RS): Sl1 wyif, *k1, sl1 wyif* to end.
Next Row (WS): K1, *sl1 wyif, k1* to end.

BO with the Italian Tubular BO method.

ATTACHED I-CORDS

You will work an attached i-cord along the edges of the fronts and around the armholes.
With RS facing, *pick up 1 st just inside of the selvage st, slide all 4 sts to the other end of the DPN, k2, k2tog tbl*. Rep *–* until the i-cord has been worked.

Front Opening

Using US 13 / 9 mm DPNs and 2 strands of Yarn A, CO 3 sts with the Long-Tail CO method.

Beg at bottom of right front hem, *pick up 1 st just inside of the selvage st, slide all 4 sts to the other end of the DPN, k2, k2tog tbl*. Rep *–* until the top of the collar has been reached. To finish, k2, BO first st, work k2tog tbl, BO second st and fasten off. Then CO 3 sts as bef, beg at top of left front collar and work down as bef.
Note! Along the edge of the fronts (worked in the Fisherman's Rib Variation patt), skip every 4th st when picking up a new st – otherwise, work the i-cord in every st.

Tip! If the i-cord seems too tight (or loose), pick up more (or fewer) sts along the fronts.

Armholes

Using US 13 / 9 mm DPNs and 2 strands of Yarn A, CO 3 sts with the Long-Tail CO method.

Beg at the bottom of the armhole, *pick up 1 st just inside of the selvage st, slide all 4 sts to the other end of the DPN, k2, k2tog tbl*. Rep *–* until the i-cord has been worked.
Note! Along the straight sides of the armhole, skip every 4th st when picking up a new st – otherwise, work the i-cord in every st all the way around. Sew ends tog neatly.

FINISHING

Weave in ends. Hide as many ends as possible inside the i-cords for a quick and easy finish. Wet block to measurements.

Sew the zipper to the fronts with 2 strands of sewing thread (to make it stronger), stitching just on the outside of the i-cord. If choosing to sew the zipper using a sewing machine, hand baste the zipper to the front first to make it as smooth as possible.

27

Scarves & Cowls

Vicky M — Lili Tobias — Natalya Berezynska

Rebekka Mauser — Julia Wilkens — Cristina Cusano — Pauliina Kuunsola

Marion Bulin — Aude Martin — Sini Kramer

Vicky M

27 Heart Scarf

This fun scarf by Vicky M – known as Vicky Knits – is an easy pattern with intarsia hearts throughout. Perfect for confident beginner-level knitters!

SIZE

One size.

FINISHED MEASUREMENTS

Length: Approx. 89" / 225 cm.
Width: Approx. 7.5" / 19 cm.

MATERIALS

Yarn: Lil' Crazy Sexy Wool by Wool and the Gang (100% wool, 87 yds / 80 m – 100 g).
Colour A: 3 balls in colourway Cameo Rose.
Colour B: 1 ball in colourway Lipstick Red.

Or approx. 230 yds / 210 m (in Colour A) and 87 yds / 80 m (in Colour B) of chunky-weight yarn. Alternative yarn suggestions are for example The Fibre Co. &Make Super Bulky, Happy Sheep Woolpower Big and Rico Design Creative Fun Felting Wool.

Needles: US 11 / 8 mm needles.

GAUGE

11.5 sts x 15 rows to 4" / 10 cm on US 11 / 8 mm needles in St St, after blocking.

CONSTRUCTION

This scarf is knitted from the bottom up. Intarsia is used for the heart pattern with a lace stitch worked at the hearts' edges. Change colours by using the intarsia method when indicated with A and B, making sure to twist the yarns together to avoid holes at the join.

DIRECTIONS

BODY

With A, US 11 / 8 mm needles and the Long-Tail CO method, CO 23 sts.

K 3 rows.

Next, est 2 selvage sts at either side:
Next Row (RS): K to end.
Next Row (WS): K2, p19, k2.
Rep last 2 rows twice more.

Using either the chart for rows 1–22 or the written instructions, start working the heart pattern, using A and B, as foll:
Row 1 (RS): With A k11, with B k1, with A k11.
Row 2 (WS): With A k2, p8, with B p3, with A p8, k2.
Row 3: With A k10, with B k1, yo, ssk, with A k10.
Note! To avoid long floats in this area, start using a second ball of A.

Note! To avoid long floats in this area, start using a little ball of A for the small section in the middle of the heart.

Row 21: With A k6, with B k1, yo, k3tog, yo, with A k3, with B yo, k3tog, yo, k1, with A k6.
Row 22: With A k2, p4, with B p4, with A p3, with B p4, with A p4, k2.

The heart is completed. Cut B.

Row 23 (RS): K to end.
Row 24 (WS): K2, p19, k2.
Rows 25–32: Rep rows 23 and 24 another 4 times.

Rep rows 1–32, another 8 times.
On the next rep, finish after row 28, then k 4 rows.

BO all sts.

FINISHING

Weave in the ends. Wet block to measurements.

Row 4: With A k2, p8, with B p3, with A p8, k2.
Row 5: With A k9, with B k2tog, yo, k1, yo, ssk, with A k9.
Row 6: With A k2, p7, with B p5, with A p7, k2.
Row 7: With A k8, with B k2tog, yo, k3, yo, ssk, with A k8.
Row 8: With A k2, p6, with B p7, with A p6, k2.
Row 9: With A k7, with B k2tog, yo, k5, yo, ssk, with A k7.
Row 10: With A k2, p5, with B p9, with A p5, k2.
Row 11: With A k6, with B k2tog, yo, k7, yo, ssk, with A k6.
Row 12: With A k2, p4, with B p11, with A p4, k2.
Row 13: With A k5, with B k2tog, yo, k9, yo, ssk, with A k5.
Row 14: With A k2, p3, with B p13, with A p3, k2.
Row 15: With A k4, with B k2tog, yo, k11, yo, ssk, with A k4.
Row 16: With A k2, p2, with B p15, with A p2, k2.
Row 17: With A k4, with B k1, yo, ssk, k4, yo, ssk, k3, k2tog, yo, k1, with A k4.
Row 18: With A k2, p2, with B p15, with A p2, k2.
Row 19: With A k5, with B k1, yo, ssk, k1, k2tog, yo, k1, yo, ssk, k1, k2tog, yo, k1, with A k5.
Row 20: With A k2, p3. with B p6, with A p1, with B p6, with A p3, k2.

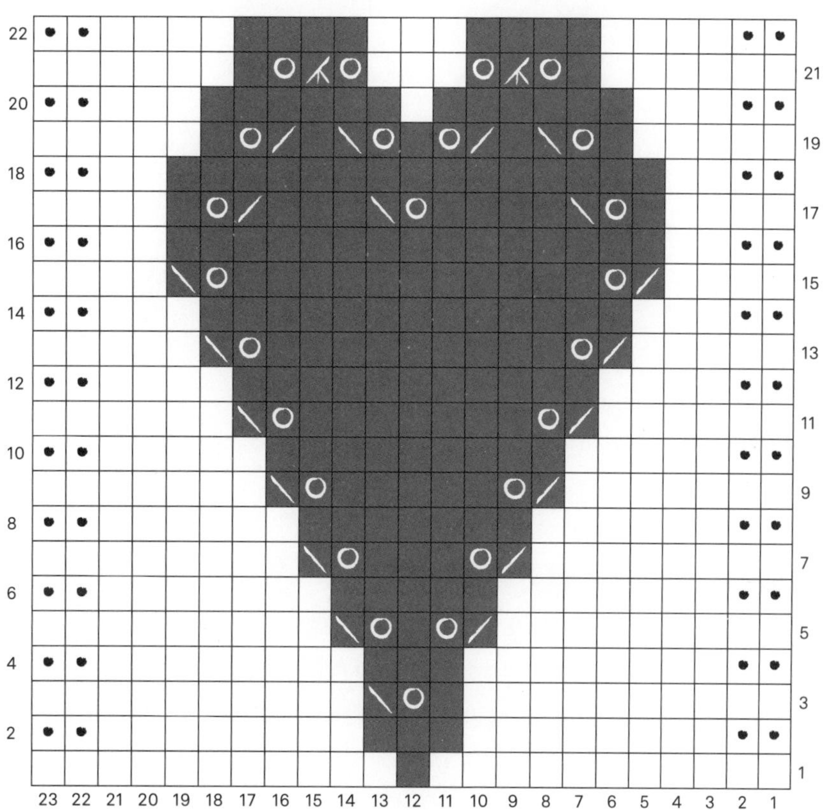

- RS: knit / WS: purl
- • RS: purl / WS: knit
- O yo
- \ ssk
- / k2tog
- k3tog
- Colour A
- Colour B

Lili Tobias

28 One Chevron Scarf

A seemingly simple idea creates a fun and exciting shape for this cosy, oversized scarf. Designed with a single-ply super-chunky yarn, it is perfect for the coldest winter days!

SIZE

One size.

FINISHED MEASUREMENTS

Length (Excluding Tassels): 84.5" / 214.5 cm.
Width: 9.5" / 24 cm.

MATERIALS

Yarn: 6 skeins of Super Soft Merino by Purl Soho (100% merino, 87 yds / 79 m - 100 g), colourway Pink Starfish.

Or approx. 515 yds / 471 m of super-bulky-weight yarn. Alternative yarn suggestions are for example Bernat Softee Chunky, Malabrigo Chunky and Drops Snow.

Needles: US 11 / 8 mm 24" / 60 cm circular needles.

Notions: Stitch marker, piece of cardboard (to make tassels).

GAUGE

16.5 sts x 15.5 rows to 4" / 10 cm on US 11 / 8 mm needles in 1 x 1 rib, after blocking.

CONSTRUCTION

This scarf is knitted flat beginning at the forked end of the scarf. Three stitches for the left point are cast on and a simple 1 x 1 ribbing is worked while increasing at one edge. Similar steps are repeated for the right point, and once both points are of equal length, the points are joined together. From here, the scarf's main body is worked in a chevron pattern with increases at the edges and a double decrease at the centre. Once the scarf nears its final length, increases are omitted to form the final, central, point. As a final touch, three tassels are attached, one to each point.

DIRECTIONS

LEFT POINT

With the Long-Tail CO method, CO 3 sts.

Set-Up Row (WS): Sl1, k1, sl1.

Row 1 (RS): K1, m1r(p), p1, k1. (4 sts)
Row 2 (WS): Sl1, k2, sl1.
Row 3: K1, p1, m1r, p1, k1. (5 sts)
Row 4: Sl1, k1, p1, k1, sl1.
Row 5: K1, p1, k1, m1r(p), p1, k1. (6 sts)
Row 6: Sl1, k2, p1, k1, sl1.
Row 7: *K1, p1* to 2 sts bef end, m1r, p1, k1. (7 sts)
Row 8: Sl1, k1, *p1, k1* to 1 st bef end, sl1.
Row 9: *K1, p1* to 3 sts bef end, k1, m1r(p), p1, k1. (8 sts)
Row 10: Sl1, k2, *p1, k1* to 1 st bef end, sl1.
Rep rows 7–10, 8 more times. (16 sts inc'd) (24 sts)

Do not turn at end of last row. Cut yarn.

RIGHT POINT

Keeping the left point on the same needle, CO 3 sts to unoccupied needle. Then, slide left point onto the cord of the circular needle.

Set-Up Row (WS): Sl1, k1, sl1.

Row 1: K1, p1, m1l(p), k1. (4 sts)
Row 2: Sl1, k2, sl1.
Row 3: K1, p1, m1l, p1, k1. (5 sts)
Row 4: Sl1, k1, p1, k1, sl1.
Row 5: K1, p1, m1l(p), k1, p1, k1. (6 sts)
Row 6: Sl1, k1, p1, k2, sl1.
Row 7: K1, p1, m1l, *p1, k1* to end. (7 sts)
Row 8: Sl1, *k1, p1* to 2 sts bef end, k1, sl1.
Row 9: K1, p1, m1l(p), k1, *p1, k1* to end. (8 sts)
Row 10: Sl1, *k1, p1* to 3 sts bef end, k2, sl1.
Rep rows 7–10, 8 more times. (16 sts inc'd) (24 sts)

JOIN POINTS

Joining Row (RS): K1, p1, m1l, *p1, k1* to 2 sts bef end of right point, p1, k2tog (last st of right point and first st of left point), p1, PM, *k1, p1* to 2 sts bef end, m1r, p1, k1. (1 st inc'd) (49 sts)

Next Row (WS): Sl1, k1, *p1, k1* to 1 st bef m, p1, SM, k1, sl1, *k1, p1* to 2 sts bef end, k1, sl1.

CONTINUE CHEVRON

Row 1 (RS): K1, p1, m1l(p), *k1, p1* to 4 sts bef m, k1, CDD, RM, k1, PM, *p1, k1* to 2 sts bef end, m1r(p), p1, k1.
Row 2 (WS): Sl1, k2, *p1, k1* to m, SM, p1, sl1, *p1, k1* to 2 sts bef end, k1, sl1.
Row 3: K1, p1, m1l, *p1, k1* to 4 sts bef m, p1, CDD, RM, p1, PM, *k1, p1* to 2 sts bef end, m1r, p1, k1.
Row 4: Sl1, *k1, p1* to m, SM, k1, sl1, *k1, p1* to 2 sts bef end, k1, sl1.
Rep rows 1–4 until scarf measures 72.5" / 184 cm from the tip of either point, ending on a 4th row.

DECREASE TO POINT

Row 1: *K1, p1* to 4 sts bef m, k1, CDD, RM, k1, PM, *p1, k1* to end. (2 sts dec'd)
Row 2: Sl1, *k1, p1* to 1 st bef m, k1, SM, p1, sl1, *p1, k1* to 1 st bef end, sl1.
Row 3: *K1, p1* to 3 sts bef m, CDD, RM, p1, PM, *k1, p1* to last st, k1. (2 sts dec'd)
Row 4: Sl1, *k1, p1* to m, SM, k1, sl1, *k1, p1* to 2 sts bef end, k1, sl1.
Rep rows 1–4 until 13 sts rem, ending on a row 4. (36 sts dec'd)

FINAL DECREASES

Row 1: *K1, p1* to 4 sts bef m, k1, CDD, RM, k1, *p1, k1* to end. (11 sts)
Row 2: Sl1, k1, p1, k1, p1, sl1, *p1, k1* twice, sl1.
Row 3: *K1, p1* twice, CDD, *p1, k1* twice. (9 sts)
Row 4: *Sl1, k1, p1, k1*, rep *–* twice, sl1.
Row 5: K1, p1, k1, CDD, k1, p1, k1. (7 sts)
Row 6: Sl1, k1, p1, sl1, p1, k1, sl1.
Row 7: K1, p1, CDD, p1, k1. (5 sts)
Row 8: Sl1, k1, sl1, k1, sl1.
Row 9: K1, CDD, k1. (3 sts)
Row 10: Sl3.
Row 11: Sl2 tog kwise, sl1 pwise, pass first 2 slipped sts over and off needle. (1 st)

FINISHING

Cut yarn and pull through remaining stitch. Weave in all ends except for the end attached to each of the three points of the scarf. Spray block scarf.

Use a piece of cardboard to make three 4.5" / 11.5 cm long tassels (wrapping the yarn 20 times around the cardboard). Use remaining three ends to attach tassels to each point of scarf.

Natalya Berezynska

29 Stacked Lines

This contemporary scarf was inspired by urban architecture and the Stacking Stool: a timeless design by the Finnish architect and designer Alvar Aalto.

SIZES

Scarf (Wrap)

FINISHED MEASUREMENTS

Length: 79 (67)" / 200.5 (170) cm.
Width: 9 (17)" / 23 (43) cm.

MATERIALS

Yarn: 5 (10) skeins of Luft by Woolfolk (55% Ovis 21 Ultimate Merino, 45% organic Pima cotton, 109 yds / 100 m – 50 g), colourway L14.

Or approx. 545 (1090) yds / 500 (1000) m of light-weight bulky-weight yarn. Alternative yarn suggestions are for example We are Knitters The Double Trouble Yarn, Gepard Garn PuF and Katia Concept Cotton Merino.

Needles: US 10 / 6 mm 16" / 40 cm circular needles.

Notions: Row counter (optional).

GAUGE

16 sts x 24.5 rows to 4" / 10 cm in Garter St, after blocking.

NOTES

The 3 first and 3 last stitches of each row form an i-cord edge.

The pattern is written for the scarf size sample (shown in the pictures). However, the pattern can be used to make a larger wrap. Please see the wrap modifications at the end of the pattern.

CONSTRUCTION

This scarf is worked from end to end. It features sets of slip-stitch columns on a background of classic Garter Stitch. I-cord edges provide a finished look and flawless structure.

DIRECTIONS

BODY

Using the Long-Tail CO method, CO 40 sts.

Row 1 (RS): K1, sl1 wyif, k to last 3 sts, sl1 wyif, k1, sl1 wyif.
Row 2 (WS): Rep row 1.
Row 3: K1, sl1 wyif, k1, k3, sl1 wyib, k17, sl1 wyib, k12, sl1 wyif, k1, sl1 wyif.
Row 4: K1, sl1 wyif, k1, k12, p1, k17, p1, k3, sl1 wyif, k1, sl1 wyif.
Rows 5–10: Rep rows 3–4.
Row 11: K1, sl1 wyif, k1, k3, (sl1 wyib, k2) twice, k12, (sl1 wyib, k2) twice, k7, sl1 wyif, k1, sl1 wyif.
Row 12: K1, sl1 wyif, k1, k7, (k2, p1) twice, k12, (k2, p1) twice, k3, sl1 wyif, k1, sl1 wyif.
Rows 13–18: Rep rows 11–12.
Row 19: K1, sl1 wyif, k1, k6, (sl1 wyib, k2) twice, k12, (sl1 wyib, k2) twice, k4, sl1 wyif, k1, sl1 wyif.
Row 20: K1, sl1 wyif, k1, k4, (k2, p1) twice, k12, (k2, p1) twice, k6, sl1 wyif, k1, sl1 wyif.

Rows 21–26: Rep rows 19–20.
Row 27: K1, sl1 wyif, k1, k9, (sl1 wyib, k2) twice, k12, (sl1 wyib, k2) twice, k1, sl1 wyif, k1, sl1 wyif.
Row 28: K1, sl1 wyif, k1, k1, (k2, p1) twice, k12, (k2, p1) twice, k9, sl1 wyif, k1, sl1 wyif.
Rows 29–34: Rep rows 27–28.
Row 35: K1, sl1 wyif, k1, k12, sl1 wyib, k17, sl1 wyib, k3, sl1 wyif, k1, sl1 wyif.
Row 36: K1, sl1 wyif, k1, k3, p1, k17, p1, k12, sl1 wyif, k1, sl1 wyif.
Rows 37–42: Rep rows 35–36.
Rows 43–44: Rep rows 1–2.
Rep rows 1–44, 10 times more (11 reps total).
Rep rows 1–43.

BO all sts kwise.

FINISHING

Weave in all ends. Gently block to measurements.

MODIFICATION: WRAP

Using the Long-Tail CO method, CO 74 sts.

Follow the directions for the scarf, rep patt sts (sts between the 3 first and 3 last sts of each row) twice.
Rep rows 1–44, 9 times total.
Rep rows 1–43 once.

BO all sts kwise.

Rebekka Mauser

30 Vice Versa

In the Vice Versa scarf, vertical lines alternate with almost three-dimensional structures. The random shifting of colours creates exciting effects in the simplest ways.

SIZE

One size.

FINISHED MEASUREMENTS

Length: 70" / 180 cm.
Width: 15.75" / 40 cm.

MATERIALS

Yarn: Chunky Andean Wool by KAOS Yarn (100% Peruvian Highland wool, 109 yds / 100 m – 50 g).
C1: 4 balls of colourway Zealous.
C2: 4 balls of colourway Vivacious.
Or approx. 350 yds / 320 m of each colour of aran-weight yarn.

Plus 1 extra ball (in the sample C2 was used) or approx. 70 yds / 70 m of aran-weight yarn for the i-cord edging.

Alternative yarn suggestions are for example Schoppel Wolle Reggae, CaMaRose Snefnug, Sandnes Garn Kos and Hobbii Tweed Delight.

Needles: US 10 / 6 mm 32" / 80 cm circular needles, a US J / 6 mm crochet hook for the Provisional Cast-On.

Notions: Stitch markers, stitch holders or waste yarn.

GAUGE

16 sts x 21 rows to 4" / 10 cm on US 10 / 6 mm needles in St St, after blocking.

12 sts x 28 rows to 4" / 10 cm on US 10 / 6 mm needles in Double Tuck St Patt, after blocking.

SPECIAL ABBREVIATIONS

The main stitch pattern as well as all special abbreviations needed for working tuck stitches are taken from *Tuck Stitches: Sophistication in Handknitting* by Nancy Marchant.

The sl1yo is the action that creates the shawled stitch. This action works differently for a knit row than for a purl row, but one manipulation remains standard: the working yarn must always be in front before slipping the next stitch. On a purl row, the working yarn is in place before slipping the stitch but in a knit row, you need to first bring the yarn to the front and then slip the stitch. This worked stitch with its yarn over shawl(s) is considered one stitch.

Sl1yo: *Following a knit stitch:* Bring the working yarn under the needle to the front of the work, sl the next st pwise, then bring the yarn over the needle (and over the sl st) to the back, in position to work the following k st.

Following a purl stitch: Working yarn is already in front of the work, sl the next st pwise, then bring the yarn over the needle (and over the slipped st), then to the front, in position to work the following p st.

Sl1^{1}yo: With yarn in front, sl the st with its yarn over pwise and give it a second yarn over.

Brp1^2: P the st tog with its 2 yo's.
Brk1^2: K the st tog with its 2 yo's.

STITCH PATTERN

Double Tuck Stitch

Worked over a multiple of 6 sts.

Row 1 (RS): Sl1yo, p1, sl1yo, brp1^{2}, k1, brp1^{2}.
Row 2 (WS): K1, p1, k1, sl1^{1}yo, k1, sl1^{1}yo.
Row 3: Brk1^{2}, p1, brk1^{2}, sl1yo, k1, sl1yo.
Row 4: Sl1^{1}yo, p1, sl1^{1}yo, p1, k1, p1.

SPECIAL TECHNIQUES

I-Cord Bind-Off

Step 1: CO 3 sts and sl these sts from RHN to LHN.
Step 2: K2, k2tog tbl (1 st dec'd/BO).
Step 3: Sl 3 sts from RHN to LHN.
Rep steps 2–3 until all sts have been BO.

NOTES

Colours are changed on every other row. Twist yarns at every colour change by placing the new colour over the previous used thread.

Both width and length can be adjusted easily by adding more pattern repeats.

When joining a new ball of yarn, do this at the beginning or end of a row, as the loose ends can be hidden in the i-cord edging.

CONSTRUCTION

The stitch pattern for this generously sized scarf creates a fabric that is the same on both sides – only the colours are reversed. A few stitches worked in Moss Stitch frame the main part on both sides and give it stability. A neat i-cord edging completes the piece.

The scarf begins with a Provisional Cast-On. The easy-to-remember Double Tuck Stitch pattern, in which the colours alternate every other row, is worked all over the body of the scarf. To keep knitting exciting, shift the colours at irregular intervals. When the required total length has been reached, the stitches are bound off with an i-cord bind-off. The bind-off is done along the long side with the selvage stitches as a base until you reach the Provisional Cast-On and then back up along the other long side.

DIRECTIONS

BODY

With C1, CO 47 sts using the Provisional Crochet CO method.

Set-Up Row 1 (RS): With C1, (k1, p1) x 2, *k1, p1, k1, sl1yo, k1, sl1yo*, rep until 7 sts rem, (k1, p1) x 3, k1.
Set-Up Row 2 (WS): With C1, (k1, p1) x 2, *p1, k1, p1, sl1^{1}yo, p1, sl1^{1}yo*, rep until 7 sts rem, (k1, p1) x 3, k1.
Row 1 (RS): With C2, (k1, p1) x 2, *work row 1 of Double Tuck Stitch Patt*, rep until 7 sts rem, sl1yo, p1, sl1yo, (p1, k1) x 2.
Row 2 (WS): With C2, (k1, p1) x 2, sl1^{1}yo, k1, sl1^{1}yo, *work Row 2 of Double Tuck Stitch Patt*, rep until 4 sts rem, (p1, k1) x 2.
Row 3: With C1, (k1, p1) x 2, *work row 3 of Double Tuck Stitch Patt*, rep until 7 sts rem, brk1^{2}, p1, brk1^{2}, (p1, k1) x 2.
Row 4: With C1, (k1, p1) x 2, p1, k1, p1, *work row 4 of Double Tuck Stitch Patt*, rep until 4 sts rem, (p1, k1) x 2.
Rep rows 1–4 until the scarf measures approx. 70" / 180 cm, or until desired length.

Note! Change the colour sequence randomly after a complete patt rep or follow a defined stripe sequence, depending on your taste. In any case, the colour change must take place after a row 4.
In the sample shown 128 pattern repeats have been worked in total and 17 colour changes have been made, with changes after 12 / 5 / 9 / 11 / 4 / 9 / 12 / 7 / 9 / 4 / 11 / 7 / 4 / 2 / 10 / 5 / 7 pattern repeats (rows 1–4 = 1 repeat).

Next Row (RS): With the next colour (C2 was used in the sample), (k1, p1) x 2, *k1, p1, k1, brp1^{2}, k1, brp1^{2}*, rep until 7 sts rem, k1, (p1, k1) x 3.

Work the transition between short side and long side as bef, working the 3 i-cord sts twice.

Cont working the i-cord BO along the rem long side of the scarf as foll:
K2, sl 1 st from LHN to RHN, with the needle tip, pick up the very top loop of yarn in the garter bump of the next selvage st AND (from with the second BO row onwards) the carried strand of yarn, sl this new st plus the carried strand onto the LHN, sl 1 st back from RHN to LHN and join the i-cord edging by working k2tog tbl. This way the carried yarn will be hidden at the inside of the i-cord.
Rep along the long side of the scarf up to the beg of the i-cord.

Work 1 i-cord rnd without binding off. Graft the rem 3 sts from the i-cord BO tog with the beg of the i-cord.

FINISHING

Weave in ends. Wet block to measurements.

I-CORD EDGING

Cont with the colour chosen for the i-cord (worked along all sides of the scarf). Cut yarn if necessary.

With RS facing, CO 3 sts using the Long-Tail CO method, sl these 3 sts from RHN to LHN and start to BO all sts using the i-cord BO method (see Special Techniques).
Note! To make the transition between the short and long side of the scarf more flexible, work the 3 i-cord edging sts twice, without working the k2tog dec's.

Cont working the BO along the long side of the scarf as foll:

K2, sl 1 st from LHN to RHN and with the needle tip, pick up the very top loop of yarn in the garter bump of the next selvage st, sl this new st onto LHN needle, sl 1 st back from RHN to LHN and join the i-cord edging by working k2tog tbl.
Rep along the long side of the scarf down to the second short side.

Work the transition between long side and short side as before, working the 3 i-cord sts twice.

Unravel the Provisional CO and sl the live sts back onto the LHN ready to work the BO along the short side.

Julia Wilkens

31 Le Pompom

Double knitting creates an extra-warm fabric for this fluffy scarf. Although this technique is known for being time-consuming, Le Pompom knits up quickly.

SIZE

One size.

FINISHED MEASUREMENTS

Length (excl. Pompom): 50" / 127 cm.
Width: 6.5" / 16 cm.

MATERIALS

Yarn: 2 balls of Eco Soft by Isager (56% baby alpaca, 44% organic pima cotton, 137 yds / 125 m – 50 g), colourway E6s.

Or approx. 274 yds / 250 m of aran-weight yarn. Alternative yarn suggestions are for example Katia Air Alpaca Natural Colors and Biches et Bûches Le Gros Silk & Mohair.

Approx. 40 g of yarn of choice for pompoms. If pompom is made with same yarn as scarf consider an extra ball or approx. 137 yds / 125 m scrap yarn for colour pops.

Needles: US 8 / 5 mm 24" / 60 cm needles.

Notions: Cardboard or pompom maker.

GAUGE

24 sts x 40 rows to 4" / 10 cm in double knitting after blocking (count 2 sts and 2 rows for each visible st and row on either side).

NOTES

In double knitting only every other stitch is knitted while the other stitches are slipped.

CONSTRUCTION

This scarf is knitted from end to end in one piece, flat. It is worked in double knitting creating identical sides. To finish, pompoms are added to the gathered ends.

DIRECTIONS

BODY

With the Long-Tail CO method, CO 40 sts with enough yarn to leave a tail of approx. 12" / 30 cm.

Row 1: *K1, sl1 wyif * to end.
Rep row 1 for double knitting until scarf measures approx. 50" / 127 cm.

BO Row: K1, *k2tog, sl second st on RHN over first st on RHN*, rep *–* until last st, BO last st.

Cut yarn leaving a tail of approx. 12" / 30 cm.

FINISHING

Gathering
Using the tail left from CO and a tapestry needle, *sew through every other st of the CO edge using running st. Gently pull tight so that the end of the scarf is gathered.* Rep *–* in opposite direction twice more to secure gathered end. Weave in end.

Work other ends alike.

Block scarf to measurements.

Pompom
Use a pompom maker or prepare a cardboard template of the desired size. The pompom on the sample measures approx. 4" / 10 cm in diameter. For a speckled pompom, use different colours on varying sections of the cardboard ring.

Make a second pompom.

Attach a pompom to each end of the scarf using the yarn tail to secure it.

Cristina Cusano

32 Basketweave

This dickey is cute and practical, and it's sure to keep the cold at bay. It features an uncomplicated yet engaging basketweave pattern.

SIZE

One size.

FINISHED MEASUREMENTS

Width: 11.5" / 29 cm.
Length (without Collar): 11.25" / 28 cm.
Height of Ribbed Collar: 2.5" / 6.5 cm.
Neck Circumference: 19" / 47.5 cm.

MATERIALS

Yarn: 2 skeins of Cardo by Manos del Uruguay (100% non-sw Uruguayan Corriedale wool, 109 yds / 100 m – 100 g), colourway Peach Blossom.

Or approx. 218 yds / 200 m of bulky-weight yarn. Alternative yarn suggestions are for example Cascade Yarns 220 Grande, Malabrigo Mecha and Berroco Lanas Quick.

Needles: US 10.5 / 6.5 mm 32" / 80 cm circular needles and US 10 / 6 mm DPNs or preferred needles for working small circumferences in the round (for the ribbed collar).

Notions: Stitch holders or waste yarn, stitch marker.

GAUGE

13.5 sts x 21 rows to 4" / 10 cm on US 10.5 / 6.5 mm in Basketweave St patt, after blocking.

SPECIAL ABBREVIATIONS

ICRS: I-cord on RS: K1, sl1 wyif, k1.
ICWS: I-cord on WS: Sl1 wyif, k1, sl1 wyif.
PSO: Pass last st on RHN over st just slipped. (1 st dec'd)

STITCH PATTERN

Basketweave Stitch

Row 1 (RS): ICRS, k to 3 sts bef end, ICRS.
Row 2 (WS): ICWS, k4, *p3, k5* 3 times, p3, k4, ICWS.
Row 3: ICRS, p4, k3, *p5, k3* 3 times, p4, ICRS.
Row 4: ICWS, k4, *p3, k5* 3 times, p3, k4, ICWS.
Row 5: ICRS, k to 3 sts bef end, ICRS.
Row 6: ICWS, p3, k1, *k4, p3, k1* 3 times, k4, p3, ICWS.
Row 7: ICRS, k3, p4, *p1, k3, p4* 3 times, p1, k3, ICRS.
Row 8: ICWS, p3, k1, *k4, p3, k1* 3 times, k4, p3, ICWS.

CONSTRUCTION

This dickey is knitted from the bottom up in pieces. The front and back are knitted separately in a Basketweave Stitch pattern featuring an integrated i-cord edging. The neck is shaped using a sloped bind-off. The shoulders are grafted together, and the collar is picked up along the neckline and knitted in 1 x 1 ribbing.

DIRECTIONS

BACK

With US 10.5 / 6.5 mm circular needles, CO 41 sts using the Long-Tail CO method. This counts as row 1 (RS) of the Basketweave St patt.

Work rows 2–8 of Basketweave St patt once.
Rep rows 1–8, 5 more times.
Work rows 1–4 once.
A total of 52 rows (including CO row) have been worked.

Shape Left Side of Back Neckline

Row 1 (RS): ICRS, k7, kfb, k1, pass the inc'd st from the kfb over the first st on the RHN (the last st knitted), BO 19 sts (including first st on RHN, leaving 11 sts on RHN before BO), k7, ICRS. (11 sts on each side of the central 19 BO neck sts)

Pl the first set of 11 sts on a st holder or waste yarn for right shoulder and cont on left shoulder sts only.

Row 2 (WS): ICWS, p3, k4, tw (leaving last st unworked).
Row 3 (RS): Sl1 wyib (RHN now has 2 sts), PSO, p3, k3, ICRS. (10 sts)
Row 4: ICWS, p3, k3, tw (leaving last st unworked).
Row 5: Sl1 wyib, PSO, k5, ICRS. (9 sts)
Row 6: ICWS, k4, p2.
Row 7: K2, p4, ICRS.
Row 8: ICWS, k4, p2.

Pl all sts on a st holder or waste yarn. Cut yarn. These live shoulder sts will be grafted later.

Shape Right Side of Back Neckline

Transfer right shoulder sts from st holder back onto needles. With WS facing, join yarn at neck edge.

Row 1 (WS): K5, p3, ICWS.
Row 2 (RS): ICRS, k3, p4, tw (leaving last st unworked).
Row 3: Sl1 wyif, PSO, k3, p3, ICWS. (10 sts)
Row 4: ICRS, k6, tw (leaving last st unworked).
Row 5: Sl wyif, PSO, p1, k4, ICWS. (9 sts)
Row 6: ICRS, p4, k2.
Row 7: P2, k4, ICWS.

Pl all sts on a st holder or waste yarn. Cut yarn, leaving a long tail for grafting the live shoulder sts later.

FRONT

With US 10.5 / 6.5 mm circular needles, CO 41 sts using the Long-Tail CO method.
This counts as row 1 (RS) of the Basketweave St patt.

Work rows 2–8 of Basketweave St patt once.
Rep rows 1–8, 5 more times.
A total of 48 rows (including CO row) have been worked.

Note! Keep in mind that the orientation of the front neck and shoulders is opposite that of the back neck and shoulders. When working on the back with RS facing, the sts of the right shoulder were on your right. In contrast, when RS of front is facing, the sts of the right shoulder are on your left.

Shape Right Side of Front Neckline

Row 1 (RS): ICRS, k9, kfb, k1, pass the inc'd st from the kfb over the first st on the RHN (the last st knitted), BO 15 sts (including first st on RHN, leaving 13 sts on RHN bef BO), k9, ICRS. (13 sts on each side of the central 15 BO neck sts)

Pl the first set of 13 sts on a st holder or waste yarn for left shoulder and cont on right shoulder sts only.

Row 2 (WS): ICWS, k4, p3, k2, tw (leaving last st unworked).
Row 3: Sl1 wyib (RHN now has 2 sts), PSO, p1, k3, p4, ICRS. (12 sts)
Row 4: ICWS, k4, p3, k1, tw (leaving last st unworked).
Row 5: Sl1 wyib, PSO, k7, ICRS. (11 sts)
Row 6: ICWS, p3, k4, tw (leaving last st unworked).
Row 7: Sl1 wyib, PSO, p3, k3, ICRS. (10 sts)
Row 8: ICWS, p3, k3, tw (leaving last st unworked).
Row 9: Sl1 wyib, PSO, k5, ICRS. (9 sts)
Row 10: ICWS, k4, p2.
Row 11: K2, p4, ICRS.
Row 12: ICWS, k4, p2.

Pl all sts on a st holder or waste yarn and cut yarn. These live shoulder sts will be grafted later.

Shape Left Side of Front Neckline

Transfer left shoulder sts from st holder back onto needles. With WS facing, join yarn at neck edge.

Row 1 (WS): K3, p3, k4, ICWS.
Row 2 (RS): ICRS, p4, k3, p2, tw (leaving last st unworked).
Row 3: Sl1 wyif, PSO, k1, p3, k4, ICWS. (12 sts)
Row 4: ICRS, k8, tw (leaving last st unworked).
Row 5: Sl1 wyif, PSO, k4, p3, ICWS. (11 sts)
Row 6: ICRS, k3, p4, tw (leaving last st unworked).
Row 7: Sl1 wyif, PSO, k3, p3, ICWS. (10 sts)
Row 8: ICRS, k6, tw (leaving last st unworked).
Row 9: Sl1 wyif, PSO, p1, k4, ICWS. (9 sts)
Row 10: ICRS, p4, k2.
Row 11: P2, k4, ICWS.

BASKETWEAVE STITCH PATTERN (INCLUDES INTEGRATED I-CORD EDGE)

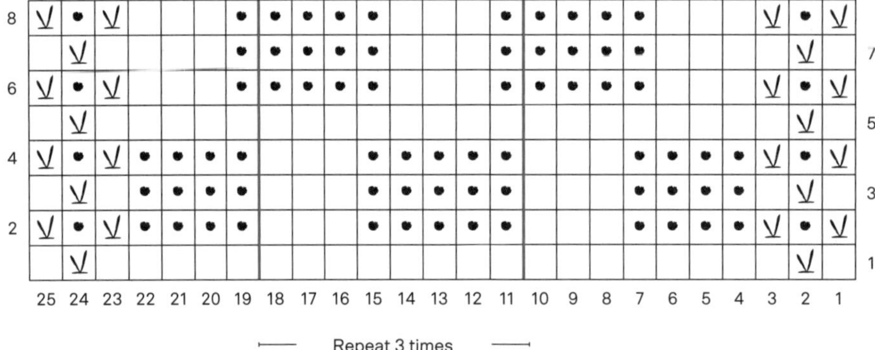

- [ ] (empty square) RS: knit / WS: purl
- • RS: purl / WS: knit
- V sl1 wyif

Cut yarn, leaving a long tail for grafting the live shoulder sts in the next step.

FINISHING

Transfer live shoulder sts back onto needles and graft sts together for each shoulder.

With US 10 / 6 mm DPNs or preferred needles for working small circumference in the round, beg at centre back, pick up and k 74 sts evenly around the neckline. (You may use the following st counts as a guide when picking up and knitting these sts: 11 sts from centre back along left half of back BO edge; 18 sts along left neckline shaping; 17 sts along front BO edge; 18 sts along right neckline shaping; 10 sts along rem half of back BO edge.) PM for BOR and join to work in the rnd.

Set-Up Rnd: *K1tbl, p1tbl* to end.
Rib Rnd: *K1, p1* to end.
Work in est rib until collar measures 2.5" / 6.5 cm.
Note! For a consistent ribbed fabric, tug your yarn gently at the back after completing each p st.

BO in patt.

Weave in ends. Block gently to measurements.

Pauliina Kuunsola

33 Camellia

Worked in 1 × 1 rib and mainly large cable turns, the Camellia scarf is perfect TV knitting – easy and addictive. It exudes gentle warmth and is fully reversible.

SIZE

One size.

FINISHED MEASUREMENTS

Length: 75" / 188 cm.
Width: 15.5" / 38.5 cm.

MATERIALS

Yarn: 5 skeins of Poppy by Sandnes Garn (50% superfine alpaca, 35% cotton, 15% merino, 120 yds / 110 m – 50 g), colourway 4315.

Or approx. 600 yds / 550 m of bulky-weight yarn. Alternative yarn suggestions are for example Rowan Cocoon and Woolfolk Luft.

Needles: US 10 / 6 mm 32" / 80 cm circular needles.

Notions: Stitch markers, cable needle (or a single DPN).

GAUGE

13 sts x 18 rows to 4" / 10 cm in 1 x 1 rib, after blocking.

SPECIAL ABBREVIATIONS

1/1 LC: Sl 1 st to CN, hold in front, p1, k1 from CN.

1/1 RC: S 1 st to CN, hold in back, p1, k1 from CN.

4/4 RC: Sl 4 sts to CN, hold in back, work 4 sts in rib, work 4 sts in rib from CN.

6/4 RC: Sl 4 sts to CN, hold in back, work 6 sts in rib, work 4 sts in rib from CN.

10/10 LC: Sl 10 sts to CN, hold in front, work 10 sts in rib, work 10 sts in rib from CN.

NOTES

All cable turns are worked on RS rows. To help keep track of the sides, it may be helpful to place a locking stitch marker on the RS.

Markers are placed to help see the placement of the left and right cable block. Always slip markers when coming across them.

CONSTRUCTION

This long, rectangular scarf is worked in one piece from end to end, flat. It features 1 x 1 ribbing and a cable pattern. Both ends have a stripe of 1/1 cable turns.

DIRECTIONS

CAST-ON

CO 50 sts with the Long-Tail Cast-On or preferred method.

Rib Row (RS): *K1, p1* to end.
Rib Row (WS): *K1, p1* to end.
Work in est 1 x 1 rib for 12 rows.

Next, work small cable turns as foll:
Row 1 (RS): *1/1 LC* to end.
Row 2 (WS): *P1, k1* to end (i.e. work sts as they appear).
Row 3: *1/1 RC* to end.
Row 4: *K1, p1* to end (i.e. work sts as they appear).

Work in 1 x 1 rib for 19 rows. On the next WS rows, PM as foll:
Next Row (WS): Work 4 sts in rib, PM, work 20 sts in rib, PM, work 22 sts in rib, PM, work 4 sts in rib to end.

CABLE PATTERN

Note! In this section, always slip markers not mentioned in the instructions when you come to them.

Left Cable Block
Row 1 (RS): Work in 1 x 1 rib to 2nd m, SM, 10/10 LC in rib, SM, work in 1 x 1 rib to end.
Rows 2–24: Work in 1 x 1 rib.
Row 25: Rep row 1.
Row 26: Work in 1 x 1 rib.

Right Cable Block
Rows 1–8: Work in 1 x 1 rib.
Row 9: Work 16 sts in 1 x 1 rib, 6/4 RC, work in 1 x 1 rib to end.
Rows 10–16: Work in 1 x 1 rib.
Row 17: Work in 1 x 1 rib to first m, SM, 4/4 RC, work 1 x 1 rib to end.
Rows 18–22: Work in 1 x 1 rib.

Work Left Cable Block followed by a Right Cable Block 4 more times. Then work 1 more Left Cable Block.

Note! If wanting to make a longer or shorter scarf, work more or fewer repeats of the Left and Right Cable Blocks.

BIND-OFF

Work in 1 x 1 rib for 20 rows.

Then, work small cable turns as foll:
Row 1 (RS): *1/1 LC* to end.
Row 2 (WS): *P1, k1* to end of row (i.e., work sts as they appear).
Row 3: *1/1 RC* to end.
Row 4: *K1, p1* to end (i.e., work sts as they appear).

Work in 1 x 1 rib for 12 rows.

BO loosely.

FINISHING

Weave in ends. Block to measurements.

Marion Bulin

34 Bobble Kite

This cosy, reversible shawl is fun to knit and wear! It is all about the yarn – a chunky mohair – and the eye-catching bobble i-cord edges.

SIZE

One size.

FINISHED MEASUREMENTS

Left Edge (Sections 1 and 2): 75.5" / 192 cm.
Shortest Edge (Section 1): 35.5" / 90 cm.
Right Edge (Section 2 and BO Edge): 58.25" / 148 cm.

MATERIALS

Yarn: 3 skeins of Big Fiffi by Frida Fuchs (78% mohair, 13% merino, 9% nylon, 219 yds / 200 m – 100 g), colourway Anis.

Or approx. 657 yds / 600 m of chunky-weight yarn. Alternative yarn suggestions are for example Malabrigo Mecha or 2 strands of Wooldreamers Manchelopi held with 1 strand of a lace-weight silk mohair.

Needles: US 10 / 6 mm 40" / 100 cm circular needles.

Notions: Waste yarn, stitch marker.

GAUGE

12 sts x 18 rows to 4" / 10 cm in Garter St, after blocking.

SPECIAL ABBREVIATIONS

MB: Make Bobble. Kfb into the next st 2 times (you made 4 sts from 1 st). *Sl these 4 sts back onto LHN, k4*, rep *–* once more, sl these 4 sts back onto LHN, k2tog 2 times, sl these 2 sts back onto LHN, k2tog.

NOTES

If modifying the shawl, make sure to not use more than 35% of the yarn for Section 1 – otherwise you might run out of yarn in Section 2.

CONSTRUCTION

This Garter Stitch shawl has a kite shape and begins with a Provisional Cast-On after which the 3-stitch i-cord bobble edge is established. The shawl is worked flat, in two sections, with the 3-stitch i-cord bobble edge at either side. In Section 1, increases are worked on every row while, at the same time, a central double decrease is worked in the centre on every WS row. In Section 2, increases are only worked at the left edge. The total number of stitches of Section2 stays the same until the bind-off, which is a continuation of the 3-st i-cord bobble edge.

DIRECTIONS

CAST-ON AND ESTABLISHING I-CORD

With waste yarn and US 10 / 6 mm needles, use the Provisional CO method to CO 3 sts. Change to working yarn.

Work 3 rows of i-cord as foll: *K3, sl these 3 sts back onto LHN*, rep *–* 2 times for a total of 3 rows.

Next, work an i-cord row with a bobble as foll: K1, MB, k1, sl these 3 sts back onto LHN.

Work 3 more regular i-cord rows.

Next, work a partial i-cord bobble row as foll: K1, MB, k1. (Do not sl sts back onto LHN and do not turn.)

Now pick up and k 5 sts from the i-cord edge, making sure to pick up the 3rd of those 5 sts from the i-cord bobble row, hold yarn in front, tw. (8 sts)

Next Row (WS): Carefully remove the waste yarn from the Provisional CO and pl these 3 sts at the start of the LHN, making sure they appear as knit sts (not purls). Working these new sts first, k1, MB, k1, then k1, m1l, k2, PM, k1, m1l, k1, sl3 wyif. (13 sts)

SECTION 1

Row 1 (RS): K3 i-cord sts, sl these 3 sts back onto LHN, k3 i-cord sts again, k1, m1l, k to 4 sts bef end, m1l, k1, sl3 wyif. (2 sts inc'd)
Row 2 (WS): K3 i-cord sts, sl these 3 sts back onto LHN, k3 i-cord sts again, k1, m1l, k to 2 sts bef m, sl2 tog as if to k, RM, k1, p2sso, PM, k to 4 sts bef end, m1l, k1, sl3 wyif.
Row 3: Rep row 1. (2 sts inc'd)
Row 4: Rep row 2.
Row 5 (Bobble Row): K1, MB, k1, sl these 3 sts back onto LHN, k3 i-cord sts again, k1, m1l, k to 4 sts bef end, m1l, k1, sl3 wyif. (2 sts inc'd)
Row 6 (Bobble Row): K1, MB, k1, sl these 3 sts back onto LHN, k3 i-cord sts again, k1, m1l, k to 2 sts bef m, sl2 tog as if to k, RM, k1, p2sso, PM, k to 4 sts bef end, m1l, k1, sl3 wyif.
Rep rows 1–6, 16 more times. (18 bobbles on each side plus central one, at CO edge) (115 sts in total: 57 sts bef m and 58 after m, seen from the RS)

SECTION 2

Row 1: K3 i-cord sts, sl these 3 sts back onto LHN, k3 i-cord sts again, k to 4 sts bef end, m1l, k1, sl3 wyif. (1 st inc'd)
Row 2: K3 i-cord sts, sl these 3 sts back onto LHN, k3 i-cord sts again, k1, m1l, k to 2 sts bef m, sl2 tog as if to k, RM, k1, p2sso, PM, k to 3 sts bef end, sl3 wyif. (1 st dec'd)
Row 3: Rep row 1. (1 st inc'd)
Row 4: Rep row 2. (1 st dec'd)
Row 5 (Bobble Row): K1, MB, k1, slip these 3 sts back onto LHN, k3 i-cord sts again, k to 4 sts bef end, m1l, k1, sl3 wyif. (1 st inc'd)
Row 6: K1, MB, k1, sl these 3 sts back onto LHN, k3 i-cord sts again, k1, m1l, k to 2 sts bef m, sl2 tog as if to k, RM, k1, p2sso, PM, k to 3 sts bef end, sl3 wyif. (1 st dec'd)
Rep rows 1–6 until 4 sts (1 st plus 3 i-cord sts) rem bef marker after working a row 4 (seen from the RS). (115 sts in total: 111 sts on the left side of the m and 4 sts on the right side of the m, seen from the RS)

The final row has no m1l:
Next Row (RS, Bobble Row): K1, MB, k1, slip these 3 sts back onto LHN, k3 i-cord sts again, k1, RM, k2tog, k to 3 sts bef end, sl3 wyif. (114 sts)

BIND-OFF

Tw for the i-cord bobble BO which is worked on the WS. BO all sts as foll: *K1, MB, ssk, sl these 3 sts back onto LHN, (k2, ssk, sl these 3 sts back onto LHN) 5 times*, rep *–* until 6 sts rem in total.

Break yarn leaving a 12" / 30 cm long thread. Use this tail to graft the 3 sts from one side tog with the 3 sts from the other side.

FINISHING

Weave in ends. Block to measurements.

Aude Martin

35 Grid

Grid combines knitting and crochet in a stylish, lightweight scarf. It features knitted horizontal lines and is completed with vertical lines, crocheted on after the knitting is finished.

SIZE

One size.

FINISHED MEASUREMENTS

Length: 69" / 175 cm.
Width: 19.75" / 50 cm.

MATERIALS

Yarn: MC: 7 balls of Air by Drops (65% alpaca, 28% polyamide, 7% wool, 164 yds / 150 m – 50 g), colourway 31 Black.
CC: 1 ball of Nepal by Drops (65% wool, 35% alpaca, 82 yds / 75 m – 50 g), colourway 0100 Off White.

Or approx. 1105 yds / 1010 m (in MC) and 75 yds / 70 m (in CC) of similar aran-weight yarn. Alternative yarn suggestions are for example Sandnes Garn Kos or Isager Alpaca 3 (for MC) and Katia Concept Essential Alpaca or Filcolana Peruvian Highland Wool (for CC).

Needles: US 8 / 5 mm needles.

Notions: Row counter, US 6 / 4 mm crochet hook.

GAUGE

Knit gauge
23 sts x 24 rows to 4" / 10 cm in 1 x 1 rib with MC, after blocking.

Crochet gauge
Approx. 15 sts to 4" / 10 cm in Surface Slip-Stitch with CC, after blocking.

NOTES

Instead of a single CC, you could use scraps of aran-weight yarn.

CONSTRUCTION

This scarf features both knitting and crochet. First, the entire piece is knitted flat in 1 x 1 ribbing with contrasting horizontal lines created with a special colourwork technique. After the scarf has been knitted, vertical lines are crocheted over the knit stitches following a chart, creating a grid pattern.

DIRECTIONS

PART 1: KNITTING

With MC and US 8 / 5 mm needles, CO 113 sts with the Cable CO method.

Rib Row 1 (RS): *K1, p1* to 1 st bef end, k1.
Rib Row 2 (WS): *P1, k1* to 1 st bef end, p1.
Work rows 1–2 in est 1 x 1 rib for another 14 rows.

Next, following the Stripe Sequences, work as described in next 2 rows:
Row 1 (RS): In MC, work indicated number of sts in 1 x 1 rib, *join CC and work indicated number of sts in 1 x 1 rib, cut CC, slide CC sts back onto LHN, with MC work 1 x 1 rib over CC sts*, rep *–* as instructed, cont to end with MC in 1 x 1 rib.
Row 2 (WS): In MC, work 1 x 1 rib to end.

Stripe Sequence 1
Row 1 (RS): Work 12 sts in MC, work 31 sts in CC, work in MC over CC sts and cont to end.
Rows 2–12: In MC, work in 1 x 1 rib.

Stripe Sequence 2
Row 1 (RS): Work 42 sts in MC, work 45 sts in CC, work in MC over CC sts and cont to end.
Rows 2–8: In MC, work in 1 x 1 rib.

Stripe Sequence 3
Row 1 (RS): Work 8 sts in MC, work 19 sts in CC, work in MC over CC sts, work 23 sts in MC, work 57 sts in CC, work in MC over CC sts and cont to end.
Rows 2–16: In MC, work in 1 x 1 rib.

Stripe Sequence 4
Row 1 (RS): Work 32 sts in MC, work 63 sts in CC, work in MC over CC sts and cont to end.
Rows 2–28: In MC, work in 1 x 1 rib.

Stripe Sequence 5
Row 1 (RS): Work 18 sts in MC, work 43 sts in CC, work in MC over CC sts, work 15 sts in MC, work 13 sts in CC, work in MC over CC sts and cont to end.
Rows 2–8: In MC, work in 1 x 1 rib.

Stripe Sequence 6
Row 1 (RS): Work 12 sts in MC, work 31 sts in CC, work in MC over CC sts, work 25 sts in MC, work 41 sts in CC, work in MC over CC sts and cont to end.
Rows 2–6: Work 4 rows in 1 x 1 rib in MC.

Stripe Sequence 7
Row 1 (RS): Work 27 sts in MC, work 47 sts in CC, work in MC over CC sts and cont to end.
Rows 2–16: In MC, work in 1 x 1 rib.

Stripe Sequence 8
Row 1 (RS): Work 52 sts in MC, work 45 sts in CC, work in MC over CC sts and cont to end.
Rows 2–14: In MC, work in 1 x 1 rib.

Stripe Sequence 9
Row 1 (RS): Work 16 sts in MC, work 15 sts in CC, work in MC over CC sts, work 15 sts in MC, work 35 sts in CC, work in MC over CC sts and cont to end.
Rows 2–8: In MC, work in 1 x 1 rib.

Stripe Sequence 10
Row 1 (RS): Work 12 sts in MC, work 59 sts in CC, work in MC over CC sts and cont to end.
Rows 2–20: In MC, work in 1 x 1 rib.

Stripe Sequence 11
Row 1 (RS): Work 16 sts in MC, work 43 sts in CC, work in MC over CC sts, work 19 sts in MC, work 25 sts in CC, work in MC over CC sts and cont to end.
Rows 2–16: In MC, work in 1 x 1 rib.

Stripe Sequence 12
Row 1 (RS): Work 38 sts in MC, work 49 sts in CC, work in MC over CC sts and cont to end.
Rows 2–10: In MC, work in 1 x 1 rib.

Stripe Sequence 13
Row 1 (RS): Work 26 sts in MC, work 17 sts in CC, work in MC over CC sts, work 27 sts in MC, work 25 sts in CC, work in MC over CC sts and cont to end.
Rows 2–6: In MC, work in 1 x 1 rib.

Stripe Sequence 14
Row 1 (RS): Work 52 sts in MC, work 47 sts in CC, work in MC over CC sts and cont to end.
Rows 2–12: In MC, work in 1 x 1 rib.

Stripe Sequence 15
Row 1 (RS): Work 16 sts in MC, work 41 sts in CC, work in MC over CC sts and cont to end.
Rows 2–4: In MC, work in 1 x 1 rib.

Stripe Sequence 16
Row 1 (RS): Work 66 sts in MC, work 15 sts in CC, work in MC over CC sts and cont to end.
Rows 2–18: In MC, work in 1 x 1 rib.

Work Stripe Sequences 1–16 once more (202 rows).

On next RS row, BO in patt. Weave in ends.

PART 2: CROCHET

Vertical lines are now worked on the RS, using the Surface Crochet Slip-Stitch technique. Refer to the chart for placement of vertical lines, and begin at the bottom left of the chart.

Note! The chart is for guidance rather than precise placement.

Working from the CO edge up, hold CC yarn on the WS of the scarf, insert crochet from RS in a purl st and pull a CC loop from WS up to RS. Crochet 1 sl-st upwards over 2 p rows, being careful not to crochet too tightly, in order to prevent puckering of the knitted fabric.

FINISHING

Weave in ends. Block scarf to measurements.

CROCHET STITCH PLACEMENT

Work a total of 2 times from bottom up

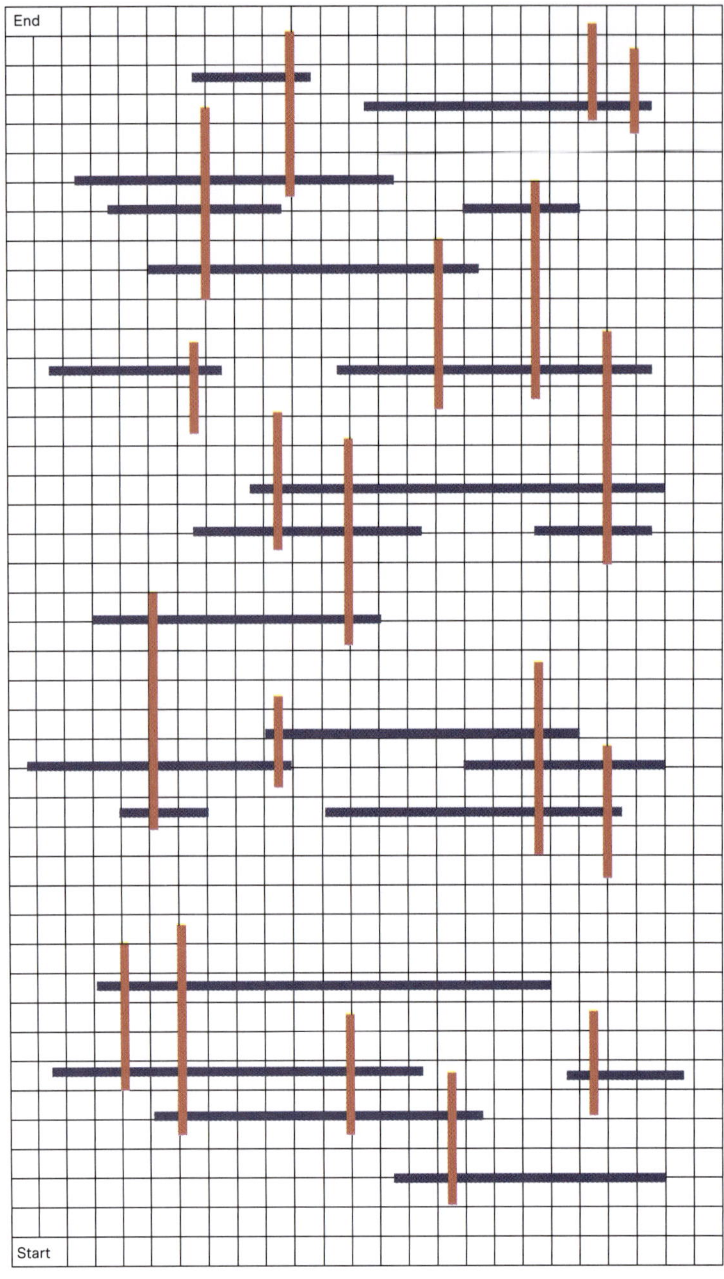

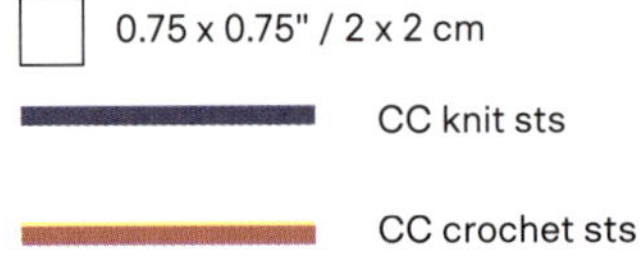

0.75 x 0.75" / 2 x 2 cm

CC knit sts

CC crochet sts

Sini Kramer

36 Ingrid

This beginner-friendly, squishy cowl in Half-Fisherman's Rib was named after the Danish artist Ingrid Vang Nyman, who illustrated Astrid Lindgren's Pippi Longstocking books.

SIZE

One size.

MEASUREMENTS

Length (Grafted): 27" / 68 cm.
Width: 13" / 33 cm.

MATERIALS

Yarn: 4 balls of Love Wool by Katia (85% virgin wool, 15% alpaca, 55 yds / 50 m – 100 g), colourway 114 Medium Orange.

Or approx. 437 yds / 400 m of super chunky -weight yarn. Alternative yarn suggestions are for example Gedifra Perulana, Cascade Yarns Spuntaneous and Lion Brand Wool Ease.

Needles: US 15 / 10 mm needles.

GAUGE

5 sts x 14 rows to 4" / 10 cm in Half-Fisherman's Rib, after light steaming.

NOTES

When starting a new ball of yarn, join it with the Spit Splice method to avoid knots or ends that need to be woven in.

CONSTRUCTION

This cowl is worked in one piece, flat and features a squishy Half-Fisherman's Rib pattern. Once the preferred length has been achieved, the two ends are grafted together to form a cowl.

DIRECTIONS

BODY

CO 19 sts with the Long-Tail CO method.

Start to work the body in Fisherman's Rib.
Row 1 (WS): Sl1 pwise wyif, k to end.
Row 2 (RS): Sl1 pwise wyif, *k1b, p1* to 2 sts bef end, k1b, k1.
Rep rows 1–2 until the work measures approx. 54" / 137 cm.

BO kwise, loosely. Cut yarn leaving a long enough tail for seaming, at least 3 times the width of the BO edge.

FINISHING

Seam the ends together using the BO tail.

Weave in ends. Lightly steam block to open up the stitch pattern.

37

Mittens

Julia Wilkens — Kajsa Vuorela — Lotta H Löthgren — Ayako Mizuno — Tiia Pyykkö

Julia Wilkens

37 Cookie

These super-soft mittens will keep your fingers nice and warm! The garter slip-stitch pattern brings to mind the ribbed edges of cookies – hence the name.

SIZES

1 (2, 3)

Recommended ease: Approx. 1" / 2.5 cm of positive ease.

FINISHED MEASUREMENTS

Length: 8.25 (10.5, 11.5)" / 21 (26.5, 29) cm.
Hand Circumference: 7 (7.5 9)" / 18 (20.5, 23) cm.
Thumb Circumference: 2.75 (3, 3.5)" / 7 (7.5, 9) cm.
Thumb Length: 2.25 (2.5, 3)" / 6 (7, 7.5) cm.

MATERIALS

Yarn: 1 cake of Manchelopis by Wooldreamers (100% Manchega wool, double sliver, 252 yds / 230 m – 100 g), colourway 6 s.

Or approx. 90 (120, 150) yds / 83 (110, 140) m of worsted-weight yarn. Alternative yarn suggestions are another worsted-weight unspun yarn or for example Wooldreamers Mota and De Rerum Natura Gilliatt.

Needles: US 6 / 4 mm 32" / 80 cm circular needles and 1 extra needle of same size for 3-Needle BO or DPNs.

Notions: 3 removable stitch markers, waste yarn or stitch holder.

GAUGE

16 sts x 36 rows to 4" / 10 cm in Garter Slip-St patt, unblocked.

18 sts x 40 rows to 4" / 10 cm in Garter St, unblocked.

STITCH PATTERNS

Garter Slip-Stitch
Rnd 1: K to end.
Rnd 2: *Sl1 wyib, p3 (5, 5)*, rep *–* to end.
Rnds 3–4: Rep rnds 1 and 2.
Rnd 5: K to end.
Rnd 6: *P2 (3, 3), sl1 wyib, p1 (2, 2)*, rep *–* to end.
Rnds 7–8: Rep rnds 5 and 6.

Garter Stitch
Rnd 1: K to end.
Rnd 2: P to end.

NOTES

Working with unspun yarn (also referred to as pencil roving) requires a bit of practice. To prevent the yarn from breaking put the yarn cake on a flat surface and unspool only as much yarn at a time as needed to knit a round. Knit up this length and unspool the following length of yarn.

Should a strand break, both ends can easily be 'glued' back together by rubbing them together between palms and a drop of water (or spit).

The Manchelopis yarn, used for the sample pair, appears as 2 strands of unspun pencil roving wound together. The complete pattern is worked with both of these strands throughout.

CONSTRUCTION

These textured mittens are worked in the round starting from the cuff. A garter slip-stitch pattern knits up into an elastic and soft fabric ideal for adjusting to individual hand shapes. There is minimal shaping. The left and right mitten are identical.

DIRECTIONS

CUFF

With the Long-Tail CO method, CO 28 (30, 36) sts. Join to work in the rnd being careful not to twist sts. PM for BOR.

Work in Garter Slip-St patt for 23 (29, 29) rnds, or until cuff measures approx. 2.5 (3, 3)" / 6 (8, 8) cm ending with an odd-numbered (k) rnd.

THUMB INCREASE

Note! Left / right are interchangeable.

The first and last st of the rnd will now be incorporated into the thumb. As a result, the Garter Slip-St patt for the body of the mitten will beg with the second st of the patt and end 1 st bef the full 4 (6, 6) st patt rep. The thumb is worked in Garter St while the rest of the body cont to be worked in Garter Slip-St patt.

Rnd 1: P1, yo, PM, cont with 2nd st of Garter Slip-St patt to1 st bef BOR, PM, yo, p1. [4 sts for thumb, 26 (28, 34) sts for body]
Rnd 2: K to last st bef m, k1tbl, SM, work in Garter Slip-St patt to m, SM, k1tbl, k to end.
Rnd 3: P to m, SM, work in est patt to m, SM, p to end.
Rnd 4: K to end, slipping markers.
Rnd 5: P to m, yo, SM, work in est patt to m, SM, yo, p to end. (2 sts inc'd)
Rnd 6: K to last st bef m, k1tbl, SM, work in est patt to m, SM, k1tbl, k to end.
Rep rnds 3–6 for 1 (2, 3) more time(s). [8 (10, 12) sts for thumb, 26 (28, 34) sts for body]

DIVIDING THUMB FROM BODY

Rnd 1: P to m, RM, work in est patt to m, RM, sl 8 (10, 12), including BOR m to waste yarn or st holder for thumb, with the Backwards Loop CO method CO 1 st, PM (new BOR for body of mitten), CO 1 st, work in est patt to end. [8 (10, 12) sts for thumb, 28 (30, 36) sts for body]

Work in est patt until mitten is 7.25 (9.25, 10)" / 19 (23, 26) cm long or approx. 1.25 (1,25, 1.5)" / 3 (3, 4) cm shorter than desired finished length, ending with an odd-numbered rnd.

TIP BODY

Set-Up Rnd: Work in est patt for 14 (15, 18) sts, PM, work in est patt to end.

Sts of mitten are now divided in back and front by two m's.

Next Rnd: *SM, k1, ssk, k to 3 sts bef m, k2tog, k1*, rep *–* once more. (4 sts dec'd).
Next Rnd: Work in est patt.
Rep prev 2 rnds 3 (3, 4) more times. [12 (14, 16) sts]

Turn mitten inside out and join front and back sts tog using the 3-Needle BO method.

THUMB

Pl sts and m held for thumb back onto US 6 / 4 mm needles. Starting with the sts on the right of the m, p to m (BOR), SM, k to end of thumb sts, (optional: pick up and k 2 extra sts in both corners between the live sts and picked up sts and dec these on the 2nd rnd to avoid holes), pick up and k 2 sts along the CO edge of the main body, k to m. BOR is positioned at the outer edge of the thumb. [10 (12, 14) sts]

Work 1.75 (1.75, 2.25)" / 4 (4, 5) cm in Garter St or 0.5 (0.5, 0.75)" / 1 (2, 2) cm less than desired finished thumb length ending with a p rnd.

Set-Up Rnd: K5 (6, 7) sts, PM, k to end.

Thumb sts are now divided into back and front by two m's.

Dec Rnd 1: *SM, ssk, k to 2 sts bef m, k2tog*, rep *–* once more. [6 (8, 10 sts]
Rnd 2: P to end.

Size 3 only
Work rnds 1–2 once more. [– (–, 6) sts]

All sizes resume
Next Rnd: *K2tog* to end and RMs. [3 (4, 3) sts]

Cut yarn and thread through rem sts using a tapestry needle. Pull tightly to close top.

FINISHING

Weave in ends. Block to measurements.

Kajsa Vuorela

38 Outside the Box

In this modern colourwork design, a playful plaid pattern is paired with bold boxes in a contrasting colour. The mittens offer endless options for playing with colours.

SIZES

1 (2, 3)

Recommended ease: 0–2" / 0–5 cm of positive ease.

FINISHED MEASUREMENTS

Hand Circumference: 9 (9.75, 10)" / 23 (24.5, 25.5) cm.
Hand Length (Above Cuff): 8.5 (8.75, 9.25)" / 21.5 (22, 23.5) cm.
Thumb Length: 3.25 (3.25, 3.5)" / 8 (8, 9) cm.
Total Length (from Cuff to Top): 10.5 (10.75, 11.5)" / 26.5 (27.5, 29.5) cm.

MATERIALS

Yarn: Vams by Rauma Garn (100% Norwegian wool, 91 yds / 83 m – 50 g).
MC: 1 ball of colourway 311 Fersken.
CC1: 1 ball of colourway 115 Salvie.
CC2: 1 ball of colourway 307 Myr.

Or approx. 70 (72, 76) yds / 64 (66, 70) m (in MC), 36 (38, 44) yds / 33 (35, 40) m (in CC1) and 44 (44, 44) yds / 40 (40, 40) m (in CC2) of bulky-weight yarn. Suggested alternatives are for example Sandnes Garn Fritidsgarn, Viking Garn Hobbygarn and Novita Isoveli.

Needles: US 9 / 5.5 mm circular needles for Magic Loop, or a set of DPNs.

Notions: Stitch marker, waste yarn or stitch holder.

GAUGE

14 sts x 18 rnds to 4" / 10 cm on US 9 / 5.5 mm needles in stranded colourwork, after blocking.

CONSTRUCTION

These mittens are worked in the round starting from the cuff. A Reversed Stockinette Stitch cuff is worked followed by a stranded colourwork hand and thumb in 3 colours. No more than two colours are used on a single round. The thumb stitches are placed on hold while the hand is worked and finished. Lastly, the thumb is worked.

DIRECTIONS

CUFF

With US 9 / 5.5 mm needles, MC, and using the Long-Tail CO method, CO 26 (28, 30) sts. Join to work in the rnd and PM for BOR.

Working in the rnd, p all sts until the work measures approx. 2 (2.25, 2.5)" / 5 (5.5, 6) cm.

Next Rnd (Inc): K2 (2, 3), *m1r, k4* 2 (1, 0) time(s), *m1r, k5* 2 (4, 5) times, *m1r, k4* 1 (0, 0) time(s), m1r, k2. (6 sts inc'd) [32 (34, 36) sts]

HAND

Note! The Hand Chart is the same for both hands. Make the left mitten by placing sts for thumb on hold at the red marker line. To make the right mitten, place sts for thumb on hold at the black marker line. Make sure to work your second mitten differently to the first.

Work Hand Chart for chosen size until the marker line for thumb.

Pl 7 (7, 8) sts for thumb onto a stitch holder or waste yarn and leave on hold. CO 7 (7, 8) sts using the Backwards Loop CO method in the colourway the chart shows.

Cont working Hand Chart until end.

Break yarns, pull MC yarn through rem 4 sts and fasten off.

THUMB

The thumb is worked in the rnd, following the chart for left or right thumb.

Set-Up Rnd: Pl the 7 (7, 8) thumb sts back onto the needles and work from row 1 of correct Thumb Chart, pick up 1 st from gap at side and work it according to the chart, pick up 7 (7, 8) sts from thumb CO edge and work them according to row 1 of the Thumb Chart, pick up 1 last st from gap at side and work it according to row 1 of the Thumb Chart. PM for BOR. [16 (16, 18) sts in total]

Cont working Thumb Chart until end.

Break yarns, pull MC yarn through rem 4 sts and fasten off.

FINISHING

Weave in all ends. Wet block to measurements.

SIZE 1 - HAND CHART

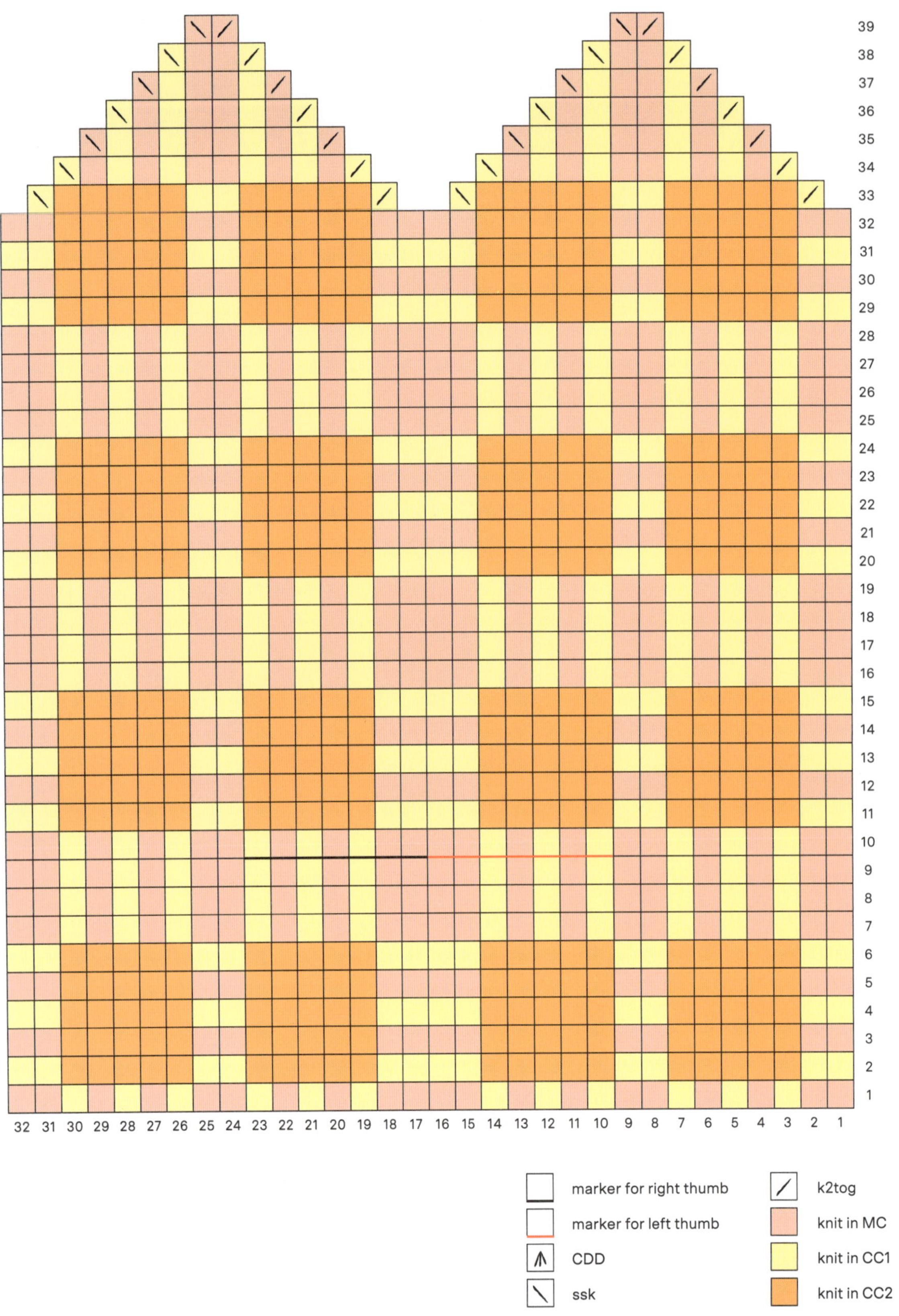

SIZE 2 - HAND CHART

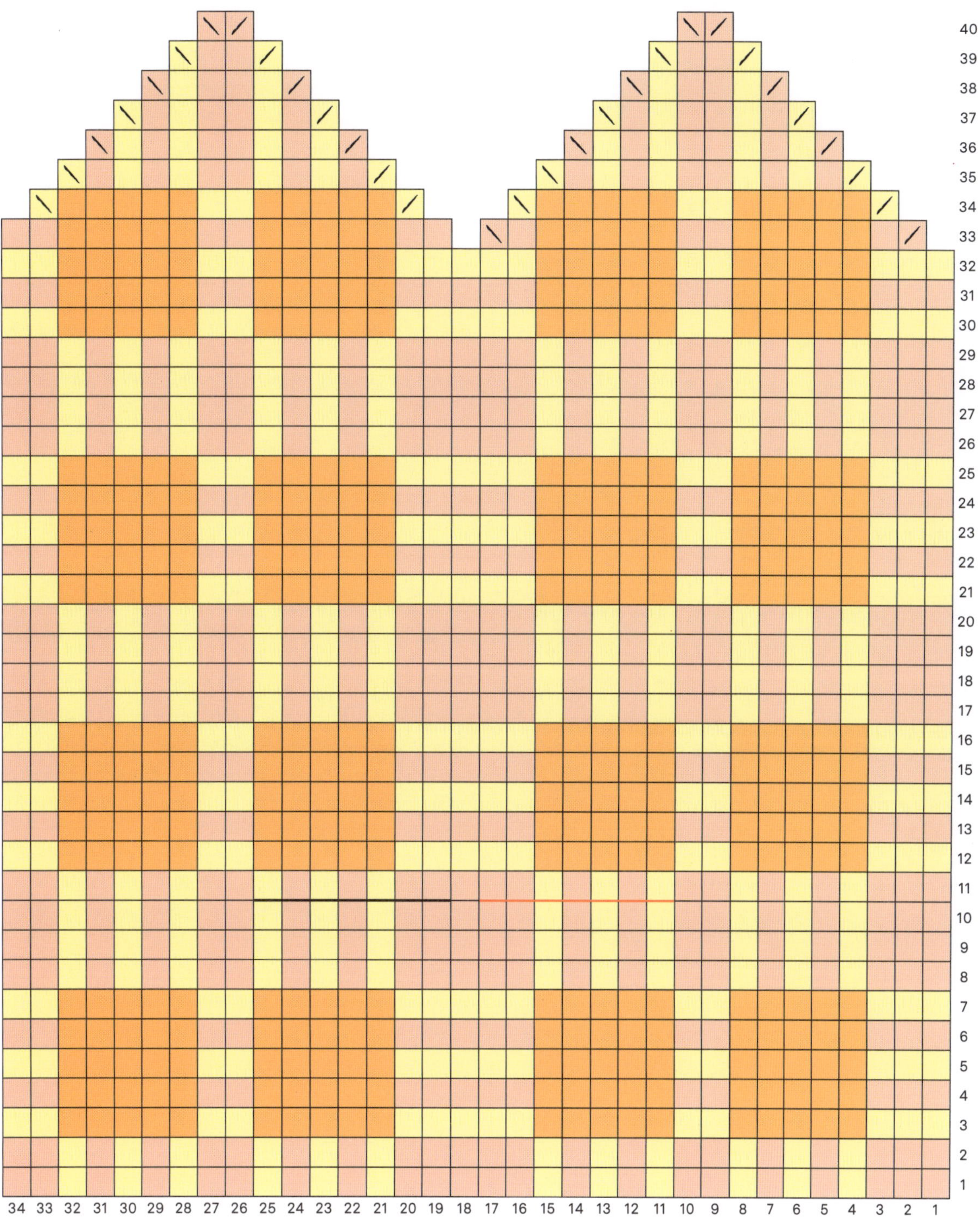

SIZE 3 – HAND CHART

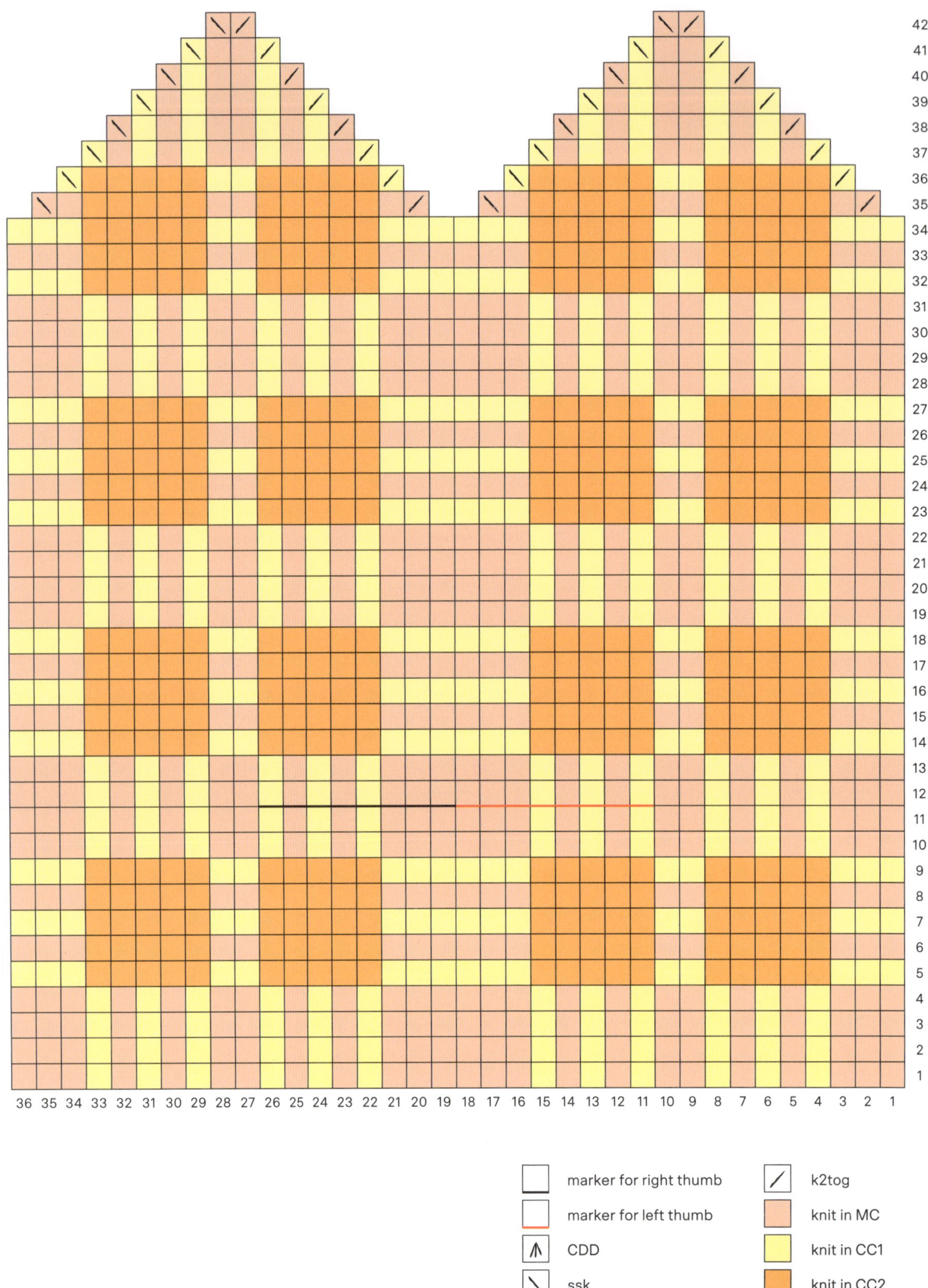

SIZES 1 AND 2 – LEFT THUMB

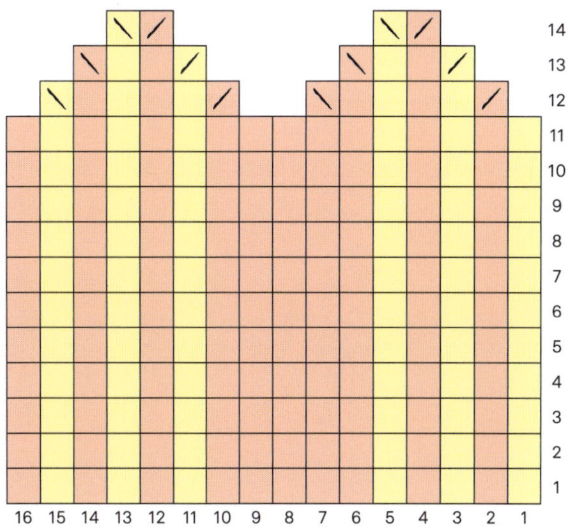

SIZES 1 AND 2 – RIGHT THUMB

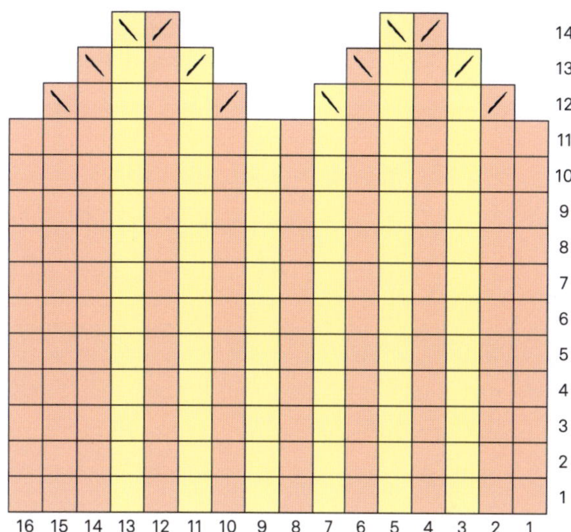

SIZE 3 – LEFT THUMB

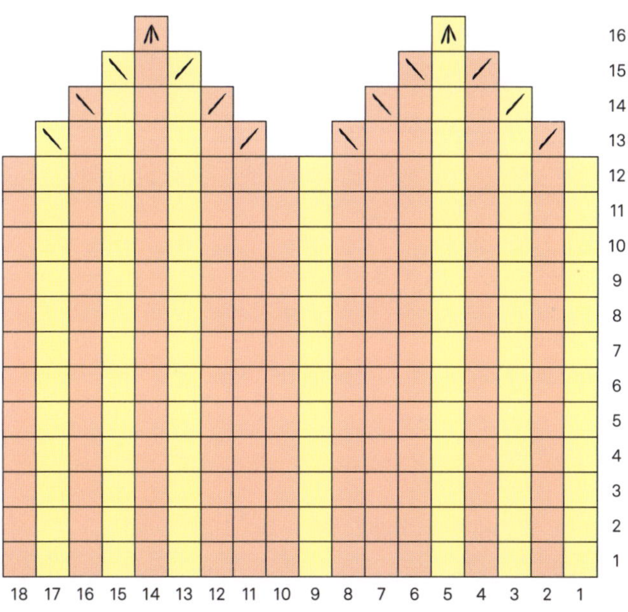

SIZE 3 – RIGHT THUMB

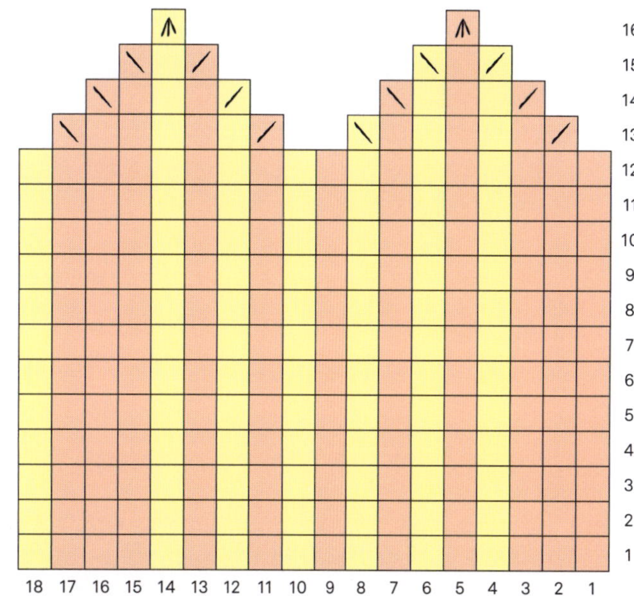

Lotta H Löthgren

39 Forest Floor

The diagonal stitch pattern of the Forest Floor mittens reminded the designer of the busy life among moss and fallen leaves. The long cuff can be folded or worn as-is.

SIZES

1 (2, 3)

Recommended ease: 0.75–1.5" / 2–4 cm of positive ease.

FINISHED MEASUREMENTS

Hand Circumference: 8 (9, 10.25)" / 20 (23, 26) cm.
Total Length (Excluding I-Cord): 9.75 (10, 10.5)" / 24.5 (25.5, 26.5) cm.
Thumb Circumference: 2.75 (3.25, 3.25)" / 7 (8.5, 8.5) cm.
Thumb Length: 2.25 (2.25, 2.75)" / 6 (6, 7) cm.

MATERIALS

Yarn: Lore by The Fibre Co. (100% Kent Romney wool, 273 yds / 250 m – 100 g). 1 skein of each colourway Ambitious and Comfort.

Or approx. 131 (142, 158) yds / 120 (130, 145) m of dk-weight yarn in each colourway. Alternative yarn suggestions are for example Wool Dreamers Mota and West Yorkshire Spinners The Croft DK.

The yarns are held double throughout the pattern.

Needles: US 10.75 / 7 mm 36" / 80 cm circular needles or DPNs. A spare circular needle a few sizes smaller than the working needle or 2 DPNs for picking up thumb sts (optional).

Notions: Stitch markers, scrap yarn in a contrasting colour.

GAUGE

14 sts x 21 rnds to 4" / 10 cm on US 10.75 / 7 mm needles in st patt, after blocking.

NOTES

The fabric created with the Split Slip-Stitch pattern is dense. Make sure to check gauge. If between sizes, size up. The fabric relaxes a bit during blocking and using mitten blockers (or a sturdy piece of cardboard cut to size) is recommended.

The pattern is written for the Magic Loop technique. If using DPNs, the first and second needle will be referred to as 'the first needle', and the third and fourth needle as 'the second needle'.

The Diagonal Slip-St pattern is worked from Charts A and B. When slipping stitches, separate the two strands of yarn and hold one strand to the RS of the fabric, while the other strand stays on the WS.

In the sample mittens, the colour Ambitious was held to the front of the work on the back side of the mitten, while the colour Comfort was held to the front of the work on the palm side of the mitten. Feel free to play with alternating colours on each row or hold the same colour to the front of the work on both the back and palm side.

CONSTRUCTION

These mittens are knitted in the round from the bottom up in an all-over textured pattern and an afterthought thumb. Two strands of yarn are held together throughout the pattern and separated when working the Slip-Stitch pattern: one of the strands is held to the front and the other to the back of the work while slipping two stitches at a time. Stitches for the thumb opening are first worked in scrap yarn, and then picked up and worked after the upper mitten is finished (afterthought thumb method). The thumb is worked in Stockinette Stitch. The mittens are finished with an applied i-cord at the bottom edge for extra stability.

DIRECTIONS

BODY

With both yarns held tog and using the Long-Tail CO method, CO 28 (32, 36) sts. PM for BOR and join to work in the rnd being careful not to twist sts. Divide sts equally, 14 (16, 18) sts on each needle. The sts on the first needle will be the back of the mitten, and the sts on the second needle will be the palm of the mitten.

Set-Up Rnd: *P1, k to last st on the needle, p1* twice.

Diagonal Slip-St Patt

Chart A is worked for the left mitten and Chart B for the right.

Sizes 1 and 3 only

Rnd 1: *P1, rep 4-st rep of chart to last st on the needle, p1* twice.

Size 2 only

Rnd 1: *P1, rep 4-st rep of chart to last 3 sts on the needle, work last 2 sts of chart, p1* twice.

Rep rnd 1, working the foll rnd in the appropriate chart, until piece measures 4.25" / 12 cm from CO, or to where you want your thumb to start.

Thumb Opening

Left mitten

Work in patt as est across first needle. On the second needle, work in patt as est to last 6 (7, 7) sts. K the next 5 (6, 6) sts with a piece of scrap yarn. Pl the sts just knitted back on the LHN and k across them with working yarn, p1. [28 (32, 36) sts]

Right mitten

Work in patt as est across first needle. On the second needle, p1, k the next 5 (6, 6) sts with a piece of scrap yarn. Place the sts just knitted back on the LHN and k across them with working yarn. Work in patt as est to end. [28 (32, 36) sts]

Upper Mitten

Both mittens

Work in patt as est, maintaining the Slip-St patt, until piece measures approx. 3.75 (4, 4.25)" / 9.5 (10, 10.5) cm from thumb opening, or until the mitten reaches just above the tip of pinky finger. End after a chart rnd 4 for left mitten and rnd 3 for right.

Shaping the Top

Note! When patt indicates to work a sl2 but only 1 st is available to work, work a sl1 in its place.

CHART A - LEFT MITTEN

CHART B - RIGHT MITTEN

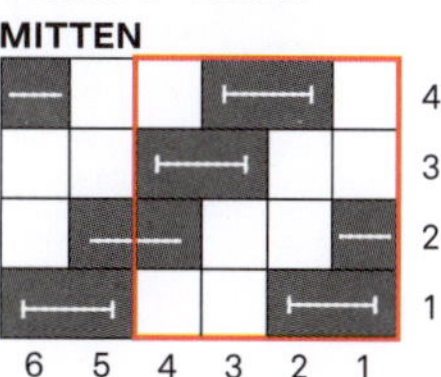

- knit with both yarns held tog
- hold one yarn to the front and one to the back of work, sl2
- hold one yarn to the front and one to the back of work, sl1
- pattern repeat

Dec Rnd: *P1, ssk, work in patt as est to 3 sts bef end of needle, k2tog, p1* twice. (4 sts dec'd)
Rep dec rnd until 4 sts rem on each needle. Cut yarns and pull the tails through the last 8 sts, closing the gap.

THUMB

Using the smaller spare needle, pick up the right leg of each of the 5 (6, 6) sts below the sts worked with scrap yarn at the thumb opening. Pick up the right leg of each of the 5 (6, 6) sts above the sts worked with scrap yarn. Carefully remove the scrap yarn. [10 (12, 12) sts]

Using the working needle and both yarns held together, pick up and k 1 st where the thumb meets the upper mitten, k across the 5 (6, 6) sts on the spare needle, pick up and k 1 st between two sets of picked up sts, k across the 5 (6, 6) sts on the spare needle. Join to work in the rnd. PM for BOR. [12 (14, 14) sts]

Next Rnd: *K2tog, k4 (5, 5)* twice. (2 sts dec'd) [10 (12, 12) sts]

Work in St St until thumb measures 2.25 (2.25, 2.5)" / 5.5 (5.5, 6.5) cm or 0.25" / 0.5 cm less than desired thumb length.

Dec Rnd 1: *K2tog, k1 (2, 2), k2tog* twice. (4 sts dec'd) [6 (8, 8) sts]
Dec Rnd 2: K2tog to end. [3 (4, 4) sts]

Cut yarns and pull the tails through the last sts, closing the gap.

I-CORD EDGE

With both yarns held tog CO 3 sts. With RS of mitten facing, *Pick up and k 1 st from the CO edge, slide these 4 sts back to the opposite end of the needle, k2, k2tog*, rep *-* until all CO sts have been worked. Break yarn and pull through the last sts.

Use the tail to sew the ends of the i-cord tog.

FINISHING

Weave in ends. Block to measurements.

Ayako Mizuno

40 Tsubomi

These mittens feature distinctive twist cables and a decorative cast-on edge. 'Tsubomi' means 'bud' in Japanese, a hint of spring in the colder months.

SIZES

1 (2, 3)

Recommended ease: 0.25–1.25" / 0.5–3 cm of positive ease.

FINISHED MEASUREMENTS

Hand Circumference: 8 (9.25, 10.25)" / 20.5 (23, 26) cm.
Length: 8 (9.5, 10.5)" / 20.5 (24, 26.5) cm (adjustable).

MATERIALS

Yarn: 2 balls of Spanish Merino by Daruma (100% merino, 77 yds / 71 m – 50 g), colourway Marine Blue.

Or approx. 105 (124, 154) yds / 97 (114, 142) m of bulky-weight yarn. Alternative yarn suggestions are for example De Rerum Natura Cyrano and Lang Merino 70.

Needles: US 10 / 6 mm DPNs or 32" / 80 cm circular needles.

Notions: Stitch markers, cable needle, stitch holders or waste yarn.

GAUGE

14 sts x 22 rnds to 4" / 10 cm in Reverse St St, after blocking.

22 sts x 21 rnds to 4" / 10 cm in 1 x 1 rib, after blocking.

9 sts to 1.75" / 4.5 cm and 24 rnds to 4.25" / 11 cm in Twist Cable patt, after blocking.

SPECIAL ABBREVIATIONS

Twist-cw: Sl 4 sts kwise one at a time to CN and twist CN 180 degrees clockwise, sl 4 sts pwise back to LHN (the 4th st becomes the first st), k4.

Twist-ccw: Sl 4 sts pwise to CN and twist CN 180 degrees counter-clockwise, sl 4 sts pwise back to LHN (the 4th st becomes the first st), k4tbl.

Twist-cw-ssk: Sl 4 sts kwise one at a time to CN and twist CN 180 degrees clockwise, sl 4 sts pwise back to LHN, k3, ssk. (1 st dec'd)

Twist-ccw-k2tog: (Started 1 st bef the Twist-cable st). Sl 1 st pwise to RHN, sl 3 sts to CN, then sl next st to CN inserting CN from back to front through the back loop (4 sts on CN), twist CN 180 degrees counter-clockwise, sl 5 sts pwise (the twist cable and first slipped st) back to LHN, k2tog, k3tbl. (1 st dec'd)

STITCH PATTERN

Twist Cable

Rnds 1–5: K4, p1, k4.
Rnd 6: Twist-ccw, p1, twist-cw.
Rep rnds 1–6 for patt.

SPECIAL TECHNIQUES

Double Strand Double Start Cast-On

Measure a length of yarn approx. 8 times the length of the hand circumference

and fold in half. With this doubled yarn and the yarn from the ball (3 strands), make a slip knot close to the tail end and place on needle (this slip knot will be dropped later bef joining in the rnd). Hold the yarn in a slingshot position as for the Long-Tail CO method with the single-strand (from the ball) over your index finger and the doubled strand over your thumb.

Step 1: CO 1 st as you normally would for the Long-Tail CO method.
Step 2: Reposition the yarn on your thumb so that the yarn from the needle wraps clockwise around the thumb (rather than counter-clockwise as for the standard Long-Tail CO method). Insert needle tip under the doubled yarn at back of thumb then over the single yarn between the needle and index finger catching the single strand bringing it up through the thumb loop. Drop the yarn off your thumb and tighten the loop on the needle. (1 st CO)

Repeat steps 1 and 2 until you have the required number of sts. Note that sts will appear paired but should be counted as 2 separate sts. Do not include the slip knot in the st count.

CONSTRUCTION

These mittens are worked in the round from the bottom up and have a thumb gusset. Except for the position of the thumb, the palm and back of the hand feature the same pattern.

DIRECTIONS

CUFF

CO 36 (44, 52) sts using the Double Strand Double Start CO method. Drop slip knot, PM for BOR and join to work in the rnd.

Rnds 1–5: *[K1, p1] 2 (3, 4) times, [k4, p1] 2 times, [k1, p1] 2 (3, 4) times*, rep *–* once more.
Rnd 6: *[K1, p1] 2 (3, 4) times, twist-ccw, p1, twist-cw, [p1, k1] 2 (3, 4) times, p1*, rep *–* once more.
Rnds 7–11: Rep rnds 1–5.

THUMB GUSSET

Note! Divide sts evenly between two needles, placing 18 (22, 26) sts on first needle (N1) and 18 (22, 26) sts on second needle (N2). If using DPNs, divide sts evenly onto 4 needles and designate first 2 needles as N1 and last 2 needles as N2.

Right Mitten: *N1:* Back of hand sts; *N2:* Palm sts.
Left Mitten: *N1:* Palm sts; *N2:* Back of hand sts.

Right Mitten

Working from correct chart for chosen size, work as foll:
Rnd 1: *N1:* Work rnd 1 of chart;
N2: PM, m1r(p), k1, m1l(p), PM, starting at 2nd st of chart, work rnd 1 of chart to end. (2 sts inc'd)
Rnd 2: *N1:* Work next rnd of chart;
N2: SM, *p1, k1* to 1 st bef m, p1, SM, starting at 2nd st of chart, work next rnd of chart to end.
Rnd 3: *N1:* Work next rnd of chart;
N2: SM, m1r, *p1, k1* to 1 st bef m, p1, m1l, SM, starting at 2nd st of chart, work next rnd of chart to end. (2 sts inc'd)
Rnd 4: *N1:* Work next rnd of chart;
N2: SM, *k1, p1* to 1 st bef m, k1, SM, starting at 2nd st of chart, work next rnd of chart to end.
Rnd 5: *N1:* Work next rnd of chart;
N2: SM, m1r(p), *k1, p1* to 1 st bef m, k1, m1l(p), SM, starting at 2nd st of chart, work next rnd of chart to end. (2 sts inc'd)
Cont working in patt and rep rnds 2–5, 1 (2, 2) more time(s). [11 (15, 15) sts between markers on N2].

Next Rnd: *N1:* Work next rnd of chart;
N2: SM, *p1, k1 * to 1 st bef m, p1, SM, starting at 2nd st of chart, work next rnd of chart to end.
Rep last rnd 4 (1, 2) more rnd(s), ending with rnd 14 (15, 16) of chart.

Next Rnd: *N1:* Work rnd 15 (16, 17) of chart;
N2: Pl sts between markers onto stitch holder or waste yarn (removing m's), CO 1 st using the Backwards Loop CO method, starting at 2nd st of chart, work rnd 15 (16, 17) of chart to end.

Proceed to Mitten Body.

Left Mitten

Rnd 1: *N1:* Work rnd 1 of chart to 2 sts bef end, PM, m1r(p), k1, m1l(p), PM, p1;
N2: Work rnd 1 of chart to end.
Rnd 2: *N1:* Work next rnd of chart to m, SM, *p1, k1* to 1 st bef m, p1, SM, p1;
N2: Work next rnd of chart to end.
Rnd 3: *N1:* Work next rnd of chart to m, SM, m1r, *p1, k1* to 1 st bef m, p1, m1l, SM, p1;
N2: Work next rnd of chart to end.
Rnd 4: *N1:* Work next rnd of chart to m, SM, *k1, p1* to 1 st bef m, k1, SM, p1;
N2: Work next rnd of chart to end.
Rnd 5: *N1:* Work next rnd of chart to m, SM, m1r(p), *k1, p1* to 1 st bef m, k1, m1l(p), SM, p1;
N2: Work next rnd of chart to end.

SIZE 1

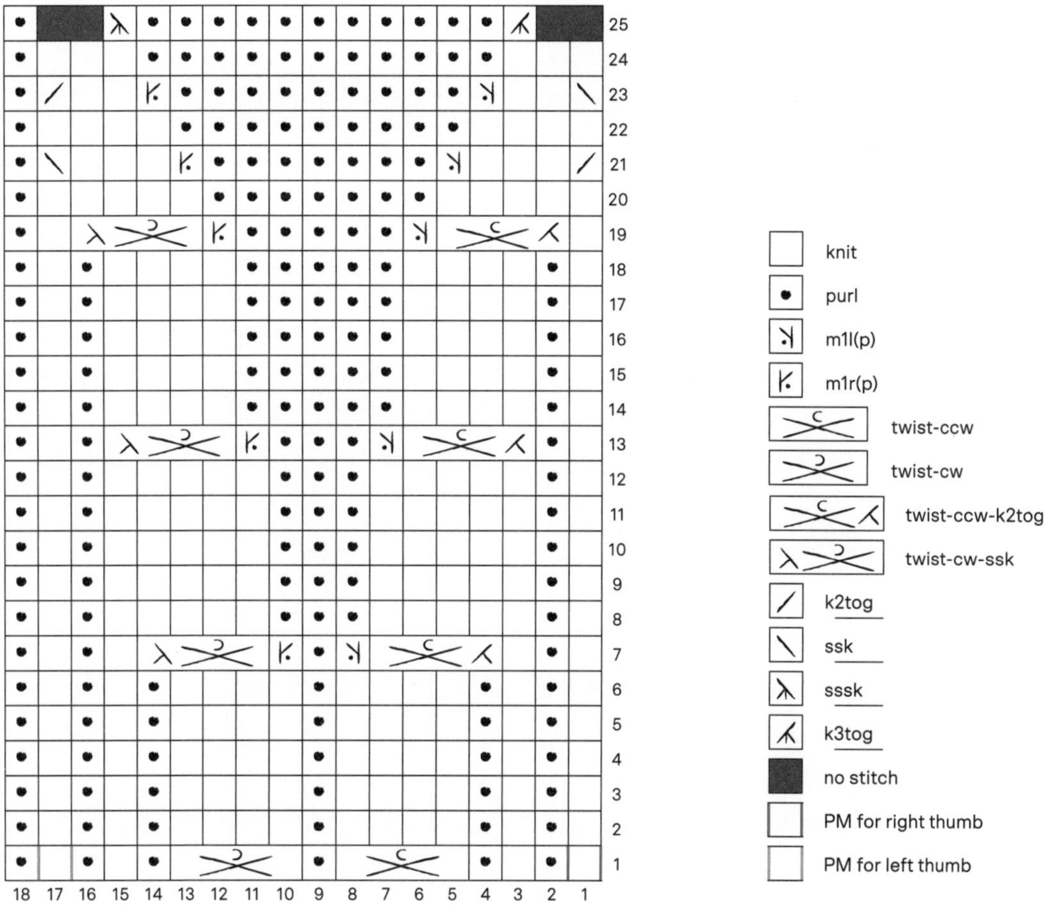

- knit
- purl
- m1l(p)
- m1r(p)
- twist-ccw
- twist-cw
- twist-ccw-k2tog
- twist-cw-ssk
- k2tog
- ssk
- sssk
- k3tog
- no stitch
- PM for right thumb
- PM for left thumb

Cont working in patt and rep rnds 2–5, 1 (2, 2) more time(s). [11 (15, 15) sts between markers on N1]

Next Rnd: *N1:* Work next rnd of chart to m, SM, *p1, k1 * to 1 st bef m, p1, SM, p1;
N2: Work next rnd of chart to end.
Rep last rnd 4 (1, 2) more rnd(s), ending with rnd 14 (15, 16) of chart.

Next Rnd: *N1:* Work rnd 15 (16, 17) of chart to m, pl sts between markers onto stitch holder or waste yarn (removing markers), CO 1 st using the Backwards Loop CO method, p1;
N2: Work rnd 15 (16, 17) of chart to end.

MITTEN BODY

Next Rnd: *N1:* Work next rnd of chart to end;
N2: Work next rnd of chart to end.
Work as est until the chart is complete. [28 (32, 36) sts]

Next Rnd: *N1:* P to end;
N2: P to end.
Rep last rnd until the length is approx. 6.5 (8, 9)" / 16.5 (20, 22.5) cm or 1.5" / 4 cm shorter than tip of middle finger.

Shape Top of Mitten

Dec Rnd: *N1:* P2tog, p to 3 sts bef end, ssp, p1;
N2: P2tog, p to 3 sts bef end, ssp, p1. (4 sts dec'd)
Rep dec rnd every 3rd rnd 2 times, then every 2nd rnd once, and then every rnd 1 (2, 3) time(s). (8 sts)

Cut yarn, thread through rem sts and pull tightly to close.

SIZE 2

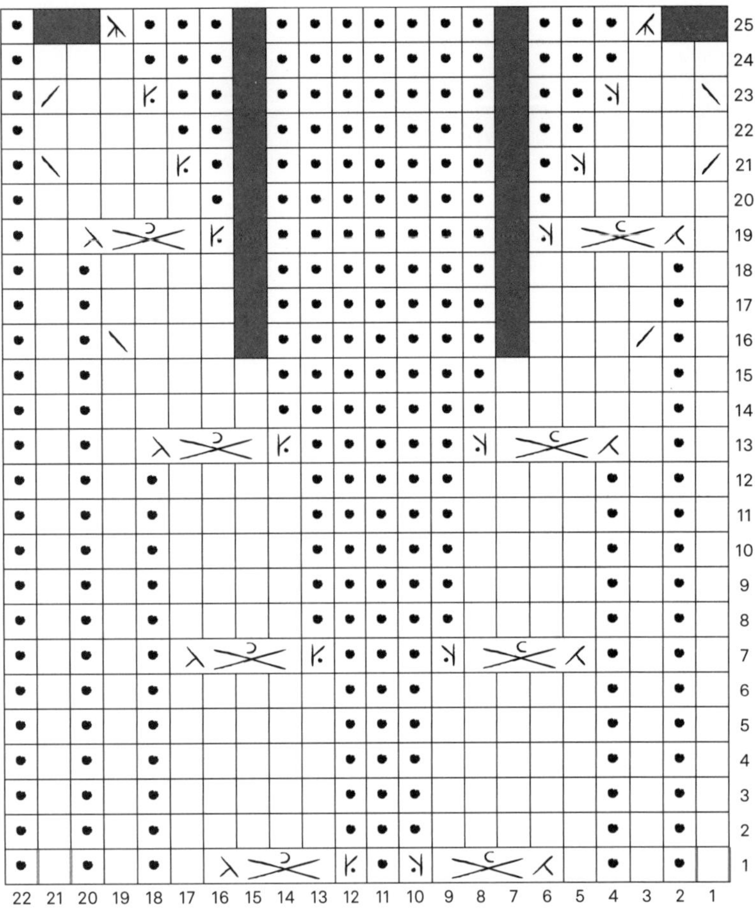

THUMB

Pl held thumb sts back onto needles.
Rnd 1: *P1, k1* to 1 st bef end, p1, pick up and k 1 st from the Backwards Loop CO. [12 (16, 16) sts]

PM for BOR and join to work in the rnd.
Rnd 2: *P1, k1* to end.
Rep rnd 2 until the thumb measures 2.5" / 6.5 cm, or your thumb is covered when you try on the mittens.

Shape Top of Thumb

Rnd 1: *K2tog* to end. [6 (8, 8) sts]

Size 1 only
Rnd 2: *K2tog, k1* to end. (4 sts)

Sizes 2 and 3 only
Rnd 2: *CDD, k1* to end. (4 sts)

Cut yarn, thread through rem sts and pull tightly to close.

FINISHING

Weave in ends. Block to measurements.

SIZE 3

31
30
29
28
27
26
25
24
23
22
21
20
19
18
17
16
15
14
13
12
11
10
9
8
7
6
5
4
3
2
1
26 25 24 23 22 21 20 19 18 17 16 15 14 13 12 11 10 9 8 7 6 5 4 3 2 1

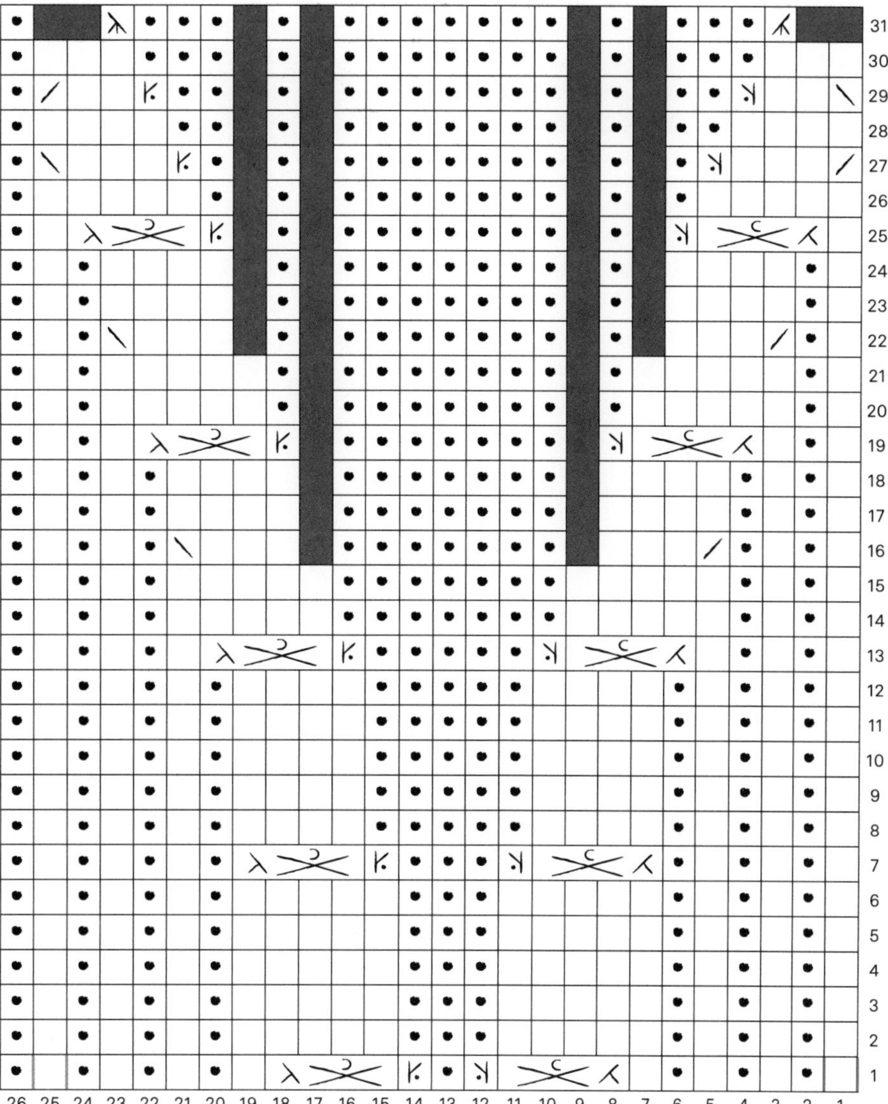

Tiia Pyykkö

41 Inkeri

If cold weather catches you by surprise, a pair of quick and simple mittens is the answer! Worked in cosy garter stitch, this pattern beautifully showcases the rustic woollen yarn.

SIZES

1 (2, 3)

Recommended ease: Little to no ease.

FINISHED MEASUREMENTS

Hand Circumference: 7 (7.75, 8.75)" / 18 (19.5, 22.5) cm.
Hand Length (Adjustable): 7 (8.25, 9.75)" 18 (21, 24.5) cm.

MATERIALS

Yarn: 2 (3, 3) balls of Fritidsgarn by Sandnes Garn (100% Norwegian wool, 76 yds / 70 m – 50 g), colourway 3021.

Or approx. 105 (155, 190) yds / 115 (170, 210) m of bulky-weight yarn. Alternative yarn suggestions are for example Biches & Bûches Le Gros Lambswool and Berroco Mercado.

Needles: US 8 / 5 mm 32" / 80 cm circular needles. The pattern has been written for the Magic Loop method but you can instead use DPNs, if preferred.

Notions: Stitch markers, stitch holder or waste yarn.

GAUGE

16 sts x 32 rnds to 4" / 10 cm in Garter St, after blocking.

STITCH PATTERNS

Garter Stitch
In the rnd.
Rnd 1: K to end.
Rnd 2: P to end.
Rep rnds 1–2 for patt.

CONSTRUCTION

These mittens are worked seamlessly, starting from the cuff, and feature a thumb gusset. The cuff is worked in 2 x 2 ribbing and can be folded double. The rest of the mittens are worked in Garter Stitch.

DIRECTIONS

CUFF

CO 28 (32, 36) sts using the German Twisted CO method. Divide sts evenly onto 2 needles. Sts for the palm will be on N1 and sts for the back of the hand on N2. Join to work in the rnd and PM for BOR at the start of N1.

Rib Rnd: *K2, p2* to end.
Cont to work in est 2 x 2 rib until the rib measures approx. 4.25" / 11 cm.

Next, work 2 rnds of Garter St bef beg the thumb gusset.

THUMB GUSSET

Right mitten
Rnd 1 (Inc): *N1:* K1, PM, m1r, k2, m1l, PM, k to end;
N2: K to end. (2 sts inc'd) [30 (34, 38) sts]
Rnd 2: P to end.
Rnd 3 (Inc): *N1:* K to m, SM, m1r, k to m, m1l, SM, k to end;

N2: K to end. (2 sts inc'd)
Rep rnds 2–3, maintaining Garter St, until there are 14 (16, 18) sts between thumb m's. [42 (48, 54) sts]

P 1 rnd.

Next Rnd: K to m, RM, pl sts between thumb m's onto a st holder or waste yarn, RM, CO 2 sts using the Backwards Loop CO method, k to end. [28 (32, 36) sts]

Cont to work all sts in Garter St, until the mitten measures 6 (7, 8)" / 15 (17.5, 20) cm from start of thumb gusset, or your index finger is covered when you try on the mittens, ending after a p rnd.

Left mitten
Work the first rnd of the thumb gusset as foll:
Rnd 1 (Inc): *N1:* K11 (13, 15), PM, m1r, k2, m1l, PM, k1;
N2: K to end. (2 sts inc'd)
Then work as for the right mitten from start of rnd 2.

DECREASES

Beg to work dec's at the sides of the hand as foll, maintaining Garter St:
Dec Rnd 1: *N1:* K1, k2tog, k to 3 sts bef end, ssk, k1;
N2: K1, k2tog, k to 3 sts bef end, ssk, k1. (4 sts dec'd)

Dec Rnd 2: *N1:* P1, p2tog, p to 3 sts bef end, ssp, p1;
N2: P1, p2tog, p to 3 sts bef end, ssp, p1. (4 sts dec'd)

Rep dec rnds 1–2 until 8 sts rem.

Cut yarn, thread it through the rem sts and pull to close. Pull the yarn end through the tip to the WS.

THUMB

Pl the held sts onto the needles, dividing the sts evenly over 2 needles. Pick up an additional 3 sts across the CO sts at the thumb opening to avoid a hole. BOR is after the picked-up sts. PM if desired. [17 (19, 21) sts]

K 1 rnd.

Next Rnd (Dec): P to 6 sts bef end, *p2tog* 3 times. [14 (16, 18) sts]

Cont to work in Garter St for 1.5 (2.25, 2.75)" / 4 (6, 7) cm, or until your thumb is covered when you try on the mittens.

Next Rnd (Dec): *K2tog* to end. [7 (8, 9) sts]

Cut yarn, thread it through the remaining sts and pull to close. Pull the yarn end through the tip to the WS.

FINISHING

Weave in ends. Wet block to measurements.

42

Hats

Claudia Joyal Laplante — Andrea Aho — Sini Kramer
Jonna Helin — Pauliina Kuunsola — Faye Kennington

Claudia Joyal Laplante

42 Hiver

Wear this chunky beanie when you need something extra cosy! Thanks to the texture of the bouclé yarn, the colourwork creates a houndstooth look without a complicated chart.

SIZES

1 (2, 3)

Recommended ease: 0–2" / 0–5 cm of negative ease.

FINISHED MEASUREMENTS

Circumference: 19 (21, 23)" / 48 (53, 58) cm.
Height (with Brim Unfolded): 14.5 (15, 15.5)" / 37 (38, 39) cm.

MATERIALS

Yarn: Boucle by Julie Asselin (70% alpaca, 30% Highland Peruvian wool, 240 yds / 220 m – 100 g).
MC: 1 skein of colourway Biscotti (see notes for size 3).
CC: 1 skein of colourway Cobalt.

The yarns are held together throughout the pattern.

Or approx. 220 (230, 240) yds / 200 (210, 220) m (in MC) and 66 (77, 87) yds / 60 (70, 80) m (in CC) of worsted or aran-weight yarn held double.

Or approx. 110 (115, 120) yds / 100 (105, 110) m (in MC) and 33 (39, 44) yds / 30 (35, 40) m (in CC) of bulky-weight yarn held single.

Alternative yarn options are for example Drops Alpaca Bouclé (held double) and Rowan Soft Bouclé (held single).

Needles: US 8 / 5 mm and US 10 / 6 mm 16" / 40 cm circular needles. US 10 / 6 mm DPNs.

Notions: Stitch markers, tapestry needle.

GAUGE

12 sts x 14 rows to 4" / 10 cm on US 10 / 6 mm needles in charted patt, after blocking.

NOTES

The largest size uses an entire 100 g skein of the recommended MC. To ensure to not run out of yarn, it is possible to cast on and knit a few rows of the brim in CC before switching to MC or to knit the brim shorter for a double (instead of triple) fold.

CONSTRUCTION

This hat is knitted in the round from the bottom up. It is worked with two strands of boucle yarn held together throughout the pattern and features a 1 x 1 ribbing for the brim and stranded colourwork for the body. The crown decreases are worked with ssk and k2tog decreases. Once finished, the brim is folded twice.

DIRECTIONS

BRIM

With US 8 / 5 mm needles and the Long-Tail CO method, CO 56 (64, 72) sts with a double strand of MC. PM and join to work in the rnd being careful not to twist sts.

Rib Rnd: *K1, p1* to end.
Work in est 1 x 1 rib until the brim measures 8" / 20.5 cm from the CO edge.

Change to US 10 / 6 mm circular needles.

BODY

Using MC and CC double-stranded, work chart in St St until the work measures approx. 12" / 30.5 cm from the CO edge, ending after a rnd 4.

CROWN

Note! Two dec sections and two 10-st sections will be worked. Every dec rnd dec's 4 sts. Pay attention to the written instructions carefully, as chart position varies. After slipping a m or working a dec, start at the beg of the chart rnd mentioned in order to maintain the colour patt. Change to DPNs as needed.

Rnd 1: *Ssk in MC, work 14 (18, 22) sts foll rnd 1, k2tog in MC, PM, work 10 sts foll rnd 1*, PM, rep *–* to end. [52 (60, 68) sts]
Rnd 2: *Ssk in CC, work to 2 sts bef m foll rnd 8, k2tog in CC, SM, work 10 sts foll rnd 2*, SM, rep *–* to end. [48 (56, 64) sts]
Rnd 3: *Ssk in CC, work to 2 sts bef m foll rnd 7, k2tog in CC, SM, work 10 sts foll rnd 3*, SM, rep *–* to end. [44 (52, 60) sts]
Rnd 4: *Ssk in MC, work to 2 sts bef m foll rnd 6, k2tog in MC, SM, work 10 sts foll rnd 4*, SM, rep *–*to end. [40 (48, 56) sts]
Rnd 5: *Ssk in CC, work to 2 sts bef m foll rnd 5, k2tog in CC, SM, work 10 sts foll rnd 5*, SM, rep *–* to end. [36 (44, 52) sts]
Rnd 6: *Ssk in CC, work to 2 sts bef m foll rnd 4, k2tog in CC, SM, work 10 sts foll rnd 6*, SM, rep *–* to end. [32 (40, 48) sts]
Rnd 7: *Ssk in MC, work to 2 sts bef m foll rnd 3, k2tog in MC, SM, work 10 sts foll rnd 7*, SM, rep *–* to end. [28 (36, 44) sts]
Rnd 8: *Ssk in CC, work to 2 sts bef m foll rnd 2, k2tog in CC, SM, work 10 sts foll rnd 8*, SM, rep *–* to end. [24 (32, 40) sts]

Sizes 2 and 3 only
Rnd 9: *Ssk in MC, work to 2 sts bef m foll row 1, k2tog in MC, SM, work 10 sts foll rnd 1*. SM, rep *–* to end. [– (28, 36) sts]
Rnd 10: *Ssk in MC, work to 2 sts bef m foll row 8, k2tog in MC, SM, work 10 sts foll rnd 2*, SM, rep *–* to end. [– (24, 32) sts]

Size 3 only
Rnd 11: *Ssk in CC, work to 2 sts bef m foll rnd 7, k2tog in CC, SM, work 10 sts foll rnd 3*, SM, rep *–* to end. [– (–, 28) sts]
Rnd 12: *Ssk in MC, k2tog in MC, SM, work 10 sts foll rnd 4*, SM, rep *–* to end. [– (–, 24) sts]

All sizes resume
Cut CC.

K1 in MC, then adjust sts so the next 12 sts are on one needle and the rem 12 sts on the other needle. Cut MC leaving a 14" / 35 cm long tail.

Graft 2 sets of 12 sts tog to close as outlined below.

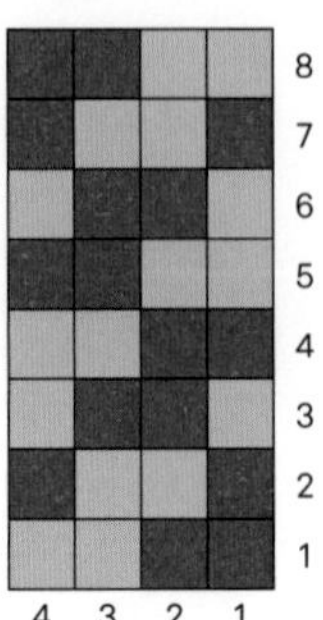

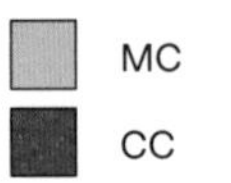

Note! There are no set-up steps or second pass on the last st of each needle in order to round off the corners.

Step 1: Pass tapestry needle through the first st on the front needle kwise and sl that st off the needle.
Step 2: Pass tapestry needle through the next st on the front needle pwise and leave the st on the needle.
Step 3: Pass tapestry needle through the first st on the back needle pwise and sl that st off the needle.
Step 4: Pass tapestry needle through the next st on the back needle kwise and leave the st on the needle.

Rep steps 1–4 until 1 st rem on each needle then slip them off the needles.

FINISHING

Weave in ends. Block to measurements.

Fold the brim twice.

Andrea Aho

43 Cloudsteek

This balaclava was designed to allow knitters to practise different colourwork techniques in a small, approachable project. There's stranded knitting in the round, in rows and, finally, steeking!

SIZE

One size.

FINISHED MEASUREMENTS

Circumference: 25.5" / 65 cm.
Height: 16" / 40.5 cm.

MATERIALS

Yarn: Cyrano by De Rerum Natura (100% merino, 164 yds / 150 m – 100 g).
C1: 2 skeins of colourway Granit.
C2: 2 skeins of colourway Sel.

Or approx. 240 yds / 219 m (in C1) and 170 yds / 155 m (in C2) of aran-weight yarn. Alternative yarn suggestions are for example Quince & Co. Osprey, West Yorkshire Spinners The Croft Aran Tweed and Brooklyn Tweed Quarry.

Needles: US 10 / 6 mm 16" / 40 cm circular needles and 2 DPNs (for i-cord, optional).

Notions: US J-10 / 6 mm crochet hook.

GAUGE

15 sts x 17 rows to 4" / 10 cm in colourwork, after blocking.

SPECIAL TECHNIQUES

Steeking

Depending on the yarn chosen, use different methods of steeking. Woolen spun non-superwash yarns will 'stick' together and make for a secure steek once enforced using the crochet reinforcement method. Other reinforcement methods can be used as well.

Crochet Slip-Stitch Reinforcement

Set-Up: With C1, make a slip knot and place on crochet hook. With RS facing, insert hook from back to front through the CO edge at the base of the 4th st of the steek column. Yarn over hook and draw a loop through the CO edge as well as the slip knot on hook.

Right Slip-Stitch Column
With RS facing and keeping working yarn at front, insert hook through the left leg of the 4th st of the steek column and the right leg of the 3rd st, yarn over hook and draw a loop through both sts as well as the loop on hook (one slip-st made). *Working into row above last slip-st, insert hook into left leg of 4th st and right leg of 3rd st, yarn over hook and draw a loop through both sts as well as the loop on hook.* Rep *–* up entire length of steek column. Cut yarn and draw tail through last loop on hook.

Left Slip-Stitch Column
Turn work 180 degrees to work in opposite direction. Work set-up, joining yarn to the BO edge. Work as given for Right Slip-Stitch Column, working into left leg of 2nd st and rem right leg of the 3rd st (right and left as viewed in this new orientation).

Cutting
Cut the bar that is visible across the third steek st up the length of the steek.

NOTES

Remember to always read the written

instructions even when working from the chart.

Steek Column (worked over 5 sts)
Every Rnd: K1 with C1, k1 with C2, k1 with C1 (this is the st that will be cut), k1 with C2, k1 with C1.

CONSTRUCTION

This balaclava is worked from bottom up and consists of three sections, each featuring a different colourwork technique. Section 1 is worked in the round. Section 2 is also worked in the round but contains a column of stitches to be steeked. Section 3 is knitted flat. An applied i-cord edge is knitted to neatly finish the face opening.

DIRECTIONS

NECK RIB

With C1, CO 96 sts using the Long-Tail CO method. Join to work in the rnd being careful not to twist sts. PM for BOR.

Rnd 1: *K2, p2* to end.
Cont in est 2 x 2 rib until work measures 1.25" / 3 cm from CO edge.

Set-Up Rnd: K to end.

SECTION 1

On the next rnd, introduce C2 and beg working from Chart A. Be careful not to pull the long floats tightly and catching (trapping) the floats when necessary.

Rnd 1: Working in St St, beg Chart A introducing C2 when called for. 8 sts of Chart A will be repeated 12 times within the rnd.
Rep rnds 1–8 of Chart A 4 times (32 rnds total).

SECTION 2

Rnd 33 (Set-Up): Work Chart A rnd 1 for 36 sts, cut C2. With C1, k24, reintroduce C2 and cont working rnd 1 of Chart A to end.
Rnd 34: Work Chart A rnd 2 for 36 sts, cut C2. With C1 BO 24 sts loosely, reintroduce C2 and work rnd 2 of Chart A to end. (72 sts)
Rnd 35: Work Chart A rnd 3 for 36 sts, With C1 CO 5 sts (these sts will form the steek column) and join to cont working rnd 3 of Chart A to end of rnd. (77 sts)
Rnds 36–64: Work next rnd of Chart A for 36 sts, work 5 steek sts as described in notes, work next rnd of Chart A to end.

From here, beg working from Chart B in St St.
Rnd 65: Work Chart B rnd 1 for 12 sts (working 8-st rep only and disregarding 2 selvage sts at each end of chart), PM, cut C2. With C1 k53, reintroduce C2 and work Chart B rnd 1 to end.
Rnd 66: Work Chart B rnd 2 for 12 sts, cut C2. With C1, BO 53 sts loosely (including the steek sts), reintroduce C2 and work Chart B rnd 2 to end, RM, cut C1 and C2. (24 sts)

SECTION 3

In this section, the colourwork is knitted flat. RS rows are knitted and WS rows are purled. Work Chart B accordingly noting there are 2 selvage sts CO on either edge of the work that are knit in a checkerboard patt and will eventually be sewn into the seam. This helps make the colourwork look neat at the edges.

Row 67 (RS): Beg with first of the 24 sts on needle (not former BOR), work row 3 of Chart B (8 st rep will be worked 3 times), with C1 CO 2 sts. (26 sts)
Row 68 (WS): Work row 4 of Chart B, with C1 CO 2 sts. (28 sts)
Rows 69–96: Work next row of Chart B (8 rows of Chart B will be worked 4 times total).

Row 97 (RS): Cut C2. With C1, k to end.

With C1, BO all sts from the WS.

FINISHING

Wet block to even out the colourwork prior to steeking and seaming.

Steek Section 2 of the balaclava (see Special Techniques). Seam the side edges of Section 3 to the BO edges at the top of Section 2, bringing 2 edge

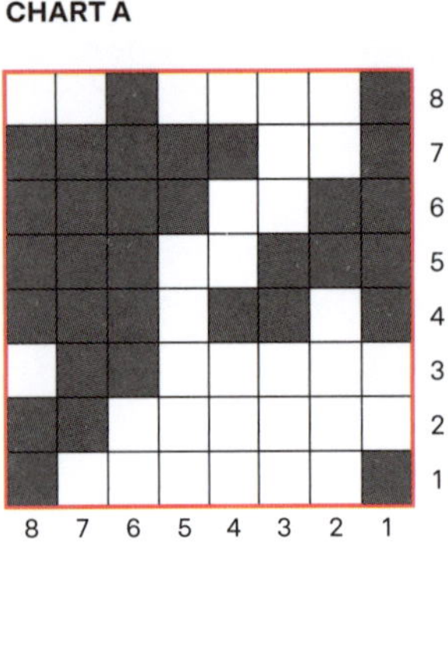

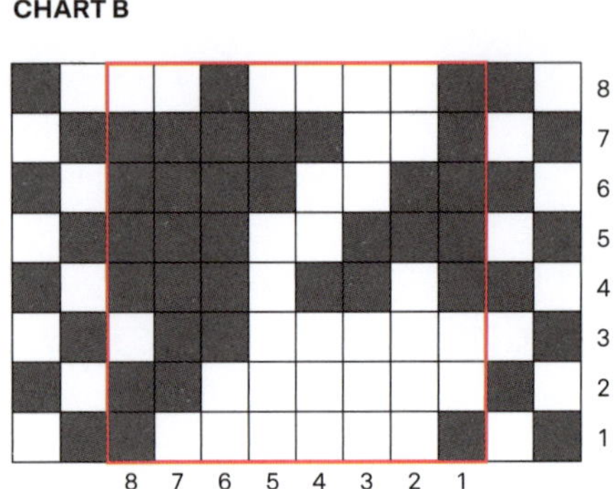

(C1) RS: knit / WS: purl

(C2) RS: knit / WS: purl

pattern repeat

sts into seam and taking care to make sure the edges stay aligned and even.

Applied I-Cord Edge

Using DPNs or circular needles, C1 and a Provisional CO method of your choice, CO 3 sts. Do not turn the work and slide the sts back to the other end of the needle so that the first CO st is ready to be knitted.

With the working yarn coming from the far-left st on the needle and wyib, k2, sl1 pwise, yo, pick up and k1 st at the bottom centre edge of the balaclava (5 sts on the needles), pass the sl st and yo over last knit st (3 sts on the needles), slide the sts back down to the right end of the needles. Rep *–* around the balaclava's face opening. On the steeked edges, be sure to pick up sts into the outermost steek column sts (these should be in C1). Once the Provisional CO has been reached, graft the two ends tog.

Pick up 5 sts for every 7 rows along the vertical edges and between each st for the horizontal edges.

Weave in ends and wet block again to measurements. Be careful not to stretch the colourwork out of shape but stretch it just enough to even out the fabric.

Sini Kramer

44 Poppy

The ribbed Poppy hat is a perfect basic beanie that is easy and meditative to knit! The combination of alpaca silk and wool creates a dreamy fabric that feels soft against the skin.

SIZES

1 (2, 3)

Recommended ease: 3–4.5" / 7.5–12 cm of negative ease.

FINAL MEASUREMENTS

Circumference (Lightly Stretched): 15.5 (16.75, 18)" / 39 (42.5, 46) cm.
Full Height: 16.5 (17, 17.25)" / 42 (43, 44) cm.
Height (with Brim Folded Triple): Approx. 9 (9.5, 9.75)" / 23 (24, 25) cm.

MATERIALS

Yarn: Yarn A: 1 skein of Corrie Worsted by La Bien Aimée (75% Falkland Corriedale, 25% Gotland wool, 250 yds / 230 m – 100 g), colourway Coquelicot.

Yarn B: 1 skein of Kumo by La Bien Aimée (74% Suri alpaca, 26% mulberry silk, 328 yds / 300 m – 50 g), colourway Coquelicot.

The yarns are held double throughout the pattern.

Or approx. 170 (210, 230) yds / 170 (190, 210) m of worsted-weight (for Yarn A) and 170 (185, 210) yds / 155 (170, 190) m of similar lace-weight silk/mohair yarn (for Yarn B). Alternative yarn suggestions are for example La Bien Aimée Wensley Worsted, De Rerum Natura Gilliatt or Hudson + West Co. Forge (for Yarn A) and The Farmer's Daughter Fibers Oh Dang!, Drops Alpaca Silk or Lana Grossa Setasuri (for Yarn B).

Needles: 5 mm 16" / 40 cm circular needles and DPNs.

Notions: Stitch markers.

GAUGE

17 sts x 22 rnds to 4" / 10 cm in 1 x 1 rib, blocked and lightly stretched.

CONSTRUCTION

This hat is worked seamlessly in the round from the bottom up in 1 x 1 ribbing. The crown is shaped with simple k2tog and ssk decreases at three points.

DIRECTIONS

BRIM AND BODY

With Yarns A and B held tog, CO 66 (72, 78) sts using the German Twisted CO method. PM for BOR.

Rib Rnd: *K1, p1* to end.
Work in est 1 x 1 rib until the work measures approx. 15" / 38 cm, or until desired length.

CROWN SHAPING

Pl 5 markers as foll to mark crown dec points:
[*K1, p1* 2 times, k1, PM, p1, *k1, p1* 8 (9, 10) times, PM] 2 times, *k1, p1* 2 times, k1, PM, p1, *k1, p1* 8 (9, 10) times.

Rnd 1 (Dec): [Work in est rib to m, SM, p1, k1, k2tog, work in est rib to 4 sts bef m, ssk, k1, p1, SM] 3 times. (6 sts dec'd)
Rnd 2: Work sts as they appear.
Rnd 3 (Dec): [Work in est rib to m, SM, p1, k2tog, work in est rib to 3 sts bef m, ssk, p1, SM] 3 times. (6 sts dec'd)
Rnd 4: Rep rnd 2.
Rep rnds 1–4, 3 times in total, changing to DPNs when this is more comfortable. (36 sts dec'd) [30 (36, 42) sts]

Size 2 only
Next Rnd (Dec): [Work in est rib to m, SM, p1, k1, p3tog, k1, p1, SM] 3 times. (6 sts dec'd) [– (30, –) sts]
Next Rnd: Work sts as they appear.

Size 3 only
Rep rnds 1–4 once more. (12 sts dec'd) [– (–, 30 sts)]

All sizes
Next Rnd (Dec): *K3tog, p1*, rep *–* to 2 sts bef end, ssk. RM as you reach them. (15 sts dec'd) [15 (15, 15) sts]

Cut yarn. Thread it through a tapestry needle and pull it through the remaining stitches.

FINISHING

Weave in ends. Wet- or steam-block to measurements.

Jonna Helin

45 Aure

The thick Aure beanie will surely keep the frost away. The double-folded, triple-thick ribbed brim is wonderfully chunky, and the playful pompom on top brings a smile to winter lips.

SIZE

One size.

Fits head circumferences of approx. 21–23" / 54–59 cm.

FINISHED MEASUREMENTS

Head Circumference (Lightly Blocked): 17.75" / 45 cm.
Total Height: 17" / 43 cm.
Height (with Brim Folded Twice): Approx. 9.5" / 24 cm.

MATERIALS

Yarn: Yarn A: 1 ball of Snorre by Viking Garn (100% merino, 110 yds / 100 m - 100 g), colourway 208.
Yarn B: 2 balls of Alpaca Maya by Viking Garn (82% alpaca, 13% merino, 5% nylon, 175 yds / 160 m - 50 g), colourway 708.

Three strands of yarn are held together throughout the pattern: 1 strand of Yarn A and 2 strands of Yarn B.

Or approx. 110 yds / 100 m of super bulky-weight yarn (Yarn A) and 220 yds / 200 m of bulky-weight yarn (Yarn B). Alternative yarn suggestions are for example Rico Creative Fun Felting Wool or Ístex Álafosslopi (for Yarn A) and Sandnes Garn Børstet Alpakka or Schulana Alparino (for Yarn B). You can also knit the beanie using a single suitable super bulky-weight yarn, such as Wool and the Gang Crazy Sexy Wool.

Needles: US 15 / 10 mm 16" / 40 cm circular needles.

Notions: 5 stitch markers.

GAUGE

9 sts x 13 rows to 4" / 10 cm in St St, after blocking.

CONSTRUCTION

This beanie is knitted in the round from the bottom up. It begins with a twisted ribbed brim, which is eventually folded twice. The ribbing is followed by Stockinette Stitch. The crown is shaped with simple k2tog decreases. The hat is finished with a pompom.

DIRECTIONS

CO 44 sts using the German Twisted Cast-On method with all three yarn strands held together. PM and join to work in the rnd.

Rib Rnd: *K1, p1tbl* to end.
Work in est rib for 23 more rnds, or until the rib measures approx. 8" / 20 cm.

Next Rnd: K.
Cont in St St (k every rnd) for 22 more rnds, or until the beanie measures approx. 15" / 38 cm in total height.

CROWN SHAPING

Set-Up Rnd: You are at the BOR m. Now, pl the rem 4 m's to mark the crown dec points as foll: K9, PM, k9, PM, k9, PM, k9, PM, k8. You are again at the BOR m.

Dec Rnd 1: *K to 2 sts bef m, k2tog*, rep *–* 4 times. You are again at the BOR m.
Rep the dec rnd 6 more times. 9 sts rem.

Note! If working with 16" / 40 cm circular needles becomes difficult, switch to DPNs or use a longer circular needle for magic loop.

Cut yarn and thread it through the remaining stitches using a tapestry needle. Pull tight but gently to secure.

FINISHING

Weave in the ends and wet block to measurements.

If desired, make a pompom and attach it to the top of the beanie.

Pauliina Kuunsola

46 Hike

Hike is worked with an assortment of yarns held together. It is perfect for scrap yarn and lonely skeins in your stash – basically anything you can get gauge with!

SIZES

1 (2, 3)

Recommended ease: 4–6" / 10–15 cm of negative ease.

FINISHED MEASUREMENTS

Circumference: 15.25 (16.75, 18)" / 38.5 (41.5, 45) cm.
Height: 9.5" / 23.5 cm.

MATERIALS

Yarn: Approx. 100 g of yarn held together gives the correct gauge.

The sample was knitted using Nest Worsted by Magpie Fibers (in colourway Castaway), Mondim by Rosa Pomar (in colourway 109), Highland Wool by Isager (in colourway Sand) and Blacker Swan 4-ply by Blacker Yarns (in colourway Pale Maiden), i.e. 1 lace, 2 fingering and 1 worsted-weight yarn.

Needles: US 13 / 9 mm 16" / 40 cm circular needles, US 13 / 9 mm DPNs for crown.

Notions: Stitch marker.

GAUGE

12 sts x 17 rnds to 4" / 10 cm in st patt in the rnd, after blocking.

NOTES

The height can be adjusted by working more or less of the 2-round pattern repeats.

CONSTRUCTION

This hat is worked from the bottom up. It can be made in any yarn you can get gauge with: holding multiple strands together, like for the sample, or with a chunky-weight yarn held single. The hat is finished with k2tog decreases at the crown.

DIRECTIONS

CO 46 (50, 54) sts with preferred CO method for rib. Join to work in the rnd and PM for BOR.

Rib Rnd: *K1, p1* to end.
Work the rib rnd a total of 4 times.

Rnd 1: K to end.
Rnd 2: *K1, p1* to end.
Rep rnds 1–2 a total of 15 times, or until the hat's height is 1.5" / 3.5 cm less than desired.

CROWN DECREASES

Rnds 1–2: K to end.
Rnd 3 (Dec): K2tog to end. [23 (25, 27) sts dec'd] [23 (25, 27) sts]
Rnd 4: K to end.
Rnd 5 (Dec): K2tog to last st, k1. [11 (12, 13) sts dec'd] [12 (13, 14) sts]
Rnd 6: K to end.

Cut yarn and pull the tail through the sts on the needle. Pull to close the hole.

FINISHING

Weave in ends. Block to measurements.

Faye Kennington

47 Gull

Elevate your winter style with this sweet hat, which boasts a wide ribbed brim, an eye-catching two-colour stitch pattern and a large pompom.

SIZES

1 (2, 3)

Recommended ease: 1.5–2.5" / 4–6.5 cm of negative ease.

FINISHED MEASUREMENTS

Circumference: 18 (19.75, 21.5)" / 45.5 (49.5, 53.5) cm.
Height: 9 (10, 10.75)" / 23 (25.5, 27) cm.

MATERIALS

Yarn: Arbor Lodge by Brooklyn Tweed (100% American Targhee wool, 125 yds / 114 m – 100 g).
MC: 1 (1, 2) skein(s) of colourway Barely There.
CC: 1 skein of colourway Burnished.
Or approx. 172 (207, 245) yds / 157 (189, 224) m of chunky-weight yarn: 89 (113, 139) yds / 81 (103, 127) m (in MC) and 83 (94, 106) yds / 76 (86, 97) m (in CC). Alternative yarn suggestions are for example Kelbourne Woolens Germantown Bulky and Erika Knight Big Vintage Wool.

Needles: US 9 / 5.5 mm and US 10 / 6 mm 16–20" / 40–50 cm circular needles and US 10 / 6 mm DPNs.

Notions: 1 stitch marker, cable needle, extra-large pompom maker.

GAUGE

17 sts x 24 rnds to 4" / 10 cm on US 10 / 6 mm needles in Gull St patt, after blocking.

SPECIAL ABBREVIATIONS

1/1 LC: Left Cross. Sl next st to CN and pl at front of work, k1, then k1 from CN.
1/1 RC: Right Cross. Sl next st to CN and pl at back of work, k1, then k1 from CN.

1/2 LC: Left Cross. Sl next st to CN and pl at front of work, k2, then k1 from CN.
1/2 RC: Right Cross. Sl next 2 sts to CN and pl at back of work, k1, then k2 from CN.

STITCH PATTERNS

2 x 1 Rib Stitch

In the rnd over a multiple of 6 sts.
Rnd 1: *K1, p1, k2, p1, k1*, rep *–* to end.
Rep rnd 1 for patt.

Gull Stitch

In the rnd over a multiple of 7 sts.

Rnd 1 (MC): K to end.
Rnds 2–3 (CC): *K1, sl1, k4, sl1*, rep *–* to end.
Rnd 4 (MC): *K1, 1/2 LC, 1/2 RC*, rep *–* to end.
Rep rnds 1–4 for patt.

NOTES

It is possible to add an extra four rounds of the Gull Stitch pattern for a deeper hat. Just keep in mind that this affects required yardage.

CONSTRUCTION

This hat is knitted seamlessly in the round from the brim to crown. It features a fascinating two-colour textural pattern, a wide, folded ribbed brim and a large pompom.

DIRECTIONS

BRIM

With MC and US 9 / 5.5 mm needles, CO 66 (72, 78) sts. Join to work in the rnd being careful not to twist sts. PM for BOR.

Rnd 1 (MC): *K1, p1, k2, p1, k1*, rep *–* to end.
Rep rnd 1 until work measures 5 (5.5, 6)" / 12.5 (14, 15) cm from CO edge.

MAIN BODY

Switch to US 10 / 6 mm needles.

Set-Up Rnd (MC): *M1r, k6* to end. [77 (84, 91) sts]
Rnds 1–2 (CC): *K1, sl1, k4, sl1*, rep *–* to end.
Rnd 3 (MC): *K1, 1/2 LC, 1/2 RC*, rep *–* to end.
Rnd 4 (MC): K to end.
Rep rnds 1–4, 4 (5, 6) more times, or until work measures 3.5 (4.25, 4.75)" / 9 (11, 12) cm from beg of main body section.

CROWN

Note! Switch to DPNs when the number of sts is too small for circulars.

Rnd 1 (CC): *K1, sl1, k4, sl1*, rep *–* to end.
Rnd 2 (CC): *K1, sl1, k2tog, ssk, sl1*, rep *–* to end. [55 (60, 65) sts]
Rnd 3 (MC): *K1, 1/1 LC, 1/1 RC*, rep *–* to end.
Rnd 4 (MC): K to end.
Rnd 5 (CC): *K1, sl1, k2tog, sl1*, rep *–* to end. [44 (48, 52) sts]
Rnd 6 (CC): *K1, sl1* to end.

Cut CC and complete final rnds with MC.
Rnd 7: *K1, sl1, k2tog, psso*, rep *–* to end. [22 (24, 26) sts]
Rnd 8: K to end.
Rnd 9: *K2tog* to end. [11 (12, 13) sts]
Rnd 10: K1 (0, 1), *k2tog* to end. [6 (6, 7) sts]

Cut yarn and pull through the rem sts.

FINISHING

Weave in ends. Wet block to measurements and fold the brim double.

Make a pompom using CC. Secure to crown.

Jonna Helin

48 Halla

The Halla hat is a quick knit – a perfect choice for your first brioche project! It is knitted with large needles and divine, hand-dyed yarns.

SIZE

One size.

FINISHED MEASUREMENTS

Circumference: 20" / 51 cm.
Total Length of Fabric (Before Folding in Half): 31.5" / 80 cm.

MATERIALS

Yarn: MC: 1 skein of Merino Singles by Qing Fibre (100% superwash merino, 400 yds / 366 m – 100 g), colourway Cactus. MC is held triple throughout the pattern.

CC: 1 skein of Melted Baby Suri by Qing Fibre (65% baby suri alpaca, 20% merino, 15% silk, 191 yds / 175 m – 50 g), colourway Nest.

Or approx. 383 yds / 350 m in total of fingering-weight yarn (in MC) and 66 yds / 60 m of similar type of fingering-weight baby suri yarn (in CC). Alternative yarn suggestions are for example La Bien Aimée Merino Singles or Sysleriget Singles (for MC) and La Bien Aimée Kumo held double, Sandnes Garn Børstet Alpakka held single or silk mohair yarn held double or triple (for CC).

Needles: US 10.75 / 7 mm 16–24" / 40–60 cm circular needles.

Notions: 1 stitch marker, waste yarn.

GAUGE

9 sts x 10 rows to 4" / 10 cm in Brioche st, after blocking.

SPECIAL ABBREVIATIONS

brk: Brioche knit.
brp: Brioche purl.
sl1yo: Sl 1 st wyif, yo.

NOTES

A brioche knit (brk) round is worked first with the MC. After that, a brioche purl (brp) round is worked with the CC. Don't cross your threads when changing colours at the beginning of a round.

At the end of a MC round, the last stitch is a sl1yo. After that, leave the MC hanging at the front of the work. Pick up the CC (hanging at the back) and work the next round.

The MC yarn is held triple and the CC yarn single throughout the pattern. The sample was knitted in one colour of MC

held triple. However, you can also use three different colours, one strand of each colour, for a fascinating effect. In this case, you will need approx. 110 yds / 120 m / 30 g of each colour or thread.

CONSTRUCTION

This two-colour brioche hat is worked in the round from one end to the other as a tube. Once the tube has been knitted to the desired length, it is folded double, creating a double-layered fabric. Lastly, the brim is folded double.

DIRECTIONS

Before you begin, wind up the MC skein (merino singles) into three equally-sized (approx. 30 g) balls. You will hold MC triple throughout the pattern.

With US 10.75 / 7 mm circular needles, provisionally CO 50 sts. PM for BOR and join to work in the rnd.

Set-Up Rnd 1: With MC, *k1, p1* to end.
Set-Up Rnd 2: With CC, *sl1yo, p1* to end.
Rnd 3 (MC): With MC, *brk1, sl1yo* to end.
Rnd 3 (CC): With CC, *sl1yo, brp1* to end.

Rep rnds 3 MC and CC until the hat measures 30.5" / 77 cm.

Rnd 4: With MC, *k1, p1* to end.
Dec Rnd: *K2tog* to end. (25 sts)
Cut yarn and thread the tail through the rem sts. Pull tight to close the crown. This end will be inside the hat.

Unravel the Provisional CO and thread a yarn through all 25 stitches. Pull gently, but firmly, to close. This end will be on the outside of the hat. Fold the other end inside, placing the crowns on top of each other. Sew them together with a few stitches.

FINISHING

Weave in ends. Gently wet block.

49

52

Bags & Home Decor

Heta Puronen — Eun Mi Ahn — Dami Hunter — Sylvie Bouchard

Heta Puronen

49 Lämpö

Lämpö is a warm, chunky blanket worked in an easy stitch pattern. Take cover underneath it on a cold day, or bring it with you on a winter outing. 'Lämpö' means 'warmth' in Finnish.

SIZE

One size.

FINISHED MEASUREMENTS

Width: 47" / 119 cm.
Length: 64.5" / 164 cm.

MATERIALS

Yarn: 13 balls of Álafosslopi by Ístex (100% Icelandic wool, 109 yds / 100 m – 100 g), colourway 0054 Light Ash Heather.

Or approx. 1417 yds / 1300 m of bulky-weight yarn. Alternative yarn suggestions are for example Hjertegarn Natur Uld.

Needles: US 10 / 6 mm 40" / 100 cm circular needles.

Hook: US I-9 / 5.5 mm crochet hook.

GAUGE

13 sts x 19 rows = 4" / 10 cm on US 10 / 6 mm needles in Border and Twisted St patt, after blocking.

STITCH PATTERNS

Border

Row 1 (RS): K1, p3, *k1tbl, p1, k1tbl, p5*, rep *–* to 7 sts bef end, k1tbl, p1, k1tbl, p3, k1.
Row 2 (WS): P1, k3, p1tbl, k1, p1tbl, *k5, p1tbl, k1, p1tbl*, rep *–* to 4 sts bef end, k3, p1.

Twisted Stitch Pattern

Row 1 (RS): K1, p3, *k1tbl, p1, k1tbl, p5*, rep *–* to 7 sts bef end, k1tbl, p1, k1tbl, p3, k1.
Row 2 (WS): P1, k3, p1tbl, k1, p1tbl, *k5, p1tbl, k1, p1tbl*, rep *–* to 4 sts bef end, k3, p1.
Rep rows 1–2 once more.

Row 5: K1, p2, *k1tbl, p3, k1tbl, p3*, rep *–* to 8 sts bef end, k1tbl, p3, k1tbl, p2, k1.
Row 6: P1, k2, p1tbl, k3, p1tbl, *k3, p1tbl, k3, p1tbl*, rep *–* to 3 sts bef end, k2, p1.
Row 7: K1, p1, *k1tbl, p5, k1tbl, p1*, rep *–* to 1 st bef end, k1.
Row 8: P1, *k1, p1tbl, k5, p1tbl*, rep *–* to 2 sts bef end, k1, p1.
Rep rows 7–8 once more.
Row 11: Rep row 5.
Row 12: Rep row 6.

SPECIAL TECHNIQUES

Crab Stitch Edging

In Crab Stitch, also known as Reverse Single Crochet, single crochet is worked backwards, from left to right. Take the crochet hook through the edge stitch onto the WS with the hook pointing downwards, yarn over and pull it through to the front of the work. Yarn over again and pull it through both loops on the hook. When working the crab stitch, make sure that the edge you are working on remains straight.

CONSTRUCTION

This blanket is knitted flat and in one piece. An approx. 5.5" / 14 cm wide border is worked on both ends. The middle part of the blanket is worked in Twisted Stitch pattern. Lastly, the long edges are finished with a crochet crab stitch edging. This prevents the edges from curling.

DIRECTIONS

FIRST END

Using US 10 / 6 mm circular needles, CO 155 sts using the Knitted CO method.

Beg working the border from row 1 (RS) following either the written instructions or Chart 1. Rep rows 1–2, 13 times in total (26 rows).

MIDDLE PART

Start the Twisted St patt from row 5 (RS) following either the written instructions or Chart 2. Cont to work rows 6–12. Next, rep rows 1–12 another 21 times.

SECOND END

Beg working the border from row 1 (RS) following either the written instructions or Chart 1. Rep rows 1–2, 13 times in total (26 rows).

BO all sts.

FINISHING

Weave in all ends.

Work a crab stitch edging onto the long edges.

Gently wet block to measurements. Make sure to straighten the edges.

CHART 1 - BORDER

Row	19	18	17	16	15	14	13	12	11	10	9	8	7	6	5	4	3	2	1
2		•	•	•	ϱ	•	ϱ	•	•	•	•	•	ϱ	•	ϱ	•	•	•	
1		•	•	•	ϱ	•	ϱ	•	•	•	•	•	ϱ	•	ϱ	•	•	•	

CHART 2 - TWISTED STITCH PATTERN

Row	19	18	17	16	15	14	13	12	11	10	9	8	7	6	5	4	3	2	1
12		•	•	ϱ	•	•	•	ϱ	•	•	•	ϱ	•	•	•	ϱ	•	•	
11		•	•	ϱ	•	•	•	ϱ	•	•	•	ϱ	•	•	•	ϱ	•	•	
10		•	ϱ	•	•	•	•	•	ϱ	•	ϱ	•	•	•	•	•	ϱ	•	
9		•	ϱ	•	•	•	•	•	ϱ	•	ϱ	•	•	•	•	•	ϱ	•	
8		•	ϱ	•	•	•	•	•	ϱ	•	ϱ	•	•	•	•	•	ϱ	•	
7		•	ϱ	•	•	•	•	•	ϱ	•	ϱ	•	•	•	•	•	ϱ	•	
6		•	•	ϱ	•	•	•	ϱ	•	•	•	ϱ	•	•	•	ϱ	•	•	
5		•	•	ϱ	•	•	•	ϱ	•	•	•	ϱ	•	•	•	ϱ	•	•	
4		•	•	•	ϱ	•	ϱ	•	•	•	•	•	ϱ	•	ϱ	•	•	•	
3		•	•	•	ϱ	•	ϱ	•	•	•	•	•	ϱ	•	ϱ	•	•	•	
2		•	•	•	ϱ	•	ϱ	•	•	•	•	•	ϱ	•	ϱ	•	•	•	
1		•	•	•	ϱ	•	ϱ	•	•	•	•	•	ϱ	•	ϱ	•	•	•	

- ☐ RS: knit / WS: purl
- • RS: purl / WS: knit
- ϱ RS: k1tbl / WS: p1tbl
- ☐ pattern repeat

Eun Mi Ahn

50 Bottari

Inspired by a traditional Korean bag people used to carry their belongings in, Bottari is a bindle-style bag that amplifies the beauty of chunky yarn, exuding a rustic yet contemporary look.

SIZE

One size.

FINISHED MEASUREMENTS

Width: 17.25" / 44 cm.
Depth: 10.5" / 27 cm.
Length (after Knotting Shoulder Strap): 24.5" / 62 cm.

MATERIALS

Yarn: Cobertor by Rosa Pomar (100% Portuguese wool, 131 yds / 120 m – 100 g).
MC: 2 balls of colourway 804 Castanho Natural.
CC: 2 balls of colourway 801 Branco Natural.

Or approx. 504 yds / 462 m of bulky-weight yarn: 252 yds / 231 m (in MC) and 252 yds / 231 m (in CC). Alternative yarn suggestions are for example Ístex Álafosslopi and Cascade 220 Grande.

Needles: US 10.5 / 6.5 mm 32" / 80 cm circular needles, US 9 / 5.5 mm 32" / 80 cm circular needles.

Notions: Removable stitch markers, stitch holder or waste yarn, sewing pins, erasable fabric marking pen, cotton fabric for lining: 19.75 x 53.25" / 50 x 135 cm.

GAUGE

13 sts x 18 rows to 4" / 10 cm on US 10.5 / 6.5 mm needles in St St, after blocking.

NOTES

To avoid the bag from stretching excessively, use a 100% wool yarn, preferably non-superwash wool.

CONSTRUCTION

This lined bag is worked in two pieces from the bottom up. Each piece features two colours and is worked in intarsia. Decreases are worked to shape the bag. At the end, the remaining stitches are grafted together and a knot is tied at the shoulder strap. An i-cord is worked around the openings for a smooth edge. Lastly, the lining is sewn in to finish the bag.

DIRECTIONS

BODY

Using MC, US 10.5 / 6.5 mm needles and the Long-Tail CO method, CO 21 sts.

Row 1 (RS): K to end.
Row 2 (WS): P to 2 sts bef end, m1l(p), p2. (1 st inc'd)
Row 3: K2, m1r, k to end. (1 st inc'd)
Row 4: P to 2 sts bef end, m1l(p), p2. (1 st inc'd)
Rep rows 3–4, another 3 times. (30 sts)

Pl all sts on hold on a spare needle or waste yarn and set aside.

Using CC, US 10.5 / 6.5 mm needles and the Long-Tail CO method, CO 21 sts.

Row 1 (RS): K to end.
Row 2 (WS): P2, m1r(p), p to end. (1 st inc'd)
Row 3: K to 2 sts bef end, m1l, k2. (1 st inc'd)
Row 4: P2, m1r(p), p to end. (1 st inc'd)
Rep rows 3–4, another 3 times. (30 sts)

JOINING THE TWO PANELS

Note! When changing colours, the yarn must be twisted at the colour change on every row to avoid holes.

Set-Up Row (RS): With CC k30, pl the sts from hold onto LHN, with MC k30. By twisting the yarn at the colour change, the last st of CC and first st of MC have been joined into a single row. (60 sts)
Set-Up Row (WS): With MC p30, change to CC, p30.

Row 1 (RS): With CC k30, change to MC, k30.
Row 2 (WS): With MC p30, change to CC, p30.

Work rows 1–2 a total of 18 times (36 rows), or until the piece measures approx. 10.5" / 27 cm, ending after a WS row.

Pl removable markers at each side of the last row worked to later identify where to stop sewing the sides.

SHOULDER STRAP

Row 1 (RS): With CC k2, ssk, k to last CC st, change to MC and k to 4 sts bef end, k2tog, k2. (2 sts dec'd)
Row 2 (WS): With MC, p to last MC st, change to CC, p to end.
Row 3: With CC, k to last CC st, change to MC, k to end.
Row 4: Rep row 2.
Rep rows 1–4 another 9 times. (40 sts)
Rep rows 3–4 another 14 times. (12 sts)

Pl removable m's at each side of last row worked to later identify where to end when picking up the sts for i-cord.

Next Row (RS): With CC, k6, change to MC, k6.
Next Row (WS): With MC, p6, change to CC, p6.
Work last 2 rows a total of 8 times.

Break yarns and transfer all sts onto a spare needle or waste yarn.

Create another piece the same way, leaving a long CC tail on one panel for the grafting later. Break yarns.

BLOCKING

Bef moving on to the next step, block the pieces to exactly the same size. Be careful when blocking to avoid changes in size and gauge.

PREPARE LINING

Note! The final section of the shoulder strap is not lined, as it is used for the knot. When tracing the outline of the bag, stop at the second m (indicating where to stop picking up sts).

Cut the lining into two pieces each measuring 19.75 x 26.75" / 50 x 68 cm. Place the lining pieces on a flat surface, with the WSs facing up, then place the knitted pieces on top with RS facing upwards. Trace the outline of the knitted pieces onto the lining with an erasable fabric marking pen. Cut along the lines, ensuring the lining pieces align with all st m's on the panels. Set aside.

SHAPE KNOT

With the WS of the pieces tog, pl the 12 sts from each piece onto separate needles. Graft the 2 sets of 12 sts tog. Weave in the ends. When the RS facing, the colours of each panel should be in reverse order from one another. Tie a firm knot, to create a shoulder strap. Ensure the RS of the knotted fabric is visible rather than the WS. It is important that all 4 removable m's are still visible once the knot has been made.

SEW THE SIDES AND BOTTOM

With RS facing, sew both side seams using Mattress st, from the bottom up to the first m, which should be at the first dec row. RM. Rep the same process for the other side seam.

For the bottom, with RS still facing, sew the bottom seam using Mattress st along the edge of the inc rows through to the other end. This will create nicely curved side edges at the bottom. Weave in the ends.

I-CORD EDGE

Next, work an applied i-cord, picking up sts between 2 of the rem 4 m's as foll: Approx. 55 sts down one edge of the shoulder strap and then another approx. 55 sts up the other edge until reaching the other m. There are now approx. 110 sts in total for the i-cord. If there are any spare sts between the knot and the m, pick up sts here too.

Pick up the sts and work i-cord as foll: With yarn in same colour as shoulder strap and US 9 / 5.5 mm needles, CO 2 sts, *pick up 1 st (skip 1 st every 4 sts) and k, sl all 3 sts from the RHN to the LHN, k1, k2tog tbl*, rep *–* until reaching the middle of the edge, where the colour changes. Change to the other colour and cont working on the i-cord edge up the other side. BO and break the yarn.

Turn the bag over and rep the same process. Remove all m's.

FINISHING

Weave in all ends.

Lining

The lining is worked in a similar way as the bag, with a 0.5" / 1 cm seam allowance. Sew the lining as foll:

Step 1: With the RS of the lining fabric facing each other, sew both sides tog from the bottom to the first m.

Step 2: Position the sewn parts so they match the shape of the bag. Sew the bottom.

Step 3: Fold 0.5" / 1 cm of all unworked edge parts (shoulder straps) to the WS and sew all the way.

Step 4: Insert the lining into the bag with the RS facing, so the WS of the bag and the WS of the lining are facing each other. Sew the corners of the bottom of the lining to the corners of the bottom of the bag with small sts. Sew the edge of the lining to the underside of the WS of the i-cord edge on the bag using a similar colour of cotton thread as the yarn colour.

Dami Hunter

51 Ondata

In the Ondata cushion, mosaic knitting is used for colour and a chunky yarn for texture. The fun wave pattern adds a modern twist.

SIZE

One size.

FINISHED MEASUREMENTS

Width: 19" / 48.5 cm.
Height: 11" / 28 cm.

MATERIALS

Yarn: Quartet Bulky by Magpie Fibers (100% superfine sw American merino, 106 yds / 97 m – 100 g).
MC: 2 skeins of colourway Desert Rose.
CC: 2 skeins of colourway Fior di Latte.

Or approx. 210 yds / 192 m (in MC) and 120 yds / 110 m (in CC) of chunky-weight yarn. Alternative yarn suggestions are for example Malabrigo Chunky and Harrisville Designs Turbine.

Needles: US 10 / 6 mm needles.

Notions: 4 stitch markers.

Pillow insert: 20 x 12" / 50 x 30 cm (1" / 2.5 cm more than finished pillow cover).

GAUGE

13 sts x 17 rows to 4" / 10 cm in mosaic patt, after blocking.

NOTES

Mosaic knitting is an easy way of creating colourwork patterns using slipped stitches. Unlike stranded colourwork, only one colour of yarn needs to be handled on each row. The first block of the pairs of colourwork rows designates the colour used for those rows – the stitches in the other colour will be slipped. Stitches are always slipped purlwise with yarn on the WS, allowing the pattern to show on the front.

The chart has been split into two sections. Follow Chart 1 to the end of row 32, then immediately begin Chart 2, working from row 1 to the end of row 34.

CONSTRUCTION

This pillow cover is worked flat. Two identical side pieces are created using two colours and the mosaic knitting technique. After blocking, the two pieces are seamed together on three sides using Mattress Stitch. A pillow insert is then put in and the fourth side is seamed. The four seams add structure to the pillow.

DIRECTIONS

SIDE PIECE (MAKE 2)

Using MC and the Long-Tail CO method, CO 61 sts.

Set-Up

Row 1 (WS): P to end.
Row 2 (RS): K6, PM, *k16, PM* 3 times, k7.

Work in St St for 5 more rows.

Charted Pattern

Now work Chart 1, repeating columns 7–22 between markers 3 times, slipping markers as you come to them. You will alternate MC and CC every 2 rows. On WS rows, work sts the same colour as working yarn and slip sts in opposite colour. When switching colours, carry yarn up the side, bringing yarn up behind the just-dropped yarn to create a tidy edge. Be careful to keep floats loose to prevent puckering of finished piece.

Follow Chart 1 to the end of row 32, then immediately begin Chart 2.

After row 34 of Chart 2, break CC and work 7 rows of St St, removing markers and ending after an RS row.

BO and cut yarn. Leave a 72" / 180 cm tail for seaming on one piece.

FINISHING

Weave in ends, reserving the long one for seaming. Wet block both pieces to 1" / 2.5 cm larger than finished measurements (seams will each use approx 0.5" / 1.25 cm). When completely dry, proceed with seaming.

With RSs outwards, arrange pieces so CO edges are together and BO edges are together. Using the long MC tail, mattress stitch 3 sides. On selvage edges, pick up every bar in MC, matching column 2 from one side and column 28 from the other. Gently tighten the Mattress Sts as you go to maintain even tension throughout the seam.

Put in the pillow insert, mattress stitch the final side and weave in the end.

CHART 1

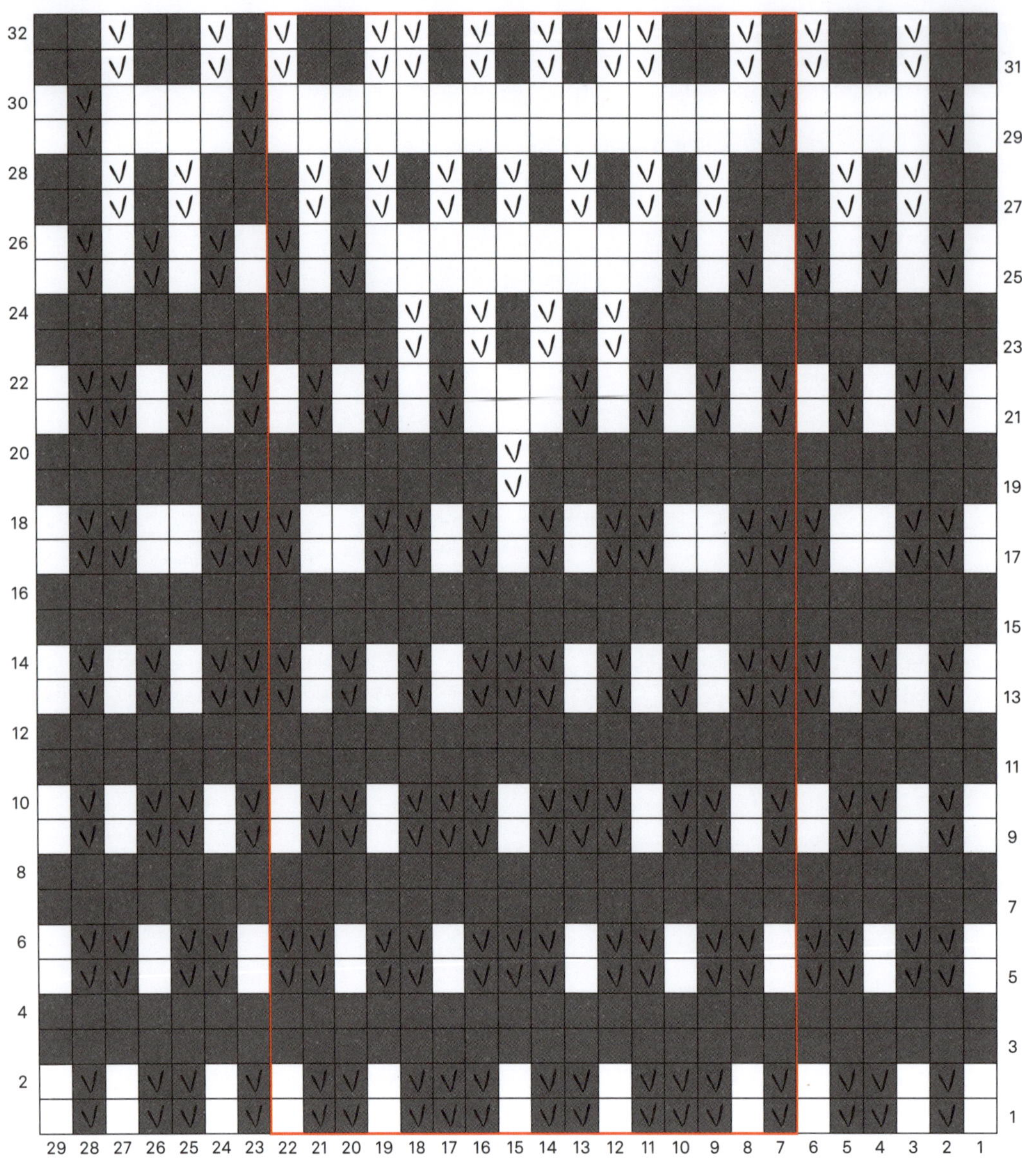

- RS: knit / WS: purl
- sl1
- MC
- CC
- pattern repeat

CHART 2

34
33
32
31
30
29
28
27
26
25
24
23
22
21
20
19
18
17
16
15
14
13
12
11
10
9
8
7
6
5
4
3
2
1
29 28 27 26 25 24 23 22 21 20 19 18 17 16 15 14 13 12 11 10 9 8 7 6 5 4 3 2 1

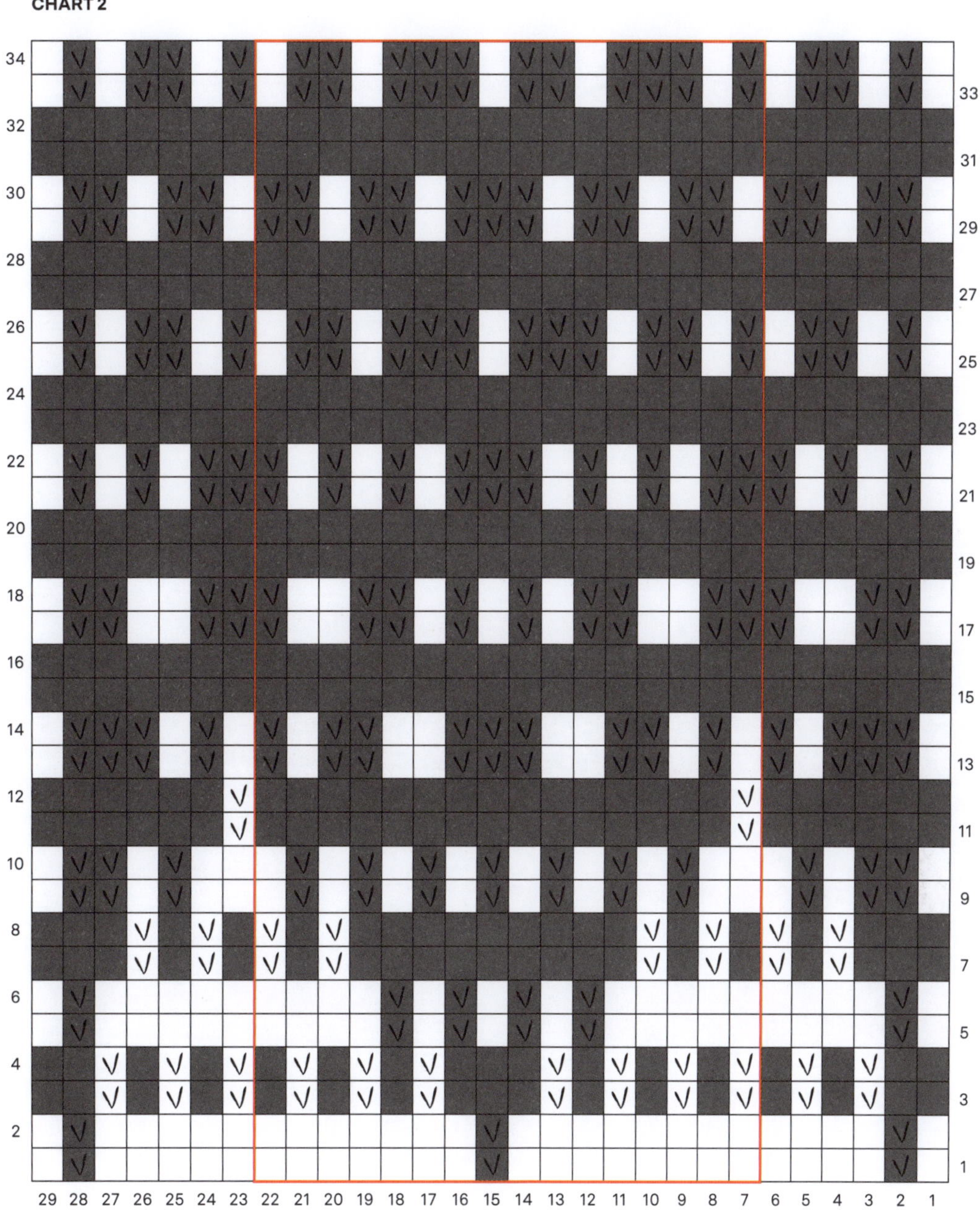

Sylvie Bouchard

52 Main Street

This intarsia cushion, inspired by roads, plays with textures as well as colours. Follow the path and see where the pattern leads you!

SIZE

One size.

FINISHED MEASUREMENTS

Height: 20" / 50 cm.
Width: 20" / 50 cm.

MATERIALS

Yarn: Yarn A: 3 skeins of 220 Grande by Cascade Yarns (100% Peruvian Highland wool, 220 yds / 200 m – 200 g), colourway 8012 Doeskin Heather.

Yarn B: 1 skein of Orséto by Fibre Carpe Diem (70% wool, 30% alpaca, 86 yds / 79 m – 100 g), colourway Bois d'Épave.

Or approx. 485 yds / 440 m (in Yarn A) and 55 yds / 50 m (in Yarn B) in bulky-weight yarn of similarly contrasting textures.

Alternative yarn suggestions are for example Berroco Lanas Quick or Rowan Brushed Fleece for Yarn A and Gepard Garn Teddy Dear for Yarn B.

Needles: US 9 / 5.5 mm needles.

Notions: US 9 / 5.5 mm crochet hook, 20 x 20" / 50 x 50 cm cushion pad.

GAUGE

13.5 sts x 19 rows to 4" / 10 cm with Yarn A in St St, after blocking.

11 sts x 20 rows to 4" / 10 cm with Yarn B in Garter St, after blocking.

Note! Pay attention to row gauge, as it is crucial.

SPECIAL ABBREVIATIONS

sl1: On RS: Sl 1 kwise wyib.
On WS: Sl 1 pwise wyif.

SPECIAL TECHNIQUES

Intarsia

At a colour change, cross the old colour over the new colour, drop the old colour and start working with the new colour (it will be coming from underneath the old colour). Crossing the old colour over the new one will twist them together at the colour change.

Weaving in

For short sections, the pattern calls to 'weave in' a yarn. Work as foll: Cross Yarn A over Yarn B, with Yarn B, k1, *insert RHN in the next st kwise, bring Yarn A over RHN, k1 with Yarn B*, rep *–* for specified number of sts.

NOTES

Be sure to cast-on and bind-off as specified in the pattern.

Work a selvage stitch as specified at the beginning of every RS and WS row

and make sure to slip them as specified for RS/WS throughout (see Special Abbreviations). Selvage stitches will be used to sew the cushion at the end.

CONSTRUCTION

This cushion is worked flat in two pieces, front and back. First, the back is worked with Yarn A in Stockinette Stitch. Then, the front is worked with both yarns using intarsia over Stockinette Stitch and Garter Stitch. Finally, three sides are seamed using crochet in the selvage stitches, the cushion pad is inserted and the final edge is seamed.

DIRECTIONS

BACK

With Yarn A, CO 70 sts using the Long-Tail CO method.

Set-Up Row (WS): Sl1, p to end.

Row 1 (RS): Sl1, k to end.
Row 2 (WS): Sl1, p to end.
Rep rows 1–2, 49 more times.

Next Row (RS): Sl1, k to end.

BO pwise.

FRONT

With Yarn A, CO 70 sts using the Long-Tail CO method.
Note! Yarn A is always used for St St, and Yarn B always for Garter St.

Set-Up Row (WS): Sl1, p to end.

Section 1

Row 1 (RS): Sl1, k to end.
Row 2 (WS): Sl1, p to end.
Rows 3–6: Rep rows 1 and 2, twice.

Section 2

Row 7 (RS): With A, sl1, k22, drop A and join B, k1, k2tog, *k4, k2tog* 7 times, k2. (8 sts dec'd) (62 sts)
Row 8 (WS): With B, sl1, k38, bring B to WS, cross B over A, with A, p23.
Row 9: With A, sl1, k22, cross A over B, with B, k39.
Rows 10–13: Rep rows 8 and 9, twice.
Row 14: Rep row 8.

Section 3

Row 15 (RS): Cut B. With A, sl1, k23, *kfb, k4* 7 times, kfb, k2. (8 sts inc'd) (70 sts)
Row 16 (WS): Rep row 2.
Rows 17–22: Rep rows 1 and 2, 3 times.

Section 4

Row 23 (RS): With A, sl1, k34, drop A and join B, k1, *k2tog, k4* 5 times, k2tog, k2. (6 sts dec'd) (64 sts)
Row 24 (WS): With B, sl1, k28, bring B to WS, cross B over A, with A, p35.
Row 25: With A, sl1, k34, cross A over B, with B, k29.
Rows 26–29: Rep rows 24 and 25, twice.
Row 30: Rep row 24.
Row 31: With A, sl1, k34, cross A over B, with B, k7 weaving in A, drop B, with A, k1, *kfb, k4* 4 times, k1. (4 sts inc'd) (68 sts)
Row 32: With A, sl1, p25, leave A at WS, cross B over A, with B, k7, bring B to WS, (make a long float and don't pull the yarn too much) with A, p35.
Row 33: With A, sl1, k34, leave A at WS, cross B over A, with B, k7 weaving in A, drop B, with A, k26.
Rows 34–37: Rep rows 32 and 33, twice.
Row 38: Rep row 32.
Row 39: With A, sl1, k34, cross A over B, with B, k8, *k2tog, k4* 4 times, k1. (4 sts dec'd) (64 sts)
Rows 40–45: Rep rows 24 and 25, 3 times.
Row 46: Rep row 24.

Section 5

Row 47 (RS): With A, sl1, k34, *kfb, k4* 5 times, kfb, k3. Cut B. (6 sts inc'd) (70 sts)
Row 48 (WS): Rep row 2.
Rows 49–54: Rep rows 1 and 2, 3 times.

Section 6

Row 55 (RS): With A, sl1, k13, drop A and join B, *k2tog, k3* 10 times, k2tog, k2, k2tog. (12 sts dec'd) (58 sts)
Row 56 (WS): With B, sl1, k43, bring B to WS, cross B over A, with A, p14.
Row 57: With A, sl1, k13, cross A over B, with B, k44.
Rows 58–61: Rep rows 56 and 57, twice.
Row 62: Rep row 58.

Section 7

Row 63 (RS): Cut B. With A, sl1, k13,

kfb, k3 10 times, *kfb, k1* twice. (12 sts inc'd) (70 sts)
Row 64 (WS): Rep row 2.
Rows 65–70: Rep rows 1 and 2, 3 times.

Section 8

Row 71 (RS): Rep row 7.
Rows 72–77: Rep rows 8 and 9, 3 times.
Row 78: Rep row 8.
Row 79: With A, sl1, k22, cross A over B, with B, k7 weaving in A, drop B, with A, *k6, kfb* 4 times, k4. (4 sts inc'd) (66 sts)
Row 80: With A, sl1, p35, leave A at WS, cross B over A, with B, k7, bring B to WS (make a long float and don't pull the yarn too much) with A, p23.
Row 81: With A, sl1, k22, leave A at WS, cross B over A, with B, k7 weaving in A, drop B, with A, k36.
Rows 82–85: Rep rows 80 and 81, twice.
Row 86: Rep row 80.
Row 87: With A, sl1, k22, cross A over B, with B, k13, *k2tog, k6* 3 times, k2tog, k4. (4 sts dec'd) (62 sts)
Rows 88–93: Rep rows 8 and 9, 3 times.
Row 94: Rep row 8.

Section 9

Row 95 (RS): Cut B. With A, sl1, k23, *kfb, k4* 7 times, kfb, k2. (8 sts inc'd) (70 sts)
Row 96 (WS): Rep row 2.
Rows 97–100: Rep rows 1 and 2, twice.
Row 101: Rep row 1.

BO pwise.

FINISHING

Weave in ends. Block to finished measurements (it will then be nice and snug after seaming).

ASSEMBLY

Preparation

All seams will be worked with Yarn A.

Place the front and back piece side by side with RS facing: CO edges at the bottom, BO edges at the top. Put the right edge of the front piece slightly on top of the back piece so it overlaps by 0.5" / 1 cm.

Step 1: Starting at the right bottom corner, insert the crochet hook under the selvage 'V' on both front and back, catch the yarn and draw a loop through. *Go under the next selvage 'V' on front and back, draw up a new st and pull it through the loop already on the hook*. Rep *–* until reaching the upper right corner.

Step 2: When at the right top corner, rep *–*, but use the 'V' from the BO edges.
Step 3: Rep step 1 until reaching the left bottom corner. Insert the cushion pad.

Step 4: Rep *–* but use the 'V' from the CO edges.

Weave in the last end.

Category Index

This edition published in 2025 by Hardie Grant Books, an imprint of Hardie Grant Publishing
First published in 2024 by Laine Publishing Oy
Published by arrangement with Rights & Brands

Hardie Grant Books (Melbourne)
Wurundjeri Country
Level 11, 36 Wellington Street
Collingwood, Victoria 3066

Hardie Grant North America
2912 Telegraph Ave
Berkeley, California 94705

hardiegrant.com/books

A catalogue record for this book is available from the National Library of Australia

52 Weeks of Chunky Knits
ISBN 9781761452154

10 9 8 7 6 5 4 3 2 1

Concept: Jonna Helin & Sini Kramer
Photography: Riikka Kantinkoski & Sini Kramer
Graphic Design: Tiina Vaarakallio & Irina Kauppinen
Editors: Maija Kangasluoma, Sini Kramer, Pauliina Kuunsola & Tiia Pyykkö
Stylist: Ida Bergfors (except pp. 229, 243, 251, 255, 267 & 269)
Hair & Makeup: Jennifer Appleton
Models: Emilia Lönnberg / Paparazzi Model Management & Trilce Teivainen / Brand Model Management
Clothing: Calla, Jeans & Towels, Marimekko, Karhu, Terhi Pölkki, R-Collection, Kristiina Laakso, Vimma, Muji

Colour reproduction by Splitting Image Colour Studio
Printed in China by Leo Paper Products LTD.

The paper this book is printed on is from FSC®-certified forests and other sources. FSC® promotes environmentally responsible, socially beneficial and economically viable management of the world's forests.